KB035575

우루과이라운드

규범 제정 및
투자 협상

우루과이라운드

규범 제정 및 투자 협상

| 머리말

우루과이라운드는 국제적 교역 질서를 수립하려는 다각적 무역 교섭으로서, 각국의 보호무역 추세를 보다 완화하고 다자무역체제를 강화하기 위해 출범되었다. 1986년 9월 개시가 선언되었으며, 15개 분야의 교섭을 1990년 말까지 진행하기로 했다. 그러나 각 분야의 중간 교섭이 이루어진 1989년 이후에도 농산물, 지적소유권, 서비스무역, 섬유, 긴급수입제한 등 많은 분야에서 대립하며 1992년이 돼서야 타결에 이를 수 있었다. 한국은 특히 농산물 분야에서 기존 수입 제한 품목 대부분을 개방해야 했기에 큰 경쟁력 하락을 겪었고, 관세와 기술 장벽 완화, 보조금 및 수입 규제 정책의 변화로 제조업 수출입에도 많은 변화가 있었다.

본 총서는 우루과이라운드 협상이 막바지에 다다랐던 1991~1992년 사이 외교부에서 작성한 관련 자료를 담고 있다. 관련 협상의 치열했던 후반기 동향과 관계부처회의, 무역협상위원회 회의, 실무대책회의, 규범 및 제도, 투자회의, 특히나 가장 많은 논란이 있었던 농산물과 서비스 분야 협상 등의 자료를 포함해 총 28권으로 구성되었다. 전체 분량은 약 1만 3천여 쪽에 이른다.

2024년 3월
한국학술정보(주)

| 일러두기

· 본 총서에 실린 자료는 2022년 4월과 2023년 4월에 각각 공개한 외교문서 4,827권, 76만여 쪽 가운데 일부를 발췌한 것이다.

· 각 권의 제목과 순서는 공개된 원본을 최대한 반영하였으나, 주제에 따라 일부는 적절히 변경하였다.

· 원본 자료는 A4 판형에 맞게 축소하거나 원본 비율을 유지한 채 A4 페이지 안에 삽입하였다. 또한 현재 시점에선 공개되지 않아 '공란'이란 표기만 있는 페이지 역시 그대로 실었다.

· 외교부가 공개한 문서 각 권의 첫 페이지에는 '정리 보존 문서 목록'이란 이름으로 기록물 종류, 일자, 명칭, 간단한 내용 등의 정보가 수록되어 있으며, 이를 기준으로 0001번부터 번호가 매겨져 있다. 이는 삭제하지 않고 총서에 그대로 수록하였다.

· 보고서 내용에 관한 더 자세한 정보가 필요하다면, 외교부가 온라인상에 제공하는 『대한민국 외교사료요약집』 1991년과 1992년 자료를 참조할 수 있다.

| 차례

정 리 보 존 문 서 목 록

기록물종류	일반공문서철	등록번호	2019090026	등록일자	2019-09-04
분류번호	764.51	국가코드		보존기간	영구
명 칭	UR(우루과이라운드) / 규범제정 및 투자 협상 그룹 회의, 1991. 전2권				
생 산 과	통상기구과	생산년도	1991~1991	담당그룹	국제경제
권 차 명	V.1 2-10월				
내용목차	* 1991.4월 협상그룹 조정으로 종전의 MTM 협정, GATT 조문, 보조금/상계관세, 세이프가드, 원산지규정, 선적전 검사, 무역관련 투자협상 등 11개 분야가 '규범제정 및 투자분야'로 통합 * 보조금.상계관세 분야는 'UR / 보조금.상계관세 회의, 1991 (2019100005)' 참조				

0001

외 무 부

종   별 :

번   호 : GVW-0347   일   시 : 91 0222 1830

수   신 : 장 관(통기,경기원,재무부,농림수산부,상공부,특허청)

발   신 : 주 제네바 대사대리

제   목 : UR/TRMIS 및 TRIPS 협상

    2.22(금) DUNKEL 의장 (TNC 의장 자격)은 브랏셀 회의 결과 의장이 부여한 MANDATE에 따라 표제 회의를 개최한다고 선언하고 아래 요지와 같이 향후 회의일정 및 회의 진행절차에 관해 설명하였음. (참석 박영우 공사, 엄낙용재무관, 김준규서기관)

    1. TRIMS 및 TRIPS 협상에 관한 회의를 91.3.18(월) 오후에 개최함.

    2. TRIMS: 브랏셀 회의에 제출할 합의된 협상기초가 없었고 COMMENTARY (갓트문서 MTN.TNC/2/35/REV.1 페이지 238)만 있었다고 말하고 각국대표들이 TRIMS 협상에 대한 의견 개진과동 COMMENTARY 에 의거 기술적 차원에서의 협상을 진행토록 제의함.

    TRIPS: 브랏셀 회의에 제출한 협상문서 (갓트문서 MTN.TNC/W/35.REV. 1 페이지194-195)가 향후 협상의 기초가 될것이며 협상진행은 현재까지의 TRIPS 협상 현황을 검토하고 현단계에서 진행할 기술적 차원의 작업분야 확인등을 의제로 토의를 진행토록 제의 함.

    첨부: 의장 발표문 1부

    (GVW(F)-0077). 끝

    (대사대리 박영우-국장)

통상국   2차보   경기원   재무부   농수부   상공부   특허정

22.2.91
10.30

GVW (π) - 0077
10222 / 8 00
GVW - 307 72 4

TRIMS AND TRIPS

Friday, 22 February 1991, a.m.

Note for Chairman

1. In his closing remarks at the Brussels Ministerial Meeting, Minister Gros Espiell requested me to pursue intensive consultations with the specific objective of achieving agreements in all the areas of the negotiating programme in which differences remain outstanding. These consultations will, he said, be based on document MTN.TNC/W/35/Rev.1, dated 3 December 1990, including the cover page which refers to the Surveillance Body and the communications which various participants sent to Brussels. He added that I would also take into account the considerable amount of work carried out at the Brussels meeting, although it did not commit any delegation.

2. I suggest that the meeting first address TRIMs and then take up TRIPs.

Trade-Related Investment Measures

3. Unlike in most other areas of the negotiations, it did not prove possible to transmit a draft text of an agreement on TRIMs to Ministers in Brussels. The commentary on TRIMs on page 238 of MTN.TNC/W/35/Rev.1 simply enumerates the points on which basic divergences of view exist. These are: coverage; level of discipline; developing countries and restrictive business practices.

4. When work restarts on TRIMS on Monday, 18 March in the afternoon I suggest that the delegations be given an opportunity to comment on the present status of negotiations on TRIMs. We should also try to identify technical work that can usefully be done in this area at the present stage of our negotiations.

0003

5.   On this latter point, I suggest that agreement could be assisted by discussions of a technical nature, building as appropriate on work already undertaken as reflected in the draft texts referred to in the commentary on page 238 of W/35/Rev.1.   Technical discussions to elaborate a workable "effects test" would, for example, be a useful contribution in the level of discipline area.

Trade-Related Aspects of Intellectual Property Rights

6.   The text sent forward to Brussels in TNC/W/35/Rev.1 listed on pages 194-195 the outstanding issues on which decisions were required in the TRIPs negotiations.   These issues remain unsettled, and the basis for future work is the draft text as contained in that document.

7.   When work restarts on TRIPs - again in the afternoon of 18 March - I suggest that delegations be given an opportunity to consider the present state of the negotiations in this area, taking into account the work done in Brussels, and to identify any areas in which technical work could usefully be undertaken at this stage.

외 무 부

종 별 :

번 호 : GVW-0503   일 시 : 91 0319 1000

수 신 : 장관(통기, 경기원, 재무부, 농림수산부, 상공부, 특허청)

발 신 : 주 제네바 대사

제 목 : UR/TRIMS.TRIPS 주요국 비공식 협의

3. 18. DUNKEL 사무총장 주재로 개최된 표제 협의토의 결과 아래 보고함. (본직, 엄재무관, 김준규 서기관 참석)

1. 무역관련 투자 조치

0 의장(DUNKEL 총장)은 MTN/TNC/W/69 의 37개내지 39항의 내용을 상기 시키면서이를 기초로 하여 향후 기술적 분야에 대한 논의를 진행할 예정인바 구체적 논의대상에 대한 발언을 요청함.

0 이에 대해 스웨덴은 구체적인 정의 규정 및 COVERAGE 등에 대한 합의가 없는상 태에서논의 대상인 기술적인 부문을 정하기는 어려운 문제이나 W/69 에 언급된부자조치의 EFFECT TEST가 가능한 논의 대상임을 제안한바 미국, EC, 일본등이 이를 지지함.

0 호주, 인도는 기술적인 문제와 정치적 결정을 요하는 문제간에 그 구분 한계가 불분명하여 기술적 분야에의 논의는 정치적 결정을 요하는 부문에 곧 접하게 되므로 스웨덴이 제안하는 접근 방법에 부정적 입장을 표명하였으며, 브라질, 멕시코, 이집트, 필리핀 등도 EFFECT TEST 가 기술적 부문에 대한 논의의 출발점이 될수있다는데는 반대하지 않았으나 COVERAGE 에 대한 합의가 없는 상태에서의 이들 부문에 대한 논의 진행의 실익에 의문을 표시 하였음.

0 의장은 차기 협의 의제를 1990. 11.9 의장 초안중 CHAPTER II 에 규정된 4가지 유형의 무역 왜곡효과 분석. 검토로 정하기로 하고 그 이외 무역 왜곡효과 LIST에 관심이 있는 국가는 이를 제출할수 있다 하였음.

2. 무역관련 지적 재산권

0 던켈 의장은 MTN/TNC/W/69 의 40 및 41항에 관한 내용을 언급하고 앞으로 TRIPS 협상을 더욱 진전시키기 위해 구체적으로 논의할 사항에 관하여 각 대표들에게발언을

통상국   경기원   재무부   농수부   상공부   특허청

요청함.

ㅇ 이집트는 아직 TRIPS 협상에서 기술적인 문제에 관해 개도국을 위해 타협된 것이 없으며, 향후 토의에서 선.개도국 간에 이문제에 관한 구체적 토의가 진행되어야 할것이라 제안하자 이에 대해 스위스는 지금까지 실질적인 문제에 관해 합의된것이 없으며, 어느것이 기술적인 문제에 해당하는지 그 범위를 한정하기 어렵다고함.

ㅇ 놀웨이는 제 73조 (기존 지적 재산권 보호)에 관하여 기술적인 토의보다 정치적인 토의가 진행되어야 한다고 언급하고 현단계에서 다른협상 그룹의 진전상황과병행하여 TRIPS 협상을 진행해야 한다고 하였으며, 콜럼비아는 협상 균형면에서 볼때 보호수준이 증대 되었음을 지적하고 개도국에 대한 경과조치(제 6장), 분쟁해결 절차등에 관해 토의가 진행되어야 한다고 언급함.

ㅇ 던켈 의장은 TRIPS 에 관해서는 실질적이고 진전된 TEXT 를 만들어야 하며, 현단계에서 기술적인 문제에 관해 토의할 생각을 강하게 느끼지 않고 있으나 TRIPS 협상에 도달하기 위한 DEADLINE 이 없으며, 토의가 진전되지 않을 것이므로 토의진전을 위해 DEADLINE 설정의 필요성을 검토할 것이라고 함.

3. 차기 회의 일정

ㅇ 추후 통보 예정이라 하고 금번 회의 종료함.

끝

(대사 박수길-국장)

외 무 부

종 별 :

번 호 : GVW-1087 　　　　　　　　　　 일 시 : 91 0611 1800

수 신 : 장관(통기,경기원,재무부,상공부)

발 신 : 주 제네바대사

제 목 : UR/ 규범제정 협상 그룹회의

　　표제 회의가 MACILL 의장 주재로 6.10-11 간 개최된바 요지 하기임.

　　(본직, 강상무관 참석)

　　1.　금번　회의는　실질문제에　대한　토론없이　향후협상　진행방식에　관한 절차문제를협의한바 6.10 오전의 공식회의에 이어 6.10 오후 및 6.11. 오후 주요국간 비공식회의를 개최하여 다음과 같이 합의하고 이를 6.12.오후 개최되는 공식회의에서 채택키로 함

　　(합의사항)

　　- 규범제정　그룹　소관　11개　분야중　보조금　및　상계관세,　반덤핑, 세이프가드,무역관련 투자 조치, BOP 등 5개분야를 중요분야 (SUBSTANTIAL ITEM)로 하고 이를우선 협의함

　　- 상기 5개 분야에 대해 우선순위 없이 7월 22일 주간에 개최되는 규범제정 그룹회의에서 이슈별로 토의함

　　- 7월회의에서는 공식회의 개최후 주요국간 비공식 협의를 주로함

　　- 7월 회의는 협상의 시작보다는 협상현황에 대한 각국의 평가를 위한 것임.

　　- 각국의 평가 과정에서 협상 가능한 요소가 발견되면 이에대한 협상을 시작할수 있음

　　- 9월회의에서 본격적인 협상을 시작함

　　2.　관찰

　　0 6.11. 오후 주요국간 비공식 회의가 상기 사항이 합의되기 전인 6.10.오후 회의 에서 MARCILL 의장은 상기 5개 중요 이슈에 대해서도, (1) 보조금및 상계관세 (2) 반 덤핑 (3) 무역관련 투자조치(4) BOP (5) 세이프가드 순으로 우선 순위를 설정하여 이를 순서대로 논의할 것을 제의하였음.

통상국　　2차보　　경기원　　재무부　　상공부

0 이에대해 많은 국가가 상기 순서가 이슈의 중요성에 입각한 순서가 아니라는점, 이슈간 토론순서에 있어 신축성을 유지하여야 한다는 전제하에이의 수락의사를밝혔으나 EC,카나다, 미국, 홍콩등의 반대로 상기 5개 이슈에 대한 우선순위 없이 7월 회의에서 토론키로 되었음.

0 EC 는 5개 이슈의 동시접근 방식을 주장하고, 홍콩, 카나다는 현단계에서 덤핑논의 필요성에 의문을 표시 하였으며, 미국은 덤핑 논의를 뒤로 미루고 보조금 및 상계관세는 즉각 토론 용의가 있음을 주장함.

0 상기 토론 과정에 비추어 볼때 주요국이 핵심이슈에 대한 기존입장을 고집하고일보 전진할려는 의사가 희박한 것으로 보이며, 따라서 7월 개최되는 회의에서도농산물 협상등에 극적인 변화가 없는한 기존입장의 반복으로 큰 진전을 기대해는어려울 것으로 보임.

    끝

    (대사 박수길-국장)

외 무 부

종   별 :

번   호 : GVW-1092 　　　　　　　　　　　　일   시 : 91 0612 1800

수   신 : 장 관(봉기/경기원,재무부,상공부)

발   신 : 주 제네바 대사

제   목 : UR / 규범제정 그룹 공식 회의

　　표제회의가 6.12(수) MACIEL 의장 주제로 개최된바 요지 하기임.

　　0 의장은 지난 2일간 향후 협상 진행 방식에 관해 주요국과 비공식 협의 결과 합의된 사항을 다음과 같이 제시함.

　　- 보조금,상계관세, 반덤핑,무역관련 부자 조치,BOP. 세이프가드가 우선적으로 다루어야 할 가장중요한 분야임.

　　- 상기 5개 분야 이슈간에 우선 순위는 없음.

　　- 7월 회의(7.22-7.26) 에서는 상기 5개 이슈중 세이프가드를 제외한 4개 이슈를 논의하되 협상상황 평가및 문제 해결을 위한 적극적인 노력을 비공식 협의 형식으로 진행 할 것임.

　　- 7월 회의의 구체적 일정은 추후 통보 함.

　　- 보조금,상계관세 및 반덤핑에 대해서는 의장보좌역인 RAMSAUER (스위스 공사)가 비공식접촉을 할것임.

　　0 상기 의장 제의에 대해 각국은 특별한 의견제시 없이 이를 수락하였으나, 일본, 칠레,아르헨티나가 규범제정 분야의 중요성과 협상진전부진에 대해 우려를 표명하는 간단한 언급을 함.

　　0 의장은 선적간 검사 협정 초안(MTN/TNC/W/35 REV1) 제 5조(재심 절차)의 시행과 관련 국제상공회의소 (INTERNATIONAL CHAMBER OF COMMENCE) 와국제 검사기관 연맹(INTERNATIONAL FEDERATION OF INSPECTION AGENCY) 의 공동제안에 대해 7.10 까지 의견이 있는 국가의 의견 제시를 요청함.끝

　　(대사 박수길-국장)　attention

통상국	차관	2차보	정와대		경기원	재무부	상공부

0009

PAGE 1 　　　　　　　　　　　　　　　　　91.06.13 ', 06:24 FO

외신 1과 통제관

외 무 부

종 별 :

번 호 : GVW-1283　　　　　　　　　　일 시 : 91 0710 1800

수 신 : 장 관(봉기, 경기원, 재무부, 상공부)

발 신 : 주 제네바 대사

제 목 : 규범제정 협상회의

　　　7.22 주간 개최 예정인 규범제정 협상에 대한 회의진행 방식 및 주요 논의 사항을 동협상의장 보좌관인 RAMSAUER 에게 탐문한 결과하기 보고함.

　　0 회의일정

　　- 7.22(월) 15:00 : 전체공식회의

　　- 7.23(화) 반덤핑

　　- 7.24(수)보조금, 상계관세

　　- 7.25(목) TRIMS

　　- 7.26(금) BOP

　　- 7.26(금) 오후 : 전체공식회의

　　0 7.23-7.26 간의 이슈별 회의는 주요국 비공식협의를 주로하되 회의진행의 명료성 확보를 위해 각 일자별로 오후에 간단한 공식회의를 개최할 가능성이 있음.

　　0 상기 4분야에서 무엇이 논의될지에 대한 질의에 대해 동인은 반덤핑의 경우 그동안 7개의 TEXT가 마련되었으나 어느것도 협상의 기초로 합의된것이 없으므로 동 분야에 대한 실질적 논의는 기대하기는 어려울 것이며 보조금 상계관세의 경우 보조금에 대한 CRITERIA 문제에 대한 논의가 있을것이라고 함. TRIMS 의 경우 참가국의 태도에 따 라 실질적 토의 여부가 결정될 것이며, BOP 는 비교적 간단히 회의가 진행될것으로 예상함. 끝

　　(대사 박수길-국장)

통상국	차관	1차보	2차보	외정실	분석관	정와대	안기부	경기원
재무부	상공부							

PAGE 1　　　　　　　　　　　　　　　　　　　91.07.11　　06:08 FN

외신 1과 통제관

0010

상 공 부

국 협 28140-⟨281⟩　　　　　(2396)　　　　　1991. 7. 19

수 신　외무부장관

제 목　UR/규범제정분야 회의 참석

　　　'91. 7. 22 (월) ~ 7. 26 (금)간 스위스 제네바에서 개최되는
UR 규범제정분야 회의에 참가하기 위하여 다음과 같이 출장코자 하오니
정부대표 임명등 필요한 조치를 하여 주시기 바랍니다.

　　　　　　　　　" 다　　　　　음 "

　　1. 출장개요

직　　위	성　　명	출 장 기 간	비　　고
국제협력관실 행정 사무관	김　영　민	'91. 7. 20 (토) ~ 　　7. 28 (일)	UR 규범제정분야 회의 참가

　　2. 예산근거 : 상공부 예산

첨　부 : 아국 입장 1부.

　　　　상　공　부　장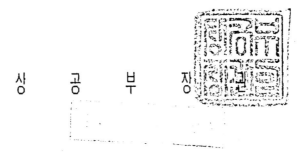

0011

UR/규범제정 및 투자분야협상 (7.22~26)에 대한 입장
===

1. 전반적인 입장

   o 규범제정 분야는 장기적인 관점에서 우리의 이익에 직결되는 중요한 협상 분야임

      - 특히, 반덤핑 협정 개정을 통해 기존 규범을 강화함으로써 공정한 무역질서를
        확립하고, 긴급수입제한조치의 명료화를 통해 선진국의 수입규제 대응해
        나갈 수 있도록 아국이 적극적인 입장을 취하고 있는 분야이며,
      - 보조금/상계관세 협상은 동 협상 결과에 따라 우리나라 산업정책의 전반적인
        방향을 수정해야 할 중요한 분야임

   o 현재 규범 제정 분야에서의 대부분 쟁점은 기술적인 문제가 아닌 정치적인 절충을
     요하는 사항이므로 농산물 협상에서 돌파구를 찾아 UR 전체 협상의 분위기
     전환이 없는 한 각국의 기존 입장만 되풀이 할 것으로 보이며,

      - 금번 7월회의에서도 각국이 기존 입장의 타협을 기대할 수 없을 것으로
        전망되며 각 분야별로 정치적 타결을 요하는 쟁점만 확인할 것으로 예상됨

   o 기본적으로 금번 협상에서는 기존의 입장을 유지하고, 선진국과 개도국간의
     중도적 입장에서 협상의 성공적인 타결을 위해서 노력하고 있다는 입장을 밝힘
      - 한국은 UR협상이 성공적으로 타결되어 갓트를 중심으로 한 세계자유무역체제가
        강화되어야 한다고 믿고, 그동안 협상타결을 위해 노력해 왔고, 앞으로도
        노력할 것임을 강조
      - 규범제정분야는 실질적으로 다자간 무역체제 확립을 위한 가장 중요한 분야로서
        아직까지 협상의 기초가 마련되지 않은 분야는 각국이 자국의 기대수준을
        낮춤으로써 협상 타결에 기여토록 노력할 필요성을 강조하고,
        수출국과 수입국, 선진국과 개도국간의 이익이 균형있게 반영된 협상text
        마련 필요성 언급

   o 농산물 협상에서 돌파구가 마련될 경우 규범제정 분야는 주요국간 정치적 타협을
     통해 급속도로 진행될 가능성이 있으므로 이에 대비하여 각 분야별로 필히
     반영하여야 할 정치적 쟁점 및 우선순위 재점검

0012

2. 반덤핑 협정

  o 반덤핑 조치의 남용 방지를 위해 현행 협정을 강화하고 명료성을 확보하자는
    아국의 기존 입장 유지

    - 덤핑, 피해 판정 기준의 공정성 및 객관성 확보
    - 조사 개시 요건등 조사 절차의 강화
    - 소멸 시효의 설정

  o 선진 수입국 (미국, EC)이 주장하는 우회덤핑 방지 조항 도입을 최대한 저지토록 함

    - 다만, 순수한 우회덤핑 (수출국내 단순조립)의 경우는 규제 인정 가능하나
      남용 방지를 위해 그 기준 설정을 엄격히 해야함

  o 주요 항목별 입장 (별첨)

3. 보조금. 상계관세 협상

  o 금번 회의시 UR/보조금.상계관세협상에 관한 각국의 기본입장 및 현재의 협상
    상황에 대한 개괄적 평가가 있을 경우

    - 이번. 회의가 브랏셀 각료회의후 재개되는 성격임을 감안하여 아국은 본 협상의
      성공적인 타결을 위해 노력하고 있음을 홍보
    - 현재 협상의 기초가 되는 브랏셀 각료회의 의장 보고서는 그간의 쟁점사항을
      종합화한 점에서 긍정적으로 평가하나, 아직 개선의 여지가 많음을 언급
    - 주요국의 입장 및 협상 동향을 면밀히 파악하여 향후 아국의 최종안 수립에
      참고토록 준비

  o 세부 쟁점별 공식. 비공식 협의가 진행될 경우 첨부한 쟁점별 아국 입장에
    의거, 적의 대처

0013

4. TRIMs 협상

o 투자제한조치 협상 타결시 아국기업의 해외투자 환경개선을 기대할 수 있는 반면
  외국인 투자를 추가로 개방하여야 하는 부담이 거의 없으므로 아국으로서는 협상이
  타결되는 것이 유리

o 협상결과에 선진국 및 일부개도국만 참여하고 다수 개도국이 불참하는 경우에도
  아국으로서는 참여가 불가피한 바 이 경우 ①아국의 대개도국 투자환경 개선을
  기대할 수 없고 ② 선진국에 비하여 상대적으로 제한조치가 많은 아국이 개선
  요청을 많이 받을 것으로 예상할 때 아국으로서는 다수 개도국이 참여하는 것이
  유리함

  - 그러나 선.개도국간 입장차이가 현격하므로 이에 대한 노력 필요

o 주요 항목별 입장 (별첨)

5. BOP 조항

o BOP 조항은 선진. 개도국간의 첨예한 의견 대립을 보이는 미묘한 문제이고
  아국은 이미 BOP 조항을 졸업한만큼 구체적인 입장 표명 자제

  - BOP 조항 개정 가능성은 거의 없으며, 다만 선진국들이 섬유 협상등 여타
    협상 분야와 연계 카드로 사용

  - BOP 조항 개정 찬성시 개도국들이 우리에게 강력히 반발할 것이므로 찬성
    의사 표명 자제 (별첨 BOP 논의 현황)

0014

UR 규범제정 및 투자분야 협상 회의 참가자료

('91. 7. 22 ~ 7. 26)

91. 7

상 공 부
국 제 협 력 관 실

0015

I. 회의개요

o '91년 4월 UR 협상 그룹이 7개로 통합된 이후에 MTN 협정, GATT조문, 보조금 상계관세 협정, 세이프가드, 원산지 규정, 선적전 검사 및 무역관련 투자 협상 분야가 규범제정 및 투자분야 그룹에서 논의되고 있음

   - 규범제정 및 투자분야 의장 : Marciel (브라질 전 제네바 주재대사)

o 지난해 말 개최된 브라셀 각료회의에서도 규범제정 분야가 통합되어 협상이 진행된 바 있으며, 최근 공식.비공식 회의가 6월에 제네바에서 개최됨

   - 지난 6월 회의에서 규범제정 분야의 협상진행방안에 대하여 논의하여 아래와 같이 결정함

     . 규범제정 분야 소관 11개 분야중 반덤핑, 보조금/상계관세, 세이프가드, 국제수지(BOP), 무역관련 투자조치 등 5개 분야를 우선적으로 다루어야 할 중요분야로 선정함 (5개 분야에 대한 우선 순위는 없음)

o 금번 공식/비공식 회의는 반덤핑, 보조금/상계관세, 무역관련투자조치, BOP조항에 대하여 91.7.22 - 26간 제네바에서 개최될 예정

   - 7. 22 : 전체 공식회의,   7. 23 : 반덤핑,   7, 24 : 보조금/상계관세,   7. 25 : 무역관련 투자조치(TRIMs),   7, 26 : BOP, 전체 공식회의 순으로 진행될 예정

   - 금번회의에서는 협상진전상황 평가 및 의제별 주요쟁점 확인 정도에 그칠 전망임

0016

II. 의제별 주요쟁점 및 입장

가. 반덤핑

1) 진전 상황

o 그동안 5차례의 의장안이 제시되었음에도 불구하고, 수출국. 수입국간의
  첨예한 이해 대립으로 협상의 기초로 할 Text에도 합의를 보지 못하고 있음

  - 수출국 (일본, 북구 및 한국, 홍콩등 개도국)
    : 덤핑 및 피해 판정기준의 합리화, 조사절차의 강화, 소멸시효 설정
      등으로 현행 반덤핑 협정을 강화하여 선진국의 자의적인 반덤핑
      관세 발동 방지 주장

  - 수입국 (미국, EC)
    : 반덤핑 규제를 회피하려는 우회덤핑 행위등 새로운 형태의 무역활동을
      효율적으로 규제하기 위한 새로운 규정 (New issue)의 도입을 주장

o 지난 브랏셀 각료 회의에서 조사 절차의 명료성 확보와 관련된 7개 항목에
  대해서는 잠정 합의를 보아 핵심쟁점에 대한 협상의 초석은 마련함

  ① 각종 쟁점을 단계적으로 구분하여 협상을 추진키로 잠정 합의

  ② 첫 단계로 반덤핑 조사절차의 명료성 확보와 관련한 일부쟁점 합의

    - 반덤핑 조사를 위한 증거 확보의 명료성 및 효율성 제고
    - 잠정조치의 요건 강화
    - 수출업자의 가격인상 약속 요건의 강화
    - 반덤핑 판정의 공표 및 설명 의무화
    - 사법적 조사절차 도입
    - 반덤핑 현장조사 절차의 구체화
    - 이용 가능한 정보 사용의 남용방지

0017

2) 미결 쟁점 및 아국 입장

가) 국내가격 결정시 원가이하 판매 (Sales below Cost)를 정상적 거래로의
인정 여부

   o 수출국 (일본, 북구 및 한국등 개도국) : 신제품 출하시 또는 시황이
   불황인 경우는 일시적으로 국내판매가격이 원가보다 낮을 수 있으므로
   비용 회수의 여부는 제품의 Life cycle 또는 산업의 Business cycle을
   기초로 하여 판정

   o 미국, EC : 제품의 Life cycle은 각 기업의 판매전략, 제품의 종류에
   따라 상이하여 일정한 기준 설정이 곤란하므로 조사대상 기간
   (미국 : 6개월, EC : 1년)을 기준으로 비용 회수 여부 판단

나) 구성가격 (Constructed Value) 산정시 이윤.산정기준

   o 수출국 (한국) : 회계장부상의 실제 Data로 이윤 산정이 어려운 경우 당해
                   수출업자가 동일 부류의 제품 판매에서 실현한 이윤을
                   우선 적용

   o E C : 수출국내 당해 제품을 생산하는 여타 생산자의 가중평균 이윤을 적용

   o 미국 : Benchmark (총 생산비의 8%) 설정이 명료성, 예측가능성
           측면에서 합리적

다) 가중평균에 의한 수출가격과 정상가격의 비교 (Negative Dumping 인정 여부)

   o 수출국 (한국) : 수출가격과 정상가격 (국내가격 등)의 비교는 동일한
                   기준을 기초로 해야 하므로 양시장 가격을 가중평균치로 비교하여
                   Negative Dumping의 경우도 덤핑마진 산정시 인정
                   (단, Selective 덤핑의 방지를 위한 예외인정 가능)

   o 미국, EC : 수출가격을 가중 평균치로 하는 경우 수출업자가 특정기간
               동안 특정모델에 대해 덤핑 행위를 하는 경우 (Selective
               Dumping) 이를 방지할 수 없으므로 국내가격을 가중평균으로
               하고 수출 가격은 개별거래 가격을 기준으로 비교   0018

라) 피해의 누적 (Cumulation)

  o 수출국 (한국) : 피해 판정은 원칙적으로 각 수입원에 대해 독립적으로
                  이루어져야 함.   단, 예외적인 경우에 한하여 Cumulation 인정 가능

  o 미국, EC : 피해의 누적 효과로 인한 국내산업의 피해를 구제할 수
              있도록 Cumulation을 일반적으로 허용해야 함.
              단, De minimus 덤핑 마진이나 수입규모가 미미한 경우는
              Cumulation에서 제외 가능

마) De minimus 덤핑 마진 및 덤핑 수입량

  o 수출국 (한국) : de minimus에 대한 계량화를 통하여 객관적인 기준 설정
                  (덤핑마진 : 5%, 덤핑수입량 : 수입국 시장점유율 3%)

  o 미국, EC

   - 덤핑마진 : De minimus의 계량화에 대해서는 긍정적이나 그 수준은
               매우 낮게 설정 (0.5% 정도)

   - 덤핑 수입량 : 누적 효과를 통하여 국내산업에 피해 우려가 있고 소규모
                 수출국가에 반덤핑 관세를 부과하지 않는 경우 시장대체
                 가능성이 존재하므로 계량화 반대

바) 제소자격

  o 수출국 (한국) : 과반수 지지 요건을 원칙 (국내 총생산의 50%)

  o 미 국 : 관행상 침묵을 지지로 보고 있으며, 과반수지지 요건 반대.
           노동조합의 제소자격 부여 주장

사) 소멸시효 설정 (Sunset Clause)

  o 수출국, EC등 대부분의 국가 3-5년의 소멸시효 설정

   - EC, 카나다, 일본, 홍콩 : 5년

   - 한국, 노르딕, 뉴질랜드 : 3년

  o 미국 : 자국 제도상 연례 재심의 실질적 운용으로 충분하므로 소멸시효
          설정 반대

0019

사) 우회덤핑 규제 (Anticircumvention)조항 설정

　　o 미국, EC : 제 3국 조립도 규제 대상에 포함하고, 수입 부품의 완제품에서
　　　　　　차지하는 비중 (X%)은 40~50% 정도
　　　　　　(EC : 조립수준 비교 기준을 수입품 가격과 조립에 사용된
　　　　　　전체 부품 가격 비교)

　　o 캐나다 및 수출국 (한국) : 제 3국 조립은 제외하고 X%는 90%로 하며,
　　　　　　　　　　　수입국내 조립 제품 가격과 수출국 국내
　　　　　　　　　　　가격과의 비교 요건도 추가되어야 함

3) 협상 전망

　　o 주요 개정대상 잇슈에 대한 기술적인 논의는 이미 완료된 상태로 향후 협상은
　　　수출입국이 주장하는 기존규제강화 잇슈와 새로운 잇슈의 협상에의 반영 정도를
　　　정치적으로 타협하는 문제가 쟁점이 될 것임

　　o 미국, EC의 완강한 입장으로 현행 협정의 강화는 어려울 것으로 전망됨

4) 협상 대응 방향

　　o 현 협정의 강화와 관련된 우리의 우선반영 이슈와 미국, EC 주장인 우회덤핑
　　　방지조항이 적절히 반영되는 수준에서 합의 도출
　　　- 단, 우회덤핑 방지조항은 순수한 우회덤핑 (수입국내 단순조립 행위)만을
　　　　대상으로 하고 그 규제요건도 엄격히 해야 된다는 전제

　　o 공동협조 강화
　　　- 기존에 협조체제를 유지하고 있는 "주요 수출국간 반덤핑 비공식협의회
　　　　(일본, 북구, 홍콩, 싱가폴 등 9개국)"와 공동 대응 추진

0020

나. 보조금. 상계관세

1) 진전상황

o 주요 협상경과

- '89.4 무역협상위원회 (Trade Negotiation Committee)에서 협정골격 (Framework)에 합의함

```
┌─────── 〈협정 Framework〉 ───────────────────────────┐
│                                                        │
│  - 내 용                                                │
│    . 금지보조금 (Prohibited Subsidies)                  │
│    . 상계가능보조금 (Actionable Subsidies)              │
│    . 허용보조금 (Non-Actionable Subsidies)              │
│    . 개도국 우대                                         │
│    . 통보 및 다자간 감시                                 │
│    . 분쟁해결절차                                        │
│  - 특 징                                                │
│    . 보조금 지급에 대한 규율과 상계조치 발동 규율을 동시에 강화   │
│      함으로써 양자간 균형 유지                            │
│    . 현행 협정은 보조금의 효과에 따라 규제하고 있으나, 새로운 협정은 │
│      각 보조금의 성격에 따라 일률적으로 규제함              │
│                                                        │
└────────────────────────────────────────────────────┘
```

- '90.5 의장 협상안 배포

    . 그동안의 협상 과정에서 나타난 각국의 입장을 감안하여 협상그룹의 의장이 협정문 초안을 작성함

    . 1차 수정 (9.4), 2차 수정 (11.2), 3차 수정 (11.7)

- '90.12.3 ~ 7 브랏셀 각료회의시 협상그룹 의장 보고서 채택

0021

o 합의사항

  - 명시적으로 합의된 사항은 없음

  - 브랏쉘 각료회의시 채택된 의장보고서는 향후 협상의 기초가 될 뿐이며
    주요 쟁점들은 미합의 상태임

o 미합의 사항

  - 정치적 결정사항

    . 일부 보조금의 심각한 손상 추정
    . 수량기준 채택 여부
    . 허용보조금의 요건 및 중복지급 허용
    . 농산물 보조금에 대한 본 협정 적용 여부
    . 개도국 우대조치
    . 보조금액 계산방법

  - 기술적 사항 → 91년 상반기중 우선 논의키로 함 (91.3.25 TNC 비공식 회의)

    . 이중 가격제도 및 정부물품 공급제도 (멕시코 주장)
    . 시장경제체제 전환국가 우대 (헝가리 주장)
    . 보조금액 산정방법 (인도 주장)

0022

2) 미결쟁점 및 아국입장

```
┌─────────────────────────────┐
│  쟁점 1) 농산물 보조금 포함 여부  │
└─────────────────────────────┘
```

o 의장안 내용

- 언급 없음

o 주요국 입장

- <브라질등 개도국 및 미국, 호주등 농산물 수출국> : 동 협정안은
  농산물 보조금에도 적용됨

- <일본, EC, 한국, 북구> : 농산물 보조금은 농산물 그룹에서 별도로
  다룰 것을 주장

o 아국입장

- 농산물 협상 그룹은 농산물 교역과 관련된 모든 측면에 대하여
  일차적인 책임을 지고 있으며 지금까지 본 협상과 별도로 논의를
  진행시켜 왔으므로, 현 시점에서 농산물 보조금에 대한 논의는
  농산물 협상그룹에 일임하도록 함.

- 보조금 협상 그룹은 농산물 협상 그룹이 합의한 결과를 수용함으로써
  농산물 보조금에 대해서도 규율할 수 있음.

- 아국입장 및 우선순위
  . 농산물 보조금은 별도의 농산물 협상 그룹의 결과 수용
  . 우선순위 : 적극 반영

0023

쟁점 2) 개도국 우대조치 (제27조)

- **의장안 내용**

  o 개도국에게는 금지보조금인 수출보조금을 줄 수 있도록 함.

  · 최빈개도국(Annex7 에 열거된 29개국)은 수출보조금을 지급할 수 있음.

  · 기타 개도국(Annex 8에 열거)은 단계적으로 수출보조금을 감축하도록
     하고, 조치가능보조금의 구제절차를 적용함 (국가별로 4구분하여 감축
     기간을 다르게 하여, 한국등 선발개도국은 수출보조금을 줄수 없도록 함)

  o 기타 우대내용

  · 심각한 손상 추정(제6.1조)의 적용을 배제

  · 아래의 경우에는 상계조치를 하지 못하도록 함.

     (a) 소액보조금 (보조비율 미정)

     (b) 수입국의 시장점유율이 일정수준 이하인 품목에 대한 보조금, 단
         이러한 품목들이 복수의 국가들로부터 수입될때는 총수입액이 시장
         점유율의 일정비율을 초과하지 않아야 함.

- **주요국 입장**

  o 〈선발 개도국을 제외한 모든 국가〉

  · 개도국은 경제발전 정도에 따라 국제사회에서의 의무를 분담해야 하며,
     따라서 개도국별 차별대우를 규정한 의장안에 찬성

  o 〈미국, 북구, 스위스등 선진국〉

  · 선진국과 경쟁관계에 있는 한국등 선발개도국은 선진국과 동일한 의무를
     부담해야 함

  o 〈한국, 싱가폴, 말레이지아〉

  · 개도국 분류는 각료선언에서 본협상에 위임된 사항이 아님.

0024

- 아국입장

  o 개도국 분류는 본 협상에의 위임사항이 아니며, 이는 보다 전문적인
    기관에 의한 전반적, 객관적 판단을 필요로 하며

  o 또한, 본 협상에서의 개도국 분류는 중요한 선례로서 일반적인 국제
    관계에 영향을 미치기 때문에 임의적인 개도국 분류에 반대함.

  o 서면으로 대안 제시
    · 최저개도국을 제외한 개도국은 일률적으로 일정기간내 수출보조금 폐지를
      약속
    · 다만 동기간 만료시점에 가서 경제개발의 낙후등으로 이를 이행 수 없는
      국가의 대해서는 기간 연장 허용

  o 그러나, <u>개도국 분류를 통해 혜택이 박탈되는 국가는 한국·싱가폴·말련 등
    극소수 국가이고, 따라서 이같은 아국등의 입장은 선진국이나 후진국 어느쪽
    으로 부터도 지지를 받기가 힘들 것으로 예상</u>

- 아국 입장 및 우선순위

  o (제1안) : <u>상기 아국이 서면으로 제출한 대안</u>
  o (제2안) : <u>의장안을 수용하고 Annex 8 개도국 List에 아국포함</u>

0025

쟁점 3) 심각한 손상(Serious prejudice) 추정(제6.1조)

- 의장안 내용

  o 아래 보조금은 조치가능보조금으로 하되, 이들은 무조건 심각한 손상을 초래하는 것으로 간주함.

  o 따라서, 위의 보조금을 지급하는 국가는 이들 보조금이 심각한 손상을 입히지 않았음을 입증해야하는 부담을 지게되며(6.2조), 이러한 입증이 없을 경우 구제절차에 의해 대응조치가 가능함.

    · 물품의 보조금액 비율이 [5]%를 초과하는 보조금
    · 특정산업에서 발생하는 영업손실을 보전하기 위한 보조금
    · 어떤 기업의 영업손실을 보전하기 위한 보조금
    · 직접적인 채무감면

- 동 조항의 배경

  o 의장안은 국내보조금의 금지화를 주장하는 미국입장과 이에 반대하는 EC 등의 주장을 절충한 것임.

- 주요국의 입장

  o 〈미국〉 : 아래의 국내 보조금은 금지보조금으로 분류주장.
    · 영업손실을 보전하기 위한 무상지원
    · 채무의 직접 감면
    · 조달 및 관리비용 이하의 금리에 의한 정부 대출
    · 손실이 예상되는 부문에 대한 지분 투자
    · 적정비용보다 낮은 보증료에 의한 대출 보증
    · 생산 성과부 보조금

0026

o 〈EC · 일본 · 개도국〉 : 국내보조금의 금지화에 반대

· E C : 보조금 규율은 무역에 미치는 부정적 효과에 따라 대처하는
방식이어야 함.

· 일 본 : 보조금 규율강화와 함께 대응조치 남용방지대책도 필요

· 헝가리 : 국내보조금의 금지 완화 주장

- 아국입장

o 아국은 해당보조금 지급국가에게 과도한 입증책임을 지게하고, 분쟁의 소지를
제공한다는 이유에서 적극적으로 이에 반대해 왔음.

o 그러나, 심각한 손상추정은 개도국 우대조항(제27 제4항)에 의해 개도국에는
적용되지 않으므로,

o 아국이 추후 개도국 List (Annex8)에 포함될 경우 동 규정은 아국에 대해
적용되지 않음.

- 아국 입장 및 우선순위

o (1안) : 제6.1조 삭제지지(적극적 반대입장 유보)

o (2안) : Annex 8의 개도국 List에 포함될때, 의장안 수용

0027

쟁점 4) 수량기준 채택여부 (제6.1조 (a))

- 의장안 내용

  o 보조금액 비율이 [5]%를 초과할 경우 심각한 손상이 있는 것으로 추정함

- 주요국 입장

  o <미국, 북구, 캐나다, 호주, 뉴질랜드, 스위스등> : 찬성국가

    · 미국 : 보조금 규율강화를 위해서는 반드시 채택필요

    · 북구 : 수량기준이 문제를 갖고 있으나, 보조금 규율강화를 위한 별도의
    대안이 없음

  o <EC, 일본, 한국, 싱가폴, 개도국등> : 반대국가

    · E C : 다른 수단을 통한 보조금 규율강화 주장, 도입하더라도 기존
    보조금에 대해서는 관용필요

    · 일본 : 원칙적으로 반대. 도입하더라도 천재지변등의 경우에 지급되는
    보조금은 제외되어야 함

- 아국입장

  o 적극적으로 반대하여 왔음.

  o 보조금은 무역효과에 따라서 규제되어야 하는데, 수량기준은
  이러한 보조금과 무역효과간의 상관관계를 무시하는 것이며,
  시행상 수출기업에게 심각한 손상을 끼치지 않았음을 증명해야
  하는등 과도한 업무부담을 초래함.

0028

o 그러나 보조금 규율강화를 주장하는 미국 등의 입장이 강경하고, 이를
   반대하던 EC·일본도 수량기준의 채택가능성을 암시하고 있으므로
   아국이 강경입장을 견지하더라도 관철될 가능성이 크지 않을 것으로 예상됨

o 또한 개도국 우대조항(제27조제4항)에 의하면 수량기준에 의한 심각한
   손상추정은 개도국에게는 적용되지 않으므로, 수량기준이 채택되더라도
   아국이 개도국 분류에 포함될 경우 동 조항은 적용되지 않음.

- 아국 입장 및 우선순위

   o (1안) : 제6.2조(a) 삭제지지(적극적 반대입장 유보)

   o (2안) : 수량기준의 상향조정 여부가 논의될 경우, 상향조정 지지

쟁점 5) 허용보조금의 요건(제8조)

- 의장안 내용

   o 특정성있는 다음 보조금은 제한된 조건, 특히 수치상한을 두어 허용

      · 연구개발보조금 : 기본적인 산업연구는 소요비용의 [20]% 초과금지
                          응용연구개발은 소요비용의 [10]% 초과금지

      · 구조조정보조금 : 생산시설의 감축, 폐기위한 비용의 [X]% 초과금지

      · 환경보호보조금 : 소요비용의 [20]% 초과금지

      · 지역개발보조금 : 전국평균보다 [15]%이상 낙후지역의 개발만 허용

- 주요국 입장

   o 〈미 국〉: 허용보조금의 범위가 지나치게 확대되었음

   o 〈개도국〉: 허용보조금의 요건이 지나치게 엄격함

0029

- 아국입장

　o 아국의 경우 <u>연구개발, 구조조정, 지역개발, 환경보호</u>등은 필수적인 것으로 향후

　　<u>이들 지원사례가 증가할 것</u>을 예상되므로, <u>가능한 한 허용보조금의 요건을</u>

　　<u>완화하는 것이 바람직함</u>.

- 아국입장 및 우선순위

　o 허용보조금의 요건완화 여부가 논의될 경우 요건완화 입장 지지

　　· (1안) : <u>수치한도 삭제 지지</u>
　　· (2안) : <u>수치한도 상향조정 지지</u>

> **쟁점 6) 복수의 허용보조금 수혜(제8.5조)**

- 의장안 내용

　o 특정기업이 복수의 허용보조금을 수혜할 경우, 단지 한가지 보조금만을

　　허용보조금으로 봄

- 주요국 입장

　o 〈미　국〉: 복수의 허용보조금 수혜금지

　o 〈EC, 일본, 한국등〉: 복수의 허용보조금 수혜가능

- 아국입장

　o <u>각 허용보조금은 상당히 제한적인 요건을 충족하는 경우에만 허용되므로,</u>

　　<u>한가지 보조금만 허용하는 것은 지나친 제한임</u>

　o 허용보조금은 보조금 자체의 성질에 따라 허용되는 것이므로, 중복지급

　　된다 하더라도 허용보조금의 성질이 변하는 것이 아니므로 허용되어야 함

- 아국입장 및 우선순위

　o 동 조항 (8.5조) 삭제

0030

- 의장안 내용

o 보조금액 계산방법은 각국 법령에 규정하되 명료하고(transparent), 적정
하여야(adquately)하며, 다음 지침에 부합하여야 함

(a) 정부의 투자는 민간투자가들의 통상적인 투자관행과 비교

(b) 정부의 대출은 당해 대출금리와 시장금리를 비교

(c) 정부의 대출보증은 당해 대출이자율과 동 보증이 없었을 경우의 이자율을
비교

(d) 정부에 의한 재화, 용역의 공급 또는 구매의 경우는 시장가격과 비교
결정

(e) 시장가격이 존재하지 않을 경우(정부가 유일한 공급자 또는 수요자인
경우) 차별여부에 의해 구분

→ 상기 의장안은 원칙적으로 수혜자 수익기준(시장가격과 비교)을 채택
하고 있음

- 주요국 입장

o 〈미 국〉

· 의장안이 수혜자 수익개념에 충실치 못함

· 보조금은 일반 민간투자자의 합리적 투자 및 대출원칙 등을 기준으로
산정되어야 함(수익기준 강화)

o 〈북구, EC, 카나다, 일본〉

· 북 구 : 보조금 산정기준의 명확화 주장, 정부비용개념 지지

· EC, 카나다, 일본 : 의장안이 수익기준에 근거하고 있어 기술적으로
보조금액 산정을 더욱 어렵게 하므로, 동 기준은
정부 비용개념을 채택하여야 함

0031

- 아국입장

    o 수익기준의 불합리성

    (ⅰ) 복잡한 실제 시장에서 적절한 비교대상 시장가격을 안다는 것이
        불가능한 경우가 많고

    (ⅱ) 시장가격에는 기업의 정상이윤이 포함되고 있으므로 이를 기준으로 할
        경우 이윤부분도 보조금으로 간주될 가능성이 있음.

    o 정부비용기준의 장점

    (ⅰ) 비용파악이 비교적 용이하고,

    (ⅱ) 보조금 부분이 축소되는 효과가 있음

- 아국입장 및 우선순위
    · (1안): 정부비용기준 채택 주장
    · (2안): 수익기준 채택 수용

0032

- 의장안 내용

  o 특정지역내에 있는 기업에게 주는 보조금은 지급기관에 관계없이 특정적인
  것으로 봄. 단, 허용대상 지역개발보조금에는 본규정 적용 배제

- 주요국 입장

  o 〈카나다, 호주〉

  · 지방정부도 중앙정부와 같은 수준의 의무를 부담하는 것이므로,

  · 지방정부가 관할내에 있는 모든 기업에게 지급하는 보조금은 특정성이 없음.

  o 아직까지 협상에서 본격적으로 쟁점화 되지는 않고 있음.

- 아국입장

  o 아국의 경우 장기적 측면에서 지방자치제의 정착이후, 지방정부의 보조금 활용
  가능성도 고려할 필요가 있으나,

  o 아국과 같이 지방의 재정자립도가 낮고, 중앙집권적인 국가에서는 사실상
  지방정부가 독자적으로 재원을 확보해서 지원하는 순수한 지방정부보조금은
  많지 않을 것으로 생각됨

  o 반면, 지방정부의 재정자립도가 비교적 높은 수준에 있는 연방국가의 경우
  지방정부 보조금을 규제밖에 둘 경우 보조금 규제의 실효성이 약화됨.

  o 따라서 의장안 제2.1조d 규정상 특정지역이 특정지방정부를 포함하는 것으로
  해석된다면, 아국입장과 일치됨

- 아국입장 및 우선순위

  o (1안) : 의장안 2.1(d) 존속 지지 (적극적 주장은 유보)

  o (2안) : 반대입장 수용가능

0033

3) 아직까지 논의안된 쟁점 및 아국입장

1) 경미한 보조금에 대한 조사 중단요건 (제11.7조)

- 의장안 내용
  - o 조사당국이 보조금지급 및 피해사실에 관한 충분한 증거가 없다고 판단할 경우에는 즉시 조사신청을 기각하고 조사중단
  - o 보조금액, 피보조수입량 및 보조금 지급으로 인한 피해가 경미한 경우에도 즉시 조사중단
    - · 보조금액이 경미한 경우 : 보조비율이 [×]% 이하
    - · 피보조수입량이 경미한 경우 : 수입국내 유사물품 시장에서의 동 수입 비중이 [Y]% 이하로서, 이들 국가들로부터의 전체수입비중이 동 국내 시장의 [Z]% 이상이 아닌 경우

- 아국입장
  - o 이에 대해서 아직까지 전혀 논의된 바가 없으므로 어느 정도의 수준으로 이들 비율이 결정될 것인지 예측이 곤란하나, 제6.1조 수량기준에 의한 심각한 피해 추정 보조비율이 [5%]에 불과하므로, 이는 매우 낮은 수준이 될 것으로 예상됨
  - o 다만, MTN 반덤핑협상에서는 덤핑율이 경미할 경우 조사중단이 논의되고 있는 바, 아국은 5%를 주장하였으나, 미국, EC 등은 동 비율이 지나치게 높음을 이유로 반대하고 있음.

- 아국입장 및 우선순위
  - o 경미한 보조 비율
    - · (1안) : 5% 주장 (MTN 반덤핑협상의 아국입장)
    - · (2안) : 5% 미만 수용
  - o 수입비중 기준 : 가능한한 높은 수준 지지
    - · (1안) : 2% 주장
    - · (2안) : 2% 미만 주장
  - o 국내시장 점유비중 : 가능한한 높은 수준 지지

0034

2) 보호대상 국내산업의 최저생산비율(제16조)

- 의장안 내용

  o 본 협정의 목적상 "국내산업"이라 함은 유사물품의 국내 생산자 전부 또는
    이들 물품의 국내 총생산의 상당부분(major proportion)을 생산하는 생산자
    집단을 의미함

  o 단, 생산자가 피보조물품, 유사물품의 수출자 또는 수입자와 특수관계에
    있거나, 그 자신이 수입자인 경우는 국내산업에서 제외

  o "상당부분"이라 함은 유사물품의 국내총생산의 가액대비, 적어도 [×]%
    이상을 의미함

- MTN 반덤핑협상의 논의

  o 종전 반덤핑 Code에는 major proportion의 정의가 없었으나,
    신협정에서는 수량화된 기준을 채택하기로 하였으며, 아국과 개도국은
    50%를 주장하는데 반해, 미국, EC 등은 이의 하향조정을 주장

- 아국입장

  o 제소권자의 범위를 국내산업의 50%이상인 자로 한정시켜 무분별한 상계관세
    의 제소를 방지함.
    . 세부적인 수치가 논의될 경우 50% 주장

0035

3) 우회수출 판정기준(제21.1조)

- **의장안 내용**

    o 본 협정에 의한 상계관계가 부과된 이후

    (ⅰ) 상계관세 대상국으로부터 상계 대상물품을 가공, 조립하기 위한

    부품이 수입되고, 동부품 가액이 조립, 완성된 물품 가액과 동일

    하거나 [X]%를 초과하는 경우 또는

    (ⅱ) 상계관세 대상국으로부터 상계 대상물품을 가공, 조립하기 위한

    부품이 제3국으로 수출되고, 그 제3국이 조립, 완성된 물품을

    다시 수출할 때 부품가액이 조립, 완성된 물품가액과 동일하거나

    [X]%를 초과하는 경우에는

    o 체약국은 본조 제2항과 제3항에 규정된 조건에 따라 제4항과 제5항에

    정해진 조치를 적용할 수 있음

- **MTN 반덤핑협상 내용**

    o 대상부품이 조립, 완성된 물품가액의 주요비율(predominant

    proportion) [전체부품가액의 (75)%이상]을 차지하고, 이들 부품이 당해

    완성물품을 위한 핵심부품일 것. 단, 조립공정으로 인한 부가가치가

    수입국내에 조립, 완성되는 유사물품의 공장도가격(ex-factory cost)의

    [20]% 이상인 경우에는 조치대상이 아님(제12.1조(v))

    o 아국은 MTN 반덤핑협상에서 90% 주장함.

    o 보조금·상계관세 협상과 반덤핑협상의 규정형태가 상이함을 이유로 상기

    비율 축소를 주장할 경우

    · 보조금협상안은 전체물품가액 기준 당해부품가액 비율

    · 반덤핑협상안은 전체부품가액 기준 당해부품가액 비율

    → 이 경우 낮은 수준으로 절충가능

- **아국입장 및 우선순위**

    o (1안): 90% 주장 (MTN 반덤핑협상의 아국입장)
    o (2안): 하향조정 가능

0036

3) 협상전망

　ｏ 91년 상반기중에는 각국의 정치적 절충이 요구되는 주요 쟁점에 대한 협상은
　　 유보되고, 기술적 사항만이 주로 논의될 것임
　　　 - 이중 가격제도 및 정부 물품 공급 제도의 보조금 여부
　　　 - 시장체제 전환국가 우대
　　　 - 보조금액 산정방법

　ｏ 91년 하반기중에 각 국가 그룹별로 주요 협상 쟁점에 대해 정치적 절충이
　　 이루어질 것으로 예상됨
　　　 - 보조금 규제강화 요구 국가들 : 미국, 호주, 카나다 등
　　　 - 보조금 규제강화 반대 국가들 : EC, 일본, 한국, 개도국 등

　ｏ 지금까지 보조금 규제 강화를 요구하는 국가들이 협상을 주도해 왔으며,
　　 이들의 주장이 UR 협상의 기본 정신인 무역자유화에 부응하므로
　　 이들의 의도대로 타결될 가능성이 높음
　　　 - 단, 새로운 규제 수단이 도입되더라도, 그 수치적 한도등은 다소
　　　　 완화될 것임
　　　 - 보조금 규제 강화에 따라 상계관세 부과에 대한 규제도 강화될 것임

4) 협상 대응 방향

　ｏ 협상과정
　　 - 규제대상 보조금은 가능한 한 수출보조금에 국한하는 것으로 시도
　　 - 상계관세등 대응조치 발동 요건의 엄격화, 합리화
　　 - 협정상 용어 및 조건을 명확히 하여 적용상 문제점 축소

　ｏ 협상이후
　　 - 정부부처 및 민간기업에 대한 홍보를 통해 대응태세 구비
　　 - 기존 산업지원 제도의 분석 검토 → 수정. 보완
　　 - 보조금 관련 대외업무 전담기구 보강
　　 - 외국의 보조금 지원사례 및 본 협정 시행에 따른 대응책 연구

0037

라. 무역관련 투자제한조치 (TRIMs)

1) 진전상황

o 주요협상 경위

- UR/TRIMs 협상은 서비스. 지적소유권과 함께 GATT 협상의 새로운 분야
  (new issue)로써 외국인 투자에 대한 각종 규제와 제한을 철폐함으로써
  국제간 투자를 촉진하고 세계무역 증진을 도모하기 위하여 UR 협상에 포함,
  '87.4월부터 협상을 개최한 이후, '90년말까지 20여 차례의 실무자간
  협상과 수차례의 Green Room 회의를 가졌음

- 그러나, 기본적으로 자국기업의 해외투자를 촉진. 보호하여야 할 입장에
  있는 선진국이 투자대상국 (Host Country)의 투자제한조치 (TRIMs)를
  규제하여야 한다고 주장하는 반면, 해외투자 실적이 거의 없고 자국
  산업을 보호해야 할 입장에 있는 개도국이 투자제한 조치에 대한 규제를
  반대하고 있는등 주요 쟁점에 대하여 선진국과 개도국간에 입장 차이가
  현격함

- 지난해 브랏셀 각료 회의에서도 선진국과 개도국간의 입장 조정에 실패

2) 미결쟁점 및 아국 입장

가) 협상의 범위

o 선진국 입장

- TRIMs은 신규투자뿐 아니라 기존 외국인 투자기업의 전반적인 영업
  활동과 관련하여 부과되는 제한 조치를 폭넓게 포함하여야 함

- 보조금등 특혜부여의 조건으로 부과되는 조치도 규제대상이 되어야 함

0038

o 개도국 입장

- TRIMs은 신규투자와 관련 부과되는 경우만 포함
- 보조금등 특혜부여와 관련 부과되는 조치는 보조금. 상계관세협상
  그룹에서 논의할 사항임

o 아국입장

- 투자제한조치중 내.외국 기업에 동등하게 부과하는 경우에는 TRIMs
  범위내에서 제외 되어야 함
- 아국은 조세감면등 혜택을 부여하면서 투자제한조치를 부과하는 사례가
  없는 반면, 개도국은 부과 사례가 많음. 따라서, 아국의 해외
  투자 측면을 고려할때 이들 TRIMs에 포함 규제 대상이 되어야 함

나) 규제의 방법

o 선진국 입장

- 국산부품사용 조건등과 같이 GATT 제 3조, 제 11조에 위반되는
  TRIMs은 금지 대상이 되도록 규정하여야 함
- 수출이행 조건도 무역왜곡 효과가 심각하므로 금지 대상이 되어야 함

o 개도국 입장

- 어떤 경우도 TRIMs을 일반적인 금지 대상으로 할 수는 없으며,
  Case by Case로 검토후 무역왜곡 효과를 치유토록 하여야 함
- 수출이행 조건은 GATT의무 위반이 아니므로 규제 대상이 될수 없음

o 아국입장

- 무역왜곡효과가 직접적이고 심각한 TRIMs은 금지대상으로 하되
  개도국에 대한 예외 범위를 확대
- 수출이행 조건도 TRIMs으로 규제대상이 되어야 하나, 개도국의
  국제수지 개선등의 목적상 불가피한 경우 예외 인정

0039

다) 개도국에 대한 배려

　o 선진국 입장

　　- 개도국에 대한 배려는 GATT 제 18조 (개도국에 대한 예외)의 규정에
　　　따라 잠정적이고 제한적이어야 함

　o 개도국 입장

　　- 개도국의 경제개발 필요성등을 고려, 개도국이 필요시 TRIMs을 운용할
　　　수 있도록 전반적인 예외를 인정하여야 함

　o 아국입장

　　- 개도국에 대하여는 GATT 제 18조에서 규정하고 있는 범위 이상으로
　　　TRIMs 의무에 대한 예외 인정

라) 제한적 사업관행 (Restrictive Business Practice)

　o 선진국 입장
　　- 제한적 사업관행은 '86.9월 Punta del Este 각료선언에 의한 협상범위
　　　에 포함되지 않음

　o 개도국 입장

　　- 다국적 기업등이 제한적 사업관행으로 무역을 심각하게 왜곡하는 사례가
　　　많으므로 본 협상에 포함 하여야 함

　o 아국입장

　　- 다국적 기업의 제한적 사업관행도 본 협상 범위에 포함하여야 함

0040

3) 협상 전망

o 선진국과 개도국간의 입장 차이가 현격하여 TRIMs 협상 자체로는 타결 되기가
  어려우나 농산물등 주요 분야에서 정치적인 타협이 이뤄져 UR 협상이
  전반적으로 타결되는 방향으로 합의가 되면 TRIMs 협상도 정치적 결단에
  의해 타결될 수 있을 것임

o 그러나 최빈 개도국의 경우에는 UR 협상타결 이후에도 TRIMs 협정에
  참여하지 않는 경우도 예상할 수 있음

4) 협상 대응 방향

o 투자제한조치 (TRIMs) 협상 타결시 아국기업의 해외투자 환경 개선을 기대할 수
  있는 반면, 외국인 투자를 추가로 개방하여야 하는 부담은 거의 없으므로
  아국으로서는 협상이 타결되는 것이 유리함

o 다만, 협상 결과에 선진국 및 일부 개도국만 참여하고 다수 개도국이 불참할
  경우에도 아국으로서는 참여가 불가피한 바, 이 경우 ① 아국의 대개도국
  투자환경 개선을 기대할 수 없고 ② 선진국에 비하여 상대적으로 제한조치가
  많은 아국이 개선 요청을 많이 받을 것 등을 예상할 때 아국으로서는 다수
  개도국이 참여하는 것이 유리하므로 이에 대한 노력 필요

라. BOP 조항

1) BOP 조항 개선 입장

가) 논의이유

o 갓트 12 -조 및 18조 B에 의한 갓트 일반원칙에 대한 예외는 무역체제의
중요 요소이며, 갓트 규정의 다른 쟁점처럼 다루어져야 함

o BOP 조항에 근거한 조치 특히, 무역 왜곡 조치에 대하여는 효율적인 규율
이 없으며, 갓트 의무에 대한 영구적인 예외가 되고 있고, 동 조항 적용
국가나 상대국가에 불필요한 비용을 야기하여, 다자간 체제의 약점 및
불협화음의 원인이 됨

나) EC, 카나다, 미국의 제안 요지(1979년 선언을 대체할 BOP 목적의 무역조치에
관한 새로운 선언안)

o 선진국의 BOP 목적을 이유로 한 무역제한조치 금지 공약의 강화

o 12조나 18조 B에 근거한 무역조치는 BOP 문제의 정도에 비례해야 하며
보호의 목적이 아니라 국내 구조조정정책이 효과가 있기까지의 일시적인
조치로써 사용해야 함

o 무역조치는 명료해야 하고, 무차별적이고, 제시될 철폐 및 점진적 완화
계획에 따른 기간의 제한이 있어야 함(선진국은 개도국보다 짧은 기간 허용)

 * E C : 제한조치 철폐를 위한 일반적으로 적용가능한 고정된 철폐 계획이
아닌 "합리적인" 철폐기간 계획이 제시 요구

0042

o 수량제한 조치보다 가격에 기초한 조치가 바람직

 - 수량제한 조치가 불가피한 경우에도 가격에 기초한 조치보다 빨리 철폐
   되거나 가격에 기초한 조치로 대체

o BOP 위원회에서의 협의는 제한 조치의 적용 또는 강화후 4개월 이내에 시작

 - full consultation은 2년마다 개최
 - 개도국이 제시한 철폐 계획에 따른 때에는 simplified 절차를 적용할
   수 없음

o BOP 위원회는 검토중인 조치의 갓트와의 일관성 및 적절한 수정에 관하여
  이사회에 권고하여야 함

o BOP 위원회는 협의중인 체약국의 수출 이익의 증대를 위하여 체약국단이
  취할 수 있는 조치를 제안할 수 있음

  * 카나다, 미국 : BOP 위원회 협의에서의 IMF의 역할을 좀더 분명히
                 정의해야 함. 동 위원회가 당해조치의 GATT 적합 여부
                 문제에 관한 권고에 합의할 수 없을 경우, 영향을 받은
                 체약국은 갓트 분쟁해결절차로 동 문제를 해결할 수 있음

  * E C : 특정산업의 설립을 촉진하기 위한 18조 C항에 대하여 동조에 의하여
          취해진 조치로 영향을 받은 체약국의 보복 가능성을 제한하면서
          거치 관세 인상을 용이하게 함으로써 동 조항의 원용을 쉽게 할 것을
          제안

다) 지지국가

o 대부분의 선진국이 지지.   단, 몇몇 선진국의 12조를 강화하는 것은 협의
  간 가능하나, 현 단계에서 12조를 사용하지 않겠다는 약속은 곤란하다느
  의견 제시

0043

2) BOP 조항 논의의 반대 입장 (이집트, 페루등 개도국)

　　o 1979년 "BOP 목적의 무역 조치에 관한 선언"이 채택된 이후 동 문제가
　　　　취급되어야 하는지에 의문

　　o 많은 개도국의 외적인 경제환경이 대외 부채 증가, 자본유입, 교역조건의
　　　　악화, 환율 및 이자율 불안정등 여러면에서 악화되고 있음

　　o 만약 18조 B항상의 무역 조치에 관한 협상이 있어야 한다면 그 목적이
　　　　보다 엄격한 조건을 부과하는것이 아니라 동 조항의 사용에 보다 융통성을
　　　　부여 하는데 두어야 함

　　o 기존의 규정과 BOP 위원회의 관련 절차는 잘 운용되고 있고, 그 운용상의
　　　　문제점은 UR 협상과 관련해서가 아니라 동 위원회에서 다루어저야 함

　　※ 18조 B항의 flexibility

　　o 18조 B항에 의한 개도국에 허가된 융통성은 갓트 체제하의 권리, 의무의
　　　　균형의 필수적인 요소이며, 동 규정이 정상적인 갓트 규정의 예외로
　　　　간주 되어서는 안됨

　　o 동 조항은 개도국의 국제 수지상의 문제점이 구조적이고 영속적이라는
　　　　점을 인정하여 체약국단에 의하여 합의 되었으며, 체약국단에 의하여
　　　　허락된 융통성은 국가 개발 계획의 효과적인 관리를 위하여 필요한 조건임
　　　　무역제한 조치가 오랫동안 유지되어도 좋다는 것은 국제수지 문제의
　　　　구조적인 성격을 반영하고 주요 수출 시장에 대한 개도국의 접근이
　　　　불충분하다는 사실을 반영함

　　　　- 단순화된 협의 절차는 상황과 정책이 상대적으로 안정된 국가와의 빈번한
　　　　　전체 협의에서 오는 위원회와 당해국가의 부담을 완화하기 위하여 도입
　　　　　되어야 함
　　　　- 위원회에서의 consensus에 도달하는 어려움은 실질 내용에 서로 다른 견해가
　　　　　있는 것이며, 이것이 동 절차가 취약하다는 증거로 간주되어선 안됨

0044

3) 지금까지의 논의에서 의견이 일치된 점

　가) 18조 B의 필요성

　　o 12조 및 18조 B의 내용 자체는 변화되어서는 안됨

　　o BOP상의 어려운 시기에 무역조치를 사용하는 권한이 배제되어서는 안됨

　　o 장기간의 BOP상의 어려움은 국내정책, 거시경제정책 및 무역관련 조치에
　　　의한 국내문제와 무역장벽 제거 및 채무, 금융 이동에 관한 국제문제로
　　　취급될 필요성은 인정

　나) 18조 B에 의한 무역제한 조치의 문제점 인식

　　o 제한적 무역조치는 어떤 상황에서는 피할수는 없지만 일반적으로 BOP 균형을
　　　유지, 회복하기 위해서는 비효과적인 수단임을 인정

　　o 동 조치는 특정산업이나 분야를 보호할 목적으로 사용되어서는 안됨을 인정

　　o 동조치 사용시 체약국은 무역에 가장 적게 영향을 미치는 조치를 우선
　　　하여야 함을 인정

　　o 개도국의 경우 각국의 개발, 금융, 무역상황이 고려되어야 함을 인정

4) 협상 전망

　o BOP 조항은 UR 협상 결과의 선.개도국간 균형여부등 UR 전체 협상 차원에서
　　다루어질 전망임

5) 우리나라 입장

　o BOP 조항은 선진.개도국간의 첨예한 의견 대립을 보이는 미묘한 문제이고
　　아국은 이미 BOP 조항을 졸업한 만큼 구체적인 입장 표명 자제

　　- BOP 조항 개정 가능성은 거의 없으며, 다만 선진국들이 섬유협상등 여타
　　　협상분야와 연계카드로 사용

　　- BOP 조항 개정 한정시 개도국들이 우리에게 강력히 반발할 것이므로 찬성
　　　의사 표명 자제

0045

기 안 용 지

분류기호 문서번호	통기 20644-	(전화: 720 - 2188)	시 행 상 특별취급	
보존기간	영구. 준영구 10. 5. 3. 1.	장 관		
수 신 처 보존기간				
시행일자	1991. 7.20.			

보조 기 관	국 장	전결	협 조 기 관		문 서 통 제	
	심의관	현정종				
	과 장					
기안책임자		송 봉 헌			발 송 인	

경 유 수 신 참 조	건 의	발 신 명 의	

제 목	UR/규범제정 분야 협상 회의 정부대표 임명

91.7.22-26간 스위스 제네바에서 개최되는 UR/규범제정 분야

협상 회의에 참가할 정부대표를 "정부대표 및 특별사절의 임명과

권한에 관한 법률"에 의거 아래와 같이 임명할 것을 건의하오니

재가하여 주시기 바랍니다.

/뒷면 계속/   0046

- 아   래 -
1. 회 의 명 : UR/규범제정 분야 협상 회의
- 반덤핑, 보조금/상계관세, 갓트조문(BOP),TRIM
2. 회의기간 및 장소 : 91. 7.22-26, 스위스 제네바
3. 정부대표
ㅇ 상공부 국제협력관실 사무관 김영민
ㅇ 주 제네바 대표부 관계관
4. 출장기간 : 91. 7.20-28 (8박9일)
5. 소요경비 : 소속부처 소관예산
6. 훈   령 : 별도 건의 예정.   끝.

0047

발 신 전 보

	분류번호	보존기간

번   호 : WGV-0925   910720 1259 FN 종별: 암호 반신

수   신 : 주   제네바 대사. 총영사

발   신 : 장   관 (통 기)

제   목 : UR/규범제정 분야 협상

1. 7.22-26간 귀지에서 개최되는 표제회의에 아래 정부대표를 파견하니 귀관 관계관과
    함께 참석토록 조치바람.
    ○ 상공부 국제협력관실 사무관   김영민

2. 금번 회의에는 아래 기본입장과 본부대표가 지참하는 쟁점별 세부입장에 따라
    적의 대처바람.

    가. 반덤핑
        ○ 반덤핑 조치의 남용 방지를 위해 현행 협정을 강화하고 명료성을 확보하자는
           아국의 기존 입장 유지
           - 덤핑, 피해 판정 기준의 공정성 및 객관성 확보
           - 조사 개시 요건등 조사 절차의 강화
           - 소멸 시효의 설정
        ○ 미국, EC등 선진 수입국이 주장하는 우회덤핑 방지 조항 도입을 최대한 저지
           - 다만, 순수한 우회덤핑(수출국내 단순조립)의 경우는 규제 인정
              가능하나 남용 방지를 위해 엄격한 기준 설정 필요

			보 안 통 제		

앙 고 재	91 년 월 일	통상기구과	기안자 성명 농병헌	과장	심의관 천창영	국장 전경		차관	장관	외신과통제

0048

나. 보조금.상계관세

　　○ 각국의 기본입장 및 현재의 협상 상황에 대한 개괄적 평가가 있을 경우
　　　하기 사항 언급

　　　- 아국은 본 협상의 성공적인 타결을 위해 노력하고 있음을 강조

　　　- 현재 협상의 기초가 되고 있는 의장 보고서는 그간의 쟁점사항을
　　　　종합화한 점에서 긍정적으로 평가하나, 아직 개선의 여지가 많음.

　　○ 주요국의 입장 및 협상 동향을 면밀히 파악, 향후 아국의 최종 입장
　　　수립에 참고토록 준비

다. TRIMs

　　○ 투자제한 조치 협상 타결시 아국 기업의 해외투자 환경개선을 기대할 수
　　　있는 반면 외국인 투자를 추가로 개방하여야 하는 부담은 거의 없으므로
　　　아국으로서는 협상이 타결되는 것이 유리

　　○ 협상 결과에 선진국 및 일부개도국만 참여하고 다수 개도국이 불참하는
　　　경우에도 아국으로서는 참여가 불가피한 바, 이 경우 아국으로서는
　　　대개도국 투자환경 개선을 기대할 수 없고 선진국에 비하여 상대적으로
　　　제한조치가 많은 아국이 개선 요청을 많이 받을 것으로 예상되므로
　　　다수 개도국 참여가 가능하도록 노력

라. 갓트/BOP 조항

　　○ 아국의 갓트/BOP 조항 졸업을 고려할때 동 조항 개선, 강화가 유리하나
　　　개도국과의 관계 감안, 입장 표명 유보.　　　　　끝.

（통상국장　　김 용 규）

0049

34227

기 안 용 지

분류기호 문서번호	통기 20644-	(전화: 720 - 2188)	시 행 상 특별취급	
보존기간	영구. 준영구 10. 5. 3. 1.	장 관		
수 신 처 보존기간				
시행일자	1991. 7.22.			

보 조 기 관	국 장		협 조 기 관		문 서 통 제
	심의관				'91. 7. 22
	과 장	전결			
기안책임자		송 봉 헌			발

경 유 수 신 참 조	상공부장관	발 명 의		반송 1991. 7. 2 외무부

제 목	UR/규범제정 분야 협상 회의 정부대표 임명 통보

91.7.22-26간 스위스 제네바에서 개최되는 UR/규범제정 분야

협상 회의에 참가할 정부대표가 "정부대표 및 특별사절의 임명과 권한에

관한 법률"에 의거 아래와 같이 임명 되었음을 알려 드립니다.

- 아   래 -

1. 회 의 명 : UR/규범제정 분야 협상 회의   0050

- 반덤핑, 보조금/상계관세, 갓트조문(BOP),TRIM

2. 회의기간 및 장소 : 91.7.22-26, 스위스 제네바
3. 정부대표
ㅇ 상공부 국제협력관실 사무관 김영민
ㅇ 주 제네바 대표부 관계관
4. 출장기간 : 91. 7.20-28 (8박 9일)
5. 소요경비 : 소속부처 소관예산
6. 출장 결과 보고 : 귀국후 20일이내.   끝.
0051

외 무 부

종 별 :

번 호 : GVW-1388   일 시 : 91 0723 1830

수 신 : 장 관(통기, 재무부, 상공부)

발 신 : 주 제네바 대사

제 목 : UR/ 규범제정 협상(반덤핑 관련 회의)

7.23. MACIEL 의장 주재로 반덤핑 협상에 관해 주요국 비공식 회의(오전)및 공식회의(오후) 가 개최된바 요지 하기임.

0 금번 회의에서는 실질문제에 대한 토론없이 추후 협상진행에 관해 논의하였음.

0 미국, EC 는 반덤핑 협상에 있어서 기술적토론을 충분히 하였고 5개의 TEXT 가마련되어 있으므로 앞으로 구체적 이슈에 대한 기술적 토론에 대해 부정적 견해를 표명하고 최종단계에서의 정치적 결정을 강조함.

0 아국, 홍콩, 싱가폴, 노딕등 많은 수출국들은 반덤핑의 주요 이슈들은 기술적 측면과 정치적 성격을 동시에 갖고 있으며, 협상의 활력을 유지해야 한다는 관점에서 주요 이슈에 대한 기술적 토론을 9월 이후 재개할 것을 주장함.

0 일본은 반덤핑의 미결쟁점이 대부분 정치적 결정을 요하는 사항이며 다른분야협상 진행등과 관련 반덤핑 분야에서만 성급한 결정을 요구하는 것은 문제가 있으나기술적 토론을 요하는 사항이 있으면 이의 토론이 필요하다는 견해를표시함

0 의장은 상기 견해를 참작하여 다음과 같이 제의하고 참서국간에 합의함

- 9월회의(9.23.주간 예정) 에서도 비공식 회의를 개최하되 구체적 쟁점에 대한기술적 토론이 아닌 일반적 토론을 위주로 함.

- 각국이 당면한 문제점을 평가하고 브랏셀 회의에서 토론하지 못한 쟁점을 주로 토론함

- PACHAGE 로서 가능한 해결방안을 모색함.

- 이와는 별도로 의장 또는 의장 보좌관이 기술적사항에 대해 전문가들과 접촉, 조언을 구함. 끝

(대사 박수길-국장)

통상국	2차보	구주국	분석관	청와대	재무부	상공부

PAGE 1   91.07.24   05:07 FN
                                외신 1과 통제관
                                   0052

외 무 부

종 별 :

번 호 : GVW-1433

일 시 : 91 0727 1000

수 신 : 장관(통기,경기원,재무부,상공부)

발 신 : 주 제네바 대사

제 목 : UR/TRIMS 회의

7.25 당지에서 MACIEL 의장 사회로 개최된 표제회의(비공식 및 공식) 토의 내용을 아래 보고함.(엄재무관, 상공부 김사무관 참석)

1. 당일 오전 개최된 비공식회의에서 미국, 이씨,일본, 북구, 스위스 등 선진국은 UR 협상에서 TRIM 의 중요성을 재강조하면서 금지 개념의도입, 모든 TRIM 에 대한규율의 필요성등을 주장한 반면 이집트, 필리핀, 말레이지아, 태국,멕시코, 브라질등 개도국은 금지 개념 도입 불가및 개별 사안에의 무역 저해 효과 검토등을 주장하여 브랏셀회의 이전과 동일한 대립양상을 나타냈었음. 한편 호주는 기 시행되고있는TRIM 에의 새로운 규범 적용 문제에 우려를 표시하였고 인도는 RBP 를 포함하여 규율할것을 거듭 주장하였으나 미국은 RBP 는 협상대상이 아니라고 반박하였음.

2. 의장은 토의 내용을 정리하면서 앞으로 TRIM회의에서 다음의 사항을 중심으로논의를 계속하겠다고 발표하고 회의를 종료하였음. 차기회의는 9.23 주간에 개최됨.

　- COVERAGE

　. 신규 TRIM 에 국한 할 것인가 또는 기존TRIM 에도 적용할 것인가

　. 강제적 조치만 대상으로 할 것인가 INCENTIVE등도 포함할 것인가 (의장은 개인적인 견해로강제적 조치만이 대상으로 여겨진다고 언급)

　. 지방정부등의 조치도 규율대상으로 할 것인가.

　- TRIM 의 규율방안에 금지 개념을 도입할 것인가 또는 CASE BY CASE 로 무역 저해 효과를 검토할 것인가, 금지 개념 도입시에 갓트 3조 및 11조 위반 사항만을 대상으로 할 것인지 또는 수출의무등도 포함하 것인지 여부

　- 개도국에 대한 우대 조치

통상국　　2차보　　경기원　　재무부　　상공부

PAGE 1

- 경과 규정 및 기존 TRIM 의 단계적 철폐방식
- RBP 에 대한 규율 필요 여부
- 기타 명료성, 기구설치등의 사항. 끝
(대사 박수길-국장)

0054

5. TRIMs

가. 목표

○ 투자 조치의 무역제한 왜곡효과 분석

○ 현행 GATT 규정에 의한 투자조치 규제등 가능 어부 검토

○ 필요한 경우 새로운 규정 제정 검토

나. 협상 현황

○ 90.5. 협상 Group 의장 보고서 제출
   - 선.개도국간 이견 대립 지속으로 인하여 토의 중단사태

다. 합의사항

○ 사실상 합의사항 없음

라. 주요쟁점 및 주요국 입장

○ 금지 개념
   - 선진국은 국산부품 사용의무,수출의무등 금지화
   - 개도국 및 호주는 TRIMs의 금지화에 반대하고 Case by case 별로 검토

○ Coverage
   - 선진국은 보조금등 투자유인 시책 및 기존기업에 대한 조치도 포함
     주장
   - 개도국은 반대

0055

○ 제한적 기업관행(R.B.P) 포함 여부
- 개도국, 특히 인도는 포함 주장
- 선진국은 반대

○ 지방정부 TRIMs 적용 여부
- 카나다, 호주등 : 인방국가 적용배제
- EC, 일본등 : 동일적용 주장

마. 아국 입장

○ 무역에 직접적이고 중대한 부정적 효과를 초래하는 투자조치에 대해서는
금지 개념을 도입하는데 찬성

○ 투자 유인 시책과 기존 기업에 대한 조치의 적용 대상 여부 및 제한적
기업관행 포함 여부 문제는 협상의 타결을 위하여 신축적 입장 견지

바. 협상 전망

○ 현재로서는 선진국.개도국간 입장 차이가 좁혀질 것으로 예상되지
않으므로 UR/TRIMS 협상은 협상이 연기되든가 또는 선진국과 NICs등
일부 개도국의 참여하에 타결될 것을 전망할 수 있음

0056

외 무 부

종   별 :

번   호 : GVW-1435   일   시 : 91 0727 1000

수   신 : 장관(봉기, 경기원, 재무부, 상공부)

발   신 : 주 제네바 대사

제   목 : UR/ 규범제정 협상 그룹(공식회의)

7.19 오후 MACIEL 의장 주제로 개최된 표제회의 결과 하기임.

1. 의장은 금번 주간중 반덤핑, 보조금 및 상계관세, TRIMS, BOP 에 대한 협상현황 평가 및 금후 회의 진행에 관한 토의가 있었다고 간단히 언급한후 9월 회의에 대해 다음과 같이 제의함.

O 9월 회의는 9.30 주간에 개최됨.

O 4가지 의제에 대한 비공식회의 중심으로 진행하되 구체적 일정은 다음과 같음.

- 9.30 오전: 전체공식회의

- 9.30 오후: TRIMS

- 10.1 : 반덤핑

- 10.2 : BOP

- 10.3 및 1.4 (오전): 보조금 상계관세.

- 10.4 (오후): 전체 공식회의

O 10월 회의는 10.28 주간에 개최키로 잠정제의함.

2. 이에 대해 각국은 별다른 의견 개진 없이 의장 제의를 수락하고 회의를 종료함. (단, 일본은 규범제정 그룹회의가 당초 계획된 9.23에서 9.30 일로 연기된데 대해 불만을 표시함.) 끝

(대사 박수길-국장)

통상국   2차보   경기원   재무부   상공부

외 무 부

종 별 :

번 호 : GVW-1727　　　　　　　　　　　일 시 : 91 0912 1530

수 신 : 장관(통기, 경기원, 상공부)

발 신 : 주 제네바 대사 대리

제 목 : 반덤핑 협의(비공식)

　　9.11.(수) 당지 핀랜드 대표부가 주관한 주요수출국 그룹간 반덤핑 협의가 개최되어동 분야에서의 공동입장 모색등에 대해 비공식으로 논의한 바 요지 하기임.

　　(아국,홍콩,싱가폴,인도,이집트 및 북구 3국등 13개국 실무자 참석)

　　1. 회의내용

　　가. UR 협상 전반 및 반 덤핑협상 상황

　　0 참석자들은, UR 협상에서의 주요 협상국인 미국, EC 의 기존 입장에 변함이 없으며 특히 미국은 최근 UR 협상보다 북미자유 무역협정에 관심을 집중시키고 있는 것으로 보이고, EC도 최근 소련 사태등에 억매이고 있는 점에 우려를 표시함.

　　0 지난 7월말 미국,EC,캐나다,일본등 4개국이 캐나다에서 실무급 회의를 개최하여 보조금 및 상계관세, SAFEGUARD, TRIMS, 반덤핑 및서비스분야 등에 대한 비공식 모임을 가졌으며, 특히 일본이 이 회의를 계기로 반 덤핑분야 관련 수출국 입장에서 반덤핑 조치 발동국 입장으로 선회한 것으로 보인다는 일부 지적이 있었음.

　　0 일본이 발동국 입장으로 선회함으로써 동국가들이 반덤핑분야에 대한 공동안을마련하여 협상의 기초로 삼게하려는 의도가 있을 수 있음에 유의키로 함.

　　나. 수출국 그룹 협상 전략

　　0 이에따라 수출국 그룹에서도 향후 반덤핑 협상에서 상기 4개국에 대해 주도권을 행사하고 수출국 공동 의사를 제시하기 위해 수출국 그룹의 공동안을 마련해야 한다는데 인식을 같이함.

　　0 다만 시간이 촉박함에 비추어 기 제시된 여러 대안중 칼라일 II, 맥파일 I 및맥파일III를 혼합하여 수출국 GROUP의 관심 사항을 반영시킨 초안을 차기 규범 제정회의시(10월 예상) 까지 마련키로 하였으며, 향후 비공식 회의에서 이에 대한 구체 사항을 토의키로 함.

통상국　　2차보　　청와대　　경기원　　상공부　　의관실　　분석관　　안가무

O 한편 수출국 GROUP 의 공동 입장을 MACIEL 규범 제정 의장에게 인식시키고 향후 협상 진행방식 및 정보등에 대한 의견 교환을 위해 수출국 그룹의 제네바 주재 실무자가 MACIEL 의장을 오찬에 초청하는 형식의 모임을 갖기로함.

O 또한 수출국 그룹간 향후 반덤핑 협상에 관한 정보를 공유함으로써 향후 공동입장 정립에 노력키로 함.

다. 반덤핑 분야 쟁점 사항

O 기존의 주요 쟁점을 브랏셀 회의에서 제기된 사항(AVERAGING, STANDING OF THE DOMESTIC INDUSTRY, DE-MINIMIS, NEW COMERS, 수입국 조립 우회 덤핑 문제등)과 동 회의에서 토의되지 않은 사항(피해의 결정, SUNSET, 제3국 조립우회덤핑, 분쟁해결등)으로 나누어 그동안 수출.입국이 제기된 논지를 간략히 점검함.

O 한편 차기회의(10월 예상)부터 각 쟁점 사항에 대한 기술적 토의를 하게될 경우 수출국 그룹은 공동 입장을 반덤핑 조치 발동국에 표시하기 위해, 수출국 그룹이 관심을 갖고있는 쟁점 사항들에 대해 내부적인 토론을 거쳐 문제별로 한국과 가수출국그룹 입장을 대표하여 발표키로 함.

- DE-MINIMIS, SAMPLING, CUMMULATION: 홍콩
- STANDING OF THE DOMESTIC INDUSTRY, SUNSET, 피해결정:싱가폴
- AVERAGING, 덤핑결정: NORDIC
- NEW COMERS: 말레이지아

2. 일본이 반덤핑 조치 발동 국가와 입장을 같이한다는 여타 참가국의 지적과 관련 당관이 당지 일본측 담당자와 추후 접촉한 결과, 일본은 미국,EC,카나다와 규범제정 분야 및 서비스에 대해 협의한 바는 있으나 반덤핑 분야에서 이들 국가와 입장을같이 한다는 주장은 근거 없는것이라 일축하였음. 그럼에도 불구하고 수출국들은 일본의 입장 선회를 기정 사실로 받아들이고 있는 바, 일본이 반덤핑 분야에서 이들 3국가 입장에 동조하고 여타 분야에서 자국의 이익을 확보하려는 의도가 있을수 있음을 주시해야 할것임.

3. 아국은 반덤핑 분야 쟁점 사항에 대한 우선 순위를 동 수출국 그룹에 추후 통보키로 하였으며, 공식회의에서 수출국 그룹을 대표하여 특정분야에 대한 입장 발표를 하는 문제는 추후 동그룹 의장과 협의키로 하였음.끝

(차석대사 김삼훈-국장)

attention

UR/규범제정 및 투자분야 협상대책

'91. 9. 20

대고분류 의거 재분류(1991.12.31.)
직위   성당

상 공 부

국 제 협 력 관 실

0060

목　　　　차
=======================

I. 전체 협상 진전현황 및 전망 ---------- 1

II. 의제별 진전현황 및 아국 입장 ---------- 4

0061

I. 전체 협상 진전 현황 및 전망

1. 진전 상황

   o 91.4 협상그룹이 7개로 통합되면서 종전의 MTN 협정 (반덤핑, 기술장벽,
     수입허가절차, 관세평가, 정부조달), GATT 조문, 보조금/상계관세,
     세이프가드, 원산지규정, 선적전검사, 무역관련 투자협상등 11개 분야가
     규범제정 및 투자분야로 통합

   o 협상 그룹 조정 이후 금년 상반기 6월 및 7월 두차례의 비공식 및 공식회의를
     개최하였으나 실질적 진전은 없었음

     - 6월회의 : 우선 반덤핑, 보조금/상계관세, 국제수지 (BOP), 무역관련
                 투자제한조치 (TRIMs), 세이프가드 등 5개 분야를 논의
                 하되, 세이프가드를 제외한 4개 분야를 우선 논의하기로 합의

     - 7월회의 : 상기 4개 우선 논의 분야에 대한 협상 진전상황 평가 및 하반기
                 협상 방향 협의

   o 분야별 주요 진전사항

     ① 갓트조문

       - 미합의 사항인 24조 (관세동맹 및 지역협정)와 18조 B (국제수지 조항)
         중 18조 B의 협상여부에 대하여 논의중이나 선.개도국간의 의견
         대립 심각

     ② 반덤핑

       - 5차에 걸친 협상안의 제출에도 불구하고 주요 정점에 대한 이견
         대립으로 확정된 협정 초안이 없으며, 의견 대립이 심하지 않은
         덤핑조사의 절차와 관련된 7개 항목에 대해서만 잠정적으로
         합의됨

0062

③ Safeguard

- 브랏셀 회의에서 EC가 협상의 최대 쟁점인 선별적용 허용 여부에
  대해 조건부 철회의사를 표명하였으나 구체적인 논의를 하지 못하고,
  정치적 결정이 필요한 사항으로 추후 단계에서 논의키로 됨
  . EC가 제시한 조건 : 주요 공급국에 대한 쿼타 감축 인정 및 회색
    조치중 예외적으로 특정 품목에 대해 8년의 철폐시한 인정등

④ 보조금/상계관세

- 3차례 수정을 거친 의장안을 중심으로 논의하여 왔으나, 주요 쟁점이
  농산물 협상과 연관되어 있으며, 선진국간 및 선.개도국간 이견 대립이
  지속되고 있음

⑤ 무역관련투자 제한 조치

- 선.개도국간 이견 대립으로 협상 초안조차 마련되지 못함

⑥ 기타, 기술장벽, 수입허가절차, 관세평가, 정부조달, 원산지규정, 선적전
  검사에 대하여는 의견 접근을 봄

- 다만, 현 단계에서 선적전 검사의 독립재심절차의 이행방안에
  대하여 논의중

0063

2

2. 하반기 협상전망

o 현재 규범제정 분야에서의 대부분의 쟁점은 기술적인 문제가 아닌 정치적
   절충을 요하는 사항으로 농산물 협상등 타분야 협상과 연계되어 타 분야
   에서의 실질적 진전이 있어야 정치적 절충이 가능

o 하반기 회의는 매월 1회 비공식협의 (양자, 주요국간, 다자협의)로 진행하여
   각 분야별 논란이 적은 부분부터 협의하고, 각국이 견해차를 축소하여
   금년말 협상 타결을 위한 협상 package를 마련토록 협상 추진 전망

   - 9월회의는 9.30 ~ 10.4간 반덤핑, 보조금.상계관세, TRIMs, BOP 조항을 논의

   - 10월회의는 10.28 주간 개최키로 잠정 합의

3. 협상 대응 방향

o 아국 입장 재점검 및 우선순위 확인

   - 분야별 주요 쟁점에 대한 아국 입장 재점검

   - 아국 관심사항 반영 우선순위 확인

o 주요국간 비공식 협의에 적극 참가하여 아국의 관심사항 반영

   - 반덤핑의 경우 비공식 소그룹과의 기존 협조체제 활용

   - 기타 분야도 주요국과의 양자협의 및 주요국간 비공식 협의 적극 참여

0064

3

Ⅱ. 의제별 진전현황 및 아국 입장

1. 반덤핑

가. 협상진전상황

o 그동안 5차례의 의장안이 제시되었음에도 불구하고, 수출국. 수입국간의
  첨예한 이해 대립으로 협상 Text조차 합의를 보지 못하고 있음

- 수출국 (일본, 북구 및 한국, 홍콩등 개도국)

  : 덤핑 및 피해 판정기준의 합리화, 조사절차의 강화, 소멸시효 설정
    등으로 현행 반덤핑 협정을 강화하여 선진국의 자의적인 반덤핑
    관세 발동 방지 주장

- 수입국 (미국, EC)

  : 반덤핑 규제를 회피하려는 우회덤핑 행위등 새로운 형태의 무역활동을
    효율적으로 규제하기 위한 새로운 규정 (New issue)의 도입을 주장

o 지난 브랏셀 각료 회의에서 조사 절차의 명료성 확보와 관련된 7개 항목에
  대해서 잠정적으로 합의됨

- 반덤핑 조사를 위한 증거 확보의 명료성 제고

- 잠정조치의 요건 강화

- 수출업자의 가격인상 약속 요건의 강화

- 반덤핑 판정의 공표 및 설명 의무화

- 사법적 조사절차 도입

- 반덤핑 현장조사 절차의 구체화

- 이용 가능한 정보 사용의 남용방지

o 지난 7월회의에서 동 의제의 협상진전상황을 평가하고, 하반기 협상
  방향 협의

- 미국, EC 는 그간 기술적인 문제에 대하여는 충분한 기술적 토론이
  있었으므로 이제는 정치적 절충만 남았다는 의견

0065

4

- 수출국은 주요 쟁점의 기술적 토론을 계속하여 협상대상을 명확히
   하여야 한다고 주장

나. 향후 협상전망

　o 주요 쟁점사항에 대한 각국의 입장이 분명한 상황에서 향후 협상은
   기술적인 토론보다는 정치적 타협을 위한 협상 Package 마련에 치중할
   것으로 보임

다. 주요 미결 쟁점

(1) 국내가격 결정시 원가이하 판매 (Sales below Cost)를 정상적 거래로의
   인정 여부

(가) 쟁 점

o 국내가격 산정시 국내 판매분 중 원가이하의 판매가 있을 때 동 판매가격으로
   합리적인 기간내에 비용을 회수할 수 있는 경우 정상적인 거래로 인정할 수
   있으나, 비용을 회수할 수 있는 합리적인 기간을 어떻게 설정하는냐가 쟁점임

(나) 각국입장

　o 수출국 : 신제품 출하시 또는 시황이 불황인 경우는 일시적으로 국내판매
            가격이 원가보다 낮을 수 있으므로 비용 회수의 여부는 제품의
            Life cycle 또는 산업의 Business cycle을 기초로 하여 판정

　o 미국, EC : 제품의 Life cycle은 각 기업의 판매전략, 제품의 종류에
            따라 상이하여 일정한 기준 설정이 곤란하므로 조사대상 기간
            (미국 : 6개월, EC : 1년)을 기준으로 비용 회수 여부 판단

0066

5

(다) 우리입장

o 국내판매분 중 원가이하의 판매가 있는 경우에도 합리적인 기간내에
  비용을 회수할 수 있는 경우에는 이를 정상적인 거래로 인정해야 함
  - 비용회수의 여부는 단순히 조사대상 기간을 기초로 판단해서는 안되며
    신제품의 출하시기(start - up) 또는 산업불황기 (cyclical downturn)
    등의 비용을 고려할 수 있는 충분한 기간을 기초로 판단해야 됨.

o 최종대안 : 비용회복기간이 최소 18개월 이상은 되어야 함

(2) 구성가격 (Constructed Value) 산정시 이윤 산정기준

(가) 쟁점

o 국내 판매가격이 없는 경우 조사당국은 제조원가에 합리적인 판매관리비 및
  이윤을 가산하여 국내가격을 새로이 구성할 수 있는데 이 경우 이윤산정
  기준을 무엇으로 하느냐 하는 것임.

(나) 각국입장

o 수출국 : 회계장부상의 실제 Data로 이윤 산정이 어려운 경우 당해
          수출업자가 동일 부류의 제품 판매에서 실현한 이윤을 우선 적용

o E C : 수출국내 당해 제품을 생산하는 여타 생산자의 가중평균 이윤을 적용

o 미국 : Benchmark (총 생산비의 8%) 설정이 명료성, 예측가능성 측면에서
        합리적

(다) 우리입장

o 조사대상 수출자의 동종상품에 대한 실제 DATA에 의할 수 없는 경우는
  다음 원칙을 순차적으로 적용

0067

6

(i) 당해 수출자의 수출국내 동일부류 (The same general category)의
제품판매에서 실현한 이윤

(ii) 수출국내 동종상품을 생산하는 여타 생산자의 대표적(가중평균)이윤

(iii) 수출국내 동일부류의 제품을 생산하는 여타 생산자의 대표적
(가중평균) 이윤. 단 어떠한 경우에도 benchmark 의 설정금지

o 최종대안

- 조사대상 수출자 또는 생산자의 실제 DATA 를 근거로 하고

- 이에 의할 수 없는 경우 합리적이라고 볼 수 있는 여타 방법 사용가능
단, 이 경우 수출국내에서 여타 생산자 및 수출자가 동종제품 또는
동종부류의 제품의 정상적 거래에서 실현된 이윤 및 일반판매 관리비의
가중평균액을 초과할 수 없음

(3) 가중 평균에 의한 수출가격과 정상가격의 비교 (Negative Dumping 인정 여부)

(가) 쟁 점

> o 국내 가격은 가중 평균에 의하고 수출 가격은 개별거래 가격을 기준으로
> 하므로써 덤핑 마진 산정시 부의 덤핑마진 (Negative Dumping)이 인정되지
> 않는 관행의 개선 문제

(나) 각국 입장

o 수출국 : 수출가격과 정상가격 (국내가격 등)의 비교는 동일한 가격을 기초로
해야 하므로 양시장 가격을 가중평균치로 비교하여 Negative
Dumping의 경우도 덤핑마진 산정시 인정
(단, Selective 덤핑의 방지를 위한 예외인정 가능)

o 미국, EC : 수출가격을 가중 평균치로 하는 경우 수출업자가 특정기간
동안 특정모델에 대해 덤핑 행위를 하는 경우 (Selective
Dumping) 이를 방지할 수 없으므로 국내가격을 가중평균으로
하고 수출 가격은 개별거래 가격을 기준으로 비교

0068

7

(다) 우리입장

o 덤핑 마진은 국내 가격과 수출 가격의 비교에 의해 산정되므로 양시장
  가격은 동일한 기준으로 공정하게 비교되어야 함. 따라서 국내 가격을
  가중 평균으로 사용하는 경우, 수출 가격도 반드시 가중 평균을 사용
  토록 하여 부의 덤핑 마진 (Negative Dumping)이 무시되지 않도록
  해야 함 (단, 예외적인 상황의 경우 개별거래 가격 허용 문제는 논의 가능)

o 최종대안

  - 양 시장 가격은 가중 평균치 또는 거래별로 비교하는 것을 원칙으로 함

  - 다만, 조사기간 동안 소비자에 대한 수출 가격에 상당한 변화가
    있는 경우에 한하여 개별수출 가격에 의한 비교가 가능하나 이 경우
    조사 당국은 양 시장 가격이 동시에 유사한 변화를 한다면 덤핑
    마진이 없다고 확인하고, 동 방법의 사용 이유에 대해 설명해야 함

(4) 피해의 누적 (Cumulation 인정)

(가) 쟁 점

> o 여러나라로 부터 수입된 물품이 동시에 반덤핑 조사 대상이 되는 경우 그 피해를
>   누적하여 판단할 수 있는지, 만일 누적하는 경우 어떤 조건에서만 가능한지

(나) 각국 입장

  o 수 출 국 : 피해 판정은 원칙적으로 각 수입원에 대해 독립적으로
            이루어져야 함. 단, 예외적인 경우에 한하여 Cumulation 인정 가능

  o 미국, EC : 피해의 누적 효과로 인한 국내 산업의 피해를 구제할 수
            있도록 Cumulation을 일반적으로 허용해야 함.
            단, De minimis 덤핑 마진이나 수입 규모가 미미한 경우는
            Cumulation에서 제외 가능

0069

8

(다) 우리입장

o 여러국가로 부터의 수입에 의한 피해는 각각 독립적으로 평가되는 것을
   기본원칙으로 하고 다만, 예외적인 경우에 한하여 Cumulation 인정 가능

   ⅰ) De minimis 덤핑마진 및 수입량 이상

   ⅱ) 수입제품간에 상호 경쟁하고, 국내 제품과 경쟁하는 경우

o 최종 대안

   - 덤핑 수입량이 국내 산업에 줄 수 있는 영향이 미미한 수준

     (% : De minimis 참조)인 경우 Cumulation에서 제외

(5) De minimis 덤핑 마진 및 덤핑 수입량

(가) 쟁 점

> o 덤핑 마진이나 덤핑 수입량이 미미한 경우 (negligible) 반덤핑 조사의
>   중지가 가능한데 이에 대한 구체적인 수준을 계량화 하는 문제

(나) 각국입장

o 수출국 : De minimis에 대한 계량화를 통하여 객관적인 기준 설정

               (덤핑마진 : 5%, 덤핑 수입량 : 수입국 시장 점유율 3%)

o 미국, EC

  - 덤핑마진 : De minimis의 계량화에 대해서는 긍정적이나 그 수준은

                 매우 낮게 설정 (0.5% 정도)

  - 덤핑 수입량 : 누적 효과를 통하여 국내 산업에 피해 우려가 있고 소규모

                 수출 국가에 반덤핑 관세를 부과하지 않는 경우 시장 대체

                 가능성이 존재하므로 계량화 반대가 기본 입장임

(다) 우리입장

o 덤핑 마진 및 수입량이 미미한 경우 그 수입물품은 조사 대상에서

   제외될 수 있도록 이에 대한 구체적인 기준이 설정되어야 함

   - 즉 덤핑 마진율의 경우 5% 이하

   - 덤핑 수입량의 경우는 수입국내 시장 점유율의 3% 이하

o 최종 대안

   - 덤핑 마진율 : 3%

   - 덤핑 수입량 : 수입국 시장점유율을 기준 2%, 수입국의 총 수입규모 기준 5%

9

0070

(6) 피해 판정시 덤핑마진이 가격에 미치는 영향 고려

(가) 쟁 점

> o 덤핑 수입의 국내 산업에 대한 피해 여부를 결정시 덤핑 마진이 수입국의
> 국내 가격에 얼마나 영향을 주었나를 비교하여 그 영향이 미미한 경우에는
> 비록 덤핑 마진이 있더라도 피해가 없다고 판정 할 수 있는지 여부

(나) 각국입장

o 미 국 : 덤핑 마진이 있으면 그 규모에 관계없이 피해를 주는것은 사실이며,
국내 시장가격의 underselling margin을 고려할 필요가 없음

o 카나다, 한국, 일본 등 여타국 :

- 미국을 제외하고 모든 나라가 피해 판정시 덤핑 마진의 규모를 고려하고
있고, 덤핑 수입과 피해가 인과 관계가 있는 경우에만 반덤핑 관세를 부과
하도록 되어 있는 GATT 제 6조의 규정의 취지에서 볼때 미국의 관행은
시정되어야 함

(다) 우리입장

o 덤핑 마진이 수입국 국내가격에 미친 영향 별도 고려

o 최종 대안

- 국내 가격에 영향을 주는 한 요소로써 "덤핑마진의 크기"를 추가토록 함

(7) 피해 판정시 덤핑수입 이외의 고려 요소 인정 여부

(가) 쟁 점

> o 국내산업에의 피해 판정시 덤핑 수입에 의한 피해와 다른 요인에
> 의한 피해를 비교하여 덤핑 수입에 의한 피해가 주된 요인 (material
> injury) 이라고 인정되는 경우에만 피해 판정을 할 수 있는지 여부

(나) 각국입장

o 미 국 : 현행 미국제도상 ITC가 독립된 피해 판정 기구로 되어 있고, ITC 위원은
각자 자유로운 판단에 의하여 피해 여부를 결정토록 되어 있는바,
덤핑 수입에 의한 피해와 다른 요인을 세분화(Subdivide) 하여
그 크기를 저울질 (weigh)하도록 요구하는 것은 곤란함

0071

10

o E C : 동경 Round에서도 이 문제는 논란의 여지가 많았으므로 현행
          규정대로 두는것이 바람직

(다) 우리입장

o 피해 판정의 명백한 증거로 포함되어야 할 사항으로 "국내산업에 피해를
  줄 수 있는 덤핑 이외의 기타 요소에 의한 영향"을 포함토록 함

o 최종 대안

  - 덤핑 피해의 인과관계 검토시 산업에 피해를 주고 있는 덤핑 이외의
    알려진 요소에 대해 검토하고, 동 요소에 의한 피해를 덤핑 수입에
    의한 것으로 간주해선 안됨

(8) 제소자격

(가) 쟁 점

> o 현 협정상에는 반덤핑 제소의 성립 요건으로 국내산업의 "a major proportion"
>   이 지지하도록 되어있어 이에대한 기준을 수량화하여야 하는지가 쟁점임

(나) 각국입장

  o 수출국 : 과반수 지지 요건을 원칙 (국내 총생산의 50%)

  o 미 국 : 관행상 침묵을 지지로 보고 있으며, 과반수지지 요건 반대.
            노동조합의 제소자격 부여 주장

(다) 우리입장

  o 과반수 지지요건 원칙 (국내 총생산액의 50%)

  o 최종 대안

    - 과반수 지지요건 (국내 총생산액의 50%)을 일반원칙으로 하되
    - 다수 생산자가 관련된 산업등 예외적인 경우에 한하여 50% 이하
      가능하나 최소 25% 이상이어야 함

0072

(9) 신규수출참여자 (New Comer)에 대한 취급

(가) 쟁 점

> o 조사기간 동안 수출을 하지 않은 업체가 반덤핑 조치를 받고 있는
> 제품을 새로이 수출하는 경우 어떤 덤핑 관세율을 적용해야 하는지 여부

(나) 각국입장

> o 수 출 국 : 새로이 수출하는 기업의 경우는 별도의 조사를 실시하여
> 반덤핑 관세 부과 여부를 결정해야 함

> o 미국, EC : 신규 수출자는 당해 수출국 내에서 기존 경쟁자와 유사한 가격
> 결정을 한다는 측면에서 기존 수출자의 가중 평균 덤핑 관세율 적용

(다) 우리입장

> o 신규 수출자에 대하여 조사없이 반덤핑 관세를 부과해서는 안되며, 신속한
> 별도 조사에 의해 반덤핑 관세를 부과하되 잠정 조치는 예비 판정이후로 함

> o 최종 대안
> - 조사기간 동안 수출하지 않았고, 기존 AD 관세부과 대상자와 관계가
> 없는 수출자 또는 생산자의 경우 별도의 조사없이 AD 관세 부과 금지
> - 단, 제품 수입시 부터 AD 관세를 소급적용 할 수 있도록 평가유보
> 및 적절한 보증조치 가능

(10) 소멸시효 설정 (Sunset Clause)

(가) 쟁 점

> o 단기간의 피해구제 수단인 반덤핑 관세조치가 피해가 구제된 이후에도
> 특별한 사유없이 장기간 지속되므로써 남용되는 사례를 방지하기 위하여
> 일정 기간이 지난후 자동적으로 소멸되도록 하는 장치의 설정 문제

(나) 각국입장

> o 수출국, EC등 대부분의 국가 3-5년의 소멸시효 설정
> - EC, 카나다, 일본, 홍콩 : 5년
> - 한국, 노르딕, 뉴질랜드 : 3년

0073

12

o 미국 : 자국제도상 연례 재심의 실질적 운용으로 충분 (소멸시효 설정 반대)

(다) 우리입장

　　o 소멸시효는 3년으로 하고 기산일은 덤핑 최종 판정일

　　o 최종 대안

　　　- 소멸시효 : 5년

　　　- 기산일 : 최초 반덤핑 관세 부과일

(11) 우회덤핑 규제 (Anticircumvention)

(가) 쟁 점

---

o 반덤핑 조치를 회피하기 위하여 수입국내에서 조립하거나 제 3국에서 조립
하여 당해국으로 수출하는 경우

- 수입국내 조립의 경우만 우회덤핑으로 인정하고 제 3국 조립의
경우는 통상의 반덤핑 조사절차를 취하도록 하는지 여부

- 수입국내 조립의 경우 우회덤핑 판정기준을 어떻게 설정하여야 하는지
　. 조립업자와 당초 덤핑관세 부과 대상자의 관계
　. 수입부품의 완제품에서 차지하는 비중이 x% 이상인지 여부
　. 부품 수입의 증가 상태

(나) 각국 입장

　o 미국, EC : 제 3국 조립도 규제 대상에 포함하고 수입 부품의 완제품
　　에서 차지하는 비중 (X%)은 40-50% 정도 (EC : 조립수준 비교 기준을
　　수입품 가격과 조립에 사용된 전체 부품 가격과 비교)

　o 카나다 및 수출국 : 제 3국 조립은 제외하고 x%는 90%로 하며, 수입국내
　　조립제품 가격과 수출국 국내가격과의 비교 요건도 추가 되어야 함

0074

13

(다) 우리 입장

    o 수입국내 조립의 경우만 포함

        - X%는 두가지 기준 설정 : 수입부품이 전체부품 가격 대비 75% 이상으로
          하되 수입국내 부가가치가 20% 이상인 경우는 우회덤핑으로 불인정

        - 수입국내 조립제품 가격과 수출국 국내가격을 비교하여 덤핑 여부 재검토

        - 기타 요건 추가

    o 최종 대안

        - 덤핑 마진의 결정등 한국의 주요 관심 항목의 반영 정도에 따라 제3국 조립의
          경우 포함여부 고려

        - 제 3국 조립의 경우를 포함할 경우 수입국 조립의 경우에 적용되는
          요건을 기초로 하되, 보다 엄격한 기준이 설정되어야 함

          . 특히 정상 가격은 원래의 AD 부과 대상국이 아닌 제 3국의 가격을 사용

라. 협상대응 방향

(1) 협상에 임하는 기본입장

    o 현 단계에서는 지금까지 유지해온 수출국 입장을 유지하고 최종 단계에서
     수출국입장을 그대로 반영하기 어려운 경우 우리 입장을 다소 양보한 최종
     대안 수용

    o 현 협정의 강화와 관련된 아국의 우선반영 이슈와 미국, EC 주장인
     우회덤핑 방지 조항이 적절히 반영되는 수준에서 합의 도출

        - 단, 우회덤핑 방지조항은 순수한 우회덤핑 (수입국내 단순조립 행위)만을
          대상으로 하고 그 규제요건도 엄격히 해야 된다는 전제

    o 공동협조강화

        - 기존에 협조체제를 유지하고 있는 "주요 수출국간 반덤핑 비공식협의회
          (북구, 홍콩, 싱가폴 등 9개국)"와 공동 대응 추진

0075

14

(2) 쟁점별 반영 우선 순위

　o 반영 필요 분야 (Request List)

　　ⅰ) 가중평균에 의한 수출가격, 정상가격 비교 실시

　　ⅱ) 국내가격 결정시 원가이하의 판매인정 : 원가이하의 판매가 상당수량
　　　　합리적 기간내에 총 비용을 회수하지 못하는 경우를 제외하고는
　　　　정상적 거래로 인정

　　ⅲ) 구성가격 산정시 이윤산정 기준 : 수출업자의 실제 회계자료를 기초로
　　　　할 수 없는 경우 당해 수출업자가 동일부류의 제품 판매에서 실현한
　　　　이윤을 우선 적용

　　ⅳ) De minimis 덤핑마진 (5%) 및 덤핑수입량 (수입국 시장점유율 : 3%)에
　　　　대한 기준 설정

　　ⅴ) Cumulation 인정여부 : 각국의 수입에 의한 피해는 각각 독립적으로
　　　　평가하는 것을 원칙으로 하고 Cumulation은 극히 예외적인 경우 인정

　　ⅵ) 신규 수출참여자에 대한 취급 : 별첨의 신속한 조사없이 반덤핑 관세를
　　　　부여해서는 안되고 잠정조치는 예비판정 이후에 가능

　　ⅶ) 피해 판정시 덤핑마진이 가격에 미치는 영향 고려　　*meeting competition*

　　ⅷ) 제소 자격 : 과반수 (국내 총 생산 50%) 지지를 원칙

　　ⅸ) 소멸시효의 설정 및 기간은 3년 (또는 5년)
　　　　sunset clause

　o 양보 가능 분야 (Offer List)

　　- 우회덤핑 규제조항 : 그 요건이 수입국내 단순조립 활동만을 순수히
　　　　　　　　　　　　규제할 수 있도록 설정되고, 우리의 우선반영
　　　　　　　　　　　　이슈가 포함된다는 전제하에 양보 가능

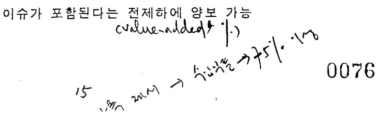

0076

마. 한. 미 양자협의 대책

(1) 미국측 예상제기 사항

o 우회덤핑 방지조항 신설

 - 반덤핑 조치를 회피하기 위하여 수입국내에서 조립하거나 제3국에서 조립하여
   수출하는 경우 덤핑으로 인정

   (수입국내 조립뿐만 아니라 제3국 조립도 포함, 수입부품의 비중은 45% ~ 50%)

(2) 아측 요구사항

o 덤핑마진 계산과 관련하여 개선되어야 할 사항

 - 구성가격 산정은 조사대상 수출자가 동종상품의 국내판매에서 실현한 실제
   이윤을 기준으로 해야함. 상기 이윤이 없는 경우 수출국 국내시장에서
   동일부류 상품판매에서 실현한 실제이윤(Benchmark 설정 반대)

 - 국내가격을 가중평균으로 사용시 수출가격도 가중평균으로 함

   (부의 덤핑 마진 (Negative Dumping) 인정)

 - 원가이하의 판매도 합리적인 기간내에 비용회수시는 정상적 거래로 인정

o 피해 판정과 관련 개선되어야 할 사항

 - 피해 판정시 인과관계 고려(덤핑마진이 가격에 미치는 영향, 덤핑이외의
   요소 고려)

 - De minimis 덤핑 마진(5%) 및 덤핑수입량(수입국 시장 점유율 3%) 인정

o 소멸시효의 설정

(3) 미측 요구에 대한 대응방안

o 아측이 요구하는 사항은 반덤핑 제도가 자의적으로 운용되는 것을 방지하고,
   조사과정에의 명료성을 제고하기 위한 것임

o 아국 요청사항의 반영정도에 따라 우회덤핑 방지조항 신설문제 수용가능

   단, 수입국내 단순조립과 같은 순수한 우회덤핑만을 인정

0077

16

(4) 미결쟁점에 대한 양국입장 비교

구 분	미 국	한 국
o 국내가격 결정시 원가이하 판매는 정상적 거래로 인정 여부	o 불인정	o 인 정
o 구성가격 산정시 이윤 산정기준	o Benchmark 설정 (총생산비 8%)	o 당해 수출업자의 이윤
o Negative Dumping 인정 여부	o 불인정	o 인 정
o 피해의 누적 허용 여부	o 인 정	o 불인정
o De minimis 덤핑마진 및 덤핑 수입량	o 덤핑마진 : 0.5% (아주낮게) o 덤핑수입량 : 불인정	o 덤핑마진 : 5% o 덤핑수입량 : 3% (수입국 시장 점유율)
o 피해 판정시 덤핑 마진이 가격에 미치는 영향 고려 여부	o 불인정	o 인 정
o 피해 판정시 덤핑 수입 이외의 고려요소 인정 여부	o 불인정	o 인 정
o 제소자격	o 과반수 지지요건 반대	o 과반수 지지요건 찬성
o 신규 수출 참여자에 대한 취급	o 기존 수출자 취급	o 별도 조사
o 소멸시효 설정	o 반대 (연례 재심으로 충분)	o 3-5년 소멸시효 설정
o 우회덤핑 규제	o 제 3국 조립도 포함 o 수입부품의 비중은 45-50% 정도	o 제 3국 조립은 제외 o 수입부품 비중은 가격 비교 75%, 부가가치 기준 20% 이상

0078

'7

2. 보조금 / 상계관세

가. 현재까지의 진전상황

1) 협상의 주요경과 및 합의사항

```
┌──────────────── 〈협상 목표〉 ────────────────┐
│                                                  │
│  - 동경라운드(79년)에서 채택된 보조금, 상계관세협정의 개선   │
│  - 국제무역에 영향을 미치는 모든 보조금과 상계조치에 관련되는 │
│    규율을 객관적이고 명확히 함                        │
│                                                  │
└──────────────────────────────────────────────────┘
```

- 주요 경과

  o 1986. 9. 우루과이 Punta del Este에서의 각료선언으로 UR 개시

  o 1989. 4. 무역협상위원회에서 기본골격 채택

  o 1990. 5. 의장 협상안을 중심으로 협상 (3차의 의장안 수정)

  o 1990. 12. 브랏셀 각료회의에서 협정채택 실패

  o 1991. 7. 협상 재개, 9월부터 본격 협상 합의

- 현재까지의 합의사항(의장 협상안)

  o 명시적으로 합의된 사항은 없으나, 다음의 미합의 사항을 제외한
    부분은 특별한 이견제시가 없는 한 묵시적으로 합의되었다고 볼수
    있음

  o 미합의사항

    . 직접적 교역효과가 없는 국내보조금의 심각한 손상 추정

    . 수량기준 채택

    . 허용보조금의 요건 및 중복지급 허용

    . 개발도상국 우대조치

    . 보조금액 산정기준

    . 농산물 보조금의 포함여부

0079

18

2) 의장협상안(3차 수정안) 기본내용

가) 보조금 분류 및 위반시 구제절차

- 보조금의 정의
    o 정부의 재정지원 또는 소득,가격지원의 존재와
    o 이로 인한 혜택이 있을 것
- 보조금의 3분류
    o 금지, 조치가능, 허용보조금

- 금지보조금 및 구제절차
  o 수출성과부 보조금과 수입대체부 보조금
  o 구제절차

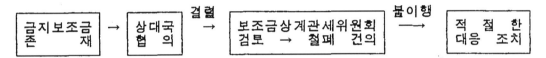

- 조치가능 보조금 및 구제절차
  o 금지 및 허용보조금 이외의 보조금
  o 구제절차

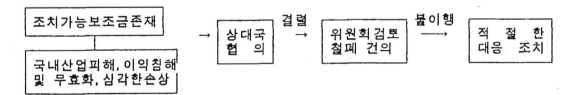

0080

19

- 허용 보조금 및 특별구제절차

    o 일반적으로 지급되는 보조금

    o 4가지 특정적인 보조금 : 연구개발, 구조조정, 환경보호, 지역개발 보조금

    o 특별 구제절차

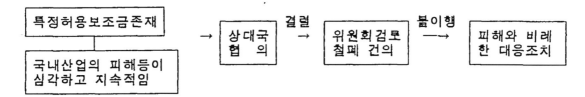

나) 상계조치

- 상계조치대상 보조금

    o 금지보조금 및 조치가능보조금 (허용보조금은 상계조치 불가)

- 상계조치 절차

```
┌─────────────────────┐      ┌──────────────────────────┐
│ 피해 국내산업에 의한 제소 │  →   │ 보조금 존재, 피해, 인과관계조사 │
└─────────────────────┘      └──────────────────────────┘

   긍정      ┌──────────────┐
  ─────→    │ 상계관세부과    │
           └──────────────┘
```

다) 개도국 우대

- 보조금 규제의 우대

    o 수출보조금의 지급가능 등 (선발개도국 제외)

- 상계조치의 적용 제한

    o 소액보조금 및 시장점유율이 낮은 물품에 대한 상계조치 금지

0081

20

나. 주요 쟁점사항 및 아국입장

1) 미결 쟁점 및 아국입장

> 쟁점 1) 동 협정의 농산물 보조금 포함여부

- 의장안 내용
  - o 언급없음

- 주요국 입장
  - o〈브라질, 미국, 호주, 카나다〉: 동 협정안은 농산물보조금에도 적용됨

  - o〈일본, EC, 북구〉: 농산물보조금 포함 반대 → 농산물 협상그룹에서
    별도로 다룰 것을 주장

- 아국입장 : 농산물 보조금의 포함 반대

  - o 농산물협상그룹은 농산물교역과 관련된 모든 측면에 대하여 일차적인
    책임을 지고 있으며 지금까지 본협상과 별도로 논의를 진행시켜 왔으므로,
    농산물 보조금에 대한 논의도 농산물협상그룹에 일임하도록 함.

  - o 보조금협상그룹은 농산물협상그룹이 합의한 결과를 수용함으로써, 농산물
    보조금에 대해서도 규율할 수 있음.

0082

ㄴ

쟁점 2)   개도국 우대조치 (제27조)

- 의장안 내용

o 개도국에게는 금지보조금인 수출보조금을 줄 수 있도록 하되,
  개도국별로 차별적인 우대
  · 최빈개도국(Annex7) →   수출보조금 지급허용
  · 기타개도국(Annex8) →   단계적으로 수출보조금 감축
  · 한국등 선발개도국 →   수출보조금 지급 금지

o 기타 우대내용 (개도국별 구분없이 일률적인 우대)
  · 심각한 손상 추정(제6.1조)의 적용을 배제
  · 아래의 경우 상계조치 불가
    (a) 소액보조금
    (b) 수입국의 시장점유율이 일정수준 이하인 품목에 대한 보조금

※   동조항의 배경
  o 의장안은 선발개도국의 개도국 우대적용 폐지(졸업)를 주장하는 미국입장과
    이에 반대하는 한국등 선발개도국의 주장을 절충한 것임.

- 주요국 입장

  o 〈선발 개도국을 제외한 모든 국가〉: 의장안 찬성
    · 개도국은 경제발전 정도에 따라 국제사회에서의 의무를 분담해야 하며,
      따라서 개도국별 차별대우를 규정한 의장안에 찬성

  o 〈한국, 싱가폴, 말레이지아〉: 의장안 반대
    · 개도국 분류는 각료선언에서 본협상에 위임된 사항이 아님.

0083

22

- 아국입장

  < 1안 > : 개도국 분류 반대 → 서면대안 (기제출)

    o 개도국 분류는 본 협상에 위임된 사항이 아니며, 이는 보다 전문적인
      기관에 의한 전반적, 객관적 판단을 필요로 함.

    o 서면 대안

      . 최저개도국을 제외한 개도국은 일률적으로 일정기간내 수출보조금 폐지
        약속

      . 다만 동기간 만료시점에 가서 경제개발의 낙후등으로 이를 이행 수 없는
        국가에 대해서는 기간 연장 허용

  < 2안 > : 의장안 수용 및 기타개도국 List (Annex 8) 에 아국 포함

    o 개도국 분류를 통해 수출보조금 지급 혜택이 박탈되는 국가는 한국·싱가폴·
      말련 등 극소수이므로 개도국 분류반대의 아국등 입장은 선진국이나 후진국
      어느쪽으로 부터도 지지를 받기 힘듬.

    o 기타 우대내용의 혜택이라도 적용받는 것이 아국에 실익이 됨.

0084

23

쟁점 3) 심각한 손상(Serious prejudice) 추정(제6.1조)

- 의장안 내용

---

o 다음의 조치가능 보조금은 그 지급만으로 무조건 심각한 손상을 초래
   하는 것으로 간주하여 보조금 지급국이 심각한 손상을 일으키지
   않았음을 입증하지 않는 경우 구제절차에 따라 대응조치함.

   · 물품의 보조금액 비율이 [5]%를 초과하는 보조금
   · 특정산업에서 발생하는 영업손실을 보전하기 위한 보조금
   · 기업의 영업손실을 보전하기 위한 보조금
   · 직접적인 채무감면

※ 동 조항의 배경
   o 의장안은 국내보조금의 금지화를 주장하는 미국입장과 이에 반대하는 EC 등의
      주장을 절충한 것임.

- 주요국의 입장
   o <미국> : 위의 국내 보조금은 금지보조금으로 분류주장.
   o <EC · 일본 · 개도국> : 동 조항은 너무 엄격한 규제임.

- 아국입장

   < 1 안 > : 의장안 반대 → 동 조항 삭제
      o 아국은 해당보조금 지급국가에게 과도한 입증책임을 지게하고, 분쟁의 소지를
         제공한다는 이유에서 적극적으로 이에 반대해 왔음.

   < 2 안 > : 개도국 List 에 포함시 의장안 수용
      o 심각한 손상추정은 개도국 우대조항에 의해 개도국에는 적용되지 않으므로,
      o 아국이 개도국 List (Annex8)에 포함될 경우 동 규정은 아국에 대해
         적용되지 않음.

0085

24

쟁점 4) 수량기준 채택여부 (제6.1조 (a))

- 의장안 내용

o 보조금액 비율이 [5]%를 초과할 경우 심각한 손상이 있는 것으로 추정함

- 주요국 입장

o 〈미국, 북구등〉 : 보조금 규율강화를 위해서는 채택 필요

o 〈EC, 일본〉 : 다른 수단을 통한 보조금 규율강화 주장

- 아국입장

〈 1 안 〉 : 의장안 반대

o 보조금은 무역효과에 따라서 규제되어야 하는데, 수량기준은 이러한 보조금과
무역효과간의 상관관계를 무시하는 것이며, 시행상 수출기업에게 심각한
손상을 끼치지 않았음을 증명해야 하는등 과도한 업무부담을 초래함.

〈 2 안 〉 : 수량기준의 상향조정(20-30%)하여 의장안 수용

o 개도국 우대조항에 의해 수량기준에 의한 심각한 손상추정은 개도국에게는
적용되지 않으므로,

o 수량기준이 채택되더라도 아국이 개도국 분류에 포함될 경우 동 조항은
적용되지 않음.

0086

25

쟁점 5) 허용보조금의 요건(제8조)

- 의장안 내용

---

o 특정성있는 다음 보조금은 제한된 조건, 특히 수치상한을 두어 허용

  · 연구개발보조금 : 기본적인 연구는 소요비용의 [20]% 초과금지
                            응용연구개발은 소요비용의 [10]% 초과금지
  · 구조조정보조금 : 생산시설의 감축, 폐기위한 비용의 [X]% 초과금지
  · 환경보호보조금 : 소요비용의 [20]% 초과금지
  · 지역개발보조금 : 전국평균보다 [15]%이상 낙후지역의 개발만 허용

- 주요국 입장

  o 〈미 국〉: 허용보조금의 범위가 지나치게 확대되었음

  o 〈개도국〉: 허용보조금의 요건이 지나치게 엄격함

- 아국입장

  〈 1 안 〉: 수치상한 삭제

  o 아국의 경우 연구개발, 구조조정, 지역개발, 환경보호등은 필수적인 것으로 향후

    이들 지원사례가 증가할 것을 예상되므로, 가능한 한 허용보조금의 요건을

    완화하는 것이 바람직함.

  〈 2 안 〉: 수치상한 상향조정

0087

26

쟁점 6) 복수의 허용보조금 수혜(제8.5조)

- 의장안 내용

o 특정기업이 복수의 허용보조금을 수혜할 경우, 단지 한가지 보조금만을
허용보조금으로 봄

- 주요국 입장

  o <미 국> : 의장안 찬성

  o <EC,일본> : 의장안 반대 → 독소조항이라 주장

- 아국입장 : 의장안 반대

o 각 허용보조금은 상당히 제한적인 요건을 충족하는 경우에만 허용되므로,
한가지 보조금만 허용하는 것은 지나친 제한임

o 허용보조금은 그 성격상 무역왜곡효과가 없어 허용되는 것이므로,
중복지급 된다 하더라도 허용보조금의 성질이 변하는 것이 아님

새

- 의장안 내용

> o 구체적인 계산방법은 각국의 법령에서 정하되 다음 지침에 부합할 것
>
> o 정부의 대출은 당해 대출금리와 상업금리 비교
>
> o 정부의 대출보증은 보증시 대출금리와 보증이 없을시 금리 비교
>
> o 정부에 의한 재화, 용역의 공급 또는 구매의 경우는 시장가격과 비교 결정
>
> → 상기 의장안은 수혜자 수익기준(시장가격과 비교)을 채택하고 있음.

※ 수혜자 수익기준 : 기업등이 정부로부터 자금을 조달받는 비용과 공개시장
　　　　　　　　　　에서 조달하는 비용간 차이

　 정부비용기준 : 정부가 부담하게 되는 비용 (예 : 정부의 자금조달이자율 -
　　　　　　　　　　　　　　　　　　　　　　　　　 대출이자율)

- 주요국 입장

　 o〈미 국〉: 의장안 원칙적 찬성 → 수혜자 수익기준보다 강화

　 o〈북구, EC, 카나다, 일본〉: 의장안 반대 → 정부비용 기준

- 아국입장 :

　〈 1 안 〉: 정부비용 기준

　　 o 수익기준은 실제 적용상 적절한 비교대상 시장가격의 파악이 어려움.

　　 o 반면 정부비용기준은 비용파악이 비교적 용이함.

　〈 2 안 〉: 의장안 수용

0089

- 의장안 내용

---
o 특정지역내에 있는 기업에게 주는 보조금은 지급기관에 관계없이 특정적인
  것으로 봄.

- 주요국 입장

  o 〈카나다, 호주〉: 의장안 반대

  · 지방정부가 관할내에 있는 모든 기업에게 지급하는 보조금은 특정성 없음.

  o 〈스위스, 북구〉: 의장안 찬성 → 지방정부 보조금도 규제

- 아국입장

  〈 1 안 〉: 의장안 찬성

  o 아국과 같이 지방의 재정자립도가 낮고, 중앙집권적인 국가에서는 사실상
    지방정부가 독자적으로 재원을 확보해서 지원하는 순수한 지방정부보조금은
    많지 않을 것으로 생각됨

  o 지방정부의 재정자립도가 비교적 높은 수준에 있는 연방국가의 경우 지방정부
    보조금을 규제밖에 둘 경우 보조금 규제의 실효성이 약화됨.

  〈 2 안 〉: 반대입장 수용 가능

  o 아국의 경우 장기적 측면에서 지방자치제의 정착이후, 지방정부의 보조금 활용
    가능성도 고려

0090

29

2? 아직까지 논의안된 쟁점

- 상계조치와 관련된 절차 및 규정을 명확히 하기 위한 세부적인
  수치를 정하는 사항들
- 상계조치와 반덤핑조치의 절차 및 규정이 매우 유사한 관계로 현재
  반덤핑협상그룹에서 논의되고 있으며, 그 결과가 도출되는 대로
  보조금·상계관세 협정에 수용될 전망임.

---

1) 상계조치 제소권자인 국내산업 제한(제16조)

- 의장안 내용

  o 상계조치의 제소는 유사물품의 국내총생산액의 [X]% 이상 생산하는

    생산자 집단이 할 수 있음.

- 반덤핑 협상의 논의

  o 아국등 개도국 : [X]% ⇒ 50% 주장

  o 미국·EC 등   : 50% 하향조정 주장

- 아국입장 : 논의시 반덤핑 협상에서의 아국입장

---

2) 경미한 보조금등에 대한 조사중단(제11.7조)

- 의장안 내용

  o 다음의 경우 상계조치의 조사 중단

    . 경미한 보조금액 : 보조비율 [X]% 이하

    . 경미한 수입량   : 수입국 시장점유율 [Y]% 이하

- 반덤핑 협상의 논의

  o 아국등 개도국 : 경미한 덤핑율 [X]% ⇒ 5% 주장,
                        시장점유율 [Y]% ⇒ 3% 주장

  o 미국·EC 등   : 하향조정 주장

- 아국입장 : 논의시 반덤핑 협상에서의 아국입장

0091

30

3) 우회수출 판정기준 (제21.1조)

- 의장안 내용
    - o 수입물품에 대해 상계관세가 부과된 이후, 상계관세를 회피하기 위해 다음과 같은 우회수출시, 우회수출된 부품액이 완성물품액의 [X]% 이상일 때 규제
        - . 수입국내에 부품 반입하여 조립, 가공하여 수출
        - . 제3국에서의 조립, 가공을 통한 우회수출

- 반덤핑 협상의 논의
    - o 아국등 개도국 : [X]% ⇒ 90% 이상
    - o 미국·EC 등 : [X]% ⇒ 40~50%

- 아국입장 : 논의시 반덤핑 협상에서의 아국입장

0092

쳐

다. 한. 미 양자협의 대책

1) 미결 쟁점에 대한 기존의 양국입장

구 분	의 장 안	미 국	한 국
조치가능 보조금	o 일정 국내보조금의 심각한 손상 추정	o 의장안 찬성	o 의장안 반대
	o 수량기준 채택	o 의장안 찬성	o 의장안 반대
허용보조금	o 일정한 제한하에 4가지 보조금의 지급허용	o 의장안보다 엄격 한 제한 주장	o 의장안 제한조건 완화 주장
	o 복수의 허용보조금 수혜 금지	o 의장안 찬성	o 의장안 반대
개도국 우대조치	o 개도국의 구분 및 차별	o 의장안 찬성	o 의장안 반대
보조금액 산정기준	o 원칙적으로 수혜자 수익기준(시장가격과 비교) 채택	o 시장가격에 의한 수익기준 강화 주장	o 정부 비용개념 기준 채택
국내산업의 정 의	o 유사물품의 국내 총생산 액의 [X]%이상 생산하는 생산자 집단	o 50% 이하의 하향 조정	o [X]%가 50% 주장
농산물 보조금 포함여부	언급 없음.	o 동 협정안은 농산물 보조금에 도 적용 주장	o 농산물 보조금은 농산물 협상그룹 에서 별도 규정 주장

2) 쟁점별 아국의 협상대책

가) 기본입장

- 보조금 상계협상이 재개되는 초기단계이므로 아국의 수정입장 제시는 시기
  적으로 적절치 않음 → 기존입장 고수
- 그러나 세부쟁점에 대한 논의가 구체화될 경우, 동 협상타결에 적극적으로
  노력하고 있다는 인식을 줄수 있도록 수정입장 제시
  o 아국의 심대한 경제적 이해가 걸린 분야는 관철
  o 아국입장 관철 불가능한 분야 및 아국에의 영향이 적은 분야는 타 쟁점과
  trade-off 하여 수용

32

나) 쟁점별 아국의 협상대책

(1) 양보할 수 없는 쟁점

쟁 점	기존입장	향후입장	고수이유
o 농산물보조금의 동협정 적용	반 대 ⇒ 농산물보조금은 농산물 협상그룹 결과 수용	기존입장 고수	o 농산물보조금 적용시 아국농업 정책이 극도로 제한됨.
o 허용보조금의 중복지급 금지	반 대	기존입장 고수	o 향후 보조금 활용 가능성 높음
o 국내산업의 정의	50% 주장	기존입장 고수	o 자의적인 상계관세 제소에 따른 수출업계의 손해 방지

(2) bargaining 할 수 있는 쟁점

쟁 점	기존입장	향후입장	수정이유
o 허용보조금의 제한조건	제한조건 완화 ⇒ 수치한도내용 삭제	제한조건 완화 ⇒ 수치한도 상향 조정	o 아국입장 관철 불가능
o 심각한 손상의 추정	반 대 ⇒ 동조항(6.1)삭제	수 용	o 개도국 우대규정 에 의해 아국에 대해서는 적용안됨
o 수량기준채택문제	반 대 ⇒ 동조항(6.1.a) 삭제	기준 상향조정하여 수용 (5%→20~30%)	o 개도국 우대규정 에 따라 아국에 대해서는 적용 안됨.
o 선발개도국 차별 취급	반 대	부속서 8에 아국 포함	o 아국입장 관철 불가능
o 보조금액 산정기준	수익기준 채택반대 ⇒ 정부비용 기준 채택 주장	수익기준 수용	o 아국입장 관철 불가능

0094

33

3. 세이프가드

가. 협상 진전상황

o 주요협상 경과

- '89.7 의장 협정안이 제시된 이후 8차에 걸친 토의 및 수정 방식으로
  협상진행

  . 선별적인 규제허용 여부 등 중요부분에 대한 합의가 이루어지지 못한
    상태에서 의장의 9차 협정안을 최종단계 협상의 working paper로
    채택하기로 결정, 각료들의 정치적 해결로 넘김 .

- 지난 브랏셀 각료회의에서

  . EC가 여타 요소에서 댓가를 기대할 수 있다면 선별적용을 철회할
    의사를 표명함에 따라 GATT 사무국이 주요국가들과 협의,
    새로운 협정안을 작성하여 Green Room 회의에 제시하였으나
    농산물 협상의 난항으로 인해 구체적인 토의는 하지 못함

- 브라셀 각료회의 이후 동 협상은 사실상 중단 상태임

  . '91.4 세이프가드 조치가 규범제정 및 투자분야로 통합됨
  . '91.6 규범분야 협상에서 동 의제는 주요분야로 논의하되 정치적
    결정이 필요한 분야로서 마지막 단계에서 논의키로 합의

o 협상진전 상황

- 지금까지 논의를 통해

  . 세이프가드 조치의 실효성 확보를 위해 GATT 19조의 규율을 명료화하고,
  . 발동 기준을 완화하고 일정한 조건을 충족할 경우에는 보상.보복을 면제
  . 회색조치는 철폐되어야 한다는 데는 의견이 접근됨

- 그러나 대다수 국가의 MFN 원칙주장과 EC의 선별적용 주장대립과 관련

  . 선별적용 관련조항을 없애는 대신, 사실상 선별적용 효과를 가져올 수
    있는 수량 규제시 쿼타의 삭감 인정여부 및
  . 회색조치에 대한 철폐시한의 예외문제에 대해 선진국(특히 EC)과
    개도국간 의견 대립 지속

0095

34

- 타결을 보지 못한 주요협상 쟁점

  . EC (관세동맹)의 지위 (2항 주석)

  . 잠정조치의 기간 (4항)

  . 국내산업의 범위 (계량화 문제) (6항)

  . 세이프가드 조치 발동시 규제조치(쿼타감축) (8항, 9항)

  . 조치의 발동기간 (최초 발동기간, 총발동기간) (10항. 12항)

  . 재발동 금지기간 (14항. 15항)

  . 보상. 보복면제조치 및 기간 (18항)

  . 구조조정 지원 조치 (삭제)

  . 개도국 우대 (예외) (19항. 20항)

  . 기존의 SG조치 철폐시한 (21항)

  . 회색조치의 철폐시한 (23항)

나. 하반기 협상전망

o 규범분야중 기타 의제에 대한 정치적 절충안이 마련된 후에 세이프가드
  협상도 선별적용 허용 여부에 대한 정치적 절충안 마련 협상 추진 예상

o 사무국안을 기초로 협상이 진행될 전망인바 EC의 선별적용 철회 의사표시에
  따른 쿼타감축을 전제로 한 MFN 원칙 수용방안이 주요 쟁점이 될 것으로 예상
  되며, 여타 협상 참가국의 반발이 커 합의 가능성이 불투명함
  다만, 동 쟁점이 해결될 경우 기타 쟁점은 융통성 있게 타결될 전망

다. 주요쟁점 사항 및 아국 입장

(1) 무차별 원칙 견지 또는 제한된 선별적용 인정 여부

  o 사무국안

  - 선별적용 규정 삭제 (MFN 원칙 견지)

  - 단, SG 조치로서 수출국별로 쿼타를 할당할 경우 관련 수출국과
    합의가 이루어지지 않았을 때에는 EC가 제안한 쿼타 감축 방안 규정

0096

35

o 주요국의 입장

  - EC : 선별조항을 없애는 대신, 사실상 선별적용 효과를 가져올 수
        있도록 하는 수량규제시 특정 수줄국이 전체 피해에 미친
        정도를 고려하여 시장 점유율의 5 % point 감축 또는 수출량의
        30% 감축중 적은 범위내에서 쿼타를 삭감 가능토록 규정

  - 대다수국가 : 무차별 원칙은 준수되어야 하며, SG 조치는 공정무역에
             대한 규제이므로 과거의 평균 수입물량은 보장

  - 미국 : 수출국별 시장점유율의 순서가 바뀌지 않는 범위내에서 최대
        X%의 쿼타량 감축 허용

o 아국입장

  - MFN 원칙 견지

  . 선별적용 허용시는 우리나라가 피 규제국이 될 가능성이 높고 수출
    장애 요소인 회색조치의 철폐효과가 반감되는 반면, 규제국으로서
    발동할 경우 선별적인 발동이 사실상 곤란한 점을 고려. 선별
    적용 반대 입장 견지

  - 선별적용 철회 조건으로 제기된 수량 규제시 쿼타 감축 반대
    (평균 수출물량 보장)

  . 선별적용 철회에 따라 명목적으로 MFN 원칙은 유지되나 우리나라등
    수출 구조상 시장점유율이 상대적으로 높은 국가에는 실질적인
    선별적용 효과가 발생되므로 최소한의 수출 물량을 보장하는
    회색지대 조치보다 심각한 타격 초래

  . 세이프가드 조치는 공정수출에 대한 규제이므로 쿼타 감축은
    과도한 규제가 됨

0097

36

(2) 회색조치의 철폐기간 및 방법

   o 사무국안 : 3년 또는 4년이내에 철폐, 최대 8년까지 예외 인정

   o 주요국의 입장

     - E C : 회색조치는 3~4년 이내에 철폐하되, 예외적으로 특정 품목에
         대해서는 8년까지 시한을 연장할 수 있는 예외적 상황 설정

     - 대다수 국가 : 3년 정도의 최대시한 설정 필요성을 지지하며 MFN
         원칙 적용시 융통성 표명 입장

   o 아국입장

     - MFN 원칙 준수시 3~4년 이내 철폐 원칙과 예외적인 8년 시한 수용

(3) 보상.보복 면제조치 및 기간

   o 사무국안 : 3년

   o 주요국의 입장

     - 대다수 국가 : 선별적용을 철회할 경우 기간에 있어서는 융통성
         있는 검토 용의 표명

     ※ 종전, 미국 : 4년, EC : 5년, 한국 : 1년, 뉴질랜드 : 시한설정 반대

   o 아국입장

     - 현실적인 보복능력 부족과 선별적인 조치 발동시의 부담을 감안,
       선별적용 철회의 조건으로 기간에 대해서는 융통성있게 대처하되,
       최대한 최초 발동기간 이내로 해야 함

(4) 구조조정 지원조치

   o 사무국안 : 삭제

   o 주요국의 입장

     - EC, 인도, 브라질 : 구조조정 지원을 Safeguard 조치의 발동 목적으로

              허용하고 수출 보조금 성격이 아닌 지원조치는 인정

     - 대다수 국가 : 보조금 협상에서 논의되고 있는 사항임을 이유로 반대

   o 아국입장

     - 실질적으로 정부지원 조치의 예외 설정이 필요하나 GATT 규정과

      일치하지 않는 보조금 지원은 곤란

     - 사무국안이 구조조정 지원조치 내용을 삭제한데 대하여 이의 제기 불필요

(5) 개도국 우대조항

   o 사무국안

     - 시장 점유율 1% 이하인 개도국에 대해서는 세이프가드 조치 발동 금지

     - 개도국의 총 발동기간 : 2년연장 가능, 총 10년 (일반은 8년)

     - 기존 SG 발동기간의 1/2기간이 경과한 후 재발동 가능, 최소 2년 경과

      (일반은 SG 조치가 취해진 기간과 동일한 기간은 재발동 금지)

   o 주요국의 입장

     - 일부 개도국을 제외하고는 대부분의 국가가 예외 인정 반대

   o 아국입장

     - 개도국 우대조치에 반대할 명분이 없으나, 개도국에 대한 예외 인정시

      우리가 피규제국 또는 발동국 입장 양 측면에서 실익이 없으므로 소극적인

      반대 유지

(6) EC (관세동맹)의 지위

  o 사무국안 : 관세동맹의 지위는 GATT 24조 8항(관세동맹)의 해석에 따름

  o 주요국의 입장
    - EC : 현재까지 EC만이 일부 회원국 또는 일부 지역을 대신하여
           EC 전체 차원의 SG 조치를 취하고, 이 경우에도 역내국간의
           교역은 피해판정 및 규제조치에서 제외할 것을 주장
    - 여타국가 : 역내국가의 제외는 사실상 선별적용임을 들어 반대

  o 아국입장
    - 우리나라로서는 역외국가에 대한 차별방지를 위해 EC를 단일주체로
      인정해온 기존 입장을 유지하되,
    - 협상타결의 장애요소가 되지 않도록 GATT 전체 차원의 문제로 관세동맹의
      지위를 24조 8항의 해석에 따르는 것으로 명시한 사무국안에 반대할
      필요는 없음

(7) 국내산업의 범위

  o 사무국안 : 피해판정시 국내산업의 범위를 국내생산의 "상당한 부분"
           [예, 통상 50% 이상, 최소한 33% 이상]을 차지하는 생산자를 의미

  o 주요국의 입장
    - 대부분의 국가 : 현실적으로 계량화가 곤란함을 표명

  o 아국입장
    - 대외무역법상 "상당한 부분"을 차지하고 있는 국내생산자 등으로
      규정하고 있고, 현실적으로 계량화가 곤란한 점을 감안, 계량화된
      표현 삭제가 바람직함
    - 단, 계량화할 경우 반덤핑 협상에서의 우리나라 입장 (50% 이상의
      국내산업)등을 고려, 적극적인 입장 표명은 자제

0100

39

(8) 조치 발동기간

  o 사무국안 : 최초 4년, 총 8년

  o 주요국 입장

    - 미 국 : 최초 5년, 연장 3년으로 총 8년

    - 일 본 : 최초, 연장 구분없이 5년

    - 대다수 국가 : 최초 3년, 연장 3년으로 총 6년

  o 아국입장

    - 대외무역법상 최대 10년 (5년 + 5년)으로 되어 있는 발동국 입장을 고려
      하여 "최소한 6년 이상" 이라는 기존 입장에 따라 융통성 있게 대처

(9) 재발동 금지기간

  o 사무국안

    - 동일 품목에 대한 SG조치 재발동은 기존의 SG조치 기간과 동일한
      기간이 경과된 후에만 가능하며, 최소한 2년 경과 후에만 가능
    - 단, 1년이 경과하고 과거 5년간 3회 이상 발동되지 않았을 경우에는
      180일 이내의 SG 조치는 발동 가능

  o 주요국 입장

    - 대부분의 국가 : 2년간 재발동 금지기간 지지
    - 카나다, 뉴질랜드, 인도등 농산물 수출국 : 180일 이내의 단기조치
      재발동 금지를 위한 예외적인 조항 지지

  o 아국입장

    - 수출국으로서의 입장과 수입국으로서의 입장을 고려할때 사무국안을
      반대할 필요는 없음

0101

40

(10) 기존의 Safeguard 조치의 철폐시한

   o 사무국안

     - 기존조치의 발동후 8년이내 또는 본협정 발효후 [5년], [6년]이내

      중 늦은 기간이내에 철폐

   o 주요국 입장

     - 미국,카나다 : 조치 발동이후 8년이내 또는 신 협정 발효후 3년이내

     - EC : 신협정 발효후 3년이내는 너무 짧은 기간임

   o 아국입장

     - 우리나라는 현재 GATT에 통보된 19조상의 SG조치를 발동하거나 규제받고

      있지 않은 상황이므로 특별한 의견제시 불필요

(11) 잠정조치 기간

   o 사무국안

     - 200일 이내로서 관세인상 형태만 인정, 피해가 없을 경우 환급

   o 주요국 입장

     - 미국, EC, 카나다 : 조사절차상 충분한 기간 허용

     - 호주 ,홍콩 : 90일 이상 허용반대

     - 뉴질랜드 : 관세형태만 인정, 피해가 없을 경우 환급

   o 아국입장

     - 수출국 측면에서 가급적 단축하는 것이 바람직함(90일 ~120일)

     - 다만, 대외무역법상 잠정조치 기간이 120 ~ 270일로 규정되어 있어

      아국제도와 유사하므로 사무국안에 이의제기 불필요

0102

니

라. 협상 대응 방향

(1) 기본입장

o 과도한 수출제한 요소는 제거하되 국내산업 피해 구제 기능 측면을 보장

  - 입장 견지 분야 : MFN 원칙. 회색지대조치 철폐
  - 입장 변경 가능분야 : 보상.보복 면제조건 완화. 조치발동기간. 회색지대
                        조치 철폐기간. 국내산업 범위
  - 기타 경미한 협상 요소는 다수의 입장에 동조하여 협상 타결 유도

(2) 협상 전략

o 선별적용 철회 조건으로 제기된 수량규제시 쿼타 감축(Cut-back)은
  아국이외의 여타 협상국이 강력히 반발하고 있어 이들 국가와 협조하여
  EC 의 주장을 철회토록 대처
    - 단, 이 경우 Leading role 로 선진국 통상압력의 Target 이 될
      이유는 없으며, 여타국의 입장에 대해 묵시적 또는 소극적 동조를
      보이며 협상흐름을 관망

o 선별적용 철회조건으로 회색지대 철폐기간의 연장, 보상, 보복 면제
  기간의 연장, 총 세이프가드 조치 발동기간 연장, 개도국 우대조치등에
  융통성있게 대처하여 협상 타결을 유도

42

0103

마. 한.미 양자협의 대책

  (1) 미국이 우리나라에 제기가능 사항

    o 선별적용과 관련한 타협안으로
      - 당사국간의 합의를 전제로 한 선별적용(Consensual Selectivity) 허용
      - 또는 수출국별 시장점유율의 순서가 바뀌지 않는 범위내에서 최대
        X%의 쿼타량 감축을 허용하는 방안 제시

    o 세이프가드조치의 구제수단의 하나로 구조조정을 포함시키는데 반대하고,
      GATT 관련 보조금규정과 일치하지 아니하는 정부지원 조치 허용 반대

    o 세이프가드 조치 발동기간을 최초 5년, 연장 3년으로 하여 총 8년을
      인정하고, 잠정조치 기간은 조사, 판정 90일, 통보 및 협의 120일등
      최대 210일 허용

  (2) 우리나라 대응방안

    o 선별적용과 관련 MFN 원칙 기본입장 견지

      - 쿼타 배분시 일정 쿼타 감축허용은 세이프가드 조치가 공정한 수출에
        대한 규제이므로 과도한 규제로서 반대

      - Consensual Selectivity 도 현실적으로 EC 의 일방적인 선별조치와
        동일한 효과 발생

    o 기타 사항은 MFN 원칙이 준수되고, 회색조치가 철폐된다면 융통성있는
      입장임을 제시

(3) 미결쟁점에 대한 양국 입장 비교

쟁 점	미 국	한 국
o 선별적용 허용여부 -사무국안 : 삭제	o MFN 원칙 준수 - 단, 수입.수출국간 상호합의하에 선별적용 허용	o MFN 원칙 준수 - 보상, 보복의무완화 등 여타요건에서 발동국 부담 완화
o 수량규제시 쿼타 감축 - 사무국안 : 허용	o 시장점유율 순서가 바뀌 지 않는 범위내에서 최대 X%의 쿼타 감축 허용	o 쿼타 감축 반대
o 회색조치 철폐기간	o 3 년	o 3 년정도의 최대시한 - 단, MFN원칙 준수시 8년 시한도 인정
o 보상, 보복 면제조치 및 기간 - 사무국안 : 3년	o 4년	o 종전 1년 - 최대한 최초 발동 기간 이내
o 구조조정 지원조치 - 사무국안 : 삭제	o 정부의 계획 또는 보조 하의 지원 반대	o SG 조치 기간중에는 구조조정이 실질적임
o 잠정조치 - 사무국안 : 200일 (관세인상 조치 한정)	o 210일 (수량제한도 허용)	o 가능한 짧은 기간이 바람직

4. GATT 조문

가. 협상 진전상황

1) 주요협상 경과

○ '88.12 중간평가를 통하여 아래 사항에 합의
 - GATT 조문의 명료화 및 개선에 협상력 집중
 - 본 협상그룹내 쟁점과 타협상 그룹 쟁점간에 관련성 고려
 - 명확한 협상쟁점 설정

○ '90.11.2. TNC 수석대표 비공식 협의에서 2조 1(B)항, 17조, 28조는 잠정합의가 이루어진 분야로, 24조, 25조 5항, 35조 및 잠정 적용 의정서는 합의된 협상 기초가 있는 분야로 분류 되었으며, 다만 BOP 조항만이 합의된 협상 기초조차 없는 분야로 분류됨.

○ 91.3.26. 주요국 수석대표급 비공식 협의에서 규범제정(Rule making) 협상 그룹의 일부로 재구성됨.

○ 91.7.30. TNC앞 협상그룹 의장 보고서는 BOP 조항만을 우선 협상 과제로 지적하고 나머지 쟁점은 기술적 사항으로서 추후 협의키로 제의함.

2) 합의사항

○ 잠정합의를 도출한 조문
 - 2조 1(B)항 : 관세 양허표상의 기타 과세 및 부과금
 - 17조 : 국영무역기업
 - 28조 : 관세 양허 재협상 절차

○ 철폐시한만 결정되면 타결될 조문
 - 25조 5항 : 웨이버
 - 잠정 적용 의정서 및 가입 의정서상의 조부 조항

○ 일부 참가국들이 초안 내용의 법적 의미에 대한 검토 완료시까지 유보한 조문
 - 35조 : GATT 협정 부적용

0106

45

3) 미합의사항
   o 24조 : 관세동맹 및 지역협정
   o 18조 B : BOP 조항

나. 주요 쟁점사항 및 주요국 동향

1) 24조 (관세동맹 및 지역협정)

   o 관세동맹 및 지역협정의 결성 및 확대에 따른 관세 조정에 대한 보상
     지불문제 (24조 6항)
     - E C : 타회원국의 동일 품목 관세인하로 부족할 경우 타회원국의
             다른 품목에 대한 관세인하분도 고려대상에 포함
     - 미국등 : 타회원국의 동일 품목 관세인하로 부족할 경우 다른 품목의
               공동 관세인하로 보상

   o 지방정부 또는 기관의 조치 및 행위에 대한 중앙정부의 GATT상 책임문제
     (24조 12항)
     - E C : 중앙정부의 책임으로 함으로써 분쟁해결 절차 명료화
     - 미국, 카나다, 인도등 : 중앙정부가 GATT 규정의 준수를 위한
               합리적인 조치를 취하는 것은 헌법상 허용된 한도내에서만 가능

2) BOP 조항

   ① 선진국(미국, 카나다, EC) 제안 요지
     o 선진국의 BOP 목적을 이유로 한 무역 제한조치 금지 공약의 강화
     o 12조나 18조 B에 근거한 무역조치는 BOP 문제의 정도에 비례해야
       하며 일시적인 조치로서 사용
     o 무역조치는 명료, 무차별적이어야 하며, 일정한 기간내 철폐 및
       점진적 완화를 약속해야 함 (선진국은 개도국보다 짧은기간내 철폐)
     o 수량제한 조치보다 가격에 기초한 조치가 바람직

0107

46

o BOP 위원회에서의 협의는 제한조치의 적용 또는 강화후 4개월
  이내에 시작

o BOP 위원회는 협의중인 체약국의 수출 이익의 증대를 위하여
  체약국단이 취할 수 있는 조치를 제안

  - BOP 위원회 협의에서의 IMF의 역할을 좀 더 분명히 정의

  - 동 위원회가 당해 조치의 GATT 적합 여부 문제에 관한 권고에
    합의할 수 없을 경우, 영향을 받은 체약국은 갓트 분쟁해결 절차
    원용 가능

② 개도국 입장

o 많은 개도국의 외적인 경제환경이 대외 부채 증가, 자본 유입, 교역
  조건의 악화, 환율 및 이자율 불안정등 여러면에서 악화되고 있음.

o 만약 BOP 조항이 협상의 대상이 된다면 그 목적은 보다 엄격한
  조건을 부과하는 것이 아니라 동 조항의 사용에 보다 융통성을
  부여하는데 두어야 함.

o 기존의 규정과 BOP 위원회의 관련 절차는 잘 운용되고 있고,
  그 운용상의 문제점은 UR 협상과 관련해서가 아니라 동 위원회에서
  다루어져야 함.

③ 지금까지의 협상 동향

(i) 18조 B의 필요성은 공감

  o 12조 및 18조 B의 내용 자체는 변화되어서는 안됨.

  o BOP상의 어려운 시기에 무역조치를 사용하는 권한이 배제되어서는
    안됨.

  o 장기간의 BOP상의 어려움은 국내정책, 거시경제정책 및 무역관련
    조치에 의한 국내문제로서 뿐만 아니라 무역장벽 제거 및 채무,
    금융 이동에 관한 국제문제로서도 취급될 필요성은 인정

(ii) 18조 B에 의한 무역제한 조치의 문제점 인식

  o 제한적 무역조치는 어떤 상황에서는 피할수는 없지만 일반적으로
    BOP 균형을 유지, 회복하기 위해서는 비효과적인 수단임을 인정

0108

41

o 동 조치는 특정산업이나 분야를 보호할 목적으로 사용되어서는
  안됨을 인정

o 동 조치 사용시 체약국은 무역에 가장 적게 영향을 미치는
  조치를 우선하여야 함을 인정

o 개도국의 경우 각국의 개발, 금융, 무역상황이 고려되어야 함을
  인정

3) 조부 조항, 웨이버

o X년이후 철폐에 합의

o 철폐에 관한 구체적 사항은 타협상그룹(특히 농산물)의 협상 결과를
  감안하여 결정

다. 아국 입장

1) 기본 입장

① 24조

o 관세동맹 및 자유무역 협정으로 인한 역외국가에 대한 불이익 최소화

② BOP 조항

o BOP 조항 개정에 불반대하나 개도국의 강한 입장을 고려 입장 표명
  유보

2) 세부 쟁점별 기존 입장

① 24조

o 관세동맹 및 지역협정의 결성과 확대에 따른 보상 지불

  - 타회원국의 동일품목의 관세 인하로 보상이 충분치 못할 경우,
    다른 품목에 대한 공동 관세인하로 보상

0109

48

o 지방정부의 기관의 조치에 대한 중앙정부의 책임

- 지방정부의 행위는 중앙정부의 책임

② BOP조항

o 구체적 입장 표명 불요

③ 조부조항, 웨이버

o 협상 결과에 따름

3) 입장 재정립 가능 분야 : 기존 입장에 따름.

49

5. 무역관련 투자제한조치 (TRIMs)

가. 협상 진전 상황

o UR/TRIMs 협상은 서비스. 지적소유권과 함께 GATT 협상의 새로운 분야
  (new-issue)로써 외국인 투자에 대한 각종 규제와 제한을 철폐함으로써
  국제간 투자를 촉진하고 세계무역 증진을 도모하기 위하여 UR 협상에 포함.

  - '87.4월부터 협상을 개최한 이후, '90년말까지 20여 차례의 실무자간
    협상과 수차례의 Green Room 회의를 가졌음

o 그러나, 선진국과 개도국간의 입장차이가 현격하여 협상의 진전이 없었음

  - 선진국 : 기본적으로 자국기업의 해외투자를 촉진. 보호하여야 할 입장으로
            투자대상국 (Host Country)의 투자제한조치 (TRIMs)의 규제 주장

  - 개도국 : 해외투자 실적이 거의 없고 자국산업을 보호해야 할 입장으로
            투자제한 조치에 대한 규제를 반대

o 지난해 브랏셀 각료 회의에서도 협상안 조차 마련되지 못하고 선진국과
  개도국간의 입장 조정에 실패

o 금년 4월 규범제정 및 투자분야로 통합되어 주요의제로 논의되고 있으나
  실질적 진전이 없음

  - 지난 7월회의에서 각국의 기존입장을 재확인하고 하반기 협상 방향을
    설정하는데 그침

0111

나. 하반기 협상 전망

o 하반기 협상은 비공식 협의 위주로 다음 쟁점에 대한 선·개도국간 견해차이를
축소하기 협상을 추진키로 함

- 하반기 주요 논의 쟁점
(i) 협정의 적용 범위, (ii) 규제 방법, (iii) 개도국 취급방법
(iv) 잠정조치, (v) 제한적 사업관행, (vi) 기타 명료성 및 향후작업을
위한 제도 정비

o 선진국과 개도국간의 입장 차이가 현격하여 TRIMs 협상 자체로는 타결 되기가
어려우나 농산물등 주요 분야에서 정치적인 타협이 이뤄져 UR 협상이
전반적으로 타결되는 방향으로 합의가 되면 TRIMs 협상도 정치적 결단에
의해 타결될 수 있을 것임

o 그러나 최빈 개도국의 경우에는 UR 협상타결 이후에도 TRIMs 협정에
참여하지 않는 경우도 예상할 수 있음

다. 주요 쟁점 사항 및 아국입장

(1) 협상의 범위

o 쟁점 :. 신규 TRIMs 에 국한할 것인지 또는 기존 TRIMs에도 적용할 것인지
여부
. 강제적 조치만 대상으로 할 것인지 또는 incentive도 포함할
것인지 여부

o 선진국
- TRIMs은 신규투자뿐만 아니라 기존의 무역관련 투자제한 조치도 포함
- 보조금등 특혜 부여의 조건으로 부과되는 조치도 규제

o 개도국
- TRIMs은 신규투자와 관련되는 분야만 포함
- 보조금등 특혜부여에 따르는 조건은 보조금 상계관세 협상에서 논의

0112

o 아국입장

  - TRIMs는 신규투자 뿐만 아니라 기존의 TRIMs조치도 포함되어야 함
    다만, 투자제한조치중 내.외국 기업에 동등하게 부과하는 경우에는
    TRIMs 범위 내에서 제외 되어야 함
  - 아국은 조세감면등 혜택을 부여하면서 투자제한조치를 부과하는 사례가
    없는 반면, 개도국은 부과 사례가 많은바 아국의 해외투자 측면을
    고려할때 incentive 조치도 TRIMs에 포함, 규제 대상이 되어야 함

(2) 규제의 방법

┌───┐
│ o 쟁점 : TRIMs 조치의 전반적인 금지개념 도입 또는 case 별로 검토 여부, │
│   수출의무도 포함여부   │
└───┘

o 선진국
  - 국내부품 사용조건 등과 같이 GATT 제 3조(내국민 대우), 제 11조(수량제한)
    에 위반되는 모든 TRIMs 조치 및 수출이행 의무 조건은 금지
  - 법령, 행정 명령등 형식에 관계없이 일률적으로 규제

o 개도국
  - case by case로 검토하여 무역왜곡 효과를 치유토록 하며 궁극적인 규제
    조치는 GATT 분쟁해결 절차에 의함
  - 수출이행 조건은 GATT 의무 위반이 아니므로 규제대상이 될수 없음

o 아국입장
  - 무역왜곡 효과가 직접적이고 심각한 TRIMs은 금지대상으로 하되 개도국에
    대한 예외 범위를 확대
  - 수출이행 조건도 TRIMs으로 규제대상으로 되어야 하나, 개도국의 국제수지
    의 개선등의 목적상 불가피한 경우 예외 인정

(3) 개도국에 대한 취급

o 개도국

- 개도국의 경제개발 필요성을 고려, 개도국이 필요시 TRIMs을 운용할 수
  있도록 전반적인 예외 인정

o 선진국

- 개도국에 대한 배려는 GATT 18조 규정(개도국에 대한 예외)의 규정에
  따라 잠정적이고 제한적 배려

o 아국입장

- 개도국에 대하여는 GATT 제 18조에서 규정하고 있는 범위 이상으로
  TRIMs 의무에 대한 예외 인정

(4) TRIMs 규제를 위한 잠정조치

o 개도국

- TRIMs의 운용은 철폐될 수 없으므로 철폐기한 도입 반대

o 선진국

- TRIMs 규제를 위한 철폐기한의 도입(선진국 X 년, 개도국 Y 년,
  최저개도국 Z 년)

o 아국입장

- 개도국에 대한 예외범위를 인정하고, TRIMs 규제를 위한 철폐
  기한 도입(개도국에는 장기간의 철폐기한 인정)

0114

(5) 제한적 사업관행 (Restrictive Business Practice)

o 쟁점 : 다국적 기업의 제한적 사업관행을 TRIMs으로 포함 여부

o 개도국
- 다국적 기업등의 제한적 사업관행은 무역을 심각하게 왜곡하는 사례가 있으므로 본 협상에 포함

o 선진국
- 제한적 사업관행 포함 반대 ('86. 9 Punta del Este 각료선언에 의한 협상범위에 포함되지 않음)

o 아국입장
- 다국적 기업의 제한적 사업관행도 본 협상 범위에 포함하여야 함

라. 협상 대응 방향

o 아국은 외국인 투자 자유화조치를 지속적으로 추진하여 왔고 해외투자가 증가되는 상황에서, 무역관련 투자제한조치를 철폐하려는 선진국 입장과 유사함

- 투자제한조치 (TRIMs) 협상 타결시 아국기업의 해외투자 환경 개선을 기대할 수 있는 반면, 외국인 투자를 추가로 개방하여야 하는 부담은 거의 없음

o 다만, 협상 결과에 선진국 및 일부 개도국만 참여하고 다수 개도국이 불참할 경우에도 아국으로서는 참여가 불가피한 바, 이 경우 ① 아국의 대개도국 투자환경 개선을 기대할 수 없고 ② 선진국에 비하여 상대적으로 제한조치가 많은 아국이 개선 요청을 많이 받을 것 등을 예상할 때 아국으로서는 다수 개도국이 참여하는 것이 유리하므로 개도국이 참여토록 개도국에 대한 특별배려 필요 주장

0115

54

외 무 부

안, 이

종 별 :

번 호 : GVW-1823   일 시 : 91 0924 1600

수 신 : 장 관 (통기)경기원,재무부,상공부)

발 신 : 주 제네바 대사

제 목 : UR/규범제정 및 TRIMS 회의 일정

　　　GATT 사무국은 표제건의 구체적 일정을 아래와 같이 잠정 결정하였으며,
전체회의는 공식, 소그룹회의는 비공식으로 개최할 예정이라 함.

　　0 9.30.오전: 전체회의 오후 : 반덤핑, 선적전 검사

　　0 10.1.오전: TRIMS 오후 : 반덤핑

　　0 10.2.오전 :TRIMS 오후 : 보조금.상계관세

　　0 10.3. 오전 : 보조금.상계관세 오후: BOPS

　　0 10.4. 오전 : BOPS 오후: 전체회의. 끝

　　(대사 박수길-국장)

통상국　　2차보　　경기원　　재무부　　상공부

91.09.25　　09:03 WG

외신 1과 통제관

0116

외 무 부

종 별 :

번 호 : GVW-1835

일 시 : 91 0925 1830

수 신 : 장 관(통기,경기원,재무부,상공부)

발 신 : 주 제네바 대사

제 목 : UR/반덤핑 협상

0 향후 반덤핑협상 진행에 관해 강상무관이 규범제정 협상그룹의장 보좌역인 RAMSAUSER 및 주요국과 접촉한 내용을 하기 보고함.

0 던켈 총장이 9.20 그린룸 회의에서 10월말 또는 11월 초까지 전 협상그룹이 TEXT 를 제출토록 촉구함에 따라 반덤핑 분야에서도 상기 일정에 맞추기 위해 9.30. 및 10.1 오후에 열리는 반덤핑 비공식회의에서는 어려운 쟁점인 8개 항목에 대해 집중토의를 하며 그목적은 PRE-DRAFTINGEXERCISE 라고 함

0 8개 항목은 비용이하 판매, 구성가격계산, 평균가격 대 평균가격 비교문제, 수입국 및 제 3국 경유 우회덤핑, 피해의 누적, DEMINIMUS, 소급적용문제 (COUNTRY HOPPING 의 경우),분쟁해결등 이라고 함.

0 이에대해 대부분 국가는 이에 찬성하고 있으나 EC 는 시기상조라는 이유로 소극적 반응을 보이고 있다고 하며 아국은 덤핑논의의 활성화 및 협상기초문안 마련을 위해 주요쟁점에 대한 토론재개를 환영하였음.

0 9.30 개최되는 반덤핑회의에서는 의장의 상기복안에 따라 회의가 진행될 것으로 보임.끝

(대사 박수길-국장)

통상국   2차보   경기원   재무부   상공부

91.09.26   09:18 WG

외신 1과   통제관

0117

기 안 용 지

분류기호 서번호	통기 20644-	(전화 : 720 - 2188)	시 행 상 특별취급	
보존기간	영구. 준영구 10. 5. 3. 1.	장 관		
수 신 처 보존기간				
시행일자	1991. 9. 28.			

보 조 기 관	국 장	전 결	협 조 기 관		문 서 통 제	
	심의관					
	과 장					
기안책임자		안 명 수			발 송 인	

경 유 수 신 참 조	내부결재	발 신 명 의	

제 목	UR/규범제정 협상참가 정부대표임명

1991.9.30(월)-10.4(금)간 스위스 제네바에서 개최되는 UR/규범

제정 협상에 참가할 정부대표를 "정부 대표및 특별사절의 임명과 권한에

관한 법률"에 의거, 아래와 같이 임명할 것을 건의 합니다.

- 아   래 -

1. 회 의 명 : UR/규범 협상

- 1 -

0118

2. 회의기간 및 장소 : 91. 9.30-10.4, 스위스 제네바

3. 정부대표 :

   o 상공부 국제협력관실 사무관   김영학

    (UR/섬유 협상그룹회의 참석차 제네바 기.출장중)

4. 출장기간 : 91.9.30-10.6

5. 소요경비 : 상공부 소관예산

6. 훈   령 : 별도 건의예정   끝.

- 2 -

0119

상 공 부

국 협 28140-375   (503 - 9446)   1991. 9. 27.

수 신   외무부 장관

제 목   UR/규범제정 및 투자분야 협상 참가 관련 출장기간 연장

　　91.9.30(월) ~ 10.4(금)간 스위스 제네바에서 개최되는 UR/규범제정 및 투자분야 협상에 참가하기 위하여 다음과 같이 출장기간을 연장코자 하오니 정부대표 임명등 필요한 조치를 하여 주시기 바랍니다.

= 다　　음 =

1. 출 장 지 : 스위스 제네바

2. 출장자 및 출장기간

소 속	직 급	성 명	출 장 기 간		비　　고
			UR/섬유협상	UR/규범제정분야	
국제협력 관실	행정 사무관	김영학	91. 9. 22 ~ 9. 29	91. 9. 30 ~ 10. 6	UR/섬유협상차 제네바에 기 출장 중

3. 소요예산 : 상공부 예산

첨 부 : 회의 참가 입장 1부.

상　　공　　부　　장
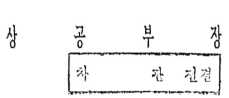

0120

UR/규범제정 및 투자분야 협상 (9.30~10.4) 입장(안)
===

1. 전반적인 입장

o 현재 규범제정 및 투자분야의 대부분의 쟁점은 기술적인 문제가 아닌 정치적
   절충을 요하는 사항으로 금년 협상은 비공식 협의를 통해 정치적 타협을 위한
   협상 package 마련에 치중할 것으로 보임

o 주요국간 공식, 비공식 협의에 적극 참여하여 아국의 관심사항이 반영될 수
   있도록 협상에 임하되, 동 분야의 협상이 재개되는 초기 단계이므로 기존의
   입장을 유지하고, 주요국의 입장 및 협상동향을 면밀히 파악하여 아국 입장
   수립에 참고토록 함

2. 반덤핑 협상

o 반덤핑 조치의 남용 방지를 위해 현행 협정을 강화하고 명료성을 확보하자는
   아국의 기존 입장 유지
   - 덤핑, 피해 판정 기준의 공정성 및 객관성 확보
   - 조사 개시 요건등 조사 절차의 강화
   - 소멸 시효의 설정

o 선진 수입국 (미국, EC)이 주장하는 우회덤핑 방지 조항 도입을 최대한 저지
   - 다만, 순수한 우회덤핑 (수입국내 단순조립)의 경우는 규제 인정 가능하나
     남용 방지를 위해 그 기준 설정을 엄격히 해야 함

o 특히, 최근 주요 수출국간 비공식 협의가 활발히 진행되고 있는바, 동 협의에
   아국이 적극 참여토록 하고 그 협상동향을 면밀히 파악토록 함

o 주요 항목별 입장 (별 첨)

0121

o 보조금. 상계관세 협상이 재개되는 초기 단계이므로 기존의 아국 입장을 고수하면서,
주요국의 입장 및 협상 동향을 면밀히 파악하여 향후 아국의 입장 수립에
참고할 수 있도록 함

o 세부 쟁점별 공식. 비공식 협의가 진행되어 논의가 구체화될 경우 협상 타결에
적극적으로 노력하고 있다는 인식을 줄 수 있도록 첨부한 쟁점별 아국 입장에
의거, 적의 대처

4. TRIM 협상

o TRIMs을 포함한 UR 협상이 전반적으로 교착상태에 처해있는 점을 감안, 아국은
TRIMs 협상이 성공적으로 타결되기를 희망한다는 점을 강조하며 다음과 같은
입장 표명
  - TRIMs 협상은 선진국. 개도국을 망라, 가급적 많은 국가가 협상 결과에 참여
    할 수 있는 방향으로 협상이 타결 되어야 함
  - 이를 위하여 협상 참가국들은 다수국가가 합의할 수 있도록 기존입장을 양보.
    조정하여야 할 것임
  - 한국 정부는 다수 참가국이 합의하는 내용이면 적극 참여하는 방향으로
    검토 할 것임

5. BOP 조항

o BOP 조항은 선진. 개도국간의 첨예한 의견 대립을 보이는 미묘한 문제이고
아국은 이미 BOP 조항을 졸업한만큼 구체적인 입장 표명 유보
  - BOP 조항 개정 가능성은 거의 없으며, 다만 선진국들이 섬유 협상등 여타
    협상 분야와 연계 카드로 사용
  - BOP 조항 개정 찬성시 개도국들이 우리에게 강력히 반발할 것이므로 찬성
    의사 표명 자제

0122

47237

기 안 용 지

분류기호 서번호	통기 20644-	(전화 : 720 - 2188)	시 행 상 특별취급	
보존기간	영구. 준영구 10. 5. 3. 1.	장 관		
수 신 처 보존기간				
시행일자	1991. 9.28.			

보조 기관	국 장	전 결	협 조 기 관		문 서 통 제
	심의관				
	과 장				
기안책임자		안 명 수			발 송 인

경 유 수 신 참 조	상공부장관	발 신 명 의	

제 목	UR/규범제정 협상참가 정부대표임명

91.9.30(월)-10.4(금)간 스위스 제네바에서 개최되는 UR/규범

제정 협상에 참가할 정부대표를 "정부 대표및 특별사절의 임명과 권한에

관한 법률"에 의거, 아래와 같이 임명되었음을 통보합니다.

- 아 래 -

1. 회 의 명 : UR/규범 협상

- 1 -

0123

2. 회의기간 및 장소 : 91.9.30-10.4, 스위스 제네바
3. 정부대표 :
○ 상공부 국제협력관실 사무관   김영학
(UR/섬유 협상그룹회의 참석차 제네바 기.출장중)
4. 출장기간 : 91.9.30-10.6
5. 소요경비 : 상공부 소관예산   끝.
- 2 -   0124

발 신 전 보

분류번호	보존기간

번 호 : WGV-1310   910930 1535   DW   종별 : 암호송신

수 신 : 주 제네바   대사. 총영사

발 신 : 장 관 (통 기)

제 목 : UR/규범제정 협상

1. 9.30-10.4간 귀지 개최 UR/규범제정 협상그룹 회의에 참석할 본부대표로 상공부
   국제협력관 김영학 사무관(UR/섬유 협상그룹 회의 참가차 귀지 출장중)이 추가
   임명된바, 귀관 관계관과 함께 참석토록 조치바람.

2. 훈 령

   가. 주요국간 공식, 비공식 협의에 참여하여 아국 관심사항을 적극 반영하고,
      주요국의 입장 및 협상 동향을 면밀히 파악토록 함.

   나. 의제별 토의시 세부협상 대책에 의거 대처하되, 보조금 상계관세 협의시
      기제출한 아국제안에 추가하여
      개도국 우대와 관련 대다수 국가가 의장안에 찬성하고 있음을 감안 Annex 8
      개도국 리스트에 아국이 포함되도록 할것 (이는 동건 관련 각 협상그룹에서
      통일된 입장을 견지해야 한다는 원칙 및 농산물 협상그룹에서의 개도국 우대
      확보의 필요성을 감안한 것임)

   다. 회의 종료후 갓트 사무총장의 연내 협상 타결 시도와 관련 표제 협상그룹의
      향후 전망에 대한 귀관 의견을 보고바람.   끝.

(통상국장 대리 최 혁)

	보안통제	~

앙고재	91년 9월 30일 통상기구과	기안자성명 안명수	과 장	심의관 전결	국 장	차 관	장 관	외신과통제

0125

		기 안 용 지		시 행 상	
분류기호 서번호	통기 20644-	(전화 : 720 - 2188)		특별취급	
보존기간	영구 . 준영구 10. 5. 3. 1.	장 관			
수 신 처 보존기간		*(서명)*			
시행일자	1991. 9.27.				

보 조 기 관	국 장	전 결	협 조 기 관		문 서 통 제
	심의관				
	과 장	*(서명)*			
	기안책임자	이 찬 범			발 송 인

경 유 수 신 참 조	내부결재	발 신 명 의	

제 목	UR/TRIMs 협상 정부대표 임명

1991.10.1-10.2간 제네바에서 개최되는 UR/TRIMs 협상에 참석할

정부대표를 "정부대표 및 특별사절의 임명과 권한에 관한 법률"에 의거,

아래와 같이 임명할 것을 건의하오니 재가하여 주시기 바랍니다.

- 아   래 -

1. 회 의 명 : UR/TRIMs 협상

- 1 -

0126

2. 회의기간 및 장소 : 91. 10.1-2, 스위스 제네바
3. 정부대표 :
ㅇ 재무부 경제협력국 투자진흥과 사무관   김교식
ㅇ 주 제네바 대표부 관계관
4. 출장기간 : 91.9.29-10.4 (6일간)
5. 소요예산 : 재무부 소관예산
6. 훈   령
ㅇ TRIMs 협상을 포함한 UR 협상이 전반적으로 교착상태에
처해있는 점을 감안, TRIMs 협상이 성공적으로 타결되기를
희망한다는 점을 강조하여 아래 입장 표명
- TRIMs 협상은 선진국.개도국을 망라, 가급적 많은
국가가 협상 결과에 참여할 수 있는 방향으로 협상이
타결되어야 함.

- 이를 위하여 협상 참가국들은 다수국가가 합의할 수
  보다 공통점이 있는 방상을 개시
  있도록 기존 입장을 ~~양보 조정~~하여야 할 것임.

~~- 한국 정부는 다수 참가국이 합의하는 내용이면 적극~~

~~참여하는 방향으로 검토할 것임.~~

ㅇ 주요 쟁점별 아국 입장 : 별첨 참조

첨   부 : UR/TRIMs 협상 참고자료.   끝.

- 3 -

0128

재　　무　　부

투 전 2254-1878　　　　　　(503-9276)　　　　　　1991. 9. 26.

수 신　외무부장관

참 조　통상국장

제 목　UR/TRIMs 협상참가 및 검토의견 송부

　　　1.　'91.10.1 - 10.2간 GATT에서 개최될 예정인 UR/TRIMs 협상
에 참가할 당부 대표를 다음과 같이 선정 통보하오니,

　　　2.　정부 대표 임명등 참가에 필요한 조치를 처리하여 주시기 바랍니다.
　　　　　　　　　　　　- 다　　음 -
　　　가.　출 장 자 :　경제협력국 투자진흥과 김 교식사무관
　　　나.　출 장 지 :　스위스 제네바
　　　다.　출장기간 :　'91. 9.29. - 10.4(6일간)
　　　라.　경　　비 :　당부 예산

　　　3.　이와 관련 UR/TRIMs 협상에 대한 아국의 입장을 별첨과 같이
송부하오니 대표 임명과 아울러 훈령하여 주시기 바랍니다.

첨 부 :　1.　일정표 1부.

　　　　　2.　UR /무역관련 투자조치(TRIMs)협상 대책 1부. 끝.

　재　　　무　　　부　　　장

0129

이 행 일 정 표
===============

1991. 9.29.(일)　　　서울출발

10. 1.(월)　　　Geneva 도착

10.1 - 2.　　　회의참석

10. 3.(목)　　　○ Geneva 출발
　　　　　　　　○ London 출발

10. 4.(금)　　　서울도착

0130

UR/무역관련 투자제한조치(TRIMs) 협상 자료

('91. 10. 1 ～ 10. 2.)

1. 협상진전상황

- UR/TRIMs 협상은 서비스, 지적소유권과 함께 GATT 협상의 새로운 분야(new issue)로써 외국인투자에 대한 각종 규제와 제한을 철폐함으로써 국제간 투자를 촉진하고 세계무역 증진을 도모하기 위하여 UR협상에 포함

- 그러나, 선진국과 개도국간의 입장차이가 현격하여 협상의 진전이 없었음.

  o 선진국 : 기본적으로 자국기업의 해외투자를 촉진·보호하여야 할 입장으로 투자대상국(Host Country)의 투자제한조치(TRIMs)의 규제 주장

  o 개도국 : 해외투자 실적이 거의 없고 자국산업을 보호해야 할 입장으로 투자 제한 조치에 대한 규제를 반대

- 지난해 브랏셀 각료회의에서도 협상안 조차 마련되지 못하고 선진국과 개도국간의 입장조정에 실패

- 금년 4월 규범제정 및 투자분야에 통합되어 주요의제로 논의되고 있으나, 실질적 진전이 없음.

  o 지난 7월회의에서 각국의 기존입장을 재확인하고 하반기 협상 방향을 설정하는데 그침.

2. 하반기협상 전망

- 하반기 협상은 비공식 협의 위주로 다음 쟁점에 대한 선·개도국간 견해차이를 축소하기 위한 협상을 추진키로 함.

0131

o 하반기 주요논의쟁점

(i) 협정의 적용범위, (ii) 규제방법, (iii) 개도국 취급방법, (iv)잠정조치,

(v)제한적 사업관행, (vi)기타 명료성 및 향후작업을 위한 제도정비

- 선진국과 개도국간의 입장차이가 현격하여 TRIMs협상 자체로는 타결되기가 어려우나
농산물등 주요 분야에서 정치적인 타협이 이뤄져 UR협상이 전반적으로 타결되는
방향으로 합의가 되면 TRIMs 협상도 정치적 결단에 의해 타결될 수 있을 것임.

3. 주요쟁점 사항 및 아국입장

(1) 협상의 범위

o 쟁점 :· 신규 TRIMs에 국한할 것인지 또는 기존 TRIMs에도 적용할
             것인지 여부
        · 강제적 조치만 대상으로할 것인지 또는 Incentive도 포함할
             것인지 여부

- 선진국

   o TRIMs은 신규투자뿐만 아니라 기존의 무역관련 투자제한 조치도 포함

   o 보조금등 특혜부여의 조건으로부과되는 조치도 규제

- 개도국

   o TRIMs은 신규투자와 관련되는 분야만 포함

   o 보조금등 특혜부여에 따르는 조건은 보조금 상계관세 협상에서 논의

- 아국입장

   o TRIMs 는 신규투자 뿐만 아니라 기존의 TRIMs 조치도 포함되어야 함.

      다만, 투자제한조치중 내·외국기업에 동등하게 부과하는 경우에는 TRIMs

      범위내에서 제외되어야 함.

0132

o 아국은 조세감면등 혜택을 부여하면서 투자제한 조치를 부과하는 사례가
  없는 반면, 개도국은 부과사례가 많은 바 아국의 해외투자 측면을 고려할 때
  Incentive 조치도 TRIMs에 포함, 규제대상이 되어야 함.

(2) 규제의 방법

```
o 쟁점  : TRIMs 조치도 전반적인 금지개념 도입 또는 Case 별로 검토
         여부, 수출의무도 포함여부
```

- 선진국

  o 국내부품 사용조건등과 같이 GATT 제3조(내국민대우), 제11조(수량제한)에
    위반되는 모든 TRIMs조치 및 수출이해 의무조건은 금지
  o 법령·행정 명령등 형식에 관계없이 일률적으로 규제

- 개도국

  o Case by Case로 검토하여 무역왜곡 효과를 치유토록 하여 궁극적인 규제조치
    는 GATT 분쟁해결 절차에 의함.
  o 수출이행 조건은 GATT 의무 위반이 아니므로 규제대상이 될 수 없음.

- 아국입장

  o 무역왜곡 효과가 직접적이고 심각한 TRIMs은 금지대상으로 하되 개도국에 대한
    예외 범위를 확대
  o 수출이행 조건도 TRIMs으로 규제대상으로 되어야 하나, 개도국의 국제수지의
    개선등의 목적상 불가피한 경우 예외 인정

(3) 개도국에 대한 취급

```
o 쟁점  : 개도국에 대한 전반적인 예외 인정 여부
```

0133

- 개도국

    o 개도국의 경제개발 필요성을 고려, 개도국이 필요한 TRIMs을 운용할 수 있도록
      전반적인 예외 인정

- 선진국

    o 개도국에 대한 배려는 GATT 18조 규정(개도국에 대한 예외)의 규정에 따라
      잠정적이고 제한적 배려

- 아국입장

    o 개도국에 대하여는 GATT 제18조에서 규정하고 있는 범위 이상으로 TRIMs 의무
      에 대한 예외 인정

(4) 제한적 사업관행(Restrictive Business Practice)

> o 쟁점 : 다국적 기업의 제한적 사업관행을 TRIMs으로 포함 여부

- 개도국

    o 다국적기업등의 제한적 사업관행을 무역을 심각하게 왜곡하는 사례가 있으므로
      본 협상에 포함.

- 선진국

    o 제한적 사업관행 포함반대('86. 9. Punta del Eate 각료선언에 의한 협상
      범위에 포함되지 않음.)

- 아국입장

    o 다국적기업의 제한적 사업관행도 본 협상 범위에 포함하여야 함.

0134

4. 협상대응방향

- 아국은 외국인투자 자유화조치를 지속적으로 추진하여 왔고 해외투자가 증가되는
  상황에서, 무역관련 투자제한 조치를 철폐하려는 선진국 입장과 유사함.

  o 투자제한조치(TRIMs) 협상 타결시 아국기업의 해외투자 환경 개선을 기대할 수
  있는 반면, 외국인투자를 추가로 개방하여야 하는 부담은 거의 없음.

- 다만, 협상 결과에 선진국 및 일부 개도국만 참여하고 다수 개도국이 불참할
  경우에도 아국으로서는 참여가 불가피한 바, 이 경우 ① 아국의 대개도국 투자환경
  개선을 기대할 수 없고 ② 선진국에 비하여 상대적으로 제한조치가 많은 아국이
  개선 요청을 많이 받을 것등을 예상할 때 아국으로서는 다수 개도국이 참여하는
  것이 유리하므로 개도국이 참여토록 개도국에 대한 특별배려 필요 주장

0135

UR / TRIMs협상('91.10.1) 관련 훈령 (안)

TRIMs 를 포함한 UR 협상이 전반적으로 교착상태에 처해있는 점을 감안,
아국은 TRIMs 협상이 성공적으로 타결되기를 희망한다는 점을 강조하며
다음과 같은 입장 표명

- TRIMs협상은 선진국·개도국을 망라, 가급적 많은 국가가 협상결과에
  참여 할 수 있는 방향으로 협상이 타결 되어야함.

- 이를위하여 협상참가국들은 다수국가가 합의 할수 있도록 기존입장을
  양보·조정하여야 할 것임.

- 한국정부는 다수참가국이 합의하는 내용이면 적극참여하는 방향으로
  검토 할 것임.

0136

47222

기 안 용 지

분류기호 서번호	통기 20644-	(전화: 720 - 2188)	시 행 상 특별취급	
보존기간	영구 . 준영구 10. 5. 3. 1.	장	관	
수 신 처 보존기간				
시행일자	1991. 9.30.			

보조기관	국 장	전 결	협조기관		문서통제
	심의관				검열 1991.9.30
	과 장				
기안책임자		이 찬 범			발 송 인

경 유 수 신 참 조	재무부장관 경제협력국장	발신명의	

제 목	UR/TRIMs 협상 정부대표 임명 통보

1991.10.1-2일간 제네바에서 개최되는 UR/TRIMs 협상에 참석할

정부대표를 "정부대표 및 특별사절의 임명과 권한에 관한 법률"에 의거,

아래와 같이 임명 되었음을 알려 드립니다.

- 아 래 -

1. 회의목적 : UR/TRIMs 협상 참가

- 1 -

0137

2. 회의기간 및 장소 : 91.10.1-2, 스위스 제네바

3. 정부대표

    ㅇ 재무부 경제협력국 투자진흥과 사무관   김교식

    ㅇ 주 제네바 대표부 관계관

4. 출장기간 : 91.9.29-10.4 (6일간)

5. 소요예산 : 재무부 소관예산

6. 훈   령

    ㅇ TRIMs 협상을 포함한 UR 협상이 전반적으로 교착상태에

       처해있는 점을 감안, TRIMs 협상이 성공적으로 타결되기를

       희망한다는 점을 강조하여 아래 입장 표명

    - TRIMs 협상은 선진국.개도국을 망라, 가급적 많은

       국가가 협상 결과에 참여할 수 있는 방향으로 협상이

       타결되어야 함.

- 2 -

0138

- 이를 위하여 협상 참가국들은 다수국가가 합의할 수

있도록 보다 융통성 있는 입장을 제시하여야 할 것임.

7. 출장 결과 보고 : 귀국후 20일이내.   끝.

0139

- 3 -

발 신 전 보

WGV-1306   910928 1255 BE

번   호 : _____   종별 : _____

수   신 : 주 제네바 대사. 총영사/

발   신 : 장   관 (통 기)

제   목 : UR/TRIMs 협상

_____

10.1-2간 개최되는 UR/TRIMs 협상에 참가할 본부대표로 재무부 투자진흥과 김교식 사무관이 임명 되었으니 귀관 관계관과 함께 참석토록 조치바람.

1. 훈   령

   ○ TRIMs 협상을 포함한 UR 협상이 전반적으로 교착상태에 처해있는 점을 감안, TRIMs 협상이 성공적으로 타결되기를 희망한다는 점을 강조하여 아래 입장 표명

   - TRIMs 협상은 선진국.개도국을 망라, 가급적 많은 국가가 협상 결과에 참여할 수 있는 방향으로 협상이 타결되어야 함.

   - 이를 위하여 협상 참가국들은 다수국가가 합의할 수 있도록 ~~커존 입장을 양보, 조정하여야~~ 할 것임. ~~협상~~-자세를 보여야~~ 보라 융통성잇는~~

   - ~~한국 정부는 다수 참가국이 합의하는 내용이면 적극 참여하는 방향으로 검토할 것임.~~

   ○ 주요 쟁점별 아국 입장은 본부대표가 지참함.   끝.

                                            (통상국장 대리 최 혁)

보 안 통 제	

앙 고 재	91 년 9 월 27 일	통 상 국 과	기안자 성 명 이찬벽	과 장	국 장 전결	차 관	장 관	외신과통제

0140

원 본

외 무 부

종 별 :

번 호 : GVW-1888

일 시 : 91, 1002 1730

수 신 : 장관(통기, 경기원, 재무부, 상공부)

발 신 : 주 제네바 대사

제 목 : UR/반덤핑(비공식)

10.1 표제회의가 MR. CAMPEAS 관세국장 주재로 주요국간 비공식 개최되어 맥파일III 를 기초로 AVERAGING, DEMINIMUS, 우회덤핑, 원가이하 판매 및 피해의 누적문제등을 논의하였는바, 요지 하기 보고함.

1. AVERAGING (MCPHAIL III 2,4,2)

0 국내 가격과 수출가격 비교시 그 기준을 무엇으로 할 것인지에 대해 아국, 홍콩, 싱가폴, 노르딕등 수출국들은 평균 가격 비교를 원칙으로 하고, 예외적인 경우 개별 수출 가격과 평균 국내가격이 비교되어야 함을 주장하였으며, EC, 미국, 카나다는 평균 가격을 원칙적인 비교기준으로 할 경우 TARGETED DUMPING 에 대한 만연을 초래할수 있다는 이유로 이에 반대함.

0 개도국은 TARGETED DUMPING 에 대한 개념 규정을 명확히 할것을 주장하였는바, EC 는 TARGETED DUMPING 의 구성 요소로 CUSTOMER, REGION 및 TIME에 대한 표현이 들어 있는 칼라일 I 혹은II 가 대안이 될수 있음을 주장함. 의장은 동용어에 대한 추가적 검토가 필요함을 언급함.

2. DE MINIMUS (MCPHAIL III 5.7)

0 아국을 포함한 싱가폴, 인도, 홍콩등은 덤핑마진 및 덤핑 수량을 계량화 할수있도록 규정한 OPTION I 을 찬성한 반면 미국, 카나다, EC등은 개별 수입원의 수입양은 적더라도 피해가 가능하다는 이유로 덤핑 수입량의 계량화에는 반대 입장을 표명함.

0 이에 의장은 동 문제는 정치적인 사안임을 강조하면서 무시할 만한 (NEGLIGIBLE) 덤핑수입량의 기술적 정의가 필요할 것이라고 언급함.

3. 수입국 조립 우회 덤핑(MCPHAIL III, 12, 1)

0 반덤핑 부과요건을 규정한 항목의 하나인 제5호의 'VALUE'용어에 대해서는

통상국   2차보   경기원   재무부   상공부

PAGE 1

91.10.03   09:45 DQ

외신 1과 통제관

0141

별도의 기술적 검토를 하기로 함.

카나다는 5호의 요건을 보다 엄격히 하기 위해 맥파일II(12. 1. V)에 있는 'ESSENTIAL CHARACTERISTIC'의 문장이 포함되어야 함을 주장하였으며, 이에 브라질, 일본등이 찬성하였으며, 미국이 반대함.

0 한편 노르딕은 동 조문 제 2호의 'OR 이하' 문장대신 ' OR BY SOMEONE ELSE UNDER THE CONTRACT ENTEREDINTO WITH THE RELATED PARTY FOR THE PURPOSE OF CARRYINGOUTTHE ASSEMBLY OF COMPLETION' 을 제의하였으며, 아국,홍콩등이 이를 기초로 논의할 것을 주장하였고,미국은 우회 덤핑은 계약없이도 가능하다는 이유로 동 제의를 반대함.

0 의장은 노르딕 제안을 검토할 것임을 언급함.

4. 원가이하 판매(MCPHAIL III 2.2.2.4)

0 노르딕, 브라질, 싱가폴등은 산업 불황기,출하시기 등의 비용을 고려하여 합리적 기간내에 비용 회수를 할 경우 이를 정상거래로 간주할 수 있도록 규정한 OPTION를 지지한 반면, 미국,EC, 카나다등은 조사 대상 기간동안을 기준으로 비용회수 여부를 판단하여야 한다는 주장을 계속함.

0 의장은 START UP CYCLICAL INDUSTRIES 등의 용어를 보다 명확히 할 필요가 있음을 지적함.

5. 피해의 누적(MCPHAIL III 3.6)

0 인도, 싱가폴등은 피해 판정시 원칙적으로 각수입원에 대해 독립적으로 평가하고 예외적인 상황에서만 CUMULATION 을 허용하고 있는 OPTION 2 를 지지한 반면 미국 EC 은 이에 반대함.

0 의장은 본 항목은 정치적으로 결정해야 할 사안임을 밝히면서 각국 입장을 충분히 수용할것임을 시사함.

6. 제 3국 조립 우회 덤핑(MCPHAIL III, 12.3)

0 미국은 본조문의 필요성을 강조하였고, 홍콩은III 항의 'SOURCE'는 다른 국가로부터의 수입부품도 포함하는지 문의하였으며, 카나다는 VALUE ADDED, MANUFACTURINGCOST 등의 용어를 보다 명확히 하여야 할 것을 지적함.

0 의장은 전문가와 상기 용어등에 대해 기술적 검토를 할 것임을 밝힘. 끝

(대사 박수길-국장)

PAGE 2

0142

외 무 부

종 별 :

번 호 : GVW-1900

일 시 : 91 1004 1730

수 신 : 장 관(봉기,상공부)

발 신 : 주 제네바 대사

제 목 : UR/반덤핑 주요국 비공식 회의(2)

10.2. 속개된 표제회의 에서는 COUNTRY HOPPING, 구성가격, 분쟁해결에 대해 논의하고 비공식회의를 종료하였는바 요지하기임.(강상무관 참석)

1. COUNTRY HOPPING(MACPHAIL II,10.4)

0 미국, EC는 COUNTRY HOPPING 은 제3국우회덤핑과는 다른 경우 (원수출국으로부터 주요부품등이 제3국에 수출, 조립되지 않고 제3국에 소재하는 업체로부터 수입국에 덤핑하는 경우)를 취급하는 것이며, 이에대한 적절한 규제를 위해 덤핑관세의 소급 적용이 필요함을 강조함.

0 이에대해 한국,일본, 홍콩, 노딕등은 COUNTRY HOPPING 개념이 원활한 투자 및상품이동에 미칠 부정적 영향을 강조하였으나 이문제는 기본적으로 다른 협상 이슈와의 BALACNE 차원에서 다루어야한다고 하였음.

0 아국, 일본은 COUNTRY HOPPING 의 요건으로 관련기업간의 CONTROL 관계 원수출국으로부터의 수입감소와 제 3국으로 부터의 수입증가가 동시에 이루어져야 한다는점, 제3국에 대한 투자가원덤핑조치 개시전에 이루어졌어야 한다는 점등 엄격한 요건이 유정되어야 함을 강조하고 미국은 이에대해 토론 의사를 표명함.

0 미국은 COUNTRY HOPPING 의 경우 덤핑 및 피해에 대한 별도의 조사로 덤핑 여부 및 피해에 대한 판정이 있어야 하고 이에 추가하여 상기 피해가 원덤핑조치의 구제효과를 저해하는 것이어야하는지에 대한 아국의 질의에 COUNTRY HOPPING 의 경우에는 원덤핑조사와는 별도의 조사에 의해덤깅 및 피해에 대한 판정이 있고, 이에추가적으로 상기 피해가 원덤핑 조치의 구제효과를 저해하는 것이어야 하는 DOUBLE TEST임을 명백히함

2. 구성가격(MACPHAIL III 2.2.3)

0 노딕은 비용이하 판매문제는 국내판매가격을 사용하기 위한 기준 (즉

통상국 2차보 상공부

PAGE 1

91.10.05 09:26 WG

외신 1과 통제관

0143

정상거래하의 국내시 판물량이 국내판매가격을 NORMAL VALUE 로 사용하는데 충분한 것인지 여부) 에 만 관련되는것이 아니고, 구성가격 계산시에도 고려되어야 할사항이므로 이러한 관점에서 2.2.2.의 서두가 개정되어야 함을 언급함.

0 EC 는 수출국과 원산지 국가의 비용이 구성가격 계산의 기초가 될 수 있어야함을 주장함.

0 이에대해 아국, 홍콩은 CARLISLE 11 의 2.2.4.1과 2.2.4.2 를 기초로 토의할 것을 주장함.

3. 분쟁해결

0 미국, EC 는 반덤핑의 경우 (1) 국내사법절차가 진행중인 경우 GATT 에 제소할 수 없음

(2) GATT PANEL 은 사실에 대한 판단은 하지않아야 함 (3) 최종 판정후에만 갓트에 제소가능하여야 함을 주장하였으나 아국, 홍콩, 노딕,일본등은 (1) 국내사범 절차와 GATT PANEL 은근거 법규가 다르므로 양 절차사이에 직접적인 단계가 있을수 없다는 점 (2) GATT PANEL 에서 사실에 대한 판단도 하여야 한다는 점 (3) 갓트제소는 어느 시기에도 가능해야 함을 주장함.

단 일본은 갓트 제소시기에 대해서는 더 검토가 필요하다 함.

0 EC 는 덤핑 판정의 경우에도 주관적, 재량적요소 (예: 피해가 MATERIAL 인지여부)에 대해서는 PANEL 에서 이를 취급하지 않는 것이 좋다고 함.

0 카나다는 분쟁해결에 관한 MACPHAIL III, 18.1을 지지함

4. 기타

0 MACPHAIL III 의 12.1(V)의 부가치의 개념 문제및 구성가격 산정에 대한 기술적 토의를 위해 별도의 소그룹회의를 10.3.오후 갖도록 하였으며 이에는 미국, EC, 카나다, 노딕, 일본, 홍콩, 싱가폴, 아국의 참여키로 함.

0 의장은 10.23.경 다시 회의를 개최할 예정이라고함.끝

(대사 박수길-국장)

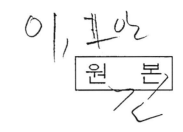

외 무 부

종 별 :

번 호 : GVW-1881   일 시 : 91 1002 1030

수 신 : 장관(통기,경기원,재무부)

발 신 : 주 제네바 대사

제 목 : UR/TRIMS 협상(1)

(1)91.9.30(월) 당지에서 개최된 표제 협상 비공식회의 토의 요지 아래 보고함.

(엄재무관 및 재무부 김사무관 참석)

1. 의장은 금년내 협상이 타결되기 위하여는 일정이 급박한바 4주내로 의장 DRAFT TEXT 를 작성하여 11월 TNC 에 제출할 예정임을 설명하고, - 그동안 협상 결과 가장중요한 쟁점은 협상의 COVERAGE, 규제 방법, 개도국에 대한 배려, 잠정기간, 사기업에 의한 제한적 사업관행 등이었던바 사무국에서 협상에서 논의된 사항을 종합한 INFORMAL PAPER 를 금회 협상자료로 활용할 것임을 설명

2. 쟁점별 협상 내용

- 협상의 범위에 관하여 멕시코, 인도, 말레이지아,중국등은 기존 TRIMS 은 포함하지 않고 새로이 부과되는 TRIMS 만을 포함하자고 주장한 반면,일본, 미국, 카나다, 스웨덴등은 기존 TRIMS 도무역 왜곡 효과는 동일 하므로 협상 범위에 포함하되, 개도국의 특별한 사정은 잠정기간을 둠으로써 배려할 것을 주장

O INCENTIVES 의 포함여부에 관하여 호주는 'LEGALLYENFORCEABLE MEASURES' 만 포함하여야 하며, SUBSIDY까지 포함할 경우, SUBSIDY 협상과의 중복 및TRIMS 의 주장.

- 규제 방법(DISCIPLINE)에 관하여 의장은 갓트3조 및 11조에 위반되는 조치는 금지되어야 하는바,구체적으로 갓트 3조, 11조를 TRIMS 에 어떻게 적용하느냐가 쟁점임 을 설명

O 호주와 BRAZIL 은 TRIMS 는 갓트 3조 및 11조에의해 직접 규제 될수 없음을

통상국   2차보   청와대   안기부   경기원   재무부

주장하고, 인도,이집트등은 INVESTMENT MEASURES 자체가 아닌 이로인한 무역 왜곡
효과를 어떻게 방지, 치유할것인가에 중점을 두어야 하고, 갓트 3조 및 11조의적용에
관한 MANDATE 또는 INTERPRETATIVE NOTE등을 작성하여 CASE BY CASE 로 규제할
것을주장

0 일본, 미국, 스웨덴등은 갓트 3조, 11조에 위반되는 TRIMS 은 금지 되어야 하고,
이러한 TRIMS 의 구체적 내용이 열거되어야 함을 주장.

0 수출 이행조건에 관하여 멕시코, 인도는 개도국경제발전을 위하여 이러한 조치가
불가피한바, 동조치는 갓트 규정상 직접 규제 대상으로 하고 있지않으므로 다국적
기업의 제한적관행(R.B.P)은 제외하면서 수출 이행조건을 규제하고자 하는
것에는반대함을 주장하였으나,미국, EC 등은 수출 이행 조건의 무역 왜곡효과가
심각하므로 금지 되어야 한다고 주장.

0 아국은 갓트 3조 및 11조에 위반되는 TRIMS 은이의 무역 왜곡 효과와
관계없이금지하되, 수출이행 조건등 기타 TRIMS 은 갓트 규정상 명시적으로 위반되지
않으므로 구체적으로 무역왜곡 효과가 있는 경우에만 규제토록하는 절충안을
제시하였음.

  - 개도국에 대한 특별 배려에 관하여 모든참가국이 동 필요성에 동의하고 구체적인
내용은 추후 논의하기로 함. 끝

  (대사 박수길-국장)

외 무 부

종 별 :

번 호 : GVW-1924   일   시 : 91 1007 1200

수 신 : 장관(봉기,경기원,재무부)

발 신 : 주 제네바 대사

제 목 : UR/TRIMS 협상(2)

9.30, 10.1 속개된 표제 협상 토의 요지 아래 보고함.

가. 무역 왜곡 효과에 대한 TEST (EFFECT TEST OFTRIMS)

0 의장은 갓트 3조 및 11조에 위반되는 TRIMS은 당연히 금지 대상이고 갓트 분쟁해결절차(22조 및 23조)에 의하여 실효성을 확보할수있으나 갓트 규정에 명문화되어있지 않은 수출이행조건은 그 범위와 금지 여부 및 실효성 확보방법등이 문제될수 있어 EFFECT TEST 가필요하다는 의견이 많음을 설명

0 일본, 미국, EC 는 수출 이행 조건은 원칙적으로 금지되어야 하고 EFFECT TEST 의절차를 거친다면 그 범위 및 절차를 명확히 규정하여야 할 것을 주장

0 캐나다, 브라질, 호주는 모든 TRIMS 은 다소간긍정적이든 부정적이든, 무역에영향을 미치는바,수출 이행 조건에 대하여만 EFFECT TEST 를거친다는 것과 이의 효율성에 회의적인 의견 표시

0 인도, 중국, 칠레는 모든 TRIMS 에 대하여EFFECT TEST 를 한후, 동 결과에 따라 규제 여부를결정할 것임을 주장

0 EFFECT TEST 의 방법 및 절차에 관하여 다수국가가 반덤핑, 상계관세, SAFEGUARD 등의방법 및 개념, 절차(LIKE PRODUCT, 산업피해등)를 원용해야 할 것임을 주장하고AGREEMENT 에 구체적으로 명시하는 방법과 후에INTERPRETATIVE NOTE 나 RECOMMENDATION 등으로 구체화하는 방법등에 대하여 논의하였음.

나. 분쟁해결(DISPUTE SETTLEMENT)절차

0 대다수의 국가가 TRIMS 의 분쟁해결 절차도 UR협상에서 일부 수정될 갓트 규정(22조, 23조)의 절차를 그대로 따른 것에 동의하였으며, EC 는 수출 이행 조건의 경우는 다소문제가 있을 것이므로 AGREEMENT 에 동 조건의 갓트 절차적용에 관하여 추가로 구체적인 내용을 명시하는것이 필요할 것임을 주장

통상국   경기원   재무부

PAGE 1   91.10.07   21:46 DU

다. 지방정부 조치에 대한 TRIMS 협정의 적용

0 갓트 24조 2 및 INTERPRETATIVE NOTE 에 명시된바와 같이 TRIMS 협정은 지방정부의 투자제한 조치에도 적용하여야 한다는데 대체로 동의함.

라. 사기업의 제한적 사업 관행(RESTRICTIVEBUSINESS PRACTICE)

0 의장은 동 쟁점에 관하여 그동안 선진국, 개도국간에 입장이 분명히 표명되었으므로 재논의는 생략하고 추후 DRAFT TEXT 에 의장이 종합한 의견을 갖고 다시 논의하기로 하였음.

마. 경과기간(TRANSITIONAL ARRANGEMENT)

0 의장은 TRIMS 협정 발효후 각국은 운용중인 모든 투자제한 조치를 갓트에 통보하여야 하고(NOTIFICATION REQUIREMENT)통보된 조치에 대하여각국의 경제 발전 정도에 따라 잠정기간을 차등적용하게 될 것임을 설명

0 각국은 갓트 통보의무 및 잠정 기간의 인정등에 일반적인 갓트 규정을 따라야한다는데 대체로 동의하였으나 일부 개도국은 잠정기간의 적용대상이 되는 TRIMS을 모든 TRIMS 이 아닌개별 TRIMS 의 CASE 별로 결정하여야 할것임을 주장

0 헝가리는 동구권 국가의 경우 개도국은 아니나 시장경제를 새로이 도입함에 따른 어려움을 극복하기 위하여 경과기간 적용에 특별한 고려가 필요함을 주장

0 아국은 다수 개도국이 TRIMS 협정에 참여개위한 방법으로 경과기간은 매우 중요하나, 추후개도국에 대한 기준등에 대하여 논의되어야 하며, 투자제한 조치의 갓트 통보는 그 내용이 상세하고명확한 경우 (EXHAUSTIVE AND TRANSPARENT)에 한하여잠정기간이 인정되어야 할 것임을 주장

바. TRIMS COMMITTEE

0 아국과 대부분의 선진국은 TRIMS 협정의운용을 위하여 COMMITTEE 설치의 필요성을주장한 반면, 인도, 이집트는 갓트 분쟁 해결절차가 있고 TRIMS 협정의 내용이 불확정한상태에서 COMMITTEE 설치 여부를 논할수 없음을주장

사. 차기회의는 10.21(월) 부터 시작되는 주간에재개키로 함.

(대사 박수길-국장)

재　　　무　　　부

투　전　2254-//ᄼᄼ7　　　(503-9276)　　　1991. 10. 9.

수　신　외무부장관

참　조　통상국장

제　목　UR　/무역관련 투자제한조치(TRIMs) 협상 참석결과 송부

　　　'91.9.30 - 10.4간 스위스 제네바 GATT본부에서 개최된 표제협상

참석 결과를 별첨 송부합니다.

　첨　부　:　UR /무역관련 투자제한조치(TRIMs) 협상 참석보고.　끝.

재　　무　　부　　장

33580　　　　　　　　　　　　　　　　　　0149

UR/ 무역관련 투자제한조치(TRIMs) 협상참석보고

1. 협상일시 및 장소

o '91.9.30(월) - 10.2(수) : 비공식협상

'91.10.4(금) : 규범제정 및 TRIMs분야 전체 공식회의

o 스위스 제네바 GATT본부에서 개최

2. 협상 참가자

o 의장 : Mr. George Maciel (전 주제네바 브라질대사)

o 아국

· 주제네바 대표부   엄 낙용 재무관

· 재무부 투자진흥과 김 교식 사무관 (9.30 - 10.2간 비공식 협상참가)

o 기타

· 미국, 일본, EC, 카나다,스웨덴(북구대표), 호주등 선진국

· 인도, 브라질, 멕시코, ASEAN 등 개도국 참가

0150

3. 협상참가 내용

   가. 금번협상의 의의

   o UR협상의 타결목표였던 '90.12 브랏셀 각료회의에서 UR협상 전체가 결실없이
     '91년 이후로 연기된 이후, '91년들어 UR/TRIMs 협상은 소강상태에 있었음.

   o 주요선진국은 그동안 수차례에 걸쳐 금년내 UR협상타결을 선언하였는바
     '91년말을 3개월 앞둔 시점에서 개최된 금번 TRIMs 협상은
     금년들어 최초의 본격적인 협상으로 각국이 적극 참여하였으며 앞으로의
     협상에 영향을 미치고 협상진전 방향을 전망 할 수 있는 협상이었음.

   o 그동안 외국인투자 자유화조치를 지속적으로 추진하여 왔고 해외투자가 매년
     증가하고 있는 아국으로서는 투자제한조치를 철폐 하고자하는 TRIMs 협상은
     다른 UR협상에 비하여 비교적 부담이 적은 협상인바,

     동협상에 참여·협상의 성공적 타결에 기여함으로써 아국의 주요 해외투자
     대상국의 투자환경 개선을 도모하는 한편, 아국의 대외신인도를 제고하고
     UR협상 실패시 강화 될 선진국의 통상압력을 사전 완화하는데 기여하는 방향으로
     참여 하엿음.

0151

나. 분야별 협상결과

i) 협상의 범위(Coverage)

┌───┐
│ ┌────────┐   │
│ │ 주요쟁점 │   │
│ └────────┘   │
│   o 협상타결시 제정될 TRIMs Agreement에 의해 규제대상이 되는 투자제한조치 │
│   (TRIMs)의 범위   │
│   │
│   · 수출이행조건의 포함여부   │
│   │
│   · 기존의 조치(Existing measures)도 포함할 것인지 또는 새로운 조치   │
│   만을 포함 할것인지 여부   │
│   │
│   · 투자Incentives 관련조치(조세감면 대가로 국산부품사용의무등)도   │
│   포함할 것인지 여부   │
└───┘

- 선진국 입장

o 규제대상 TRIMs은 GATT 3조(내국민대우) 및 11조(수량제한) 위반 TRIMs은
  물론 수출이행조건도 포함.

o 신규조치와 기존조치를 모두 포함하여 규제대상으로함

o Incentives관련조치도 무역왜곡효과가 심각하므로 규제대상에 포함

- 개도국 및 호주입장

o GATT 3조 및 11조 관련 TRIMs은 Case별로 무역왜곡효과가 심각한 경우에 규제.
  수출이행조건은 직접 GATT규정과 관련이 없으므로 불포함

o 신규조치만 규제대상 TRIMs으로 함

o Incentives관련조치는 보조금 협상에서 다룸

- 아국입장 및 발언내용

o GATT 3조 및 11조에 위반되는 TRIMs은 규제대상이 되어야하나 수출이행조건은
  GATT규정에 직접 명시되어 있지않으므로 무역왜곡효과가 있는지 여부에 대한
  검토(Effect Test)를 한후 규제여부 결정

o 신규조치와 기존조치를 모두 포함·규제대상으로함

o Incentives자체는 TRIMs으로 규제대상이 될수 없으나 동 관련조치의 무역왜곡
  효과가 심각한 경우에 관련조치만을 규제대상에 포함

0152

ii) 규제방법 (Disciplines)

┌─ 주요쟁점 ───┐
│   │
│ o 투자제한조치(TRIMs) 자체를 규제할 것인지 또는 투자제한조치로 인한   │
│   무역왜곡효과가 심각한 경우만 Case by case로 규제할 것인지 여부   │
│   │
│ o 지방정부에도 TRIMs Agreement를 적용할 것인지 여부   │
│   │
└──┘

- 선진국 입장

    o GATT 3조 및 11조 위반 TRIMs과 수출이행조건은 무역에 미치는 영향여부에
      대한 검토(Effect test) 없이 금지대상으로 함

      · 다만 수출이행조건에 예외적으로 Effect test를 하는 경우 그 범위및 방법을
        Agreement에 구체적으로 명시

    o 지방정부에도 TRIMs Agreement를 적용한다는데 대체로 동의(과거 일부국가 반대)

- 개도국 및 호주입장

    o 모든 투자제한조치는 무역왜곡효과 여부에 대한 Effect test를 거친후 직접적이고
      심각한(direct and significant) 경우에 한하여 규제대상으로 함

- 아국입장 및 발언요지

    o GATT3조 및 11조에 위반하는 TRIMs은 당연히 금지대상으로 하나 수출이행조건은
      GATT에 명시되어있지 않으므로 Effect test를 거친후 규제여부 결정

0153

iii) 개도국에 대한 배려 및 경과기간(Transitional arrangement)

```
┌─────────────────────────────────────────────────────────────────┐
│ ┌─────────┐                                                       │
│ │ 주요쟁점 │                                                       │
│ └─────────┘                                                       │
│                                                                   │
│   o Trims Agreement 에서 개도국에 대한 예외범위를 어느정도까지 인정  │
│     할 것인지의 문제                                                │
│                                                                   │
│   o 투자제한조치의 철폐기한에 대한 경과기간(Transitional arrangement)을 │
│     경제발전 정도에 따라 차등적용 할 것인지 여부                      │
│                                                                   │
└─────────────────────────────────────────────────────────────────┘
```

- 선진국입장

  o 개도국에 대한 예외는 GATT규정(18조등)에서 명시된범위에 한정

  o 각국의 경제발전정도에 따라 철폐기한(경과기간)의 차등적용에 동의

  ※ 호주 : 산업구조 조정 중이거나 개방추진과정에 있는 산업에 대하여는
          별도의 경과기간 인정 필요

- 개도국입장

  o TRIMs은 GATT에서 직적 규정하고 있지 않고있고 개도국의 급박한 경제발전의
    필요성등을 고려, GATT에서 인정된것보다 더욱 폭넓은 예외인정

  o 각국의 경제발전 정도및 각산업의 발전정도에 따라 Case 별로 경과기간 차등적용

- 항가리등 동구권 국가입장

  o 동구권국가는 개도국은 아니나 시장경제 체제를 새로이 도입한점을 고려,
    별도의 경과기간 필요

0154

- 아국입장 및 발언요지

    o 개도국의 경제발전등을 위하여 투자제한조치의 운용이 불가피 할 수있는점을 고려
       개도국에 대한 예외는 GATT 규정에 명시된 범위로 하되, 개별적으로 특별한
       고려가 필요한 경우 경과기간등에 별도의 예외 인정(예: 경과기간의 연장등)

    o 경과기간은 각국이 운용하고 있는 투자제한조치를 상세하고 명확하게
       GATT에 통보된 경우(Notified exhaustively and transparently)에 한하여
       경과기간 인정

iv) 제한적 사업관행(Restrictive Business Practices)

┌───┐
│ ┌─────────┐   │
│ │ 주요쟁점 │   │
│ └─────────┘   │
│   │
│   o 다국적기업등 사기업의 제한적 사업관행으로 인한 무역왜곡효과도   │
│   Trims Agreement 에 포함시켜 규제할 것인지 여부   │
│   │
└───┘

    ※ Restrictive Business Practices: 다국적기업이 물품의 제조에 필요한
       원료·부품의 구입이나 제품의 판매등을 타국에 소재한 자매회사간에만
       하도록 제한하는 경우등

 - 선진국 입장

    o '86년 Punta del Este 각료선언에 포함되지 않았으므로 Trims Agreement에의
       포함 반대

 - 개도국 입장

    o GATT에 규정되지 않은 수출이행조건도 TRIMs에 포함할 경우 사기업의 제한적
       사업관행도 당연히 TRIMs에 포함하여야 함

 - 아국 입장

    o 다국적기업등 사기업의 제한적 사업관행으로 인한 무역왜곡효과도 심각한 경우가
       있으므로 TRIMs에 포함 규제여부 검토필요

0155

v) 기타 쟁점

```
o 협상타결후의 TRIMs Committee 설치여부
```

o 아국 및 선진국은 설치에 찬성, 일부개도국은 GATT 분쟁해결 절차등이 있으므로
  Committee 설치에 반대

```
o 분쟁해결 절차 (Dispute  Settlement)
```

o 현재 UR 제도분야 협상에서 논의되고 있는 기존 분쟁해결절차(GATT 22,23조)의
  결과를 TRIMs 에도 그대로 적용할 것에 대체로 동의

o 다만 수출이행조건은 GATT에 규정되어 있지않으므로 분쟁해결절차의 적용에 관한
  구체적인 내용 규정필요 (EC)

0156

다. 의장 Comment

i) 주요쟁점에 대한 종합의견

o GATT 3조 및 11조에 위반되는 TRIMs은 GATT규정에 따라 금지(forbidden) 대상으로
  하되 수출이행조건은 Effect test를 거쳐서 규제여부를 결정함이 바람직

o Effect test의 절차및 개념등은 GATT/ 반덤핑·상계관세·Safeguards등에서 발달된
  개념 및 절차를 원용하되, TRIMs Agreement에 구체적으로 명시하는 방법과
  추후에 해설서(Interpretative Note)나 Recommendation등으로 보완하는 방법이
  있을 것임

o 지방정부의 투자제한조치는 GATT 24조(적용지역)및 동해설서에 의해 당연히
  TRIMs Agreement 가 적용되어야 함.

o 투자제한조치의 철폐에 관한 경과기간은 모든 투자제한조치를 GATT에 통보
  (Notification requirement)한 경우에 인정되므로 추후 명료성(Transparency)에
  대하여 논의·Agreement에 규정하여야 할것임.

ii) 향후일정등

o 여타 UR협상과 같이 TRIMs 협상도 금년 11월 TNC(무역협상위원회)에 최종 Text를
  제출하여야 하므로 그동안 논의된 내용을 종합· Draft Text를 작성 예정

o 동 Draft Text를 갖고 10.21(월) 부터 시작되는 주에 다시 논의 한후 최종 Text를
  작성· TNC에 제출할 예정임

4. 관찰 및 평가

- UR/TRIMs협상은 그동안 선진국과 개도국간의 입장이 첨예하게 대립되어 UR협상 중에서도 협상이 부진한 분야였음

- 그러나 금번협상에서는 선진국이 협상에 적극적인 자세를 취하였는바, 그 이유는

  개도국에 양보를 해서라도 TRIMs 협상을 타결하는것이, 협상이 완전 결렬되는것보다는, 선진국의 해외투자 확대등에 절대 유리하다는 방향으로 추진하는것으로 평가됨

  o 의장(Mr. Maciel) 또한 주요쟁점에 대하여 선진국과 개도국간의 의견을 적극적으로 조정하는 방향으로 협상을 진행하였음.

- 따라서, UR협상이 전반적으로 농산물협상등의 부진으로 협상타결 가능성을 예측하기는 곤란하나, TRIMs 협상자체만으로 볼때는 금번 협상은 성공가능성을 예측할수 있는 협상이었음.

- 아국입장에서 볼때, 외국인투자 자유화추진 및 해외투자의 증가추세등을 고려할때 UR/TRIMs 협상이 성공적으로 타결될 경우 아국의 동남아등에 대한 투자환경이 개선되는 점을 기대할 수있는 반면, 협상결렬시에는 쌍무적인 통상마찰이 심화될 것으로 예측되는 점등을 고려하여

  o 아국입장과 크게 상치되 않는한, 협상이 타결되는 방향으로 적극 참여 및 기여 하므로써 아국의 대외신인도를 제고하고 주요 교역국와의 통상마찰을 사전에 예방하면서 아국의 해외투자 환경개선을 도모함이 바람직 할 것으로 사료됨.

0158

외 무 부

종   별 :

번   호 : GVW-1920   일   시 : 91 1007 1100

수   신 : 장 관(통기,경기원,재무부,상공부)

발   신 : 주 제네바 대사

제   목 : UR/규범제정 협상그룹 공식회의

표제회의가 10.4. MACIEL 의장주재로 개최된바 요지 하기임.

(강상무관,김영학 사무관등 참석)

0 의장은 <u>금주중 개최된 규범제정 공식 및비공식 회의</u>에서는 각국 입장의 명료화와
기술적 토론에는 진전이 있었으나 주요 쟁점에 대한 확실한 진전(DECISIVE
PROGRESS)은 없었다고 하고 던켈 총장이 제시한 목표에 맞추기 위해서는 실질적이고
심도있는 협상이 곧시작되어야 할 것이라고 언급함.

0 이에 각국은 별다른 언급이 없었음. 단 브라질은 보조금 분야에서 자국 입장에
대해 선진국이 긍정적 자세를 보이지 않는다고 하였으며, 일본은 SAFEGUARD 에 대한
브랏셀의장 TEXT ( ) 되지 않는 부분도 미해결된부분이 많다고 하였음.

0 다음번 회의는 <u>10월 23일부터 10.31.</u>까지 개최하며 반덤핑, 보조금 및 상계관세,
BOP, TRIMS 뿐아니라 SAFEGUARD, TBT 등 모든 분야를 논의토록 함

0 의장은 선적전 검사의 재심기구 구성에 관한ICC 와 IFIA 의 공동제안 내용을 배
포함.(파편 송부 예정).끝

(대사 박수길-국장)

통상국   2차보   정와대   안기부   경기원   재무부   상공부

PAGE 1   91.10.08   06:53 FN

외신 1과 통제관
0159

외 무 부

종 별 :

번 호 : GVW-1938   일 시 : 91 1008 1700

수 신 : 장 관(봉기,경기원,재무부,상공부)

발 신 : 주 제네바 대사

제 목 : UR/규범제정 및 TRIMS 협상

　9.30-10.4 개최된 규범제정 그룹회의에 대한 평가및 전망을 하기 보고함.

　0 9.30-10.4 개최된 규범제정 그룹회의는 반덤핑, 보조금.상계관세, BOP 및 TRIMS 4 개 의제에 대한 주요국 비공식 회의 위주로 진행되었으며 주요 쟁점에 대한 각국입장의 명료화와와 기술적논의가 활발히 있었으나 MACIEL '의장도 지적하였듯이 입장의 차이를 좁히지는 못하였음.

　0 합의된 협상문서조차 마련하지 못한 반덤핑, TRIMS 및 TEXT 가 있는 보조금.상계관세, 갓트조문 (BOPS 등) 각협상 분야 공히 선.개도국간 입장 대립으로 실질 협상에서는 별다른 진전이 없었으나, 던켈이 제시한 일정에 맞추기 위해 MACIEL 의장이 단일 TEXT(개정안) 마련에 강한 의지를 보이고 있어 11월초까지 어떤 형태로든 상기분야에 대한 협상문안이 마련될 가능성이 많은 것으로 판단됨.

　0 따라서 10.23.부터 재개되는 규범제정 회의가 반덤핑을 포함한 중요 이슈에 대한 협상문안 작성 (또는 개정)을 위한 중요한 시기가 될 것으로보임.

　(대사 박수길-국장)

통상국　　2차보　　경기원　　재무부　　상공부

외 무 부

종 별 :

번 호 : GVW-2015   일 시 : 91 1016 1100

수 신 : 장관(통기, 경기원, 재무부, 상공부)

발 신 : 주 제네바 대사

제 목 : UR/규범제정 협상을 위한 비공식 만찬 협의

9.14 싱가폴 대사 주최로 열린 상기 만찬협의에서는 주로 세이프가드 및 반덤핑협상 관련 의견 교환이 있었는바, 요지 하기 보고함.(본직 및 말레이지아, 홍콩, 스웨덴, 브라질, 스위스 대표참석)

0 본협의에서는 반덤핑 협상의 중요성과 현코드의 현저한 개선이 있어야 한다는데 의견을 같이하고, 수출국 공동 이해를 반영하기 위해 규범제정 협상 그룹의 MACIEL 의장과 회동(10.22일경)관련 수출국 (약 10여개국)들이 공동입장을 개진키로 함.

0 본협의에서 본직은 SAFEGUARD 협상에 있어서 SELECTIVITY 는 받아들일수 없으며, 또한 시장접근이 아무리 보장된다 하더라도 ANTI-DUMPING관계 법규가 명백히 되지않으면 그것은 무실화 되므로 ANTI-DUMPING 문제는 협상 요소중 가장 중요하고 양보할수 없는 사항임을 강조함.

0 이와 함께 현재 GATT 에 계류중인 아국의 폴리에스터 수지 반덤핑 관세 부과 건과 관련하여, 미국.EC 등 수입 선진국에 의한 반덤핑 조치 남발이 개도국의 수출에미치는 부정적 영향을 언급하면서, 향후 분쟁해결 처리과정에서 동건에 대한 개도국들의 지지가 중요함을 강조한바, 이에 대해 SINGAPORE, BRAZIL, SWEDEN, SWISS 대표등도 아국입장에 동정과 공감을 표시하면서 CONCILIATION 에서의 사태진전을 주시하고있다고 말했음을 참고로 부언함. 끝

(대사 박수길-국장)

통상국   2차보   경기원   재무부   상공부

외 무 부

종 별 :

번 호 : GVW-2027

일 시 : 91 1017 1100

수 신 : 장 관(봉기, 경기원, 재무부, 상공부)

발 신 : 주 제네바 대사

제 목 : UR / 규범제정 그룹 회의 관련

10.23 일 부터 개최되는 상기 회의와 관련 당관 강상무관 이 그룹 의장 보좌관인 RAMSAUSER 와 면담한 결과 하기 보고함.

1. 차기 회의의 진행에 관한 사항

0 구체적인 일정은 의장인 MACIEL 이 10.21 제네바 도착후 결정될 것임.

0 10월 23일 오전에 규범제정 그룹 공식 회의를 개최하고 23일 오후 및 24, 25 일 까지 반덤핑 및 TRIMS 에 관한 비공식 회의를 가짐. 10.26 일 이후 보조금. 상계관세, SAFEGUARD 등 나머지 이슈가 필요시 주말 포함 비공식 회의에서 논의될것임.

0 반덤핑 회의에서는 일반적 입장 개진은 피하고 구체적 이슈에 대한 초안 작업에 주안을 두고 25일까지 관계국 협의에 의한 TEXT 를 마련토록 노력하고 이것이 실패할 경우 사무국이 TEXT 를 제시

0 반덤핑, 보조금 상계관세 등 모든 분야에 있어 구체적 DRAFTING 은 매우 제한된 SMALL GROUP 위주로 이루어질 것이나 관심있는 국가에 대해 의견 개진을 위한 적절한 기회가 보장될 것임.

0 이에 대해 아국은 비공식 회의에서도 가능한 많은 국가의 참여 필요성 및 관련국 합의에 의한 TEXT 마련이 바람직 하다는 의견을 개진함.

2. 반덤핑에 관한 아국 입장 개진

가. 아국은 기존 규범의 현저한 강화 및 개선이 있을시 우회 덤핑의 3가지 유형에 대해 논의 용의가 있으며, MINIMUM PACKAGE 는 의미가 없다는 기본입장을 밝힘.

나. 구체적 이슈에 대해 아국이 밝힌 입장은 하기와 같음.

0 비용 이하 판매에 대해서는 MACPHAIL 3 의 2, 2,2, 4조중 첫 OPTION 을 지지하며, 특히 START UP COST의 반영이 필요, 경기 변동 및 환율 변동에 관한 조항은 수출 국에만 이익이 되는 조항이 아니고 수출입국 공히 예측 불가능한 상황에 대한

통상국   2차보   안기부   경기원   재무부   상공부

PAGE 1

완충작용을 하는 것임.

0 구성 가격 사용에 있어서는 실제 자료가 사용되어야하며 BENCH MARK 는 수락할수 없음. 우선 순위문제(제 3국 수출 가격과 구성가격간 우선순위등)는 관련국 의견이 다르므로 공봉입장 수립이 어려움을 이해함.

0 AVERAGING 문제에 있어서는 정상가격과 수출가격이 EQUAL BASIS 로 비교되어야하며, TRAGET 덤핑 문제를 고려할 용의는 있으나 구체적 표현에 있어 LOOP HOLE 이있어서는 안됨.

0 DE MUNIMUS 에 있어서는 이의 계량화가 중요함. 그러나 협상을 위해 미국. EC등이 염려하는 시잠 점유율은 적으나 덤핑 마진이 높은 경우는 제외하는 방안을 제시한바이에 대해 RAMSAUER 는 협상 촉진을 위해 유용한 방안 이라고 언급함.

0 SAMPLING 에 포함되지 않은 기업에 대해서는 가중 평균 마진이 적용되어야 하며, ZERO 또는DE MINIMI 덤징 마진도 포함되어야 함.

0 SUNSET 의 도입은 중요한 사항임. 그러나 미국의 반대로 불가능할 시 REVIEW 관정에서 INJURYTEXT 를 강화하는 방안을 고려할수 있을 것임.

0 우회 덤핑 중 COUNTRY HOPPING 의경우 엄격한 조건이 설정되어야 함(원 수출자와 제 3국 수출자간의 CONTROL 관계, 원수출국의 수출감소와 제 3국 수출의 동시적증가등)

0 수입국 우회 덤핑 및 제 3국 우회 덤핑의 경우현 MACPHAIL III 의 조문에 많은기술적 개선및 엄격한 요건이 설정되어야 함.

3. 10.23 부터 개최되는 규범제정 회의 일정에 관해 논의하기 위해 10.17 주요국 비공식 회의가있음. 끝

(대사 박수길-국장)

외 무 부

종 별 :

번 호 : GVW-2040   일 시 : 91 1017 1930

수 신 : 장 관(통기, 경기원, 재무부, 상공부, 농림수산부)

발 신 : 주 제네바대사

제 목 : UR/규범제정 그룹회의

연: GVW-2027

대: WGV-0158(91.1.31)

10.23.부터 개최되는 연호 규범제정 그룹회의 시세이프가드 분야 논의에 대비하여, 대호 아국입장에 특별히 추가할 사항이 있으면 회시바람.끝

(대사 박수길-국장)

통상국   2차보   경기원   재무부   농수부   상공부

91.10.18   08:32 WH

외신 1과 통제관   0164

기 안 용 지

분류기호 문서번호	통기 20644-	(전화 : 720 - 2188)	시 행 상 특별취급	
보존기간	영구. 준영구 10. 5. 3. 1.	장	관	
수 신 처 보존기간				
시행일자	1991.10.21.			

보 조 기 관	국 장	전 결	협 조 기 관		문 서 통 제	
	심의관					
	과 장					
기안책임자		안 명 수			발 송 인	

경 유 수 신 참 조	내부결재	발 신 명 의	

제 목	UR/시장접근, 섬유 및 규범제정 협상그룹 회의 참가 정부대표 임명

91.10.23-30간 · 제네바에서 개최되는 표제 회의에 참가할

정부대표를 "정부대표 및 특별사절의 임명과 권한에 관한 법률"에 의거,

아래와 같이 임명할 것을 건의하니 재가하여 주시기 바랍니다.

- 아   래 -

1. 회 의 명 : UR/시장접근, 섬유 및 규범제정 협상그룹 회의

- 1 -

0165

2. 기간 및 장소 : 91.10.23-30, 스위스 제네바

3. 정부대표 :

　　ㅇ 상공부 산업정책과장　　　이재길(시장접근 및 반덤핑)

　　ㅇ 재무부 국제관세과 사무관　허용석(시장접근)

　　ㅇ 상공부 국제협력관실 사무관　윤동섭(시장접근)

　　ㅇ 상공부 국제협력관실 사무관　김영학(세이프가드 및 섬유)

4. 출장기간

　　ㅇ 상공부 산업정책과장 이재길 : 91.10.22-27

　　ㅇ 재무부 국제관세과 사무관 허용석 : 91.10.23-11.1

　　ㅇ 상공부 국제협력관실 사무관 윤동섭 : 91.10.22-11.1

　　ㅇ 상공부 국제협력관실 사무관 김영학 : 91.10.22-11.1

5. 소요예산 : 상공부 및 재무부 소관예산

6. 훈　　　령 : 별도 건의 예정.　　　　　　　끝.

0166

- 2 -

상 공 부

국 협 28140 - 420   503 - 9446   1991. 10. 21.

수 신   외무부 장관

참 조   통상기구과장

제 목   UR 협상 참가 (시장접근, 섬유, 규범제정 분야)

    91.10.23(수) ~ 10.30(수)간 스위스 제네바에서 개최되는 표제분야 UR협상 그룹 회의에 참가하기 위하여 다음과 같이 출장코자 하오니 정부대표 임명등 필요한 조치를 하여 주시기 바랍니다.

" 다   음"

    1. 출장개요

소 속	직 급	성 명	출 장 기 간	비 고
산업정책과	과 장	이 재길	91. 10. 22(화) ~ 10. 27(일)	시장접근 및 반덤핑 회의 참가
국제협력관실	행정사무관	윤 동섭	91. 10. 22(화) ~ 11. 1(금)	시장접근 회의 참가
국제협력관실	행정사무관	김 영학	91. 10. 22(화) ~ 11. 1(금)	세이프가드 및 섬유 회의 참가

    2. 예산근거 : 상공부 예산.   끝.

상   공   부   장

0167

재   무   부

국관 22710-469   503~9297   1991. 10. 21.

수신 외무부장관

참조 통상국장

제목 UR 시장접근분야 협상 참석

　　　'91. 10. 24 ~ 30 중 스위스 제네바에서 개최예정인 UR 시장접근
분야 협상에 참석할 대표를 아래와 같이 추천하오니 필요한 조치를
취하여 주시기 바랍니다.

- 아   래 -

직 책	성 명	참 석 자 격	출 장 기 간
국제관세과 사무관	허용석	UR 시장접근분야회의	'91. 10. 23~11·1

첨부 : UR 시장접근분야 협상대책. 끝.

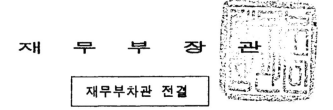

재 무 부 장 관

재무부차관 전결

0168

UR 협상 대책보고(시장접근분야)

1. 협상개요

- 일   시 : '91. 10. 24~30 (제네바)

- 아국대표 : 제네바 재무관
  국제관세과 사무관

- 주요회의 : 시장접근분야 공식회의, 무세화 협상등

2. 금차협상의 중요성

- 협상그룹별로 최종적인 협정초안 작성을 위한 회의의 성격을 가짐.

- 아국입장이 동 초안에 반영될 수 있도록 금차협상에서 적극적인 노력경주

3. 아국의 기본입장

- 11월에 제시될 시장접근분야 협정초안과 관련하여 아래입장 견지

  o 몬트리올 관세인하 목표(33% 관세인하)달성 촉구

  o 무세화등 분야별 접근방법의 보완성 및 응능부담 원칙의 강조

  o 고관세(High Tariffs/Tariff Peaks) 인하·철폐

  o 천연자원/열대산품 → 아국 현안사항 없음.

0169

4. 무세화 협상

- 종전입장을 고수하면서 협상 막바지에 각국의 태도변화등 협상동향
  을 면밀히 파악

- '91.9 회의시 수정제의된 분야에 아국입장 제시

  〈 수산물 〉 ('91.10 관계부처 회의 결과)

  ┌───┐
  │ ┌─────────────┐   │
  │ │ 수정제안내용 │   │
  │ └─────────────┘   │
  │ - 무세화 이행기간   │
  │   │
  │   ┌ 5% 이하 : 즉시   │
  │   └ 5% 초과 : 시장접근 의정서에 따름.   │
  │ - 각국의 관세, 비관세조치(NTMs), 수출보조금 등의 현황과│
  │   철폐계획을 담은 Country List/Plan을 10월말까지 제출│
  └───┘

  o 금차회의에서는 일단 종전입장(무세화 불참)을 고수하면서

    각국의 동향을 파악하고 내부적으로 협상의 급진전에 대비,

    관련자료 준비

  〈 비철금속 · 의료장비 〉

  ┌───┐
  │ ┌─────────────┐   │
  │ │ 수정제안내용 │   │
  │ └─────────────┘   │
  │ · 비철금속 : 알루미늄, 아연추가   │
  │ · 의료장비 : 의료용가구 추가   │
  └───┘

  o 수입일방분야로 참여불가 입장 견지

0170

5. 관세조화 협상

┌─────────────┐
│ 기본대응방안 │
└─────────────┘

o **목표세율이 5.5~6.5%인 분야는 참여가능하나**

o **목표세율이 무세인 분야는 참여불가**

- 미국·EC의 관세조화제안

  o 기본 대응방안으로 대처

- 일본의 화학제품 관세조화제안('91. 10)

  o 미국의 조화제안과 동일하나 필름이 추가

  o 현재 관계부처에서 검토중 → 기본 대응방안으로 대처가능시됨.

6. 양자협상

- 대미

  o 지난회의('91. 9)시 전달한 아국의 무세화 참여가능 품목리스트
    에 대한 미측 반응주시

  o 추가 Request 제시

- 대 E C/카나다

  o EC, 카나다 제시 아국 비관세조치(NTMs) 관련 질의에 대해 답변

- 대스웨덴·스위스등

  o Request 제시

0171

51619

기 안 용 지

분류기호 문서번호	통기 20644-	기 안 용 지 (전화: 720 - 2188)	시 행 상 특별취급	
보존기간	영구. 준영구 10. 5. 3. 1.	장 관		
수 신 처 보존기간				
시행일자	1991.10.21.			

보 조 기 관	국 장	전 결	협 조 기 관		문 서 통 제	검열 1991. 10. 22 공제관
	심의관					
	과 장					
기안책임자		안 명 수			발 송 인	

경 유 수 신 참 조	재무부장관, 상공부장관	발 신 명 의	

제 목	UR/시장접근, 섬유 및 규범제정 협상그룹 회의 참가 정부대표 임명

91.10.23-30간 제네바에서 개최되는 표제 회의에 참가할

정부대표가 "정부대표 및 특별사절의 임명과 권한에 관한 법률"에 의거,

아래와 같이 임명 되었음을 통보합니다.

- 아   래 -

1. 회 의 명 : UR/시장접근, 섬유 및 규범제정 협상그룹 회의

- 1 -   0172

2. 기간 및 장소 : 91.10.23-30, 스위스 제네바

3. 정부대표 :

     o 상공부 산업정책과장   이재길(시장접근 및 반덤핑)

     o 재무부 국제관세과 사무관   허용석(시장접근)

     o 상공부 국제협력관실 사무관   윤동섭(시장접근)

     o 상공부 국제협력관실 사무관   김영학(세이프가드 및 섬유)

4. 출장기간

     o 상공부 산업정책과장 이재길 : 91.10.22-27

     o 재무부 국제관세과 사무관 허용석 : 91.10.23-11.1

     o 상공부 국제협력관실 사무관 윤동섭 : 91.10.22-11.1

     o 상공부 국제협력관실 사무관 김영학 : 91.10.22-11.1

5. 소요예산 : 상공부 및 재무부 소관예산.   끝.

0173

- 2 -

발 신 전 보

분류번호	보존기간

번   호 : WGV-1445   911021 1905 FN   종별 : _____

수   신 : 주   제네바   대사. 총/영사

발   신 : 장 관 (통 기)

제   목 : UR/시장접근, 섬유 및 규범제정 협상그룹 회의

---

1. 91.10.23-30간 귀지 개최 표제 회의에 참가할 본부대표단이 아래와 같이 임명
   되었는바 귀관 관계관과 함께 참석토록 조치바람.

   ㅇ 본부대표단

      - 상공부 산업정책 과장   이재길(시장접근 및 반덤핑)

      - 재무부 국제관세과 사무관   허용석(시장접근)

      - 상공부 국제협력관실 사무관 윤동섭(시장접근)

      - 상공부 국제협력관실 사무관 김영학(세이프가드 및 섬유)

2. 훈 령

   ㅇ 10월말경까지 최종 텍스트(안) 작성을 목표로 협상그룹 회의가 개최됨을
     감안, 아국 입장을 적극 반영하고 협상 동향을 면밀히 파악할것.

   ㅇ 세부사항은 본부대표 지참 대책자료에 따라 대처할것.   끝.

(통상국장 김 용 규)

보 안	
통 제	

앙고재	91년 월 일 통상규주화	기안자 성명 안영	과장 심의반	국장 전결		차관 장관	외신과통제

0174

원 본

외 무 부

종 별 :

번 호 : GVW-2091   일 시 : 91 1022 1900

수 신 : 장관(통기, 경기원, 재무부, 상공부)

발 신 : 주 제네바 대사

제 목 : UR 분야별 협상대책(규범제정그룹 - TRIMS)

연: GVW-2083

1. 주요쟁점

가. 금지 개념

- 선진국은 국산부품 사용의무, 수입수량규제, 수출의무등의 금지 주장

- 개도국 및 호주는 TRIMS 협정이 부자조치의 무역효과에 국한하여 CASE BYCASE 로 다룰 것을 주장

나. COVERAGE

- 선진국은 보조금등 부자 INCENTIVE 및 기존 기업에 대한 조치도 다룰 것을 주장하나 개도국 반대

2. 협상진전상황

가. 그동안 MACIEL 의장 주재회의에서 협상 참가국들은 종전의 입장을 반복표명하였으나 의장이 갓트 3 조, 11 조 위반 TRIMS 을 금지시키고 수출의무는 포함시키지 않는 절충안을 제시한데 대하여 선진국을 대표하는 미국 및 강경개도국인 인도, 이집트등의 주장이 종전보다 덜 강경하여진 상태임.

나. 강경개도국의 입장이 연화된 배경에는 동 협상그룹 의장이 일본인에서 브라질인으로 교체된데 따른 개도국들의 신뢰 제고와 UR 협상 전반 PACKAGE 에서동 협상의 타결을 긍정적으로 검토코자 하는 여러 개도국의 입장 변화가 있었던 것으로 사료됨.

3. 전망 및 대책

가. UR 이 전체적으로 타결되는 경우에는 동분야 협상도 현재 MACIEL 의장이 제시하는 절충안으로 성립될 가능성이 크다고 보여짐

나. 아국은 동협상의 성공적 타결을 위하여 의장의 절충안을 지지, 선. 개도국간의

통상국	장관	차관	1차보	2차보	경제국	외정실	분석관	정와대
안기부	경기원	재무부	상공부					

PAGE 1   91.10.23   08:01

입장 대립을 해소하는데에 기여하는 것이 바람직하다고 사료됨.

　이러한 TRIMS 의 타결은 아국이 외국인 투자를 대부분 자유화 하였으므로 별다른 영향이 없는 반면 대외적으로 진출하는 아국의 해외투자여건을 개선하는데 많은 도움이 될것임.끝

　(대사 박수길-국장)

　예고:91.12.31. 까지

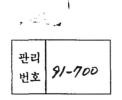

관리 번호	91-700

외 무 부

종 별 :

번 호 : GVW-2098   일 시 : 91 1023 1100

수 신 : 장관(봉기, 경기원, 재무부, 상공부)

발 신 : 주 제네바 대사

제 목 : UR/분야별 협상 대책(규범제정 분야-반덤핑)

연: GVW-2083

1. 협상 분야별 쟁점

A. 전봉이슈(기존 규범의 강화)

0 덤핑 결정(SALES BELOW COST, START UP COST, 실제 자료 이용, NEGATIVE DUMPING 처리문제등)

0 피해결정(누적 계산 인정, DEMINIMIS 제외등)

0 제소자 자격(제소자 자격의 객관적 기준 설정 여부 및 노조 포함 여부)

0 덤핑 부과 및 종료(SUNSET 도입 문제, NEW COMER 처리 문제등)

B. 세이슈

0 수입국내 조립을 통한 우회 덤핑

0 제3국 조립을 통한 우회 덤핑

0 COUNTRY HOPPING

2. 최근의 협상 동향 및 전망

0 수출국은 전봉이슈의 현저한 개선시 우회덤핑을 엄격한 기준, 요건하에 인정

0 수입국은 교역의 GLOBALIZATION 경향에 대비, 우회 덤핑 규제 필요성 강조

0 현재까지 미국, EC 등의 소극적 태도로 큰 진전 없음.

0 협상의 기초가 되는 TEXT 가 없는 상황이므로 어떤 형태로든 11 월초까지 TEXT 가 제시될 경우 코드 개선 가능성이 있음.

0 참여국간 합의에 의한 TEXT 제시를 위해 최대한 노력하고 이것이 안될시 TEXT 를 제시할 가능성이 많음.

0 내주(10.23-10.25)에 TEXT 작성을 위한 집중적인 토의 예정 및 소규모 그룹에 의한 초안 작성 작업이 진행

통상국	장관	차관	1차보	2차보	외정실	분석관	청와대	안기부
경기원	재무부	상공부	경제3					

3. 우리의 관심분야

0 기존 규범의 강화 및 개선

- SALES BELOW COST 의 인정

- START UP COST, ACTUAL DATA 및 NEGATIVE DUMPING 인정

- 제소자 자격의 객관적 기준 설정

- SUNSET CLAUSE

0 우회 덤핑에 대한 엄격한 요건 설정

- 기존 규범의 현저한 강화, 개선이 있을시 3 가지 유형의 우회 덤핑 엄격한 요건 설정

4. 관심사항 반영 방안

0 수출 개도국(홍콩, 싱가폴등)과의 공동 보조 강화로 협상 능력 강화

0 협상 막바지에서 아국의 우선적 관심사항 반영 노력

- 일본과의 계속적 유대

0 갓트 사무국 및 협상 그룹 의장과의 접촉을 통한 아국 입장 반영

0 본부 전문가 참석. 끝

(대사 박수길-국장)

예고: 91.12.31. 까지

외 무 부

종 별 :

번 호 : GVW-2110   일 시 : 91 1023 1700

수 신 : 장 관(통기,경기원,재무부,상공부)

발 신 : 주 제네바 대사

제 목 : UR/무역관련 투자 조치 협상

　　10.23 당지에서 개최된 표제 협상 주요국 비공식협의에서 MACIEL 의장은 자신의 NON-PAPER 를 배포하고 이를 기초로 협의를 진행할 예정임을 설명하면서 10.25(금) 오전에 재회합키로 함.(엄재무관, 김재무관보 참석)

　　첨부: 의장 TEXT 각 1부

　　(GVW(F)-440)

　　(대사 박수길-국장)

91.10.24   09:09 WH
외신 1과 통제관
0179

DRAFT GVW(巧)-0440 //023 //9 23 October 1991

" GVW-2110 첨부 "

TRADE-RELATED INVESTMENT MEASURES

Preamble

The CONTRACTING PARTIES;

Considering that Ministers agreed in the Punta del Este Declaration that following an examination of the operation of GATT Articles related to the trade restrictive and distorting effects of investment measures, negotiations should elaborate, as appropriate, further provisions that may be necessary to avoid such adverse effects on trade;

Desiring to promote the expansion and progressive liberalisation of world trade and the economic growth of all trading partners, and particularly developing countries, while ensuring free competition;

Taking into account the particular trade, development and financial needs of developing countries, particularly those of the least-developed countries;

Recognising that certain investment measures can cause trade restrictive and distorting effects;

decide as follows:

CHAPTER I: Coverage

1. This Decision covers investment measures related to trade in goods only (hereafter referred to as "TRIMs").

2. Nothing in this Decision shall derogate from existing obligations of contracting parties under the General Agreement or under any legal instrument negotiated under its auspices.

TM5(3)1DI

0180

/ o -'

- 2 -

CHAPTER II: National Treatment And Quantitative Restrictions

3.   No contracting party shall apply any TRIM that breaches the obligation of national treatment provided for in Article III of the General Agreement.[1]

4.   No contracting party shall apply any TRIM that breaches the obligation of the general elimination of quantitative restrictions provided for in Article XI of the General Agreement.[1]

CHAPTER III: Adverse Trade Effects

5.   In the application of any TRIM, which is enforceable or mandatory under domestic law or under administrative rulings and which requires an enterprise to export a specific product or a specified minimum volume, value or proportion of volume or value of local production, a contracting party shall avoid causing direct and significant trade restrictive and distorting effects adverse to the trade of another contracting party.[2]

6.   Such direct and significant trade restriction and distortion shall, subject to paragraph 9 below, be deemed to arise when a TRIM is demonstrated on the basis of positive evidence by the contracting party which considers its trade is being adversely affected by the TRIM, to have caused one or more of the following effects:

   (a)   imports into the market of the contracting party applying the TRIM of like products to those subject to the TRIM or of inputs into the product subject to the TRIM are impeded or displaced;

---

[1]An illustrative list of TRIMs that breach the provisions of Articles III and XI is contained in Annex I.

[2]A general prohibition to sell in the customs territory of a contracting party within the framework of an export processing zone or of other equivalent schemes (considered for customs purposes as being outside the customs territory of the contracting party) shall not be regarded as being in conflict with this Chapter.

TM5(3)1DI

16-2

0181

- 3 -

(b) exports from a contracting party other than the one applying the TRIM of like products to those subject to a TRIM are displaced in third country markets;

(c) exports of the product subject to the TRIM from the contracting party applying it are positively affected.

7.   For the purpose of measuring the effects referred to in paragraphs 6(a), 6(b) and 6(c) above, due attention should be given to any changes in the relative market share to the disadvantage of the relevant products not subject to the TRIM.

8.   The effects referred to in paragraph 6 above must be demonstrated, through clear and positive evidence, to have occurred over an appropriate period of time sufficient to make apparent clear trends in the trade flows concerned.

9.   Direct and significant trade restriction and distortion in the sense of paragraph 5 above will be considered not to have occurred if any of the following circumstances is demonstrated on the basis of positive evidence by the contracting party applying the TRIM to have occurred during the period when such trade restriction and distortion is alleged to have taken place, provided that the contracting party applying the TRIM did not provoke or cause those circumstances to occur:

(a) in the case of a displacement or impedance of imports, there is a prohibition or quantitative restriction on exports of the product in question from the complaining contracting party or existence of other arrangements limiting exports from the complaining contracting party;

(b) Natural disasters, strikes, transport disruptions or other _force majeure_ substantially affecting availability of the product for export from the complaining party;

TM5(3)1DI

0182

10-3

- 4 -

(c) Voluntary decrease in the availability for export of the product concerned from the complaining contracting party, including, _inter alia_, a situation where the complaining contracting party, or the exporting enterprises in such contracting party, autonomously reallocated exports of the product concerned to new markets;

(d) Failure to conform to standards and other regulatory requirements in the importing country.

10. In determining the causal link between a TRIM and any of the direct and significant trade restrictive and distorting effects observed, due consideration shall be given to the existence of other relevant economic, commercial and technological factors (such as contraction in demand, changes in patterns of consumption, relative competitiveness and exchange rate fluctuations in the country applying the TRIM, and technologically induced changes in demand) which can affect changes in trade flows and which were present during the period when the direct and significant trade restriction and distortion is alleged to have taken place.

11. Each contracting party in whose market the effects described in paragraph 6 are alleged to arise shall make available to the contracting party or parties making the allegation and to the GATT secretariat all relevant information that can reasonably be obtained as to the pertinent facts, including trade data on the products concerned. Nothing in paragraph 6 shall be construed to require the complaining contracting party to provide information that is not reasonably available to it. However, that contracting party shall not withhold information on the matters covered by paragraph 9.

CHAPTER IV: Exceptions

12. All exceptions under the General Agreement shall apply as appropriate to the provisions of this Decision.

TM5(3)1DI

10-4

0183

- 5 -

CHAPTER V: DEVELOPING COUNTRIES

13. A developing contracting party shall be free to deviate temporarily from the provisions of paragraphs 3 and 4 above to the extent and in such a manner as Article XVIII of the General Agreement permits the contracting party to deviate from the provisions of Articles III and XI of the General Agreement.

14. With reference to paragraph 5 above, it is understood that in considering actions that should be taken to remedy any effects adverse to the trade of another contracting party caused by a measure taken by a developing contracting party, due attention should be given to whether the TRIM in question is part of a clearly defined and time-bound programme designed to promote economic development.

CHAPTER VI: Regional And Local Governments And Authorities

15. The provisions of Article XXIV:12, as interpreted by the CONTRACTING PARTIES, shall apply with regard to TRIMs applied by regional and local governments and authorities within the territory of a contracting party.

CHAPTER VII: Transitional Arrangements

16. Contracting parties shall notify the secretariat of all measures they are applying that are not in conformity with the provisions of paragraphs 3 and 4 above. Such notifications shall be made within ninety days of the entry into force of this decision. Each such measure should be notified separately, along with its principal features.[3]

---

[3] The principal features notified should include the date of introduction of the TRIM in the case of each investment subject to it, the specific requirement involved, and the legislative or administrative basis of the measure. Business-sensitive information need not be included.

TM5(3)1DI

0184

10-5

- 6 -

17. Each contracting party shall eliminate, subject to paragraphs 12, and 13 above, all measures which are notified under paragraph 16 within one year of the date of entry into force of this Decision in the case of a developed contracting party; within two years in the case of a developing contracting party, and within three years in the case of a least developed contracting party.

18. Notwithstanding the provisions of paragraph 17, measures covered by paragraphs 3 and 4 which are subject to a contract enforceable under domestic law between an enterprise and a contracting party which was entered into prior to the entry into force of this Decision may continue to be applied for the duration of the current contract up to a maximum of five years from the date of entry into force of this Decision. No later than the expiry of this period the measure shall, subject to paragraphs 12 and 13 above, be terminated or renegotiated to bring it into conformity with the provisions of this Decision.

19. On request, the CONTRACTING PARTIES may extend the transition period for the elimination of measures notified under paragraph 16 above by up to one year for a developing contracting party, and two years for a least-developed contracting party which demonstrates particular difficulties in implementing the provisions of this Decision in the light of its development needs.

20. In considering requests referred to in paragraph 19, the CONTRACTING PARTIES shall take into account its special development, financial and trade needs.

21. During the transition period, a contracting party shall not modify the terms of any measure which it notifies under paragraph 16 above from those prevailing at the date of entry into force of this Decision so as to increase the degree of inconsistency with the provisions of paragraphs 3 and 4.

TM5(3)IDI

10-6

- 7 -

CHAPTER VIII: Transparency

22. Contracting parties reaffirm, with respect to TRIMs, their commitment to existing obligations in Article X of the General Agreement and to their undertaking on 'Notification' contained in the CONTRACTING PARTIES 1979 Understanding Regarding Notification, Consultation, Dispute Settlement, and Surveillance.

23. Each contracting party shall notify the GATT secretariat of the publications in which TRIMs of general application may be found, including those applied by regional and local governments and authorities within their territories.

24. A contracting party which considers that a TRIM of general application applied by another contracting party has not been notified may bring the matter to the attention of such other contracting party. If the TRIM is not thereafter notified promptly, the contracting party may itself notify the measure in question to the GATT secretariat.

25. A contracting party which has reason to believe that another contracting party is applying a TRIM which is inconsistent with the provisions of this Decision may make an appropriate notification to the GATT secretariat.

26. A contracting party applying a TRIM shall, at the written request of another contracting party which is able to demonstrate that it has due reason to believe that its trade may be adversely affected by the measure, provide to that party promptly and in writing all relevant information about the trade-related terms and conditions of the measure.

27. A contracting party which, pursuant to a formal written request made under the provisions of paragraph 26, has received information about measures of specific application shall not disclose such information except for the purpose of enforcing the terms of this Decision without written

TM5(3)1DI

10-1

0186

- 6 -

authorisation from the contracting party providing the information unless the particular information provided is in the public domain on or after the date on which the information is provided.

28.   The provisions of this Decision shall not require any contracting party to disclose confidential information which (a) would impede law enforcement or otherwise be contrary to the public interest or (b) would prejudice the legitimate commercial interests of particular enterprises, public or private. A contracting party may be requested to disclose information falling within (b) in connection with dispute settlement proceedings. Confidential information provided to a dispute settlement panel shall not be revealed without formal authorisation from the person or authority providing the information. Where such information is requested from a panel but release of such information by the panel is not authorised, a non-confidential summary of the information authorised by the authority or person providing the information, will be provided.

29.   Each contracting party shall accord sympathetic consideration to requests for information, and afford adequate opportunity for consultation, on any matter arising from this Decision raised by another contracting party, including such matters where they relate to practices defined as anti-competitive in the domestic law of the requesting contracting party which may be engaged in by an enterprise domiciled in its territory. In conformity with paragraph 28 above and Article X of the General Agreement no contracting party is required to disclose information which would impede law enforcement or otherwise be contrary to the public interest or would prejudice the legitimate commercial interests of particular enterprises, public or private.

CHAPTER IX: Committee On TRIMs

30.   A Committee on Trade-Related Investment Measures shall be established, open to all contracting parties to the General Agreement. The Committee shall elect its own Chairman and Vice-Chairman, and shall meet not less than once a year and otherwise at the request of any contracting party.

TM5(3)1DI

0187

- 9 -

The Committee may set up subsidiary bodies, as appropriate, which shall carry out such functions as may be given to them by the Committee.

31.   The Committee shall carry out responsibilities assigned to it by the CONTRACTING PARTIES and shall afford contracting parties the opportunity to consult on any matters relating to the operation of this Decision.

32.   The Committee shall review annually the operation and implementation of this Decision and shall report thereon annually to the CONTRACTING PARTIES.

CHAPTER X: Consultation and Dispute Settlement

33.   The provisions of Articles XXII and XXIII of the GATT, as interpreted by the CONTRACTING PARTIES, shall apply to matters arising from the operation of this Decision.

CHAPTER XI: Review

34.   Not later than five years after the date of entry into force of this Decision, the CONTRACTING PARTIES shall review its operation and, if necessary, revise its text. In the course of this review, the CONTRACTING PARTIES shall consider whether it should be complemented with provisions on restrictive business practices.

TM5(3)1DI

0188

- 10 -

ANNEX I

Illustrative List

1.   TRIMs that breach the provisions of Article III include those which are mandatory or enforceable under domestic law or under administrative rulings or compliance with which is necessary to obtain an advantage, and which:

   (a)   require the purchase or use by an enterprise of specific products or a specified volume, value or proportion of volume or value of products of domestic origin or from domestic sources;

   (b)   require the use by an enterprise of products that it produces in the territory of the contracting party applying the TRIM in place of like imported products;

   (c)   require that an enterprise's purchases or use of imported products be related to the volume, value or proportion of the volume or value of local products that it exports.

2.   TRIMs that breach the provisions of Article XI include those which are mandatory or enforceable under domestic law or under administrative rulings or compliance with which is necessary to obtain an advantage, and which:

   (a)   restrict the importation by an enterprise of products used in or related to its local production, generally or in an amount related to the volume, value or proportion of volume or value of local production that it exports;

   (b)   restrict the importation by an enterprise of products used in or related to its local production by restricting its access to foreign exchange;

   (c)   restrict the volume, value or proportion of volume or value of an enterprise's local production that is intended for exportation.

TM5(3)1DI

/ 0-/6

0189

종 별 :

번 호 : GVW-2122　　　　　　　　　　　　　일 시 : 91 1024 1230

수 신 : 장관(봉기,경기원,재무부,상공부)

발 신 : 주제네바대사

제 목 : UR/규범제정 그룹관련 회의

　　1. 규범제정 공식회의

　　10.23.MACIEL 의장 주재로 열린 표제회의 결과하기 보고함.(강상무관, 이재길과장등 참석)

　　0 의장은 10.31.까지 TNC 에 제출할규범제정분야의 TEXT 가 마련되기를기대한다면서 이를 위해 비공식협의 위주로 반덤핑, 세이프가드, TRIMS, BOP,보조금,상계관세분 야를 중점 논의하되, TBT등 다른분야의 경우도 기술적 성격의 협의가 진행될 것이라 함

　　0 의장이 밝힌 구체적 일정은 다음과 같음.

　　- 반덤핑 및 TRIMS : 10.23.오후 - 10.25

　　- TBT, BOP: 10.26-10.27

　　- 보조금,상계관세 및 세이프가드 : 10.28

　　- 수입허가 절차 협정등 : 10.29

　　0 의장은 반덤핑 협상에 있어 구체적 DRAFTING을 위해서는 SMALL GROUP 의 작업이 필요하나 다른 모든 나라에 충분한 의견 개진의 기회가 주어질 것이라고 말함.이에 대해 아국, 인도, 북구 3국은 모든 관심있는 나라의 참여 필요성을강조함.

　　0 반덤핑 비공식회의는 24일 오전 10:00 에개최키로 함.

　　2. 규정제정 관련 비공식협의

　　아국, 싱가폴, 홍콩, 말레이지아, 노르웨이, 브라질,스웨덴, 항가리, 콜롬비아등9개국은 규범제정그룹의장인 MACIEL 과 의장 보좌역 RAMSAUER를 오찬에 초청 공동 관심사항을 개진하고,향후 협상에 대해 협의한바 요지 하기임.

　　0 참가국은 규범제정 그룹의 중요성을 강조하고 보다개선된 일반 RULE 이 없을시무역자유화 노력이 선진국의 일방적이고 자의적인 규범해석과 적용에 의해

통상국　　2차보　　정와대　　안기부　　경기원　　재무부　　상공부

　　　　　　　　　　　　　　91.10.25　　00:43 DU

　　　　　　　　　　　　　　　　　　　　　外신 1과 통제관

　　　　　　　　　　　　　　　　　　　　　　　　　　　　0190

무효화될 위험성을 지적함.

0 세이프가드에 있어서는 모든 참가국이 EC 가주장하는 SELECTIVITY 를 인정할 수 없다고하였으며 이에 의장은 대부분 국가 SELECTIVITY를 받아들일수 없다는 입장임을 잘 알고있다고 함.

콜롬비아, 브라질은 EC 가 SELECTIVITY 를 협상도구로 사용하고 있다면서 EC 가 SELECTIVITY 를 포기한다 하여 이것이 EC 의 양보는 아니란 점을 명심하여야 한다고 함.

0 반덤핑에 대해 모든 참가국은 기존 규범의 현저한 개선이 있어야 하며 이를 전제로 우회덤핑문제가 다루어져야 함을 강조함. 이에대해RAMSAUER 는 덤핑 논의는 MACPHAIL III 를주된 기초로 할 수 밖에 없다고 하고 덤핑 TEXT가 ' ABOVE CERTAIN POINT' 가 아니면 개도국들이수용하지 않을 것이라는 점을 알고 있다고 하고기존 규범강화와 우회 덤핑은 연계되어 있는것으로 문제는 BALANCE 를 어떻게 취하느냐에있으며, 각 국의 타협적 의지를 강조함.끝

(대사 박수길-국장)

외　무　부

종　　별 :

번　　호 : GVW-2145　　　　　　　　　　일　　시 : 91 1025 1800

수　　신 : 장관(봉기, 경기원, 재무부, 상공부)

발　　신 : 주 제네바 대사

제　　목 : UR/반덤핑 협상 비공식 회의(1)

　　10.23-24 일간 표제 회의가 RAMSAUER 스위스 공사 주재로 개최되어 MCPHAIL III
를 기초로 조사 대상의 SAMPLING, 덤핑관세 환급 시한, 신규수출자의 취급, 제소요건,
DE MINIMUS, 조사기간의 제한등을 논의하였는바, 요지 하기보고함.(강상무관, 상공부
이재길 과장 참석)

　　1. RESIDUAL DUTY 의 취급 (MCPHAIL III 9.4 조)

　　0 수입자가 많아 SAMPLING 방법에 의하여 조사를 하는 경우 조사 받지 않은
수입자의 반덤핑 관세를 어떻게 정할 것인지에 대해 미국은 SAMPLING 대상의 가중
평균마진 계산시 DEMINIMI 마진을 포함할 수 없다고 하고 SAMPLING 조사 착수후
자발적으로 조사를 받겠다고 희망하는 업체를 조사당국이 별도로 조사토록 하는
것은 현실적으로 어렵다는 점을 들어 반대

　　2. 신규 수출자에 대한 취급(9.5 조)

　　0 개도국은 조사대상 기간중 수출하지 않은자에 대해서 까지 반덤핑 관세를
부과하는 것은 부당하다고 주장

　　0 EC 와 미국은 세관에서 누가 신규 수출자인지 잘 모를수 있고, RESIEUAL
DUTY문제와 연결해볼때 이를 악용할 소지가 많으므로 신규 수출자에 대한 반덤핑
관세부과 면제는 곤란다하고 반대입장 표시

　　0 미국은 신규 수출자에 잠정 조치를 취할때 현금 예치를 주장

　　3. 관세 환급시한(9-3-1, 2조)

　　0 반덤핑 관세는 최종 관세 결정 요청이로 부터 12개월 내에 결정하여야
하며, 최대한 18 개월을 초과할 수 없고 환급되어야 할 관세액은 최종 결정일로 부터
90일이내 에 환급되도록 합의

　　4. 제소시 증거(5-2 조)

통상국　　2차보　　정와대　　안기부　　경기원　　재무부　　상공부

PAGE 1　　　　　　　　　　　　　　　　　　　91.10.26　　07:39 DU

0 제소자로 하여금 덤핑 및 피해사실에 대한 충분한거증 자료를 제출토록 의무화하여야 한다는 개도국 주장이 받아들여져 'THE APPLICATION SHALL BE PROPERLYDOCUMENTED ...' 표현을 삽입하기로 하고 여타 문안은 더 검토키로 함.

5. DE MINIMUS (5-7조)

0 미국, EC 는 덤핑 수입량이나 덤핑 마진의 DEMINIMUS 를 계량화 하는 것은 정치적으로 민감한 부분으로 반대 입장 표시

0 미국은 덤핑 마진의 경우는 우회 덤핑과 연계시켜 해결한다는 입장을 표명

6. 조사기간(5-9)

0 반덤핑 조사는 조사 개시일로 부터 12개월 이내에 종료되어야 하며, 최장 18개월을 초과할 수 없는데 합의

7. 국내 가격을 정상가격으로 인정하기 위한 요건(2.2.1 조)

0 국내 시판 규모가 당해 덤핑 제소국으로 수출하는 금액 5 퍼센트 이상이 되면그 국내 가격을 NORMAL VALUE 로 인정하며, 설사 그 비율이 5 퍼센트미만이더라도수출 가격과 비교 가능하다는 증거가 제시되면 이를 인정해 주도록 합의

8. 평가

이번 회의에서는 주로 크게 어렵지 않은 쟁점에 대해 논의하였으며, 기술적 표현 및 일부 쟁점에 대해서는 진전이 있었으나, 여전히 중요 쟁점에 대해서는 의견차이를 크게 좁히지 못하였음. 끝

(대사 박수길-국장)

PAGE 2

0193

외 무 부

종 별 :

번 호 : GVW-2167
일 시 : 91 1028 1900

수 신 : 장 관(봉기,경기원,재무부,상공부)

발 신 : 주 제네바대사

제 목 : UR/반덤핑 협상 비공식 회의(2)

10.25.속개된 표제회의 결과, 하기보고함.(강상무관, 이재길과장 참석)

1. 가중평균(AVERAGING)에 의한 수출가격과 정상가격의 비교(2.4.2조)

0 미국은 TARGETED DUMPING 의 개념을 수출가격이 구매자 뿐만 아니라 지역, 기간별로 현저하게 다른경우에도 적용할 것을 제안

0 이에 대하여 수출국은 조사국당국의 자의적인 판단에 따라 LOOPHOLE 이 생길 가능성이 크다는 이유로 미국의 제안에 대해 엄격한 개념정립 필요성 강조

2. 수입국 조립에 의한 우회덤핑(12.1조)

0 부가가치 TEST 방법, 부가가치율, 특수관계의 범위등 주요부분에 대한 의견 불일치로 진전없음.

0 미국은 부가가치 산정에 노무비와 FACTORY OVERHEADCOST 만 포함을 주장

3. 원가이하 판매(2.2.2조)

0 EC 는 비용회수 개념자체를 부인하는등 강한 반대입장 표명

0 미국은 조사대상 기간에 한정하여 비용회수 여부를 판단하여야 한다는 종전 입장을 반복

0 미국,EC는 CYCLICAL INDUSTRY 의 경우 경기회복시와 불경기시 동일한 방법이 적용되어야 함을 주장하고 개도국은 불경기시만 과거 평균단위당 비용을 고려할 것을주장

4. 평가

0 금번 회의에서는 각국간에 의견이 크게 대립되어온 중요한 쟁점사항에서 별다른 의견접근을 보이지 못하게 됨에 따라 10.29(월) 오전에 개최 예정인 비공식회의에서 MACIEL 의장의 입장 개진이 있을 것으로 관측됨.끝

(대사 박수길-국장)

통상국   2차보   경기원   재무부   상공부

91.10.29   07:34 WH
외신 1과 통제관

0194

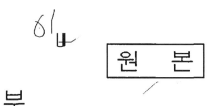

외 무 부

종 별 :

번 호 : GVW-2168   일 시 : 91 1028 1900

수 신 : 장 관(봉기,경기원,재무부,상공부)

발 신 : 주 제네바대사

제 목 : UR/규범제정 그룹(반덤핑 비공식회의- 3)

  표제회의가 10.28 규범제정 협상그룹의장 보좌역인RAMSAUER 주재로 개최된바 결과하기임(강상무관 참석)

  1. RAMSAUER 보좌역은 지난주 23일-25까지 MACPHAILIII 를 기초로 집중적인 협의를 하였으나 브랏셀회의시 합의된 쟁점(TRANCH 1)외에는 일부합의 또는 합의 가능한사항은 있으나 주요쟁점에 대해서는 여전히 입장차이를 극복하지 못하였다고 설명함.

  2. 동 보좌역은 이를 MACIEL 의장에게 보고하였으며, 상기 주요쟁점에 대한 해결을 위해서는 각국이 기존입장을 되풀이 해서는 안되며, 보다 신축성 있는 입장을 보여야 하며, 현재로선 협상을 계속할 수 있는 상황이 아니라고 함

  3. 이에 대해 브라질은 규범제정분야 특히 반덤핑에 관한 규범개선 필요성을강조하였으며, 여타 국가는 아무 발언없이 회의를 종료함

  4. RAMSAUER 보좌관이 합의가 이루어지지 않은 어려운 분야로 지적한 쟁점은 다음과 같음

  - 제 2조(원가 이하 판매, 구성가격 계산, AVERAGING)

  - 제 3조(제소자 자격, 최소 반덤핑 마진율 및시장점유율)

  - 제 9조(SAMPLING 에서 제외된 기업에 대한 덤핑 관세 부과문제 및 신규 수출자 처리문제)

  - 제 10조(소급적용문제)

  - 제 11조(SUNSET)

  - 제12조(우회덤핑)

  - 제 18조(분쟁해결)

  5. RAMSAUER 보좌관이 합의가 되었거나 가능분야로 언급한 조항은 다음과 같음

통상국   2차보   경기원   재무부   상공부

91.10.29   07:46 WH

외신 1과 통제관

0195

- 제 2조(비용이하 판매, 구성가격, AVERAGING 은제외)

- 제3조(제 6항 제외)

- 제 4조

- 제5조(제1항 및 제 7항 제외)- 제 6조, 제 7조 및 제 8조

- 제 9조 중 1항, 2항, 3-1항, 3-2항

- 제 13조 및 제 14조

6. 평가

0 반덤핑 협상은 미국, EC와 수출국간의 의견차이를 여전히 좁히지 못함으로서 관계국간 합의에 의한 TEXT 작성은 불가능할 것으로 보임

0 이경우 TEXT 의 제출시기와 그 내용은 REV 2의 전체 TEXT 와 관련, 결정될 것으로 보이며( ) 이 전혀없는 TEXT 가 될것인지는 예측하기 어려움.끝(대사 박수길-국장)

외 무 부

종 별 :

번 호 : GVW-2146　　　　　　　　　　일 시 : 91 1025 1800

수 신 : 장관(통기,경기원,상공부,공진청)

발 신 : 주제네바대사

제 목 : UR/규범제정(기술장벽협정)

　　표제 회의가 10.25.개최되어 의장 TEXT(W/35/REV.1)중 미결사항에 대해 논의한바요지 하기 보고함.(상공부 김영학 사무관,김상무관보 참석)

　　1. 협정의 위생 및 검역 규제에의 적용문제(TEXT 1조 5항)

　　0 의장은 본협정이 위생 및 동물위생 사항에 대해 적용되지 않는다는 내용의 제안(별첨FAX 송부)을 배포함.

　　0 EC 는 동 제안이 지난 브랏셀 회의전까지 많이 논의된 사항임을 언급하면서 의장 제안 내용에 찬성함.

　　0 이에 의장은 10.28(화) 회의시까지 참가국의 반대가 없을 경우 동 제안을 채택할 것임을 언급함.

　　2. 협정의 지방정부 및 비지방정부 기관에의 적용여부(TEXT 3조 및 7조)

　　0 미국은 중앙정부가 지방정부를 대신하여 동협정에 서명할 수 있는 권한이 없는자국의 국내법 체계를 이유로 동 협정의 지방정부 및 비지방 정부 기관에의 적용확대에 반대함.

　　0 EC 는 협정 목적의 명료성 확보를 위해서는 동 협정이 지방정부 및 비정부 기관에로 적용되어야 한다는 분명한 입장을 표명하였으며 핀랜드도 이에 동조함.

　　3. 분쟁해결(제 14조)

　　0 핀랜드는 제 14조 1,2,3 항 지난 브랏셀회의에서 이미 합의되었으며 제4항과관련 의무의 구체적 수준만이 미결사항임을 상기시키면서 별첨 제안(FAX 송부)을함.

　　4. 차기회의 일정

　　0 의장은 10월말까지 동 협정의 최종 TEXT 가 마련되어야 함을 강조하고 10.28(월) 개최되는 다음 회의에서는 상기 제안 및 쟁점사항에 대한 각국이 협상력을 발휘해 줄

통상국　2차보　청와대　안기부　경기원　상공부　공진청

것을 요청함.

0 상기 제안에 대해 본부 별도 의견 있을시 지침 시달바람.

(대사 박수길-국장)

GVW (전) - 0451   1105   (전→)
         ↙ GVW- 제 96 첨부 ↙

1.5 The provisions of this Agreement do not apply to sanitary and
phytosanitary measures as defined in Annex A of the Decision of the
CONTRACTING PARTIES on the Application of Sanitary and Phytosanitary
measures.

Article 14[1]

Consultation and dispute settlement

14.1 Consultations and the settlement of disputes with respect to any matter affecting the operation of this Agreement shall take place under the auspices of the Committee on Technical Barriers to Trade and shall follow, mutadis mutandis, the provisions of Articles XXII and XXIII of the GATT, including the Dispute Settlement Procedures as adopted by the CONTRACTING PARTIES.

14.2 At the request of a Party to a dispute, or at its own initiative, a panel may establish a technical expert group to assist in questions of a technical nature, requiring detailed consideration by experts.

14.3 Technical expert groups shall be governed by the procedures of Annex 2.

14.4 The dispute settlement provisions set out above can be invoked in cases where a Party considers that another Party has not achieved satisfactory results under Articles 3, 4, 7, 8 and 9 and its trade interests are significantly affected. In this respect, such results shall be equivalent to those as if the body in question were a Party.

---

[1]It is understood that the procedures on consultation and dispute settlement, including the possible role of the Committee in this context and the scope of suspension of the application of obligations under this Agreement, will be re-examined when the legal form of the agreement is decided.

0200

ANNEX 2

TECHNICAL EXPERT GROUPS

The following procedures shall apply to technical expert groups established in accordance with the provisions of Article 14.

1.   Technical expert groups are under the panel's authority. Their terms of reference and detailed working procedures shall be decided by the panel, and they shall report to the panel.

2.   Participation in technical expert groups shall be restricted to persons of professional standing and experience in the field in question.

3.   Citizens of parties to the dispute shall not serve on a technical expert group without the joint agreement of the parties to the dispute, except in exceptional circumstances when the panel considers that the need for specialized scientific expertise cannot be fulfilled otherwise. Government officials of parties to the dispute shall not serve on a technical expert group. Members of technical expert groups shall serve in their individual capacities and not as government representatives, nor as representatives of any organization. Governments or organizations shall therefore not give them instructions with regard to matters before a technical expert group.

4.   Technical expert groups may consult and seek information and technical advice from any source they deem appropriate. Before a technical expert group seeks such information or advice from a source within the jurisdiction of a Party, it shall inform the government of that Party. Any Party shall respond promptly and fully to any request by a technical expert group for such information as the technical expert group considers necessary and appropriate.

5.   The Parties to a dispute shall have access to all relevant information provided to a technical expert group, unless it is of a confidential nature. Confidential information provided to the technical expert group shall not be released without formal authorization from the government, organization or person providing the information. Where such information is requested from the technical expert group but release of such information by the technical expert group is not authorized, a non-confidential summary of the information will be provided by the government, organization or person supplying the information.

6.   The technical expert group shall submit a draft report to the Parties concerned with a view to obtaining their comments, and taking them into account, as appropriate, in the final report, which shall also be circulated to the Parties concerned when it is submitted to the panel.

0201

외 무 부

종 별 :

번 호 : GVW-2165　　　　　　　　　　일 시 : 91 1028 1900

수 신 : 장 관(봉기, 경기원, 재무부, 상공부)

발 신 : 주 제네바대사

제 목 : UR/TRIMS 협상

10.25(금) 개최된 표제협상 비공식협의 결과 토의요지 아래 보고함.

1. 토의요지

- 의장은 10.23., 배포한 자신의 TEXT 에 대한 각국의 의견개진을 요청함.

- 호주는 제 1조 COVERAGE 에 대한 자국의 안(별첨1)을 배포 설명하면서 현의장안은 TRIMS 의정의가 불명확하고 EFFECT TEST 방법이 지나치게 모호하며 수출이행 의무 는 현 GATT 조문이 적용되지 않는 부문임을 들어 의장안에 반대의견을 분명히 한 바, 필리핀, 인도, 항가리, 아르헨티나, 브라질, 말레이지아, 태국, 이집트등이 이에동조하 면서 특히 ANNEX의 삭제를 주장

- EC 는 현재의 의장안은 현행 GATT체제의 확인에 불과한 바, 수출이행 의무의 금지의의 누락과 R.B.P 가 언급된데 불만을 표시하면서 전체를 받아들일수 없다고 주장한 바 미국이 이에 동조하면서 수출이행 의무를 금지화하는 자국의 대안을 배포함.(별첨 2)

- 홍콩만이 의장안이 균형된 안임을 언급하였는 바 카나다, 뉴질랜드, 북구, 스위스등은 발언이 없었음.

- 의장은 10.31.까지 ON CALL 상태에서 한.두번의 협의를 계획하고 있으나 별다른 진전이 보이지 않을 경우에는 현 상태대로 DUNKEL 총장에게 보고 예정임을 언급함.

2. 전망

- MACIEL 의장의 의욕과 인동등 강경개도국의 일부 입장완화로 단일 TEXT 의 가능성이 커졌던 지난 주초 분위기와는 달리, 기존 GATT 제3조 및 11조에 위배되는 국산부품 사용의무는 금지화하고 현 GATT 조문으로 규제가 곤란한 수출이행의무에 대해서는 EFFECT TEST 를 규제하는 것을 주된 내용으로 하고 있는 의장안에 대하여, 오히려 종전 보다 강한 TONE 으로선. 개도국 공히 의장안에 반대하고 있음.

통상국	1차보	외정실	분석관	청와대	안기부	경기원	재무부	상공부

- 이는 동의장안의 내용이 선.개도국의 종래입장을 절충하고 있으나 11월중 REV 2 의 제출을 염두에 두고 선.개도국 공히 현 상태에서 자국입장을 최대한 반영하기 위하여 실무자간의 협상에서는 일단 의장안에 반대하고 있는 것으로 보여짐

- 따라서 현시점에서 UR 협상 전체적인 차원에서 돌파구가 마련되지 않는 한 협상 그룹차원에서 TRIMS 단일 TEXT 의 합의 도출은 쉽지 않을 것으로 전망됨.

첨부: GVW(F)-0457

끝

(대사 박수길-국장)

1. 호주제안

(handwritten: GVW-457 11-28 11-29-1991. GVW-2165 첨부)

TRADE-RELATED INVESTMENT MEASURES

1 bis.

For the purposes of this decision, a Trade-Related Investment Measure (TRIM) is any measure applied by a contracting party in connection with the making of an investment by a new or existing enterprise in its territory in the form of conditions on the quantity, origin or source of the enterprise's purchases or the quantity or destination of its sales and which can cause the restrictive and distorting effects to international merchandise trade described in paragraph 6. A TRIM "requires" an investing enterprise to fulfil such conditions where compliance with them is mandated by or enforceable under domestic law or administrative rulings of general or specific application.

9455G

3-1

0204

2. 미국 제안

U.S

Substitute for Para 5 re Export Performance Requirements:

A Contracting Party shall not apply any measure, which is mandatory or enforceable under domestic law or under administrative rulings, or compliance with which is necessary to obtain an advantage, which requires that an enterprise export a specific product, or a specific minimum volume, value, or proportion of volume or value of local production, generally or to a specific market or region.

(amend 16 to read "Contracting Parties shall notify the Secretariat of all measures they are applying that are not in conformity with the provisions of paragraphs 3, 4 <u>and 5</u> above....")

(amend para 17 to provide a transition period for the elimination of export performance requirements prohibited under   new   para   5.)

3-2

0205

New Para 21 (A) -- Competitive Disadvantage

A new clause should be added to ensure that the competitive
ability of firms which are subjected to TRIMs prohibited by
this agreement is not undermined during the transition
period. This can be either a second sentence to para 21 (as
amended) or a subsequent paragraph.

In order not to disadvantage established enterprises
during the transition period, a contracting party may
apply a notified measure to a new investment (i) where
the products of such investment are in direct competition
with those of the established enterprise, and (ii) where
necessary to avoid distorting the conditions of
competition between the new investment and the
established enterprises. Any measure so applied to the
new investment shall be notified to the CONTRACTING
PARTIES as provided for in paragraph 16. The terms of
such measures shall be the same as those applicable to
the established enterprise, and the measure shall be
phased out in the same manner.

0206

3-3

5. TRIMs

가. 목 표

o 투자 조치의 무역제한 왜곡효과 분석

o 현행 GATT 규정에 의한 투자조치 규제등 가능 여부 검토

o 필요한 경우 새로운 규정 제정 검토

나. 협상 현황

o 90.5. 협상 Group 의장 보고서 제출

o 91.4. 회의에서 규범제정 및 투자분야에 통합되어 주요의제로 논의되고 있으나 실질 진전 없음.

o 91.7. 회의에서 각국 기존 입장을 재확인하고 하반기 협상 방향을 설정하는데 그침.

o 91.9.30주 협상이 재개될 예정임.

다. 합의사항

o 사실상 합의사항 없음.

라. 주요쟁점 및 주요국 입장

o 금지 개념

  - 선진국은 국산부품 사용의무.수출의무등 금지화

  - 개도국 및 호주는 TRIMs의 금지화에 반대하고 Case by case 별도 검토

o Coverage

  - 선진국은 보조금등 투자유인 시책 및 기존기업에 대한 조치도 포함 주장

  - 개도국은 반대

0207

o 제한적 기업관행(R.B.P) 포함 여부

 - 개도국, 특히 인도는 포함 주장

 - 선진국은 반대

o 지방정부 TRIMs 적용 여부

 - 카나다, 호주등 : 연방국가 적용 배제

 - EC, 일본등 : 동일 적용 주장

마. 아국 입장

o 무역에 직접적이고 중대한 부정적 효과를 초래하는 투자조치에 대해서는
   금지 개념을 도입하는데 찬성

o 투자 유인 시책과 기존 기업에 대한 조치의 적용 대상 여부 및 제한적
   기업관행 포함 여부 문제는 협상의 타결을 위하여 신축적 입장 견지

바. 협상 전망

o 현재로서는 선진국. 개도국간 입장 차이가 좁혀질 것으로 예상되지
   않으므로 UR/TRIMS 협상은 협상이 연기되든가 또는 선진국과 NICs등
   일부 개도국의 참여하에 타결될 것을 전망할 수 있음.

o 하반기 협상은 비공식 협의 위주로 다음 쟁점에 대한 선.개도국간
   견해차이를 축소하기 위한 협상을 추진키로 함.

 - 협정의 적용범위

 - 규제방법

 - 개도국 취급방법

 - 잠정 조치

 - 제한적 사업 관행(RBP)

 - 기타 명료성 및 향후 작업을 위한 제도정비

0208

외 무 부

종 별 :

번 호 : GVW-2187

일 시 : 91 1030 1230

수 신 : 장 관(봉기,경기원,상공부)

발 신 : 주 제네바대사

제 목 : UR/규범제정(수입허가 절차)

　　표제회의가 10.29 개최되었는 바, 의장 TEXT(W/35/REV.1)상 일부용어 명료화 검토만을한후 GATT 사무국 제안문서를 채택함. 동문서는 파편 송부함.끝

　　(대사 박수길-국장)

통상국　　2차보　　　경기원　　　상공부

PAGE 1

91.10.31　　08:22 WH

외신 1과 통제관

0209

외 무 부

원 본

종 별 :

번 호 : GVW-2186   일 시 : 91 1030 1230

수 신 : 장 관(봉기,경기원,상공부,공진청)

발 신 : 주 제네바 대사

제 목 : UR/규범제정(기술장벽 협정) (2)

　　연: GVW-2146(10.25)

　　표제회의가 10.29 WILLIAMS 전 GATT 비관세국장 주재로 속개되어 브랏셀 TEXT(W/35/REV.1)상 미결사항에 대해 논의한바, 요지 하기 보고함.

　　1. 합의사항

　　0 본협정을 위생 및 검역규제 조치(제 1조 제5항)에 적용치 않기로 하였으며 분쟁해결 절차관련(제 14조) 핀랜드 제안을 채택함.

　　0 본협정과 ISO/IEC의 표준화 협약과의 관계

　　- ISO/IEC가 제정중인 표준화 관련 용어 정의에 관한 협약의 본협정에의 반영방법에 대해 GATT 사무국과 ISO/IEC 가 동문제에 대해 지속적으로 협의하고, ISO/IEC 가 동 협약을 완결한후, 기술장벽 위원회가 본협정의 운영과 관련 동 협정을 평가토록함.

　　2. 미합의 사항

　　0 본협정의 지방정부 및 비정부기관에의 적용여부(제 3조 및 제 7조)

　　- 본협정상 의무의 균형을 유지하고, 협정 목적의 명료성 확보를 위해서는 본협정이 지방정부 및 정부기관에 적용되어야 한다는 주장(EC)과 중앙정부가 지방정부 및비정부기관에 본협정준수를 강제할 수 있는 법적근거가 없음을 이유로 계속 반대하는 입장(미국)이 맞서 동문제는 합의 보지못하고 계속 괄호로 남겨둠(제3조 및 제 7조)

　　3. 기타

　　0 향후 협상계획

　　- WILLIAM 의장은 상기 논의사항 및 미결사항(제3조 및 제 7조)을 규범제정 그룹의장인 MACIEL 에게 보고하고 향후 일정등을 동인에게 위임할 예정임.

　　0 관련자료

　　- 동 협정 합의문서 및 ISO/IEC 협약등관련자료는 파편 송부함.끝 (대사총장)

―――――――――――――――――――――――――――――
통상국　　2차보　　경기원　　상공부　　공진청

PAGE 1   91.10.30　23:49 FO
                                              외신 1과　통제관
                                                    0210

216　우루과이라운드 규범 제정 및 투자 협상

정 리 보 존 문 서 목 록

기록물종류	일반공문서철	등록번호	2019090031	등록일자	2019-09-05
분류번호	764.51	국가코드		보존기간	영구
명 칭	UR(우루과이라운드) / 규범제정 및 투자 협상 그룹 회의, 1991. 전2권				
생 산 과	통상기구과	생산년도	1991~1991	담당그룹	국제경제
권 차 명	V.2 11-12월				
내용목차	* 1991.4월 협상그룹 조정으로 종전의 MTM 협정, GATT 조문, 보조금/상계관세, 세이프가드, 원산지규정, 선적전 검사, 무역관련 투자협상 등 11개 분야가 '규범제정 및 투자분야'로 통합 * 보조금.상계관세 분야는 'UR / 보조금.상계관세 회의, 1991 (2019100005)' 참조				

0001

외 무 부

종 별 :

번 호 : GVW-2223 일 시 : 91 1101 1730

수 신 : 장관(봉기,경기원,재무부,상공부)

발 신 : 주제네바대사

제 목 : UR/규범제정 및 TRIMS(공식)

MACIEL 의장 주재로 10.31.표제 회의가 개최되어 그동안 동 그룹협상 진전상황을 보고 하였는바, 요지 하기 보고함.(강상무관, 김상무관보 참석)

0 기술장벽협정 분야에서 새로운 TEXT 가 마련되었으나 주요쟁점인 동 협정의지방 정부 및 비정부기관에의 적용문제(제 3조 및 제 7조)는 여전히 미결상태로 남아 있는 바 동 쟁점 사항은 추후 해결해야 할 과제임을 언급함.

(GVW-2146,2186 참조)

0 수입허가 절차 협정 및 GATT 조문협상 그룹에서는 용어에 대한 일부 기술적인 수정이 있었음.

0 원산지 규정 협정 관련 기술적 수정사항에 대한 이견이 있을 경우 11.4까지 의견 제시를 요구함(제네경 20644-924 참조)

0 한편 반덤핑, 보조금.상계관세, 세이프가드,TRIMS,BOP 조문 협상그룹에서는 주요 쟁점사항에 대해 실질적 협상 진전이 없었으며, (TRIMS 및 BOP 조문 협상 그룹에서는 주요 쟁점사항에 대해 실질적 협상진전이 없었으며) TRIMS 및 BOP 의 경우 새로운 PAPER 가 제시되었으나 시간상 제약으로 충분한 논의를 하지 못했으며 관련국가간 이견을 축소하지 못하였음.

0 이에 따라 TNC 에 보고할 규범 제정분야 협상진전 상황을 아무것도 없으며 현재로서 동인은 규범 제정 그룹 회의를 소집할 계획이 없다함.

0 상기 의장 보고에 대해 아세안 국가를 대표하여 태국은 규범 제정분야의 중요성을 강조하면서, 동 그룹 협상 진전 상황에 실망하였다는 언급이 있었으나 다른국가들은 별다른 반응이 없었음.끝

(대사 박수길-국장)

통상국	2차보	청와대	안기부	경기원	재무부	상공부

91.11.02 08:02 DU

외신 1과 통제관

0002

외 무 부

종 별 :

번 호 : GVW-2231   일   시 : 91 1101 1930

수 신 : 장 관(봉기,경기원,재무부,상공부)

발 신 : 주 제네바대사

제 목 : UR/TRIMS 협상

10.30 개최된 표제협상 비공식회의 토의 요지아래보고함(엄재무관 참석)

가. 의장은 10.23. 배포한 자신의 TEXT를 일부수정하여 작성한 새로운 TEXT(별첨)을 배포설명하면서 각국의 의견 개진을 요청함.

- 호주는 의장의 수정 TEXT 에도 TRIMS 의정의가 없음을 지적하면서 이와같은 모호성을 전제로한 금지조치의 도입을 동의할 수 없다고 하였음.

아울러 호주는 종전 입장 TEXT 에 대한 자국수정의견을 서면 배포하였음

- 이집트, 항가리, 브라질, 아르헨티나, 말레이지아,인도, 필리핀, 태국등 개도국은 호주의 의견을 지지하였으며, 인도는 수정 TEXT T(B) 조항이 수입국산업에 피해를 야기한 경우에 한정되어야한다고 삭제를 희망하였음.

- 미국과 EC는 TRIMS 의 정의를 합의할 수가없기 때문에 규정하지 못하는 것이 현실이라고하면서, 호주 제안에 반대한다고 하였음. EC는 수출의무 규정의 금지를, 미국은 의장 TEXT내용이 너무 미약함을 각각 주장하였음.

- 아측은 의장의 TEXT 가 서로 대립된 각국간 입장의 절충을 도모하기 위한 노력의 결과라고 평가하면서 TRIMS 의 정의를 규정하는 것이 바람직 하다고 발언하였음.

나(관찰 및 평가) 금일 회의 이후 REV.2제안시까지 당분간 표제협상 그룹의 회의는 열리지 않을 것으로 보임. 의장은 TRIMS 협상에 강한 입장을 개진해온 미국, EC,호주,인도등에게 의견 절충을 위한 노력을 유도하면서, 자신의 TEXT 를 기초로한 협정(안)을 REV.2 에 포함시킬 것으로 전망됨. 의장의 TEXT 는그동안 중도적 입장에 있는 미국의 견해와 크게 상이하지 않는 내용을 담고 있다고 판단됨.

첨부: 의장 수정 TEXT(10.30)끝

(대사 박수길-국장)

롱상국   2차보   경기원   재무부   상공부

PAGE 1   91.11.02   09:09 WH

외신 1과 통제관

0003

DRAFT   16 October 1991

GVW(五)-0473   11/01 1/30

// GVW-2231 첨부 //

TRADE-RELATED INVESTMENT MEASURES

Preamble

The CONTRACTING PARTIES;

Considering that Ministers agreed in the Punta del Este Declaration that following an examination of the operation of GATT Articles related to the trade restrictive and distorting effects of investment measures, negotiations should elaborate, as appropriate, further provisions that may be necessary to avoid such adverse effects on trade;

Desiring to promote the expansion and progressive liberalisation of world trade and the economic growth of all trading partners, and particularly developing countries, while ensuring free competition;

Taking into account the particular trade, development and financial needs of developing countries, particularly those of the least-developed countries;

Recognising that certain investment measures can cause trade restrictive and distorting effects;

decide as follows:

CHAPTER I: Coverage

1.   This Decision covers investment measures related to trade in goods only (hereafter referred to as 'TRIMs').

TM5(4)

0004

O 1

- 2 -

CHAPTER II: National Treatment And Quantitative Restrictions

2.   No contracting party shall apply any TRIM that breaches the obligation
of national treatment provided for in Article III of the General
Agreement.[1]

3.   No contracting party shall apply any TRIM that breaches the obligation
of the general elimination of quantitative restrictions provided for in
Article XI of the General Agreement.[1]

CHAPTER III: Adverse Trade Effects

4.   In the application of any TRIM, which is enforceable or mandatory
under domestic law or under administrative rulings and which requires an
enterprise to export a specific product or a specified minimum volume,
value or proportion of volume or value of local production, a contracting
party shall avoid causing direct and significant trade restrictive and
distorting effects adverse to the trade of another contracting party.[2]

5.   Such direct and significant trade restriction and distortion shall,
subject to paragraph 8 below, be deemed to arise when a TRIM is
demonstrated on the basis of positive evidence by the contracting party
which considers its trade is being adversely affected by the TRIM, to have
caused one or more of the following effects:

---

[1]An illustrative list of TRIMs that breach the obligation of national
treatment provided for in Article III:4 of the General Agreement and the
obligation of the general elimination of quantitative restrictions provided
for in Article XI:1 of the General Agreement is contained in the Annex.

[2]Measures taken within the framework of an export processing zone or
of other equivalent schemes (considered for customs purposes as being
outside the customs territory of the contracting party) shall not be
regarded as being in conflict with this Chapter.

TMS(4)

0005

P-2

- 3 -

(a)   exports, of like products to those subject to a TRIM, from a
      contracting party other than the one applying the TRIM are
      displaced in third country markets;

(b)   exports of the product subject to the TRIM from the contracting
      party applying it are positively affected.

6.   The effects referred to in paragraph 5 above must be demonstrated to
have occurred over an appropriate period of time sufficient to make
apparent a clear trend in the trade flows concerned.

7.   In determining the causal link between a TRIM and any of the effects
referred to in paragraph 5 above, due consideration shall be given to the
existence of other relevant economic, commercial and technological factors
(such as contraction in demand, changes in patterns of consumption,
relative competitiveness and exchange rate fluctuations in the country
applying the TRIM, and technologically induced changes in demand) which can
affect changes in trade flows and which were present during the period when
the direct and significant trade restriction and distortion is alleged to
have taken place.

8.   Direct and significant trade restriction and distortion in the sense
of paragraph 4 above will be deemed not to have arisen if any of the
following circumstances is demonstrated on the basis of positive evidence
by the contracting party applying the TRIM to have occurred during the
period when such trade restriction and distortion is alleged to have taken
place and to have caused the effects referred to in paragraph 5 above,
provided that the contracting party applying the TRIM did not provoke or
cause those circumstances to occur:

(a)   prohibition or quantitative restriction on exports of the product
      in question from the complaining contracting party or existence
      of other arrangements limiting exports of the product from the
      complaining contracting party;

TM5(4)

0006

P - 3

- 4 -

(b) Natural disasters, strikes, transport disruptions or other _force majeure_ substantially affecting availability of the product for export from the complaining party;

(c) Voluntary decrease in the availability for export of the product concerned from the complaining contracting party, including, _inter alia_, a situation where the complaining contracting party, or the exporting enterprises in such contracting party, autonomously reallocated exports of the product concerned to new markets;

(d) Failure to conform to standards and other regulatory requirements in the importing country.

9. Each contracting party in whose market the effects described in paragraph 5 are alleged to arise shall make available to the contracting party or parties making the allegation and to the GATT secretariat all relevant information that can reasonably be obtained as to the pertinent facts, including trade data on the products concerned and information on the matters covered by paragraph 8. Nothing in paragraph 5 shall be construed to require the complaining contracting party to provide information that is not reasonably available to it.

CHAPTER IV: Exceptions

10. All exceptions under the General Agreement shall apply as appropriate to the provisions of this Decision.

CHAPTER V: Developing Countries

11. A developing contracting party shall be free to deviate temporarily from the provisions of paragraphs 2 and 3 above to the extent and in such a manner as Article XVIII of the General Agreement, as interpreted by the CONTRACTING PARTIES, permits the contracting party to deviate from the provisions of Articles III and XI of the General Agreement.

TM5(4)

00071

P- 4

- 5 -

12. With reference to paragraph 4 above, it is understood that in considering actions that should be taken to remedy any effects adverse to the trade of another contracting party caused by a measure taken by a developing contracting party, due attention should be given to whether the TRIM in question is part of a clearly defined and time-bound programme designed to promote economic development.

CHAPTER VI: Regional And Local Governments And Authorities

13. The provisions of Article XXIV:12, as interpreted by the CONTRACTING PARTIES, shall apply with regard to TRIMs applied by regional and local governments and authorities within the territory of a contracting party.

CHAPTER VII: Transitional Arrangements

14. Contracting parties shall notify the GATT secretariat of all measures they are applying that are not in conformity with the provisions of paragraphs 2 and 3 above. Such notifications shall be made within ninety days of the entry into force of this Decision. Each such measure should be notified separately, along with its principal features.[3]

15. Each contracting party shall eliminate, subject to paragraphs 10 and 11 above, all measures which are notified under paragraph 14 within one year of the date of entry into force of this Decision in the case of a developed contracting party, within two years in the case of a developing contracting party, and within three years in the case of a least developed contracting party.

---

[3] The principal features notified should include the date of introduction of the TRIM in the case of each investment subject to it, the specific requirement involved, and the legislative or administrative basis of the measure. Business-sensitive information need not be included.

TM5(4)

0008

P-5

16. Notwithstanding the provisions of paragraph 15, measures covered by paragraphs 2 and 3 which are subject to a contract enforceable under domestic law between an enterprise and a contracting party which was entered into prior to the entry into force of this Decision may continue to be applied for the duration of the current contract up to a maximum of five years from the date of entry into force of this Decision. No later than the expiry of this period the measure shall, subject to paragraphs 10 and 11 above, be terminated or renegotiated to bring it into conformity with the provisions of this Decision.

17. On request, the CONTRACTING PARTIES may extend the transition period for the elimination of measures notified under paragraph 14 above by up to one year for a developing contracting party, and two years for a least-developed contracting party which demonstrates particular difficulties in implementing the provisions of this Decision. In considering such a request the CONTRACTING PARTIES shall take into account the special development, financial and trade needs of the country in question.

18. During the transition period, a contracting party shall not modify the terms of any measure which it notifies under paragraph 14 above from those prevailing at the date of entry into force of this Decision so as to increase the degree of inconsistency with the provisions of paragraphs 2 and 3.

CHAPTER VIII: Transparency

19. Contracting parties reaffirm, with respect to TRIMs, their commitment to existing obligations in Article X of the General Agreement and to their undertaking on "Notification" contained in the CONTRACTING PARTIES 1979 Understanding Regarding Notification, Consultation, Dispute Settlement, and Surveillance.

TMS(4)

0009

- 7 -

20. Each contracting party shall notify the GATT secretariat of the publications in which TRIMs may be found, including those applied by regional and local governments and authorities within their territories.

21. A contracting party which considers that a TRIM applied by another contracting party has not been notified may bring the matter to the attention of such other contracting party. If the TRIM is not thereafter notified promptly, the contracting party may itself notify the measure in question to the GATT secretariat.

22. A contracting party which has received from another contracting party information about measures applying specifically to an enterprise shall not disclose such information, except for the purpose of enforcing the terms of this Decision, without written authorisation from the contracting party providing the information unless such information is in the public domain on or after the date on which it is provided.

23. Each contracting party shall accord sympathetic consideration to requests for information, and afford adequate opportunity for consultation, on any matter arising from this Decision raised by another contracting party, including such matters where they relate to practices defined as anti-competitive in the domestic law of the requesting contracting party which may be engaged in by an enterprise domiciled in its territory. In conformity with Article X of the General Agreement no contracting party is required to disclose information which would impede law enforcement or otherwise be contrary to the public interest or would prejudice the legitimate commercial interests of particular enterprises, public or private.

CHAPTER IX: Committee On TRIMs

24. A Committee on Trade-Related Investment Measures shall be established, open to all contracting parties to the General Agreement. The Committee shall elect its own Chairman and Vice-Chairman, and shall meet not less

TM5(4)

0010

P-7

- 8 -

than once a year and otherwise at the request of any contracting party.
The Committee may set up subsidiary bodies, as appropriate, which shall
carry out such functions as may be given to them by the Committee.

25.   The Committee shall carry out responsibilities assigned to it by the
CONTRACTING PARTIES and shall afford contracting parties the opportunity to
consult on any matters relating to the operation of this Decision.

26.   The Committee shall review annually the operation and implementation
of this Decision and shall report thereon annually to the CONTRACTING
PARTIES.

CHAPTER X: Consultation and Dispute Settlement

27.   Consultations and the settlement of disputes with respect to any
matter affecting the operation of this Decision shall be subject to the
rules and procedures of Articles XXII and XXIII of the General Agreement,
and the dispute settlement rules and procedures as adopted by the
CONTRACTING PARTIES.

CHAPTER XI: Review

28.   Not later than five years after the date of entry into force of this
Decision, the CONTRACTING PARTIES shall review its operation and, if
necessary, revise its text. In the course of this review, the CONTRACTING
PARTIES shall consider whether it should be complemented with provisions on
restrictive business practices.

TM5(4)

0011

P-8

ANNEX

Illustrative List

1.   TRIMs that breach the obligation of national treatment provided for in Article III:4 of the General Agreement include those which are mandatory or enforceable under domestic law or under administrative rulings or compliance with which is necessary to obtain an advantage, and which:

(a)   require the purchase or use by an enterprise of specific products or a specified volume, value or proportion of volume or value of products of domestic origin or from domestic sources;

(b)   require the use by an enterprise of products that it produces in the territory of the contracting party applying the TRIM in place of like imported products;

(c)   require that an enterprise's purchases or use of imported products be related to the volume, value or proportion of the volume or value of local products that it exports.

2.   TRIMs that breach the obligation of the general elimination of quantitative restrictions provided for in Article XI:1 of the General Agreement include those which are mandatory or enforceable under domestic law or under administrative rulings or compliance with which is necessary to obtain an advantage, and which:

(a)   restrict the importation by an enterprise of products used in or related to its local production, generally or in an amount related to the volume, value or proportion of volume or value of local production that it exports;

(b)   restrict the importation by an enterprise of products used in or related to its local production by restricting its access to foreign exchange;

(c)   restrict the volume, value or proportion of volume or value of an enterprise's local production that is intended for exportation.

TMS(4)

0012

P— P

4. 規範制定

主 要 爭 點	檢討意見 및 우리의 立場
① 反덤핑	
- 全般的 主要 Issue ㅇ 輸出國 : 현행 反덤핑 協定을 강화(덤핑 및 被害判定 基準 合理化등) 및 輸入國의 자의적인 反덤핑 關稅 發動防止 주장 ㅇ 輸入國 : 反덤핑規制를 회피하려는 우회덤핑행위등 새로운 형태의 貿易活動을 효과적으로 규제하기 위한 새로운 규정 도입	- 現段階에서는 輸出國立場 견지 ㅇ 최종단계에서 旣存立場 다소 양보 가능 ㅇ 즉 現協定의 강화와 관련된 我國의 關心事項과 美·EC 關心事項인 우회덤핑 방지 조항이 적절히 반영되는 수준에서 합의도출 유도
- 其他 主要爭點 ㅇ 被害判定基準의 강화여부	- 被害判定基準의 强化 및 이의 합리적 운용으로 輸入國의 자의적인 反덤핑 關稅措置 發動防止
ㅇ 제소자격(國內産業의 제소자격 認定基準)	- 國內總生産 50%이상 생산자들의 支持要件(수출국 입장)
ㅇ De minimis 덤핑마진 및 덤핑輸入量(구체적 수준을 계량화하는 문제)	- 덤핑마진 : 5%, 덤핑輸入量 : 輸入國市場占有率 : 3%(수출국 입장)

0013

主　要　爭　點	檢討意見 및 우리의 立場
○ 反덤핑 關稅의 부과 및 　評價方式과 消滅時效 설정 　여부	- 國內價格決定時 원가이하판매를 　정상적 거래로의 認定(비용회수 　與否를 제품의 life cycle 또는 　산업의 business cycle을 기초로 　판정) - 構成價格算定時 이윤산정기준 　(회계장부상의 실제자료로 이윤 　산정이 어려울 경우, 당해 輸出 　業者가 동일부류의 製品販賣에서 　실현한 이윤 우선 적용) - 가중평균에 의한 輸出價格과 　정상가격의 比較(輸出價格과 　國內價格의 비교는 同一基準으로 　하여 兩市場價格을 가중평균치로 　비교) - 消滅時效 : 3년(기산일은 덤핑 　최종 판정일)
② 補助金/相計關稅 - 貿易歪曲效果가 없는 허용 　補助金의 認定與否	- 許容補助金 認定 뿐 아니라 復數 　의 許容補助金 受惠認定 주장 　○ 각 許容補助金은 이미 제한적 　　인 요건을 충족하는 경우에만 　　허용되므로 한가지 補助金만 　　許容하는 것은 지나친 제한임

0014

主要爭點	檢討意見 및 우리의 立場
- 開途國의 優待措置	- 開途國間 分類에 반대하나 불가피할 경우 Annex Ⅷ(一般 開途國)의 범주에 아국포함 주장
- 地方政府補助金에 대한 규율	- 地方政府規制 찬성하나 신축성 있는 立場表明 강화
③ 세이프가드	
- 쿼타조정 許容與否 ㅇ 全體 輸入物量規制時 특정 輸出國이 全體被害에 미친 정도를 고려하여 최근 평균 수입물량이하로 輸入物量을 삭감할 수 있는지의 여부 (EC主張 반영여부)	- MFN原則 견지 ㅇ 輸入國의 산업피해가 있다 하더라도 이는 公正貿易에 대한 규제이므로 수입물량 삭감시 최소한 과거 평균 輸入物量(3년)은 보장 필요 ㅇ EC의 삭감주장은 사실상 選別適用效果를 초래하기 때문에 我國과 같이 수출 구조상 特定國에 대한 市場 占有率이 상대적으로 높은 국가에는 실질적 選別適用 效果 발생 우려
- 회색조치 철폐시기	- 3~4년이내 철폐원칙. 단, EC의 MFN原則適用時 特定品目에 대하여 예외적으로 8년시한 수용

主　要　爭　點	檢討意見 및 우리의 立場
④ TRIMs	
- 規制方法	
○ GATT 제3조(內國民待遇) 및 11조(數量制限)에 위배되는 모든 조치와 輸出履行義務條件 금지여부	- 貿易歪曲效果가 직접적이고 심각한 TRIMs는 禁止對象으로 하되 開途國에 대한 例外範圍 확대 　○ 輸出履行條件도 규제대상에 포함되어야 하나 開途國의 國際收支改善등 불가피한 경우 例外認定 　○ 開途國의 參與擴大 고려
- 開途國에 대한 全般的인 例外 認定 여부	- 開途國에 대하여는 GATT 제18조 (開途國 優待條項)에서 예외를 인정하고 있는 만큼 이에 상응한 優待措置 認定
⑤ GATT條文	
- 地方政府 또는 機關의 措置에 대한 中央政府의 GATT상 책임 문제	- 中央政府의 責任으로 함으로써 분쟁해결절차 명료화
- BOP條項 　○ 先進國 : BOP목적을 이유로 한 貿易制限措置 금지공약 의 강화 　○ 開途國 : 現條項 개정 불필요	- 具體的 立場表明 자제

0016

5. 知的財産權

主 要 爭 點	檢討意見 및 우리의 立場
① 著作權: 컴퓨터프로그램 보호, 貸與權	- 컴퓨터 프로그램 보호에 대해 서는 語文著作物로 保護하는 것을 반대 - 保護範圍에 있어서 Idea까지 보호하는 것에 반대하며 표현된 그 자체만을 보호 - 대여권중 報償請求權은 인정하나 報償禁止權은 반대
② 地理的 表示 : Wine에 대한 보호 및 예외	- 地理的 表示에 대해서는 중립적 입장
③ 特許 : 不特許對象, 保護期間 등	- 不特許對象 O 공서양속을 위반한 발명, 식물변종의 일부(유성생식 식물), 핵전환 제법에 의한 발명, 동물발명 및 변종 - 保護期間 O 출원일로 부터 최소 20년 으로 議長案 수용
④ 經過期間 ＊ 先進國 : 최소기간(2년), ＊ 開途國 : 최대의 기간(10년) 을 주장	- 2년이상 O 我國으로서는 최대한의 기간 을 확보하는 것이 필요 (2년이상)

0017

主 要 爭 點	檢討意見 및 우리의.立場
⑤ 經過規定 ㅇ 이미 존재하고 있는 對象에 대한 協定 適用與否 ㅇ 公衆의 領域(public domain) 에 있는 대상에.대한 協定 適用與否	- 이미 존재하고 있는 對象에 대해 協定 不適用 주장 - Public domain에 있는 대상에 대해 協定의 保護基準 및 基本 原則(MFN)을 不適用
⑥ 協定履行을 위한 制度的 裝置 마련 - 紛爭解決節次에 대해서는 特別 節次 및 報復措置 인정여부가 쟁점	- 特別節次 및 報復措置에 반대 (Gattability와 관련 大勢受容 가능)

0018

6. 制度分野

主 要 爭 點	檢討意見 및 우리의 立場
① 패널설치 및 패널보고서 채택 자동성 부여 여부	- 갓트 紛爭解決節次의 효율성 제고를 통한 多者貿易體制의 강화에는 동의하나, 갓트체제를 逸脫하는 일방조치가 존속될 경우에는 多者間 紛爭解決機能 強化는 무의미 - 따라서 紛爭解決節次의 自動化는 일방조치억제가 선행되어야만 수락 가능함.
② 開途國을 위한 1966년 紛爭解決節次의 유지여부	- 중립적 입장 견지.
③ GATT規範에 위배되지 않은 조치에 대한 紛爭解決節次	- Non-violation complaints와 관련 별도의 處理節次를 도입하는 것을 반대하며 既存節次에 의거 처리가 바람직
④ 다른분야 UR協定 각분야에서의 紛爭解決節次와의 조화문제	- 同 事項은 MTO설립에 관한 구체적 논의시 협의되어야 할 문제임.
⑤ UR協商結果의 일괄 수락 문제	- UR協商結果의 일괄수락(Single undertaking) 지지

0019

반덤핑 협상 Working Paper 검토.

I. Working Paper의 성격

o 반덤핑 협상에서 제시된 5개의 협상안중 90.11.23 제시된 Macpail III 협상안을 기초로 90년 브랏셀 각료회의시 합의된 반덤핑 조사 절차의 명료성 확보와 관련된 사항과, '91.10월말 비공식 회의시 합의사항을 반영한 협상안임

o 협상의 주요 쟁점에 대한 통일된 Text가 아니라 각 쟁점별로 [ ]또는 대안이 열거된 상태로서, 협상을 위한 종합 자료임

II. 주요 내용

1. 주요 쟁점 및 아국입장

항 목	의장안 (Working Paper)	아 국 입 장
1. Average : 가중 평균에 의한 수출. 정상가격 비교 여부	o 원칙적으로 정상가격과 수출가격은 가중 평균 또는 거래별로 비교 - 단, 예외적으로 조사 기간동안 특정 소비자에 대한 수출거래 형태가 덤핑의도의 명확한 형태가 있는 경우 (이 경우도 국내시징과 수출시장의 가격수준이 동시에 유사한 변동을 하는 경우는 덤핑 마진이 없으며, 조사 당국이 예외적인 비교를 하는 이유를 설명해야 함)	o 양시장 가격 비교는 가중 평균치 또는 거래별로 비교하는것을 원칙으로 함 - 예외 조항 삭제 o 최종 대안으로 의장안 수용 가능 (예외조항 인정)
2. 원가이하의 판매 인정 여부	o 원가이하의 판매가 인정되지 않는 경우 - 원가이하의 판매가 상당 기간이고, (통상 1년, 최소 6개월 이상) - 원가이하의 판매가 상당량이며 (동 거래의 가중 평균 가격이 단위당 비용의 가중 평균보다 낮거나 또는 원가이하의 판매량 A%인 경우)	o 합리적 기간내 비용을 회수 할 수 있는 경우는 정상적 거래로 인정 - 비용회수 여부는 단순한 조사 대상 기간이 아니라 신제품의 출하시 (strat-up) 또는 산업 불황기 등의 비용 고려

0020

항 목	의장안 (Working Paper)	아 국 입 장
	- 합리적인 기간내 비용 회수를 못하는 경우 (1안) · 신제품 출하시 : 실제 data를 기초로 판단, 상기의 방법이 적절치 못한 경우 start-up 국면의 종료시 비용 또는 조사기간 종료 시점이 빠른 경우 동 기간중 최저비용 반영 · 불황기 산업 : 최근 5년간의 평균 비용 또는 판매가격 반영 (2안) · 신제품 출하시 : start-up 종료시점 비용 또는 조사기간 종료 시점이 빠른 경우 동 기간중 최저 비용 반영 · 불황기 산업 : 최근 5년간 설비 가동율과 조사기간 설비 가동율의 비율로 조정된 조정 비용 반영	- 1안 지지 · 신제품 출하시 및 산업 불황기 산업의 비용을 보다 적절히 고려
3. 구성가격 산정시 profit의 취급	o 조사 대상 수출업자의 실제자료를 기초로 하고, 이에 의할 수 없는 경우 - 합리적이라고 볼 수 있는 방법 사용가능 (단, 이경우 수출국 국내 시장에서의 동종 상품 또는 동종부류 상품의 이윤 초과 금지)	o 조사대상 수출업자의 실제 자료를 기초, 이에 의할 수 없는 경우 (ⅰ) 당해 수출자의 수출국에 동일 부류의 제품 판매에서 실현한 이윤 (ⅱ) 수출국내 동종상품 생산자의 이윤 (ⅲ) 수출국에 동일부류 제품이 생산자의 이윤 o 최종 대안으로 의장안 수용 가능
4. 피해 판정시 덤핑 수입이외에 고려 요소 인정여부	o 덤핑 수입과 국내산업에 대한 피해의 인과 관계 존재의 입증은 조사 당국에 제시된 모든 증거에 기초 o 덤핑 수입 이외에 여타 알려진 요소에 대하여도 조사	o 의장안 지지

0021

항 목	의장안 (Working Paper)	아 국 입 장
5. Cumulation (피해의 누적) 평가 인정여부	**<1 안>** o 다음의 요건 충족시 수입효과의 누적적 평가 가능 - 수입제품간 상호경쟁, 국내 동종 상품간 경쟁 - 조사대상 동종 상품의 총수입 의 B% 이상을 차지하는 국가로 부터 수입 (개별 점유율이 B% 이하인 경우 동 국가들의 수입 을 합하여 C% 이상인 경우 누적 가능) **<2 안>** o 상이한 국가들의 수입은 별도 산정 o 예외적인 경우 피해 누적 평가 가능 - 덤핑 마진이 De minimis 이상 - 수입상품간 상호경쟁, 국내 동종 상품간 경쟁하는 증거 - 덤핑 수입에 의한 피해 및 덤핑 수입량 무시할만한 것이 아닌 경우	o 여러국가로 부터의 수입 은 독립적으로 평가 - 단, 예외적인 경우에 한하여 인정 - 1안 지지 o 최종 대안으로 2안 수용 가능
6. De minimis 인정여부	o 덤핑 마진이 De minimis (E)% 이거나 덤핑 수입량이 minimis 인 경우 조사 종결 **<1 안>** - 덤핑 수입량이 수입국내 동종 상품의 국내 시장의 x%인 경우 (단 x% 이하의 시장 점유율을 가진 국가의 수입 통계가 Y% 초과해선 안됨) **<2 안>** - 덤핑 수입량이 조사하의 동종 상품에 대한 수입국 총시장의 F% 이하인 경우	o 덤핑마진이나 덤핑수입 량이 미미한 경우 조사 종결 - 덤핑마진 E%는 5% - 덤핑수입량 X%는 3% o 최종대안으로 - 덤핑마진율 :3% - 덤핑수입량 :2% - 총수입국 규모기준:5%
7. 제소자의 대표성	**<1 안>** o major proportion이란 동종 국내 상품의 50% 이상. 단, 명백한 반대의사보다 명백한 지지의사가 많은 경우는 인정, 이 경우도 25% 이상이어야 함	o 과반수 지지요건을 원칙 으로 지지 - 다만, 예외적인 상황의 경우 25% 이상 허용 - 의장안중 1안 지지

0022

항 목	의장안 (Working Paper)	아 국 입 장
	<2 안> o 통상 50%, 예외적인 경우 25% 이상도 가능 <3 안> o 조사 지지, 국내 생산자가 반대를 표시하는 생산자들의 국내생산의 50% 이상 (단, 최소한 국내생산 의 25% 이상) o 대표적인 단체가 없는 경우 조사 당국자가 Sampling technique를 사용하여 지지 수준 결정 가능 o 노동자 단체가 지지 또는 반대 의사 표명 가능	
8. Sampling (Sampling 조사 대상이 포함되지 아니한 기업에 대한 취급)	o Sampling에 포함되지 않은 기업 에 적용되는 AD 관세는 조사받은 표본추출 생산자들의 가중평균 덤핑 마진 초과 금지 (가중 평균 산정시 zero, Deminimis, BIA 마진은 제외) - 표본 대상에 포함되지 않은 수출자로써 필요 정보를 제공 한 경우 개별 관세 적용	o 가중 덤핑 마진 초과 금지, 가중평균 산정시 zero De minimis 마진 포함, BIA마진은 제외 o 최종대안으로 의장안 수용가능
9. Sunset Clause (소멸시효 설정)	o AD 관세는 제소 자격있는 국내 산업의 요구에 의한 재심을 근거 로 계속되지 않는한 그 부과 시점으로 부터 5년내 종료	o 단기 구제 측면에서 3년 소멸 시효. 기산일은 덤핑 최종 판정일 o 최종대안으로 의장안 수용가능
10. 수입국내 조립의 우회덤핑 규제	o 수입국내 조립된 부품에 대한 우회덤핑 관세 부과 기준 - 수입국내 조립제품이 AD 부과 대상 제품과 동종제품 - 조립업자와 당초 덤핑관세 부과 대상자가 관계가 있거나 대표 되는 경우 - 수입부품의 완제품에서 차지하는 비중이 G% 이상, 부가가치가 F% 이상 - AD 조사 개시 이후 부품 수입이 실질적으로 증가 - 수입국 조립제품 가격과 수출국 국내가격을 비교하여 덤핑 증거 존재	o 의장안 수용 가능 - G%는 75% - F%는 20%

0023

항 목	의장안 (Working Paper)	아 국 입 장
11. 제 3국 조립에 의한 우회덤핑 규제	o 제 3국 조립에 의한 우회덤핑 규제 요인 - 제3국 조립제품이 AD 부과대상 제품과 동종제품 - 조립업자와 당초 덤핑관세 부과 대상자가 관계있거나 대표되는 경우 - AD 조사 개사 이후 부품 수입이 실질적으로 증가 - 수입부품의 완제품에서 차지하는 비중이 I% 이상, 부가가치가 J% 이상 - 조립된 동종상품 수출가격과 기존 AD 관세화가 대상제품의 정상가격과 비교 덤핑 증거 존재	o 제3국 조립의 경우는 본래의 반덤핑 조사 절차에 따르되 소급적용만 인정 - 잠정 조치일로부터 150일간 소급 인정 o 최종대안으로 의장안을 수용하되 보다 엄격한 기준 적용 (덤핑마진 및 피해판정 기준 강화등 전통적인 이슈에서 아국입장이 반영될 경우) - 조립된 동종상품 수준 가격과 AD 부과 대상 국이 아닌 제 3국의 정상가격 사용
12. Country hopping 의 경우 소급적용	o 의장안 : 없음 ※ Mcphail Ⅱ < 9. 6 > - 12조 우회덤핑 규제조항 이외 에도, 다음의 경우 AD 관세가 특정 수입품에 부과될 수 있음 　. 수입품이 A.D 부과 대상 제품과 동종 상품이고, 　. 동 협정에 따라 덤핑의 피해를 야기했다고 최종 결정된 것과 관련한 국가로부터 직.간접적으로 수입된 제품일 경우 < 10. 4 > - 이 협정에 의한 조사가 다음과 같은 상품과 관련된 경우 　. AD 관세가 부과되는 상품과 동종 상품이고, AD 관세가 부과되는 국가로부터 수출되었 거나 생산 되었으며, AD 관세 부과 이후 상당히 증가 하였 으며, AD 관세 부과 대상인 수출자 또는 생산자와 관련된 체약국에 의한 상품 - 조사 당국은 덤핑에 의한 피해가 기존의 AD 관세의 구제 효과를 침해하는 것으로 결정시 소급적으로 AD 관세 부과 가능 - 상기 AD 관세는 잠정조치일 이전 150일간 소급 적용 가능	o Country hopping의 개념 이 보다 분명해야 함 - 관련자의 개념 및 요건 - 덤핑마진 및 피해판정 기준 o 상기의 경우 - 12조에 의한 제 3국 우회덤핑 규제 조항이 삭제될 경우 수용가능 (다만 이경우도 본래의 반덤핑 조사에 따르 도록 해야 함)

0024

2. 합의사항

  가. 브랏셀 회의시 합의사항

    (반덤핑 조사를 위한 증거 확보의 명료성 및 효율성 제고>

    - 반덤핑 조사를 위한 증거 확보의 명료성 및 효율성 제고 (6조)

      . 질의서 답변 시한 허용 (최소 30일), 최종 판정이전 관련 정보의
        제공, 수출자 많은 경우 sampling 조사 가능, 이해 관계자의 범위
        규정, 소기업에 대한 어려움 고려 등

    - 잠정조치의 요건 강화 (7조)

      . 조사 개시후 60일 이전에 잠정조치 금지등

    - 수출업자의 가격인상 약속 요건의 강화 (8조)

      . 예비 긍정판정 이전에는 금지, 거절시 수출자에게 거절사유 제시하고
        의견제시 기회 부여 등

    - 반덤핑 판정의 공표 및 설명 의무화 (13조)

      . 예비, 확정판정 및 가격인상 약속에 대한 공표의무 부과 및 공표시 관련
        법률, 사실등에 관한 모든 정보 포함

    - 사법적 조사절차 도입 (14조)

      . 반덤핑 조사 당국과는 독립적인 사법적 재심절차 설치

    - 반덤핑 현장 조사 절차의 구체화 (ANNEX I)

      . 수출국 정부 및 기업의 사전동의, 방문전 필요 요청자료 통보

    - 이용 가능한 정보 사용의 남용 방지 (ANNEX II)

      . 조사 당국은 이해 당사자의 답변 능력 (컴퓨터 언어등)을 고려하고,
        특수한 매체 또는 컴퓨터 언어로 답변할 수 없는 경우 이를 강요해선 안됨
      . 제공된 정보가 이해 당사자의 최선의 것인 경우 무시해선 안됨
      . 정보, 증거가 채택되지 않는 경우 조사당국은 그 사유를 즉시 통보하고
        추가 설명기회 부여

0025

나. 10월말 비공식 회의시 합의사항

o 관세 환급 시한 (9.3.1.2)

- 반덤핑 관세는 최종 관세 결정 요철일로 부터 12개월 내에 결정하여야
  하며, 최대한 18개월을 초과할 수 없고 환급되어야 할 관세액은
  최종 결정일로 부터 90일 이내에 환급

o 조사기간 (5. 9)

- 반덤핑 조사는 조사 개시일로부터 12개월 이내에 종료되어야 하며
  최상 18개월은 초과할 수 없음

Ⅲ. 대응방향

o 의장안이 우회덤핑규정중 제3국조립 규제 포함등에서 아국입장이 반영되지
  않은 것을 제외하면 대부분 최종대안으로 수용할 수 있는 수준임

o 기본입장에 따라 대응하되 협상의 타결측면에서 최종대안도 수용

0026

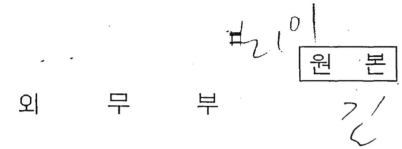

외 무 부

종   별 :

번   호 : GVW-2232   일   시 : 91 1101 1930

수   신 : 장 관(통기,경기원,재무부,농수부,상공부)

발   신 : 주 제네바대사

제   목 : UR/갓트 조문-BOP

　　대: WGV-1491

　　연: GVW-2162

　　1. 대호 BOP 비공식 협의가 금 10.31. 개최된바, 토의 결과를 아래 보고함.

　　(우성탁 서기관 참석)

　　가. MACIEL의장은 연호 초안이 각 그룹의 주장을 어느정도 반영한 것으로 본다고하면서, 각국의 입장 개진을 요청하고, 자신으로서 동 초안을 TNC에 제출할 근거로삼을 의도는 없으며, 토의의 기초로 삼고자 할뿐임을 부연함.

　　나. 이에 대한 개도국의 언급 동향

　　O 필리핀

　　- 동 초안을 의장 초안이라기 보다 NON-PAPER 라고하면서, 충분한 협의 과정없이이러한 문서가 나온데 대해 강한의념(MISGIVING)을 표하지 않을수 없다고 함.

　　- 또한 내용 측면에서도 동 초안이 EC주장을 기준으로 한 인상이며, 위원회의 공표 일정수정권한, 이사회가 특정 권고를 할 경우 이에따라 해당국의 권리, 의무가평가된다(ASSESSED)는 표현의 모호성, 협의절차관련 부분등을 볼때 BOP 조항 사용을억제하는 데만 주안점을 두었다고 비판함.

　　O 브라질, 인도, 이집트, 유고, 알젠틴, 페루

　　- 모두 구체적인 언급은 추후로 미루면서, 본초안에는 BOP 조항을 이용하는 측에어려움을 주는 내용이 있어, BOP 조항의 본질을 해치지 않고 개선하는 방향(권리와의무간 균형강조)으로 더 협의해야 한다는 입장이었으며, 전반적 거부입장은 표하지않음.

　　- 특히 인도는 본 초안과 79년 BOP 선언과의 관계에 의문을 (과거 EC초안은 79 선언을 대체하는 선언임을 명백히 하였으나 금번초안에는 전문이 생략되어 있어

통상국   2차보   경기원   재무부   농수부   상공부

이점이 불명한점을 지칭) 제기함.

- 알젠틴은 먼저 절차적 측면과 본질적 측면간의 구분을 명확히 해야 한다고 강조함.

- 한편 페루는 여타국 보다 좀더 비판적인 태도를 취하면서, 본 초안에 대한 수정안을 놓고 토의하여야 한다고 함.

0 콜럼비아, 우루과이, 헝가리

- 초안이 유용한 문건이라고 하고 토의의 기초로 하는데 동의한다고 함.

- 그러나, 우루과이는 권리,의무간 균형에도 언급함.

0 칠레

- 동 초안에 적극적인 지지를 표명(특히 명확하고 명료한 적용 가능성을 증대시키는점, 철폐일정을 정하고, 가격 조치를 선호하는 점등 지적)하고, 수량제한은 심각한 상황에서만 사용되어야 하므로 초안중 '수량제한 회피를 추구한다'는 (SHALL SEEK TO AVOID)부분을 'SHALL AVOID'로 바꿀 것을 제안함.

- 또한 전반적 제한 적용시 예외가 되는 ESSENTIAL PRODUCT를 보다 분명히 한점을 평가함.

다. EC, 미국, 카나다, 일본, 스웨덴(노르딕 국가대표), 스위스 등 선진국들의 언급 동향

0 공히 동 초안이 균형있는 내용으로서 의미있는 타협을 위한 기초가 된다고 하고, UR 막바지단계에서 이의 본격 토의 필요성을 강조함.

0 특히 미국은 동 초안이 BOP 조항적용에 있어 DISCIPLINE 을 강화 하면서, 동시에 이의발동을 제약하지 않는 원칙에 충실하다고 평가함.

0 한편 일본은 BOP 가 빠질 경우 UR 협상이 붕괴하리라고 하는등 BOP 문제에 강한 입장을 표명함.

2. 금일 회의 진행 상황과 각국 접촉결과에 따른 당관 관찰은 아래와 같음.

0 현재 BOP 조항을 협상의 대상으로 한다는데대하여는 선.개도국간 공감대가 이룩된 단계까지 진전되었으나, 일부 개도국은 상금 (절차적 개선이)상은 수락하기 어렵다는 입장임.

0 상기 초안은 EC 와 일부 개도국간 협의의 산물이나 의장의 개입정도가 적어 의장 자신의 안이라고 하기는 어려운 측면이 있으며, (비읍빈,알젠틴은 이를 NON-PAPER라고 지칭), 의장도 이점과 일부 개도국의 반발을 의식, 동 초안을 TNC에 넘길 근거로 하지

PAGE 2

0028

앓겠다고 조심스럽게 접근하는 것으로 보임.

　0 브라질, 인도등 EC와 접촉이 있었던 것으로 보이는 국가들은 강경한 입장을 취하지 않고 협의해 나가면서,수정하려는 태도였으며, 사전 협의과정에 참여치 못한 것으로 보이는 국가가 강하게 반발하는 양상이었으나, 개도국내에도입장이 서로 달라,향 후 본격적 논의가 예상됨.끝

　(대사 박수길-국장)

주 제 네 바 대 표 부

제네(경) 20644-**970**   1991. 11. 8

수 신 : 외무부장관

참 조 : 통상국장, 상공부장관

제 목 : 반덤핑 홍콩제안서

표제건 별첨 송부하니 참고 바람.

첨부 : 상기 문서 1부.   끝.

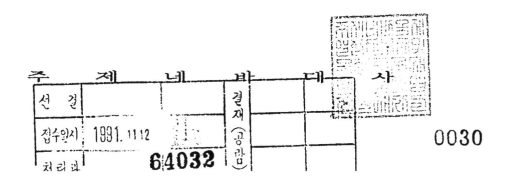

0030

Part I

ANTI-DUMPING CODE

Article 1

Principles

The imposition of an anti-dumping duty is a measure to be taken only under the circumstances provided for in Article VI of the General Agreement and pursuant to investigations initiated[1] and conducted in accordance with the provisions of this Code. The following provisions govern the application of Article VI of the General Agreement in so far as action is taken under anti-dumping legislation or regulations.

Article 2

Determination of Dumping

2.1 For the purpose of this Code a product is to be considered as being dumped, i.e. introduced into the commerce of another country at less than its normal value, if the export price of the product exported from one country to another is less than the comparable price, in the ordinary course of trade, for the like product when destined for consumption in the exporting country.

2.2 When there are no sales of the like product in the ordinary course of trade in the domestic market of the exporting country or when, because of the particular market situation or the low volume of the sales in the domestic market of the exporting country, such sales do not permit a proper comparison, the margin of dumping shall be determined by comparison with (a) a comparable price of the like product when exported to an appropriate third country, provided that this price is representative, or (b) the cost of production in the country of origin plus a reasonable amount for administrative, selling and any other costs and for profits.

---

[1] The term "initiated" as used hereinafter means the procedural action by which a Party formally commences an investigation as provided in Article 5.

0031

2.2.1 Sales of the like product destined for consumption in the domestic market of the exporting country should normally be considered a sufficient quantity for the determination of normal value if they constitute five per cent or more of the sales of the like product to the importing country, provided that a lower ratio should be acceptable where the evidence demonstrates domestic sales at such lower ratio are nonetheless of sufficient magnitude to provide for a proper comparison.

2.2.2 Sales of the like product in the domestic market of the exporting country or sales to a third country at prices below per unit cost of production plus selling, general and administrative costs may be treated as not being in the ordinary course of trade by reason of price and may be disregarded in determining normal value only if the authorities [2] determine that (a) such sales are made within an extended period of time in substantial quantities and (b) such sales are at prices which do not provide for the recovery of all actual costs within a period of time which is reasonable for the product and industry under consideration.

2.2.2.1 The extended period of time should be long enough to enable the authorities to discern whether there is a consistent pattern, in terms of quantities, of sales below per unit costs. This period shall not be less than one year and shall in any event be representative for normal selling practices for the product under consideration.

2.2.2.2 Sales below per unit cost are made in substantial quantities when the authorities establish that within the extended period of time the weighted average selling price of all arm's length transactions is below the weighted average unit cost and the volume of those sales represents a substantial proportion[3] of all sales.

2.2.2.3 Costs shall normally be calculated on the basis of records kept by the exporter or producer provided that such records are in accordance with the generally accepted accounting principles of the exporting country, and such records reasonably reflect the costs associated with the production and sale of that product. Authorities shall consider all available evidence on the proper allocation of

[2] When in this Code the term "authorities" is used, it shall be interpreted as meaning authorities at an appropriate, senior level

[3] For the purpose of this paragraph, a substantial proportion is not less than 50 per cent of all sales.

0032

costs, including that which is made available
by the exporter or producer in the course of
the investigation provided that such
allocations have been historically utilized by
the exporter or producer, in particular in
relation to establishing appropriate
amortization and depreciation periods,
appropriate cost indexation to adjust to
inflation distortions and allowances for
capital expenditures and other development
costs.

2.2.2.4 In determining whether the prices
provide for recovery of costs within a ·
reasonable period of time, the authorities
shall be guided by the pattern of prices and
costs pertaining to the product and industry in
question. In addition, the following practices
shall be observed:

i.   Producers shall be given an opportunity to
     identify those non-recurring items of cost
     which benefit current and future
     production and authorities shall adjust
     costs for the period of investigation
     appropriately.

ii. For products in the start-up phase of
     production the authorities shall determine
     if prices of the product provide for the
     recovery of all costs within a reasonable
     period of time based on actual and
     verified data of the exporter or producer
     concerning inter alia cost curve, sales
     volumes and cost recovery period for a
     prior generation or model of the product
     subject to the investigation. When this is
     not possible, the per unit costs shall
     reflect the cost at the end of the start-
     up phase or the lowest cost during the
     period of investigation, if that is
     earlier provided that there has been six
     months of commercial levels of production.

iii. In the case of cyclical industries 4 with
     high fixed cost, where sales would
     otherwise be found to be made at prices
     below per unit cost of production pursuant
     to paragraph 2.2.2, the following
     provisions shall apply:

---

4 Cyclical industries are those characterized by a
pattern of recurring market price variations, period of
significant sectoral contraction and expansion of
demand, sales and production not associated with seasonal
variations or other short term factors.

0033

a) when capacity utilization and per unit costs of production vary significantly over the business cycle and sales prices vary only moderately, the calculation of the per unit cost shall be adjusted to reflect average per unit costs for the exporter's or producer's most recent five year period for the facilities involved.

b) when the sales price varies significantly over the business cycle and the capacity utilization and the per unit costs of production vary only moderately, the calculation of the normal value shall be adjusted to reflect the average sales price for the exporter's or producer's most recent five year period for the facilities involved.

2.2.2.5 Nothing in this paragraph shall compel investigating authorities to determine sales in the domestic market of the exporting country, by reason of price, not to be in the ordinary course of trade for the purpose of establishing normal value.

2.2.3 For the purpose of paragraph 2.2, the amounts for administrative, selling and any other costs and for profits shall be the actual amount pertaining to the production and sale of the like product by the exporter or producer under investigation. When the amount for profits cannot be determined, the amount shall be based on:

i. the actual profit realized by the same exporter or producer in respect of the production and sale of products of the same general category in the domestic market of the country of export, or

ii. actual and verified data regarding weighted average representative profits normally realized by other producers in respect of the production and sale of the like product in the domestic market of the country of export.

2.2.4 If neither of the two methods mentioned in paragraph 2.2.3 can be used, the amount of profit shall be based, in order of preference, on:

i actual and verified data regarding weighted average representative profits normally realized by other producers on production and sales of products of the same general category in the domestic market of the country of export.

ii. overall profit realized by the same exporter or producer in the country of export.

2.2.5 When there are no sales in the domestic market of the exporting country the amount for administration, selling and any other costs shall be based on actual data of the exporter or producer concerned relating to export sales.

2.3 In cases where there is no export price or where it appears to the authorities concerned that the export price is unreliable because of association or a compensatory arrangement between the exporter and the importer or a third party, the export price may be constructed on the basis of the price at which the imported products are first resold to an independent buyer, or if the products are not resold to an independent buyer, or not resold in the condition as imported, on such reasonable basis as the authorities may determine.

2.4 A fair comparison shall be made between the export price and the normal value. The two prices shall be compared at the same level of trade, normally at the ex-factory level and in respect of sales made at as nearly as possible the same time. Due allowance shall be made in each case, on its merits, for all differences in conditions and terms of sale, price nominal adjustments to correct inflation distortions, taxation, levels of trade, quantities, physical characteristics, and any other differences which are affecting price comparability[5], and shall be based on actual data reflecting the costs and expenses of the exporter or producer under investigation. When considering claims for due allowance, the authorities shall treat individual categories of costs and expenses in the same manner for both the normal value and the export price. In cases referred to in paragraph 3 of Article 2 allowance for costs, including duties and taxes, incurred between importation and resale, and for profits accruing, should also be made. If in these cases price comparability has been affected, the authorities shall establish normal value at the level of trade equivalent to the level of trade of the constructed export price, and make due allowance as warranted under this paragraph. The authorities shall indicate to the parties in question what information is necessary to ensure a fair comparison and shall not impose an unreasonable burden of proof on those parties.

2.4.1 When the price comparison under this paragraph requires a conversion of currencies, such conversion should be made using the rate of exchange on the date of sale[6], provided that when a sale of

---

[5] It is understood that some of the above factors may overlap, and authorities shall ensure that they do not duplicate adjustments that have already been made under this provision.

[6] Normally, the date of sale would be the date of contract, purchase order, order confirmation, or invoice,

0035

foreign currency on forward markets is directly linked to the export sale involved, the rate of exchange in the forward sale shall be used. Fluctuations in exchange rates, whether free or induced, shall not themselves lead to a determination of dumping, and exporters shall be given at least [60] to [90] days to adjust export prices to reflect sustained movements during the period of investigation.

2.4.2   In determining the exchange rate to be applied for the conversion of currencies in economies which are experiencing high rates of inflation and accompanying sustained and frequent currency devaluation, the authorities shall use either the exchange rate in effect at the time payment is received from the customer or the exchange rate between the date of sale and the date of shipment to the customer which is most favourable to the exporter, unless it is demonstrated that the normal application of the requirements of Article 2.4.1 with respect to currency conversions will not affect the margins of dumping.

2.4.3 In cases where prices vary in both the exporting and importing country, the normal value and the export price shall be compared on the same basis. Where a number of comparisons are involved, and any comparison results in a negative margin i.e. the export price exceeds the normal value, the authorities must incorporate such negative margins into the calculation of any final dumping margin.

2.5 In the case where the like products are not imported directly from the country of origin but are exported to the country of importation from an intermediate country, the price at which the like products are sold from the intermediate country to the country of importation shall normally be compared with the comparable price in such an intermediate country. However, comparison shall be made with the price of the like product in the country of origin if, for example, the like products are merely trans-shipped through the intermediate country, or there is no comparable price for them in the intermediate country.

2.6 Throughout this Code the term "like product" ("produit similaire") shall be interpreted to mean a product which is identical, i.e. alike in all respects to the product under consideration, or in the absence of such a product, another product which, although not alike in all respects, has characteristics closely resembling those of the product under consideration.

---

whichever establishes the material terms of the sale. Where the importer is related to the exporter or producer under investigation, any conversion of currencies shall be based on the rate of exchange prevailing on the date of the sale from the exporter or producer to the importer.

0036

2.7 This Article is without prejudice to the second Supplementary Provision to paragraph 1 of Article VI in Annex I to the General Agreement.

Article 3

Determination of Injury[7]

3.1 A determination of injury for the purposes of Article VI of the General Agreement shall be based on positive evidence and involve an objective examination of (a) the volume of the dumped imports and the effect of the dumped imports on prices in the domestic market for like products and (b) the consequent impact of these imports on domestic producers of such products. It must be demonstrated that the dumped imports are, through the effects[8] of dumping, causing injury within the meaning of this Code.

> 3.1.1. With regard to the volume of the dumped imports, the authorities shall consider whether there has been a significant increase in dumped imports, either in absolute terms or relative to production or consumption in the importing country. With regard to the effect of the dumped imports on prices, the authorities shall consider whether there has been a significant price undercutting by the dumped imports as compared with the price of a like product of the importing country, or whether the effect of such imports is otherwise to depress prices to a significant degree or prevent price increases, which otherwise would have occurred to a significant degree. No one or several of these factors can necessarily give decisive guidance.

> 3.1.2 The examination of the impact of the dumped imports on the industry concerned shall include an evaluation of all relevant economic factors and indices having a bearing on the state of the industry: actual and potential decline in sales, profits, output, market share, productivity, return on investments, utilization of capacity; factors affecting domestic prices, including the magnitude of the margin of dumping; actual and potential negative effects on cash flow, inventories, employment, wages, growth, ability to raise capital or investments.

---

[7] Under this Code, the term "injury" shall, unless otherwise specified, be taken to mean material injury to a domestic industry, threat of material injury to a domestic industry or material retardation of the establishment of such an industry and shall be interpreted in accordance with the provisions of this Article.
[8] As set forth in subparagraph 1 and 2 of this paragraph.

0037

3.1.3   The demonstration of the existence of a causal relationship between the dumped imports and the injury to the domestic industry shall be based on all the evidence before the authorities. The authorities shall also take account of evidence pertaining to factors other than the dumped imports which at the same time are injuring the industry, and the injuries caused by these other fctors must not be attributed to the dumped imports. Factors which may be relevant in this respect include, <u>inter alia</u>, the volume and prices of imports not sold at dumped prices, contraction in demand or changes in the patterns of consumption, practices of domestic producers which are trade restrictive, competition between and among foreign and domestic producers, changes or developments in technology and the export performance and productivity of the domestic industry.

3.2 As a general rule, injury caused by dumped imports from different countries shall be assessed separately. However, in exceptional cases, the authorities may cumulatively assess the effects of such imports for the purposes of injury determination if the following conditions are met :-

    i.   the margins of dumping established in relation to imports from each exporter or producer is more than de minimis as defined in Article 5.7;

    ii.   there is evidence that the imported products compete with each other and with the like domestic product in terms of characteristics, price, quality and sales channels distribution and end use.

    iii. the volume of dumped imports and the injury attributable to the dumped imports from each country is not negligible as defined in Article 5.7; and

    iv.   imports from countries that are cumulatively assessed shall be imports covered under simultaneous investigation.

In any case even when the above mentioned conditions are met, the authorities shall consider the relative magnitudes of the volumes of imports from each country, and in particular whether there are significant disproportions of the volumes and the trends of volumes of imports from each such country in assessing whether imports from each country make a distinguishable contribution to injury or pose a threat of injury.

3.3   The effect of the dumped imports shall be assessed in relation to the domestic production of the like product when available data permit the separate identification of production in terms of such criteria

0038

as: the production process, the producers' realizations, profits. When the domestic production of the like product has no separate identity in these terms the effects of the dumped imports shall be assessed by the examination of the production of the narrowest group or range of products, which includes the like product, for which the necessary information can be provided.

3.4   A determination of a threat of material injury shall be based on facts and not merely on allegation, conjecture or remote possibility. The change in circumstances which would create a situation in which the dumping would cause injury must be clearly foreseen and imminent.

3.4.1 In making a determination regarding a threat of material injury, the authorities should consider inter alia such factors as:

i.   a significant rate of increase of dumped imports into the domestic market indicating the likelihood of substantially increased importations thereof;

ii.   sufficient freely disposable capacity of the exporter indicating the likelihood of substantially increased dumped exports to the importing country's market taking into account the availability of other export markets to absorb any additional exports;

iii. whether imports are entering at prices that will have a significant depressing or suppressing effect on domestic prices, and would likely increase demand for further imports; and

iv.   inventories in the importing country of the product being investigated.

No one of these factors by itself can necessarily give decisive guidance but the totality of the factors considered must lead to the conclusion that further dumped exports are imminent and that unless protective action is taken, material injury would occur.

3.5 With respect to cases where injury is threatened by dumped imports, the application of anti-dumping measures shall be considered and decided with special care.

Article 4
Definition of Industry

4.1 In determining injury the term "domestic industry" shall be interpreted as referring to the domestic producers as a whole of the like products or to those of them whose collective output of the products constitutes a major proportion of the total domestic production of those products, except that

    i.   when producers are related to the exporters or importers or are themselves importers of the allegedly dumped product, the industry may be interpreted as referring to the rest of the producers;

    ii. in exceptional circumstances the territory of a Party may, for the production in question, be divided into two or more competitive markets and the producers within each market may be regarded as a separate industry if (a) the producers within such market sell all or almost all their production of the product in question in that market, and (b) the demand in that market is not to any substantial degree supplied by producers of the product in question located elsewhere in the territory. In such circumstances, injury may be determined to exist even where a major portion of the total domestic industry is not injured provided there is a concentration of dumped imports into such an isolated market and provided further that the dumped imports are causing injury to the producers of all or almost all of the production within such market.

4.2 When the industry has been interpreted as referring to the producers in a certain area, i.e. a market as defined in sub-paragraph 1(ii), anti-dumping duties shall be levied[9] only on the products in question consigned for final consumption to that area. When the constitutional law of the importing country does not permit the levying of anti-dumping duties on such a basis, the importing Party may levy the anti-dumping duties without limitation only if (1) the exporters have been given an opportunity to cease dumping in the area concerned or otherwise give assurances pursuant to Article 8 of this Code, and adequate assurances in this regard have not been promptly given, and (2) such duties cannot be levied on specific producers which supply the area in question.

4.3 Where two or more countries have reached under the provisions of Article XXIV:8(a) of the General Agreement such a level of integration that they have the characteristics of a single, unified market, the industry in the entire area of integration shall be taken to be the industry referred to in paragraph 1 above.

4.4 For the purposes of this Code, producers shall be deemed to be related to exporters or importers only if (a) one of them directly or indirectly controls the other; or (b) both of them are directly or indirectly controlled by a third person; or (c) together they

---

[9] As used in this Code "levy" shall mean the definitive or final legal assessment or collection of a duty or tax.

0040

directly or indirectly control a third person, provided that there is evidence that the effect of the relationship is such as to cause the producer concerned to behave differently from non-related producers. For the purpose of this Code, control shall not depend on having a certain percentage of shares or stock in another company; one shall be deemed to control another when the former is legally or on a de facto basis in a position to exercise restraint or direction over the latter.

4.5 The provisions of paragraph 3 of Article 3 shall be applicable to this Article.

Article 5

Initiation and Subsequent Investigation

5.1 An investigation to determine the existence, degree and effect of any alleged dumping shall normally be initiated upon a written application by or on behalf of the domestic industry, as defined in Article 4.1.[10]

5.2 An application under paragraph 1 shall include evidence of (a) dumping, (b) injury within the meaning of Article VI of the General Agreement as interpreted by this Code and (c) a causal link between the dumped imports and the alleged injury. Simple assertion, unsubstantiated by relevant evidence, cannot be considered sufficient to meet the requirements of this paragraph. The application shall contain the following information as is reasonably available to the applicant :

    i. identity of the applicant and a description of the volume and value of the domestic production of the like product by the applicant. Where a written application is made on behalf of the domestic industry, the application shall identify the industry on behalf of which the application is made by a list of all domestic producers of the like product (or associations of domestic producers of the like product) and,

---

(10) For purposes of this Article the term "a major proportion" in Article 4 shall normally mean 50 per cent of the value of total domestic production of the like product. In exceptional circumstances where the industry is fragmented into a large number of producers who do not have a representative association, the percentage may be less than 50 per cent, but not less than 33 per cent. However an application suppported by [more than 33 per cent but] less than 50 per cent of the domestic industry shall not be accepted, or a proceeding in repect of such an application shall be terminated, whenever it becomes clear that there is more expressed opposition than expressed support.

to the extent possible, a description of the volume and value of domestic production of the like product accounted for by such producers;

2.ii. a complete description of the allegedly dumped product, the names of the country or countries of export or origin in question, the identity of each known exporter or foreign producer and a list of known persons importing the product in question;

iii. information on prices at which the product in question is sold when destined for consumption in the domestic markets of the country or countries of origin or export (or, where appropriate, information on the prices at which the product is sold from the country or countries of origin or export to a third country or countries or on the constructed value of the product) and information on actual export prices or, where appropriate, on the prices at which the product is first resold to an independent buyer in the importing country;

iv. information on the evolution of the volume of the allegedly dumped imports, the effect of these imports on prices of the like product in the domestic market and the consequent impact of the imports on the domestic industry concerned, as demonstrated by relevant factors and indices having a bearing on the state of the domestic industry, such as those listed in Article 3.1.1 and 3.1.2.

5.3 The authorities shall examine the accuracy and adequacy of the evidence provided in the application to determine whether there is sufficient evidence to justify the initiation of an investigation, provided that the authorities shall not initiate an investigation unless they are satisfied that the application for the initiation of an investigation has been made by or on behalf of the domestic industry, as provided in Article 5.1.

5.4 The authorities shall avoid, unless a decision has been made to initiate an investigation, any publicizing of the application for the initiation of an investigation. However, after receipt of a properly documented application and before proceeding to initiate an investigation, the authorities shall notify the government of the exporting country concerned.

5.5 Notwithstanding paragraph 1, if in exceptional circumstances the authorities concerned decide to initiate an investigation without having received a written application by or on behalf of a domestic industry for the initiation of such investigation, they shall proceed only if they have the same evidence of dumping, injury and a causal link, as described in

0042

paragraph 2, to justify the initiation of an
investigation.

5.6 The evidence of both dumping and injury shall be
considered simultaneously (a) in the decision whether or
not to initiate an investigation, and (b) thereafter,
during the course of the investigation, starting on a
date not later than the earliest date on which in
accordance with the provisions of this Code provisional
measures may be applied.

5.7 A written application under paragraph 1 shall be
rejected and an investigation shall be terminated
promptly as soon as the authorities concerned are
satisfied that there is not sufficient evidence of either
dumping or injury or industry support as defined in
Article 5.1 to justify proceeding with the case. There
shall be immediate termination in cases where the margin
of dumping is de minimis[10], or the volume of dumped
imports[11] , actual or potential, or the injury is
negligible.

5.8 An anti-dumping proceeding shall not hinder the
procedures of customs clearance.

5.9 Investigations shall, except in exceptional
circumstances, be concluded within one year after their
initiation and shall in any case be concluded within 18
months.

Article 6

Evidence

6.1 All interested parties in an anti-dumping
investigation shall be given notice of the information
which the authorities require and ample opportunity to
present in writing all evidence which they consider
relevant in respect of the investigation in question.

6.1.1 Exporters, importers or foreign producers
receiving questionnaires used in an anti-dumping

---

[10]For the purpose of this paragraph, a de minimis margin
of dumping is considered to be less than [5] per cent,
expressed as a percentage of the normal value.

[11]The volume of dumped imports shall be regarded as
negligible if the total volume of dumped imports from any
one country does not constitute more than [5] per cent of
the domestic market for the like product in the importing
country, unless countries with less than [5] per cent
market share collectively account for more than [20] per
cent of the domestic market for the like product in the
importing country.

0043

Article 6

Evidence

6.1 All interested parties in an anti-dumping investigation shall be given notice of the information which the authorities require and ample opportunity to present in writing all evidence which they consider relevant in respect of the investigation in question.

    6.1.1 Exporters, importers or foreign producers receiving questionnaires used in an anti-dumping investigation shall be given at least thirty days for reply.[12] Due consideration should be given to any request for an extension of the thirty day period and, upon cause shown, such an extension should be granted whenever practicable.

    6.1.2 Subject to the requirement to protect confidential information, evidence presented in writing by one interested party shall be made available promptly to other interested parties participating in the investigation.

    6.1.3 As soon as an investigation has been initiated, the authorities shall provide the full test of the written application received under Article 5.1 to the known exporters[13] and to the authorities of the exporting countries and make it available, upon request, to other interested parties involved. Due regard shall be paid to the requirement for the protection of confidential information as provided for in paragraph 5.

6.2 Throughout the anti-dumping investigation all interested parties shall have a full opportunity for the

---

[12]As a general rule, the time limit for exporters shall be counted from the date of the receipt of the questionnaire, which for this purpose shall be deemed to have been received one week from the day on which it was sent to the respondent or transmitted to the appropriate diplomatic representative of the exporting country.
[13]It being understood that, where the number of exporters involved is particulary high, the full text of the request should instead be provided only to the authorities of the exporting country or to the relevant trade association.

0044

defence of their interests. To this end, the authorities shall, on request, provide opportunities for all interested parties to meet those parties with adverse interests, so that opposing views may be presented and rebuttal arguments offered. Provision of such opportunities must take account of the need to preserve confidentiality and of the convenience to the parties. There shall be no obligation on any party to attend a meeting, and failure to do so shall not be prejudicial to that party's case. Interested parties shall also have the right, on justification, to present other information orally.

6.3 Oral information provided under paragraph 2 shall be taken into account by the authorities only insofar as it is subsequent reproduced in writing and made available to other interested parties, as provided for in subparagraph 1.2 of this Article.

6.4 The authorities shall whenever practicable provide timely opportunities for all interested parties to see all information that is relevant to the presentation of their cases, that is not confidential as defined in paragraph 5 and that is used by the authorities in an anti-dumping investigation, and to prepare presentations on the basis of this information.

6.5 Any information which is by nature confidential, (for example, because its disclosure would be of significant competitive advantage to a competitor or because its disclosure would have a significantly adverse effect upon a person supplying the information or upon a person from whom he acquired the information) or which is provided on a confidential basis by parties to an investigation shall, upon good cause shown, be treated as such by the investigating authorities. Such information shall not be disclosed without specific permission of the party submitting it.[14]

> 6.5.1 The authorities shall require interested parties providing confidential information to furnish non-confidential summaries thereof. These summaries shall be in sufficient detail to permit a reasonable understanding of the substance of the information submitted in confidence. In exceptional circumstances, such parties may indicate that such information is not susceptible of summary. In such exceptional circumstances, a statement of the reasons why summarization is not possible must be provided.

> 6.5.2 If the authorities find that a request for confidentiality is not warranted and if the supplier is either unwilling to make the information public or to authorize its disclosure in generalized or summary form, the authorities are free to disregard

---

[14] Parties are aware that in the territory of certan Parties disclosure pursuant to a narrowly drawn protective order may be required

0045

such information unless it can be demonstrated to their satisfaction from appropriate sources that the information is correct.[15]

6.6 Except in circumstances provided for in paragraph 8, the authorities shall during the course of an investigation satisfy themselves as to the accuracy of the information supplied by interested parties upon which its findings are based.

6.7 In order to verify information provided or to obtain further details, the authorities may carry out investigations in other countries as required, provided they obtain the agreement of the firms concerned and provided they notify the representatives of the government of the country in question and unless the latter object to the investigation. The procedures described in Annex I shall apply to verifications carried out in exporting countries. The authorities shall, subject to the requirement to protect confidential information, make the result of any verifications available or provide disclosure thereof pursuant to paragraph 9, to the firms to which they pertain and may make such reports available to the applicants.

6.8 In cases in which any interested party refuses access to, or otherwise does not provide, necessary information within a reasonable period, or significantly impedes the investigation, preliminary and final determinations, affirmative or negative, may be made on the basis of the facts available. The provisions of Annex II shall be observed in the application of this paragraph.

6.9 The authorities shall, before a final determination is made, inform all intested parties of the essential facts under consideration which form the basis for the decision whether to apply definitive measures. Such disclosure should take place in sufficient time for the parties to defend their interests.

6.10 The authorities shall determine an individual margin of dumping for each exporter or producer concerned of the product under investigation. In exceptional cases where the number of exporters or producers involved is so large as to make such a determination impracticable, the authorities may limit the investigation either to a reasonable number of interested parties by using statistically valid samples or to the largest percentage of the volume of the exports from the country in question which can reasonably be investigated provided that this volume is sufficiently large to be representative.

6.10.1 Any selection of exporters or producers made under this paragraph shall be chosen in consultation with and preferably with the consent of the exporters or producers concerned.

---

[15] Parties agree that requests for confidentiality should not be arbitrarily rejected.

0046

6.10.2 In cases where the authorities have limited their investigation, as provided for in this paragraph, they shall nevertheless determine an individual margin of dumping for any exporter or producer not initially selected who submits the necessary information in time for that information to be considered during the course of the investigation. The authorities shall not discourage such voluntary responses.

6.11 For the purposes of this Code, "interested parties" shall include :

    i.   an exporter or foreign producer or the importer of a product subject to investigation, or a trade or business association a majority of the members of which are producers, exporters or importers of such product;

    ii.   the government of the exporting country; and

    iii. a producer of the like product in the importing country or a trade and business association a majority of the members of which produce the like product in the importing country.

This list shall not preclude Parties from allowing domestic or foreign parties other than those mentioned above to participate as interested parties in the investigation.

6.12 The authorities shall provide opportunities for industrial users of the product under investigation, and for representative consumer organizations in cases where the product is commonly sold at the retail level, to provide information which is relevant to the investigation regarding dumping injury and causality.

6.13 The authorities shall take due account of any difficulties experienced by interested parties, in particular small companies, in supplying information requested and provide any assistance practicable.

6.14 The procedures set out above are not intended to prevent the authorities of a Party from proceeding expeditiously with regard to initiating an investigation, reaching preliminary or final determinations, whether affirmative or negative, or from applying provisional or final measures, in accordance with relevant provisions of this Code.

Article 7

Provisional Measures

7.1 Provisional measures may be applied only if:

    i.   an investigation has been initiated in accordance with the provisions of Article 5, a

0047

public notice has been given to that effect and interested parties have been given adequate opportunities to submit information and make comments;

    ii. a preliminary affirmative determination has been made of dumping and consequent injury to a domestic industry; and

    iii. the authorities concerned judge such measures necessary to prevent injury being caused during the period of investigation.

7.2 Provisional measures may take the form of a provisional duty or, preferably, a security - by cash deposit or bond - equal to the amount of the anti-dumping duty provisionally estimated, being not greater than the provisionally estimated margin of dumping. Withholding of appraisement is an appropriate provisional measure, provided that the normal duty and the estimated amount of the anti-dumping duty be indicated and as long as the withholding of appraisement is subject to the same conditions as other provisional measures.

7.3 Provisional measures shall not be applied sooner than 60 days from the date of initiation of the investigation.

7.4 The application of provisional measures shall be limited to as short a period as possible, not exceeding four months, or on decision of the authorities concerned, upon request by exporters representing a significant percentage of the trade involved, to a period not exceeding six months. When signatories, in the course of the investigation, examine whether a duty lower than a margin of dumping would be sufficient to remove injury, those periods may be six and nine months respectively.

7.5 The relevant provisions of Article 9 shall be followed in the application of provisional measures.

Article 8

Price Undertakings

8.1 Proceedings may[16] be suspended or terminated without the imposition of provisional measures or anti-dumping duties upon receipt of satisfactory voluntary undertakings from any exporter to revise its prices or to cease dumping so that the authorities are satisfied that the injurious effect of the dumping is eliminated. Price increases under such undertakings shall not be higher

---

[16] The word "may" shall not be interpreted to allow the simultaneous continuation of proceedings with the implementation of price undertakings except as provided in paragraph 4.

0048

than necessary to eliminate the margin of dumping. It is
desirable that the price increases be less than the
margin of dumping if such increases would be adequate to
remove the injury to the domestic industry.

8.2 Price undertakings shall not be sought or accepted
from exporters unless the authorities of the importing
country have made a preliminary affirmative determination
of dumping and injury caused by such dumping.

8.3 Undertakings offered need not be accepted if the
authorities consider their acceptance impractical, for
example, if the number of actual or potential exporters
is too great, or for other reasons including reasons of
general policy. Should the case arise and where
practiable, the authorities shall provide to the exporter
the reasons which led them to consider acceptance of an
undertaking as inappropriate, and shall, to the extent
possible, give the exporter an opportunity to make
comments thereon.

8.4   If the undertakings are accepted, the investigation
of dumping and injury shall nevertheless be completed if
the exporter so desires or the authorities so decide. In
such a case, if a negative determination of dumping or
injury is made, the undertaking shall automatically lapse
except in cases where such a determination is due in
large part to the existence of a price undertaking. In
such cases the authorities may require that an
undertaking be maintained for a reasonable period
consistent with the provisions of this Code. In the
event that an affirmative determination of dumping and
injury is made, the undertaking shall continue consistent
with its terms and the provisions of this Code.

8.5 Price undertakings may be suggested by the
authorities of the importing country, but no exporter
shall be forced to enter into such an undertaking. The
fact that exporters do not offer such undertakings, or do
not accept an invitation to do so, shall in no way
prejudice the consideration of the case. However, the
authorities are free to determine that a threat of injury
is more likely to be realized if the dumped imports
continue.

8.6 Authorities of an importing country may require any
exporter from whom undertakings have been accepted to
provide periodically information relevant to the
fulfillment of such undertakings, and to permit
verification of pertinent data. In case of violation of
undertakings the authorities of the importing country may
take, under this Code in conformity with its provisons,
expeditious actions which may constitute immediate
application of provisional measures using the best
information available. In such cases definitive duties
may be levied in accordance with this Code on goods
entered for consumption not more than ninety days before
the application of such provisional measures, except that
any such retroactive assessment shall not apply to
imports entered before the violation of the undertaking.

0049

8.7   Undertakings shall not remain in force any longer than anti-dumping duties could remain in force under this Code.   The authorities of an importing country shall review the need for the continuation of any price undertaking, where warranted, on their own initiative or if interested parties so request and submit positive information substantiating the need for such a review.

Article 9

Imposition and collection of anti-dumping duties

9.1   The decision whether or not to impose an anti-dumping duty in cases where all requirements for the imposition have been fulfilled and the decision whether the amount of the anti-dumping duty to be imposed shall be the full margin of dumping or less, are decisions to be made by the authorities of the importing country or customs territory.   It is desirable that the imposition be permissive in all countries or customs territories Parties to this Agreement, and that the duty be less than the margin, if such lesser duty would be adequate to remove the injury to the domestic industry.

9.2   When an anti-dumping duty is imposed in respect of any product, such anti-dumping duty shall be collected in the appropriate amounts in each case, on a non-discriminatory basis on imports of such product from all sources found to be dumped and causing injury, except as to imports from those sources, from which price undertakings under the terms of this Code have been accepted.   The authorities shall name the supplier or suppliers of the product concerned.   If, however, several suppliers from the same country are involved, and it is impracticable to name all these suppliers, the authorities may name the supplying country concerned.   If several suppliers from more than one country are involved, the authorities may name either all the suppliers involved, or, if this is impracticable, all the supplying countries involved.

9.3   The amount of the anti-dumping duty shall not exceed the margin of dumping as established under Article 2.

9.3.1   When the amount of the anti-dumping duty is assessed on a retrospective basis, the

/2 (4/3/

determination of the final liability for payment of anti-dumping duties shall take place as soon as possible, normally within ⑥ months, and in no case more than ⑫ months, after the date on which a request for a final assessment of the amount of anti-dumping duty has been made   except where one or more parties avail thenselves of judicial review. Any refund shall be made promptly and normally within 90 days following the determination of final liability made pursuant to this subparagraph.   In any case where refund is not made within 90 days, the authorities shall be obliged to provide . explanation if so requested.

9.3.2   When the amount of the anti-dumping duty is assessed on a prospective basis, provision shall be made for a prompt refund, upon request, of any duty paid in excess of the margin of dumping. A refund of any such duty paid in excess of the actual margin of dumping shall normally take place within 6 months, and in no case more than 12 months, after the date on which a request for a refund, duly supported by evidence, has been made by an importer of the product subject to the anti-dumping duty except where one or more parties avail themselves of judicial review.

9.3.3   When the export price is constructed in accordance with Article 2.3, any anti-dumping duties definitively collected in excess of the margin of dumping shall be reimbursed upon request. In determining whether a reimbursement should be made, authorities should take account of any decrease in normal value, any reduction of costs incurred between importation and resale, and any movement in the resale price, and should calculate the export price with no deduction for the amount of anti-dumping duties paid. If the result of this calculation indicates an export price that is equal to or greater than the normal value, then the full amount of the anti-dumping duty paid shall be reimbursed. If, however, the export price so calculated is less than the normal value, the amount of any refund is limited to the difference between the margin of dumping found and the amount of the anti-dumping duty paid.

9.4   When the authorities have determined margins of dumping in accordance with Article 6.10, any anti-dumping duty applied to imports from exporters or producers not included in the examination shall not exceed

(a)   the weighted average margin of dumping established with respect to the selected exporters or producers, or

(b)   where the liability for payment of anti-dumping duties is calculated on the basis of a prospective normal value, the difference between the weighted average normal value of the selected exporters or producers and the export prices of exporters or producers not individually investigated,

provided that the authorities shall disregard for the purpose of this paragraph any margins established under the circumstances referred to in Article 6.8[17]. The

[17] Parties shall come to a general understanding as to the treatment to be accorded to exporters not included in the sampling exercise where only margins established

authorities shall apply individual duties or normal values to imports from any exporter or producer not included in the examination who has provided the necessary information during the course of the investigation. Where the number of exporters or producers is so large that it is impractical to provide them all with individual margins of dumping within the time frame of the investigation, this shall be done as expeditiously as possible taking into account reasonable administrative limits for the authorities concerned.

9.5 When exporters or producers are _able to demonstrate_ that they are new exporters or producers who have not exported the product during the period of investigation and who are not related (as defined in Article 4.4) to any of the exporters or producers subject to anti-dumping duties, the authorities shall carry out an expedited investigation to determine individual margins of dumping for such exporters or producers. No anti-dumping duties shall be levied while this review is being carried out. The authorities, however, may withhold appraisement or request appropriate security (_excluding cash deposits_) to ensure that, should such an expedited investigation lead to a determination of dumping in respect of such exporters or producers, anti-dumping duties can be collected retroactively from the date of initiation of the review.

Article 10

Retroactivity

10.1 Provisional measures and anti-dumping duties shall only be applied to products which enter for consumption after the time when the decision taken under Article 7.1 and Article 9.1, respectively, enters into force, subject to the exceptions set out in this article.

10.2 Where a final determination of injury (but not of a threat thereof or of a material retardation of the establishment of an industry) is made or, in the case of a final determination of a threat of injury, when the effect of the dumped imports would, in the absence of the provisional measures, have led to a determination of injury, anti-dumping duties may be levied retroactively for the period for which provisional measures, if any, have been applied. If the anti-dumping duty fixed in the final decision is higher than the provisional duty paid or payable, the difference shall not be collected. If the duty fixed in the final decision is lower than the provisional duty paid or payable, or the amount estimated for the purpose of the security, the difference shall be reimbursed or the duty recalculated, as the case may be.

10.3 A definitive anti-dumping duty may be levied on products which were entered for consumption not more than 90 days prior to the date of application of provisional

---

under the circumstances referred to in Article 6.8 are available.

measures, provided that no duties shall be levied
pursuant to this paragraph on products which were entered
for consumption prior to the date of initiation of the
investigation, when the authorities determine :

    i.   either that there is a history of dumping which
        caused injury or that the importer was, or
        should have been, aware that the exporter
        practises dumping and that such dumping would
        cause injury, and

    ii.   that the injury is caused by sporadic dumping
        (massive dumped imports of a product in a
        relatively short time period) to such an extent
        that, in order to, preclude it recurring, it
        appears necessary to levy an anti-dumping duty
        retroactively on those imports.

10.4 Except as provided in paragraph 1 above where a
determination of threat of injury or material retardation
is made (but no injury has yet occurred) a definitive
anti-dumping duty may be imposed only from the date of
the determination of threat of injury or material
retardation and any cash deposit made during the period
of the application of provisional measures shall be
refunded and any bonds released in an expeditious manner.

10.5 Where a final determination is negative, any cash
deposit made during the period of the application of
provisional measures shall be refunded and any bonds
released in an expeditious manner.

Article 11

Duration and review of anti-dumping duties and
price undertakings

11.1 An anti-dumping duty shall remain in force only as
long as and to the extent necessary to counteract dumping
which is causing injury.

11.2 The authorities shall review the need for the
continued imposition of the duty, where warranted, on
their own initiative or, upon request by any interested
party which submits positive information substantiating
the need for a review.[18] If, as a result of the review
under this paragraph, the authorities determine that the
anti-dumping duty is no longer warranted, it shall be
terminated immediately.

11.3 Notwithstanding the provisions of paragraphs 1 and
2, any definitive anti-dumping duty shall be terminated
not later than five years from the date of its imposition

---

[18] The term "review" as used in this Article does not
include a determination of final liability for payment of
anti-dumping duties as provided for in Article 9.3.

0053

unless the authorities determine, on the basis of a
review initiated before that date upon a duly
substantiated request made in accordance with Article 5
by or on behalf of the domestic industry within a
reasonable period of time prior to that date, that the
continued imposition of the duty is necessary to offset
injurious dumping and prevent injury from recurring as a
direct result of the termination. The duty may remain in
force pending the outcome of such a review.

11.4 Any anti-dumping duty extended pursuant to paragraph
3 shall expire after an additional period of 3 years.

11.5 The provisions of Article 6 regarding evidence and
procedure shall apply to any review carried out under
this Article. Any such review shall be carried out
expeditiously and shall be concluded within twelve months
of the date of initiation of the review.

11.6 The provisions of this Article shall apply *mutatis
mutandis* to price undertakings.

Article 12

Measures to prevent circumvention of
definitive anti-dumping duties

12.1 Without prejudice to the initiation of new
investigations under Article 5 and the subsequent
imposition of anti-dumping measures in accordance with
the provisions of this Code where appropriate, an anti-
dumping measure may be imposed on an imported product
other than a like product to one which is subject to a
definitive anti-dumping duty only in accordance with the
provisions of this Article. The authorities may include
within the scope of application of a definitive anti-
dumping duty on an imported product those parts or
components destined for assembly or completion in the
importing country, provided that it has been established
that:

> i. the product assembled or completed from such
> parts or components in the importing country is
> a like product to a product which is subject
> the definitive anti-dumping duty;
> ii. the assembly or completion of the like
> product in the importing country is carried out
> by or on behalf of [19] a party which is related

[19] For the purpose of this Article, an assembly or
completion operation shall be deemed to have been carried
out by or on behalf of a party which is related to an
exporter or producer whose exports of the like product
are subject ot a definitive anti-dumping duty where it is
demonstrated that :-

> 1. the assembly or completion operation has been
> established specifically to meet the requirement of
> the exporter or producer ;

0054

20 to an exporter or producer whose exports of the like product are subject to a definitive anti-dumping duty;

iii. the parts or components have been sourced in the country to which the original anti-dumping duties apply and from the exporter or producer referred to in subparagraph (ii) above.

iv. the assembly operations in the importing country have started or expanded substantially and the imports of those parts or components have increased substantially since the initiation of the investigation which resulted in the definitive anti-dumping duty;

v. the total cost [21] of the parts or components referred to in subparagraph (iii) is not less than [G] per cent of the total cost of all parts or components used in the assembly or completion of the like product [22], and include all the principal components in subassemblies which give the product its essential characteristics, provided that in no case shall the parts and components be included within the scope of definitive measures if the total cost of the parts or components referred to in subparagraph (iii) is not less than [H]

---

2. the product specifications are determined by the exporter or producer and such exporter or producer maintains control of the manufacturing, product design, marketing, distribution, and sourcing of components; and

3. the finished like product is sold under the same brand name through the same channels of distribution as the finished like product subject to the definitive anti-dumping duty.

[20] As defined in Article 4.4
[21] The cost of a part or component is the arm's length acquisition price (i.e. price between unrelated parties and for prices between related parties, they would be regarded as arm's length if they are comparable with prices between unrelated parties) of that part or component excluding all taxes and custom duties, or in the case of related parties where arm's length acquisition price cannot be determined and in the case of parts and components fabricated internally by the party assembling or completing the product in the importing country, the total material, labour and factory overhead costs incurred in such fabrication.
[22] i.e. parts or components purchased in the importing country, parts or components referred to in subparagraph (iii), other imported parts or components (including parts or components imported from a third country) and parts or components fabricated internally.

0055

per cent of the ex-factory cost[23] of the like
product assembled or completed in the territory
of the importing country.

vi. there is indication of dumping as
determined by a comparison between the price of
the product when assembled or completed in the
importing country, and the normal value of the
original product subject to the definitive
anti-dumping order with due allowances and
adjustments to ensure a fair comparison in
accordance with Article 2 ; and

vii. a determination is made that the inclusion
of these parts of components within the scope
of application of the definitive anti-dumping
duty is necessary to offset the continuation of
the injury to the domestic industry producing a
product like the product which is subject to
the definitive anti-dumping duty.

12.2   The authorities may impose provisional measures
in accordance with Article 7.2 when they are satisfied
that there is sufficient evidence that the criteria set
out in paragraphs 12.1 (i)-(vi) are met. Any provisional
duty imposed shall not exceed the definitive anti-dumping
duty in force. The authorities may levy a definitive
anti-dumping duty once all of the criteria in paragraph
12.1 are fully satisfied. The amount of the definitive
anti-dumping duty shall not exceed the amount by which
the normal value of the original product subject to the
definitive anti-dumping order exceeds the price of the
like product when assembled or completed in the importing
country, with due allowances and adjustments to ensure a
fair comparison in accordance with Article 2, as
determined in paragraph 12.1 (vi).

12.3 An anti-dumping measure may be imposed on a
like product to one which is subject to a definitive
anti-dumping duty other than when the like product
has been imported either directly or indirectly to
the importing country from a country in respect of
which a final determination of dumping and injury
has been made pursuant to the provisions of this
Code only in accordance with the provisions of this
Article. The authorities may only include within
the scope of application of a definitive anti-
dumping duty a product exported from a country not
included within the scope of a definitive anti-
dumping duty and assembled or completed in the
exporting country, provided that it has been
established that :

---

[23] i.e. cost of materials, labour, factory overheads and
administration costs where appropriate taking into
account the company's existing practice of costing
inventories.

0056

i.   the product imported is like product to a
product which is subject to the definitive
anti-dumping duty ;

ii.   the assembly or completion of the like
product in the exporting country is carried out
by or on behalf[24] of a party which is related[25]
to an exporter or producer whose exports of the
like product are subject to a definitive anti-
dumping duty ;

iii. the parts or components used in assembling
or completing the product have been sourced in
the country to which the original anti-dumping
duties apply and from the exporter or producer
referred to in subparagraph (ii) above.

iv.   the assembly operations in the exporting
country have started or expanded substantially
and the imports of the like product have
increased substantially since the initiation of
the investigation which resulted in the
definitive anti-dumping duty whilst imports of
the like product form the exporter or producer
referred to in subparagraph (ii) above have
corresponding decrease.

v. the total costr[26] of the parts or components
referred to in subparagraph (iii) is not less than
[J] per cent of the total cost of all parts or
components used in the assembly or completion of the
like product[27], and include all the principal
components in subassemblies which give the product
its essential characteristics,   provided that in no
case shall the parts and components be included
within the scope of definitive measures if the total
cost of the parts or components referred to in sub-
paragraph (iii) is not less than [K] per cent of the
ex-factory cost[28] of the like product assembled or

---

[24] See footnote 19
[25] As defined in Article 4.4
[26] The cost of a part or component is the arm's length
acquisition proce (i.e. price between unrelated parties,
and for prices between related parties, they would be
regarded as arm's length if they are comparable with
prices between unrelated parties) of that part or
component excluding all taxes and custom duties, or in
the case of related parties where arm's length
acquisition price cannot be determined and in the case of
parts and components fabricated internally by the party
assembling or completing the product in the exporting
country, the total material, labour and factory overhead
costs incurred in such fabrication.
[27] i.e. parts or components purcahse in the exporting
country, parts or components referred to in subparagraph
(iii), other imported parts or components (including
parts or components imported from a third country) and
parts or components fabricated internally.
[28] See footnote 23.

0057

completed in the exporting country.

vi. there is indication of dumping, as determined by a comparison between the export price of the assembled or completed like product, and the normal value of the original product subject to a definitive anti-dumping order, with due allowances and adjustments including any differences in assembly costs in the country of export to ensure a fair comparison in accordance with Article 2 ; and,

vii. a determination is made that the inclusion of the like product within the scope of application of the definitive anti-dumping duty is necessary to offset the continuation of the injury to the domestic industry producing a product like the product which is subject to the definitive anti-dumping duty.

12.4 The authorities may impose provisional measures in accordance with Article 7.2 when they are satisfied that the criteria set out in paragraphs 12.3 (i)-(vi) are met. Any provisional duty imposed shall not exceed the definitive anti-dumping duty in force. The authorities may levy a definitive anti-dumping duty once all of the criteria in paragraph 12.3 are fully satisfied. The amount of the definitive anti-dumping shall not exceed the amount by which the normal value determined under subparagraph 12.3 (vi) exceeds the export price of the product when assembled or completed int he exporting country, with due allowances and adjustments to ensure a fair comparison.

12.5 The provisions of this Code concerning rights of interested parties and public notice shall apply mutatis mutandis to investigations carried out under this Article. The provisions of Article 9 and 11 regarding review and refund shall apply where appropriate to anti-dumping duties imposed, pursuant to this Article, on parts and components assembled in the importing country and any such review shall examine whether the condition set out in Article 12.1 and 12.3 are still being met.

T_n / Article 13

Public notice and explanation of determinations

13.1 When the authorities are satisfied that there is sufficient evidence to justify the initiation of an anti-dumping investigation pursuant to Article 5, the Party the products of which are subject to such investigation and other interested parties known to the investigating

0058

authorities to have an interest therein shall be notified
and a public notice shall be given.

    13.1.1 A public notice of the initiation of an
investigation shall contain or otherwise make
available adequate information on the following:

    i.   the name of the exporting country or countries
        and the product involved;

    ii.   the date of initiation of the investigation;

    iii. the basis on which dumping is alleged in the
        application;

    iv.   a summary of the factors which have led to the
        allegation of injury;

    v.   the address to which representations by
        interested parties should be directed;

    vi.   the time limit allowed to interested parties
        for making their views known.

13.2   Public notice shall be given of any preliminary
or final determination, whether affirmative or negative,
of any decisions to accept an undertaking pursuant to
Article 8, of the termination of such an undertaking, and
of the revocation of a determination. Each such notice
shall set forth or otherwise make available in sufficient
detail the findings and conclusions reached on all issues
of fact and law considered material by the investigating
authorities and shall be forwarded to the Party or
Parties the products of which are subject to such finding
or undertaking and to other interested parties known to
have an interest therein.

    13.2.1 A public notice of the imposition of
provisional measures shall set forth or otherwise
make available sufficiently detailed explanations
for the preliminary determinations on dumping and
injury (insofar as there is no separate preliminary
injury determination and a notice thereof) and shall
refer to the matters of fact and law which have led
to arguments being accepted or rejected; the notice
shall, due regard being paid to the requirement for
the protection of confidential information, contain
in particular:

    i.   the names of the suppliers, or when this is
        impracticable, the supplying countries
        involved;

    ii.   a description of the product, which is
        sufficient for customs purposes;

    iii. the margins of dumping established and a full
        explanation of the reasons for the methodology
        used in the establishment and comparison of the

0059

export price and the normal value under Article 2;

iv.   considerations relevant to the injury determination as set out in Article 3, (insofar as there is no separate notice concerning such injury determination);

v.   the main reasons leading to the determination.

13.2.2   A public notice of suspension or conclusion of an investigation in the case of an affirmative determination providing for the imposition of a definitive duty or a price undertaking shall contain or otherwise make available all relevant information on the matters of fact and law and reasons which have led to the imposition of final measures or the acceptance of a price undertaking, due regard being paid to the requirement for the protection of confidential information; it shall in particular contain the information described in sub paragraph 13.2.1 as well as the reasons for the acceptance or rejection of relevant arguments or claims made by the exporters and importers, and the basis for any decision made under Article 6.10.2

13.2.3   A public notice of the termination or suspension of an investigation following the acceptance of an undertaking pursuant to Article 8 shall include or otherwise make available the non-confidential part of the undertaking.

13.3   The provisions of this Article shall apply _mutatis mutandis_ to the initiation and completion of administrative reviews pursuant to Article 11 and to decisions under Article 10 to apply duties retroactively.

Article 14

Judicial Review

Each Party whose national legislation contains provisions on anti-dumping measures shall maintain judicial or administrative tribunals or procedures for the purpose, _inter alia_, of the prompt review of administrative actions relating to initiation, and to preliminary and final determinations and reviews of determinations within the meaning of Article 11 of this Agreement. Such tribunals or procedures shall be independent of the authorities responsible for the determination or review in question.

Article 15

Anti-dumping action on behalf of a third country

0060

[to be added]

Article 16
Developing Countries

[to be added]

PART II

Article 17

Committee on Anti-dumping Practices

[to be added]

Article 18

Consultation, Conciliation and Dispute Settlement

[to be added]

PART III

Final Provisions

[to be added, including transitional provisions]

ANNEX I

Procedures for on-the-spot investigation pursuant to Article 6:7

1. Upon initiation of an investigation, the authorities of the exporting country and the firms known to be concerned should be informed of the intention to carry out on-the-spot investigations.

2. If in exceptional circumstances it is intended to include non-governmental experts in the investigating team, the firms and the authorities of the exporting country should be so informed. Such non-governmental experts should be subject to effective sanctions for breach of confidentiality requirements.

3. It should be standard practice to obtain explicit agreement of the firms concerned in the exporting country before the visit is finally scheduled.

4. As soon as the agreement of the firms concerned has been obtained the investigating authorities should notify the authorities of the exporting country of the names and addresses of the firms to be visited and the dates agreed.

5. Sufficient advance notice should be given to the firms in question before the visit is made.

6. Visits to explain the questionnaire should only be made at the request of an exporting firm. Such a visit may only be made if the authorities of the importing country notify the representatives of the government of the country in question and unless the latter do not object to the visit.

7. As the main purpose of the on-the-spot investigation is to verify information provided or to obtain further details, it should be carried out after the response to the questionnaire has been received unless the firm agrees to the contrary and the government of the exporting country is informed by the investigating authorities of the anticipated visit and does not object to it; further, it should be standard practice prior to the visit to advise the firms concerned of the general nature of the information to be verified and of any further information which needs to be provided, though this should not preclude requests to be made on the spot for further details to be provided in the light of information obtained.

8. Enquiries or questions put by the authorities or firms of the exporting countries and essential to a successful on-the-spot investigation should,

0062

whenever possible, be answered before the visit is
made.

ANNEX II

Best information available in terms of Article 6.8

1.   As soon as possible after the initiation of the
investigation, the investigating authorities should
specify in detail the information required from any
interested party to calculate the dumping margin and/or
to assess the injury suffered by the domestic industry in
the importing country, and the way in which that
information should be structured by the interested party
in its response. The authorities should also ensure that
the party is aware that if information is not supplied
within a reasonable time, the authorities will be free to
make determinations on the basis of the facts available,
which may include as a last resort those contained in the
request for the initiation of the investigation by the
domestic industry.

2.   The authorities may also request that an interested
party provide its response in a particular medium (e.g.
computer tape) or computer language. Where such a
request is made, the authorities should consider the
reasonable ability of the interested party to respond in
the preferred medium or computer language, and should not
request the company to use for its response a computer
system other than that used by the firm. The authority
should not maintain a request for response in a
particular medium or computer language, and the response
need not be given in that particular medium or computer
language, if the interested party does not maintain
computerized accounts or if presenting the response in a
particular medium or computer language would result in an
unreasonable extra burden on the interested party, e.g.
it would entail unreasonable additional cost and trouble.

3.   All information which is verifiable, which is
appropriately submitted so that it can be used in the
investigation without undue difficulties and which is
supplied in a medium or computer language requested by
the authorities, should be taken into account when
determinations are made. If a party does not respond in
the preferred medium or computer language because of the
circumstances set out in paragraph 2, this should not be
considered to significantly impede the investigation.

4.   Where the authorities do not have the ability to
process information if provided in a particular medium
(e.g. computer tape) the information should be supplied
in the form of written material or any other form
acceptable to the authorities.

5.   Even though the information provided may not be
ideal in all respects this should not justify the

0063

authorities from disregarding it provided that the
interested party has acted to the best of its ability.

6.   If evidence or information is not accepted, the
supplying party should be informed forthwith of the
reasons thereof and have an opportunity to provide
further explanations within a reasonable period, due
account being taken of the time-limits of the
investigation. If the explanations are considered by the
authorities as not being satisfactory, the reasons for
rejection of such evidence or information should be given
in any published findings.

7.   If the authorities have to base their
determinations, including those with respect to normal
value, on information from a secondary source, which may
include as a last resort the information supplied in the
request for the initiation of the investigation, they
should do so with special circumspection. In such cases,
the authorities should check the information from other
independent sources at their disposal, such as published
price lists, official import statistics and customs
returns, and from the information obtained from other
interested parties during the investigation. It is
clear, however, that if an interested party does not co-
operate and thus relevant information is being withheld
from the authorities, this situation could lead to a
result which is less favourable to the party than if the
party did co-operate.

0064

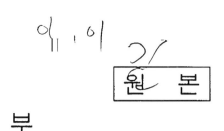

관리 번호	기-285

외 무 부

종 별 :

번 호 : GVW-2287   일 시 : 91 1108 1900

수 신 : 장관(봉기,경기원,재무부,상공부)

발 신 : 주 제네바 대사

제 목 : UR/TNC 던켈 총장 보고서 협상 분야별 분석 평가(규범제정 및 TRIMS)

연: GVW-1514

일반문서로 재분류(1991 .12 . 31.)

연호 규범제정 및 TRIMS 분야에 대한 당관 분석 평가 하기 보고함.

1. 반덤핑

0 의장 보고서는 반덤핑에 대한 주요 쟁점 사항을 열거하고 있는 것으로 향후 협상이 새로운 방향제시를 하고 있는 것은 아님.

0 그러나 반덤핑 협상의 핵심요소를 전통이슈와 뉴이슈간의 균형문제에 두고 있고, 수입국 및 수출국이 주장하는 주요 쟁점 사항을 모두 언급하고 있는 것으로 볼때, 향후 반덤핑 협정이 MINIMUM PACKAGE 로 타결되어서는 안될 것이라는 암시가 내포되어 있는 것으로 보임.

0 그러나 미국.EC 의 소극적입장을 고려할때 어느정도의 타결 수준이 될지는 예측하기 곤란함.

2. 보조금, 상계관세

0 그간 보조금 분야에서는 선진국 특히 미국, EC 간에 의견 대립을 보여온 허용 보조금의 범위 및 국내 보조금 규제 강화 문제가 핵심 쟁점으로 인식되어 왔으나, 아국이 문제를 제기하고 대부분 개도국의 지지를 얻은 개도국 분류등 개도국 우대문제가 이에 못지 않게 중요한 쟁점으로 인식되어진 것으로 평가됨.

3. 세이프가드

0 DUNKEL 의장의 평가는 3 대 주요 쟁점으로 QUOTA MODULATION, 회색 조치 철폐 시한 및 회색조치의 범위를 (W/89), 기타 쟁점으로 보복면제, 국내산업의 양적 정의, 국경조치 한정여부, 최초 및 최대 발동기간 및 개도국 우대문제를 (W/89/ADD.1) 열거함으로써 자신의 주관적 평가를 배제한 중립적 입장에서 현주소를 사실대로 언급

0 QM 문제는 EC 가 동협상 분야 또는 여타 분야에서 상당한반대급부 확보 없이는

통상국	장관	차관	1차보	2차보	경제국	외정실	분석관	청와대
안기부	경기원	재무부	상공부					

PAGE 1   91.11.09   06:57

외신 2과 통제관 BD

0065

쉽게 양보할 사항이 아니며, 회색 조치 철폐, 최초 및 최대 발동기간, 보복면제등은 이미 기본원칙에는 합의가 이루어진 사항으로 다만기간(TIME PERIOD) 관련 구체적 숫치만이 QM 과 연계되어 있기 때문에, 실무 대표급 협상에서 논의 가능한 사항은 주요 쟁점 중에서는 회색조치의 범위 문제,기타 쟁점중에서는 국내 산업의 양적 정의, 국경조치외에 보조금 지급 등 국내조치 인정 여부 문제등이 될것으로 예상

　　O 아국은 기존 혀벼상 전략대로 QM 저지에 중점을 두어 공동 이해국과 긴밀협조하여 대처해 나가되, 여타 협상 요소에는 신축적으로 대응 필요

　　4. TRIMS

　　O 현재까지는 논의되고 있는 근본적인 쟁점을 객관적으로 기술하고 있다고 보여지나 현행 GATT 규정에 위배되는 TRIMS 의 금지 여부, 수출이행 의무의 사용금지 또는 EFFECT TEST 에 의한 규제 여부, EFFECT TEST 시 그방안등이 주요 쟁점이라 기술함으로써 현행 의장 TEXT(10/25 MACIEL 의장 명의로 배포)에 기초하여 작성되어진 것으로 판단됨. 끝

　　(대사 박수길-국장)

　　예고 91.12.31. 까지

주 제 네 바 대 표 부

제네(경) 20644-*1050*   91. 12. 6

수신 : 외무부장관

참조 : 통상국장, 상공부장관

제목 : 반덤핑에 관한 수출국 공동안

연 : GVW-2567

연호 표제건 별첨 송부합니다.

첨부 : 상기문서 2부.   끝.

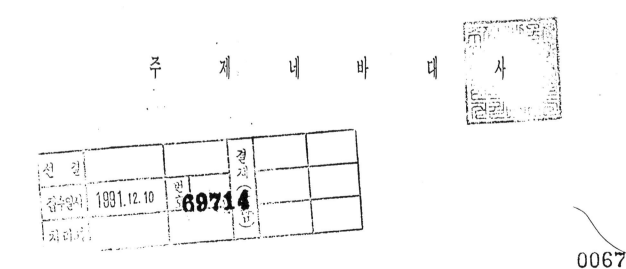

주 제 네 바 대 사

선 결			결 재		
접수일자 1991.12.10		번호 **69714**			
처리과					

0067

SECOND DRAFT (수출국)

25 November 1991

Part I

ANTI-DUMPING CODE

Article 1

Principles

The imposition of an anti-dumping duty is a measure to be taken only under the circumstances provided for in Article VI of the General Agreement and pursuant to investigations initiated[1] and conducted in accordance with the provisions of this Code. The following provisions govern the application of Article VI of the General Agreement in so far as action is taken under anti-dumping legislation or regulations.

Article 2

Determination of Dumping

2.1 For the purpose of this Code a product is to be considered as being dumped, i.e. introduced into the commerce of another country at less than its normal value, if the export price of the product exported from one country to another is less than the comparable price, in the ordinary course of trade, for the like product when destined for consumption in the exporting country.

2.2 When there are no sales of the like product in the ordinary course of trade in the domestic market of the exporting country or when, because of the particular market situation or the low volume of the sales in the domestic market of the exporting country, such sales do not permit a proper comparison, the margin of dumping shall be determined by comparison with (a) a comparable price of the like product when exported to an appropriate third country, provided that this price is representative, or (b) the cost of production in the country of origin plus a reasonable amount for administrative, selling and any other costs and for profits.

---

[1] The term "initiated" as used hereinafter means the procedural action by which a Party formally commences an investigation as provided in Article 5.

0068

2.2.1 Sales of the like product destined for consumption in the domestic market of the exporting country should normally be considered a sufficient quantity for the determination of normal value if they constitute five per cent or more of the sales of the like product to the importing country, provided that a lower ratio should be acceptable where the evidence demonstrates domestic sales at such lower ratio are nonetheless of sufficient magnitude to provide for a proper comparison.

2.2.2 Sales of the like product in the domestic market of the exporting country or sales to a third country at prices below per unit (fixed and variable) cost of production plus selling, general and administrative costs may be treated as not being in the ordinary course of trade by reason of price and may be disregarded in determining normal value only if the authorities[2] determine that (a) such sales are made within an extended period of time in substantial quantities and (b) such sales are at prices which do not provide for the recovery of all actual costs within a period of time which is reasonable for the product and industry under consideration.

2.2.2.1 The extended period of time should be long enough to enable the authorities to discern whether there is a consistent pattern, in terms of quantities, of sales below per unit costs. This period shall not be less than one year and shall in any event be representative for normal selling practices for the product under consideration.

2.2.2.2 Sales below per unit cost are made in substantial quantities when the authorities establish that within the extended period of time the weighted average selling price of all arm's length transactions is below the weighted average unit cost and the volume of those sales shall not be less than 50 percent of all sales.

2.2.2.3 Costs shall normally be calculated on the basis of records kept by the exporter or producer provided that such records are in accordance with the generally accepted accounting principles of the exporting country, and such records reasonably reflect the costs associated with the production and sale of that product. Authorities shall consider all available evidence on the proper allocation of costs, including that which is made available by the exporter or producer in the course of the investigation provided that such

---

[2] When in this Code the term "authorities" is used, it shall be interpreted as meaning authorities at an appropriate, senior level.

allocations have been historically utilized by the exporter or producer, in particular in relation to establishing appropriate amortization and depreciation periods, appropriate cost indexation to compensate for distortions caused by inflation, and allowances for capital expenditures and other development costs.

2.2.2.4 In determining whether the prices provide for recovery of costs within a reasonable period of time, the authorities shall be guided by the pattern of prices and costs pertaining to the product and industry in question. In addition, the following practices shall be observed:

i.   Producers shall be given an opportunity to identify those non-recurring items of cost which benefit current and future production and authorities shall accordingly adjust costs for the period of investigation.

ii. For products in the start-up phase of production the authorities shall determine if prices of the product provide for the recovery of all costs within a reasonable period of time based on actual and verified data of the exporter or producer concerning _inter alia_ cost curve, sales volumes and cost recovery period for a prior generation or model of the product subject to the investigation. When this is not possible, the per unit costs shall reflect the cost at the end of the start-up phase or the lowest cost during the period of investigation if that is earlier, provided that there has been six months of commercial levels of production.

iii. In the case of cyclical industries[3], where sales would otherwise be found to be made at prices below per unit cost of production pursuant to paragraph 2.2.2, the following provisions shall apply:

a) when capacity utilization and per unit costs of production vary significantly over the business cycle and sales prices vary only moderately, the calculation of the per unit cost shall be adjusted to reflect average per unit costs for the

---

[3] Cyclical industries are those characterized by a pattern of recurring market price variations, period of significant sectoral contraction and expansion of demand, sales and production not associated with seasonal variations or other short term factors.

0070

exporter's or producer's most recent five
year period for the facilities involved.

b) when the sales price varies
significantly over the business cycle and
the capacity utilization and the per unit
costs of production vary only moderately,
the calculation of the normal value shall
be adjusted to reflect the average sales
price for the exporter's or producer's
most recent five year period for the
facilities involved.

2.2.2.5 Nothing in this paragraph shall compel
investigating authorities to determine sales in
the domestic market of the exporting country,
by reason of price, not to be in the ordinary
course of trade for the purpose of establishing
normal value.

2.2.3 For the purpose of paragraph 2.2, the amounts
for administrative, selling and any other costs and
for profits shall be the actual amount pertaining to
the production and sale of the like product by the
exporter or producer under investigation. When the
amount for profits cannot be determined, the amount
shall be based on:

i.   the actual profit realized by the same exporter
      or producer in respect of the production and
      sale of products of the same general category
      in the domestic market of the country of
      export, or

ii.   actual and verified data regarding weighted
      average representative profits normally
      realized by other producers in respect of the
      production and sale of the like product in the
      domestic market of the country of export.

2.2.4 If neither of the two methods mentioned in
paragraph 2.2.3 can be used, the amount of profit
shall be based, in order of preference, on:

i   actual and verified data regarding weighted
      average representative profits normally
      realized by other producers on production and
      sales of products of the same general category
      in the domestic market of the country of
      export.

ii.   overall profit realized by the same exporter or
      producer in the country of export.

2.2.5 When there are no sales in the domestic
market of the exporting country the amount for
administrative, selling and any other costs shall be
based on actual data of the exporter or producer
concerned relating to export sales.

0071

2.2.6 The provisions of Article 2.2.2 and its sub-paragraphs shall apply <u>mutatis mutandis</u> also for constructed value calculations.

2.3 In cases where there is no export price or where it appears to the authorities concerned that the export price is unreliable because of association or a compensatory arrangement between the exporter and the importer or a third party, the export price may be constructed on the basis of the price at which the imported products are first resold to an independent buyer, or if the products are not resold to an independent buyer, or not resold in the condition as imported, on such reasonable basis as the authorities may determine.

2.4 A fair comparison shall be made between the export price and the normal value. The two prices shall be compared at the same level of trade, normally at the ex-factory level and in respect of sales made at as nearly as possible the same time. Due allowance shall be made in each case, on its merits, for all differences in conditions and terms of sale, taxation, levels of trade, quantities, physical characteristics, nominal price adjustments to compensate for distortions caused by inflation, and any other differences which are affecting price comparability[4], and shall be based on actual data reflecting the costs and expenses of the exporter or producer under investigation. When considering claims for due allowance, the authorities shall treat individual categories of costs and expenses in the same manner for both the normal value and the export price. In cases referred to in paragraph 3 of Article 2 allowance for costs, including duties and taxes, incurred between importation and resale, and for profits accruing, should also be made. If in these cases price comparability has been affected, the authorities shall establish normal value at the level of trade equivalent to the level of trade of the constructed export price, and make due allowance as warranted under this paragraph. The authorities shall indicate to the parties in question what information is necessary to ensure a fair comparison and shall not impose an unreasonable burden of proof on those parties.

2.4.1 When the price comparison under this paragraph requires a conversion of currencies, such conversion should be made using the rate of exchange on the date of sale[5], provided that when a sale of

---

[4] It is understood that some of the above factors may overlap, and authorities shall ensure that they do not duplicate adjustments that have already been made under this provision.

[5] Normally, the date of sale would be the date of contract, purchase order, order confirmation, or invoice, whichever first establishes the material terms of the sale. Where the importer is related to the exporter or producer under investigation, any conversion of

0072

foreign currency on forward markets is linked to the export sale involved, the rate of exchange in the forward sale shall be used. Fluctuations in exchange rates, whether free or induced, shall not themselves lead to a determination of dumping, and exporters shall be given at least 90 days to adjust export prices to reflect sustained movements during the period of investigation.

2.4.2 In cases where prices vary in both the exporting and importing country, the normal value and the export price shall be compared on the same basis. Where a number of comparisons are involved, and any comparison results in a negative margin, i.e. the export price exceeds the normal value, the authorities must incorporate such negative margins into the calculation of any final dumping margin.

2.5 In the case where the like products are not imported directly from the country of origin but are exported to the country of importation from an intermediate country, the price at which the like products are sold from the intermediate country to the country of importation shall normally be compared with the comparable price in such an intermediate country. However, comparison shall be made with the price of the like product in the country of origin if, for example, the like products are merely trans-shipped through the intermediate country, or there is no comparable price for them in the intermediate country.

2.6 Throughout this Code the term "like product" ("produit similaire") shall be interpreted to mean a product which is identical, i.e. alike in all respects to the product under consideration, or in the absence of such a product, another product which, although not alike in all respects, has characteristics closely resembling those of the product under consideration.

2.7 This Article is without prejudice to the second Supplementary Provision to paragraph 1 of Article VI in Annex I to the General Agreement.

---

currencies shall be based on the rate of exchange prevailing on the date of the sale from the exporter or producer to the importer.

0073

Article 3

Determination of Injury[6]

3.1 A determination of injury for the purposes of
Article VI of the General Agreement shall be based on
positive evidence and involve an objective examination of
(a) the volume of the dumped imports and the effect of
the dumped imports on prices in the domestic market for
like products and (b) the consequent impact of these
imports on domestic producers of such products. It must
be demonstrated that the dumped imports are, through the
effects[7] of dumping, causing injury within the meaning of
this Code.

3.1.1 With regard to the volume of the dumped
imports, the authorities shall consider whether
there has been a significant increase in dumped
imports, either in absolute terms or relative to
production or consumption in the importing country.
With regard to the effect of the dumped imports on
prices, the authorities shall consider whether there
has been a significant price undercutting by the
dumped imports as compared with the price of a like
product of the importing country, or whether the
effect of such imports is otherwise to depress
prices to a significant degree or prevent price
increases, which otherwise would have occurred to a
significant degree. No one or several of these
factors can necessarily give decisive guidance.

3.1.2 The examination of the impact of the dumped
imports on the industry concerned shall include an
evaluation of all relevant economic factors and
indices having a bearing on the state of the
industry: actual and potential decline in sales,
profits, output, market share, productivity, return
on investments, utilization of capacity; factors
affecting domestic prices, including the magnitude
of the margin of dumping; actual and potential
negative effects on cash flow, inventories,
employment, wages, growth, ability to raise capital
or investments.

3.1.3 The demonstration of the existence of a
causal relationship between the dumped imports and
the injury to the domestic industry shall be based
on all the evidence before the authorities. The
authorities shall also take account of evidence

---

[6] Under this Code, the term "injury" shall, unless
otherwise specified, be taken to mean material injury to
a domestic industry, threat of material injury to a
domestic industry or material retardation of the
establishment of such an industry and shall be
interpreted in accordance with the provisions of this
Article.

[7] As set forth in subparagraph 1 and 2 of this paragraph.

0074

pertaining to factors other than the dumped imports which at the same time are injuring the industry, and the injuries caused by these other factors must not be attributed to the dumped imports. Factors which may be relevant in this respect include, _inter alia_, the volume and prices of imports not sold at dumped prices, contraction in demand or changes in the patterns of consumption, practices of domestic producers which are trade restrictive, competition between and among foreign and domestic producers, changes or developments in technology and the export performance and productivity of the domestic industry.

3.2 As a general rule, injury caused by dumped imports from different countries shall be assessed separately. However, in exceptional cases, the authorities may cumulatively assess the effects of such imports for the purposes of injury determination if the following conditions are met :-

    i.   the margin of dumping established in relation to imports from each exporter or producer is more than de minimis as defined in Article 5.8;

    ii.   there is evidence that the imported products compete with each other and with the like domestic product in terms of price, quality, channels of distribution and end-use;

    iii. the volume of dumped imports and the injury attributable to the dumped imports from each country is not negligible as defined in Article 5.8; and

    iv.   imports from countries that are cumulatively assessed shall be imports covered within the same investigation.

In any case even when the above mentioned conditions are met, the authorities shall consider the relative magnitudes of the volumes of imports from each country, and in particular whether there are significant disproportions of the volumes and the trends of volumes of imports from each such country in assessing whether imports from each country make a distinguishable contribution to injury or pose a threat of injury.

3.3 The effect of the dumped imports shall be assessed in relation to the domestic production of the like product when available data permit the separate identification of production in terms of such criteria as: the production process, the producers' realizations, profits. When the domestic production of the like product has no separate identity in these terms the effects of the dumped imports shall be assessed by the examination of the production of the narrowest group or range of products, which includes the like product, for

0075

which the necessary information can be provided.

3.4 A determination of a threat of material injury shall
be based on facts and not merely on allegation,
conjecture or remote possibility. The change in
circumstances which would create a situation in which the
dumping would cause injury must be clearly foreseen and
imminent.

    3.4.1 In making a determination regarding a threat
    of material injury, the authorities should consider
    <u>inter alia</u> such factors as:

    i.   a significant rate of increase of dumped
        imports into the domestic market indicating the
        likelihood of substantially increased
        importations thereof;

    ii.   sufficient freely disposable capacity of the
        exporter indicating the likelihood of
        substantially increased dumped exports to the
        importing country's market taking into account
        the availability of other export markets to
        absorb any additional exports;

    iii. whether imports are entering at prices that
        will have a significant depressing or
        suppressing effect on domestic prices, and
        would likely increase demand for further
        imports; and

    iv.   inventories in the importing country of the
        product being investigated.

No one of these factors by itself can necessarily give
decisive guidance but the totality of the factors
considered must lead to the conclusion that further
dumped exports are imminent and that unless protective
action is taken, material injury would occur.

3.5 With respect to cases where injury is threatened by
dumped imports, the application of anti-dumping measures
shall be considered and decided with special care.

Article 4

Definition of Industry

4.1 In determining injury the term "domestic industry"[8]
shall be interpreted as referring to the domestic
producers as a whole of the like products or to those of

---

[8] The term "domestic industry" shall not be interpreted
so as to include manufacturers of products used as input
products, parts or components of the products in
question, which are not "like products" as defined in
Article 2.6.

0076

them whose collective output of the products constitutes
a major proportion of the total domestic production of
those products, except that

    i.   when producers are related to the exporters or
          importers or are themselves importers of the
          allegedly dumped product, the industry may be
          interpreted as referring to the rest of the
          producers;

    ii.   in exceptional circumstances the territory of a
          Party may, for the production in question, be
          divided into two or more competitive markets
          and the producers within each market may be
          regarded as a separate industry if (a) the
          producers within such market sell all or almost
          all their production of the product in question
          in that market, and (b) the demand in that
          market is not to any substantial degree
          supplied by producers of the product in
          question located elsewhere in the territory.
          In such circumstances, injury may be determined
          to exist even where a major portion of the
          total domestic industry is not injured provided
          there is a concentration of dumped imports into
          such an isolated market and provided further
          that the dumped imports are causing injury to
          the producers of all or almost all of the
          production within such market.

4.2 When the industry has been interpreted as referring
to the producers in a certain area, i.e. a market as
defined in sub-paragraph 1(ii), anti-dumping duties shall
be levied[9] only on the products in question consigned for
final consumption to that area. When the constitutional
law of the importing country does not permit the levying
of anti-dumping duties on such a basis, the importing
Party may levy the anti-dumping duties without limitation
only if (1) the exporters have been given an opportunity
to cease dumping in the area concerned or otherwise give
assurances pursuant to Article 8 of this Code, and
adequate assurances in this regard have not been promptly
given, and (2) such duties cannot be levied on specific
producers which supply the area in question.

4.3 Where two or more countries have reached under the
provisions of Article XXIV:8(a) of the General Agreement
such a level of integration that they have the
characteristics of a single, unified market, the industry
in the entire area of integration shall be taken to be
the industry referred to in paragraph 1 above.

4.4 For the purposes of this Code, producers shall be
deemed to be related to exporters or importers only if
(a) one of them directly or indirectly controls the
other; or (b) both of them are directly or indirectly

---

[9] As used in this Code "levy" shall mean the definitive
or final legal assessment or collection of a duty or tax.

0077

controlled by a third person; or (c) together they directly or indirectly control a third person, provided that there is evidence that the effect of the relationship is such as to cause the producer concerned to behave differently from non-related producers. For the purpose of this Code, control shall not depend on having a certain percentage of shares or stock in another company; one shall be deemed to control another when the former is legally or on a de facto basis in a position to exercise restraint or direction over the latter.

4.5 The provisions of paragraph 3 of Article 3 shall be applicable to this Article.

Article 5

Initiation and Subsequent Investigation

5.1 An investigation to determine the existence, degree and effect of any alleged dumping shall normally be initiated upon a written application by or on behalf of the domestic industry, as defined in Article 4.1[10].

5.2 An application under paragraph 1 shall include evidence of (a) dumping, (b) injury within the meaning of Article VI of the General Agreement as interpreted by this Code and (c) a causal link between the dumped imports and the alleged injury. Simple assertion, unsubstantiated by relevant evidence, cannot be considered sufficient to meet the requirements of this paragraph. The application shall contain the following information as is reasonably available to the applicant :

    i.   identity of the applicant and a description of the volume and value of the domestic production of the like product by the applicant. Where a written application is made on behalf of the domestic industry, the application shall identify the industry on behalf of which the application is made by a list of all domestic producers of the like product (or associations of domestic producers of the like product) and, to the extent possible, a description of the

---

[10] For purposes of this Article the term "a major proportion" in Article 4 shall normally mean 50 per cent of the value of total domestic production of the like product. In exceptional circumstances where the industry is fragmented into a large number of producers who do not have a representative association, the percentage may be less than 50 per cent, but not less than 33 per cent. However an application suppported by more than 33 per cent but less than 50 per cent of the domestic industry shall not be accepted, or a proceeding in repect of such an application shall be terminated, whenever it is established that there is more expressed opposition than expressed support.

0078

volume and value of domestic production of the like product accounted for by such producers;

ii. a complete description of the allegedly dumped product, the names of the country or countries of export or origin in question, the identity of each known exporter or foreign producer and a list of known persons importing the product in question;

iii. information on prices at which the product in question is sold when destined for consumption in the domestic markets of the country or countries of origin or export (or, where appropriate, information on the prices at which the product is sold from the country or countries of origin or export to a third country or countries or on the constructed value of the product) and information on actual export prices or, where appropriate, on the prices at which the product is first resold to an independent buyer in the importing country;

iv. information on the evolution of the volume of the allegedly dumped imports, the effect of these imports on prices of the like product in the domestic market and the consequent impact of the imports on the domestic industry concerned, as demonstrated by relevant factors and indices having a bearing on the state of the domestic industry, such as those listed in Article 3.1.1 and 3.1.2.

5.3 The authorities shall examine the accuracy and adequacy of the evidence provided in the application to determine whether there is sufficient evidence to justify the initiation of an investigation.

5.4 The investigating authorities shall not initiate an investigation unless they have satisfied themselves that a written request for the initiation is made by or on behalf of the domestic industry, as provided in Article 5.1.

5.5 The authorities shall avoid, unless a decision has been made to initiate an investigation, any publicizing of the application for the initiation of an investigation. However, after receipt of a properly documented application and before proceeding to initiate an investigation, the authorities shall notify the government of the exporting country concerned.

5.6 Notwithstanding paragraph 1, if in exceptional circumstances the authorities concerned decide to initiate an investigation without having received a written application by or on behalf of a domestic industry for the initiation of such investigation, they shall proceed only if they have the same evidence of dumping, injury and a causal link, as described in

0079

paragraph 2, to justify the initiation of an investigation.

5.7 The evidence of both dumping and injury shall be considered simultaneously (a) in the decision whether or not to initiate an investigation, and (b) thereafter, during the course of the investigation, starting on a date not later than the earliest date on which in accordance with the provisions of this Code provisional measures may be applied.

5.8 A written application under paragraph 1 shall be rejected and an investigation shall be terminated promptly as soon as the authorities concerned are satisfied that there is not sufficient evidence of either dumping or injury to justify proceeding with the case. There shall be immediate termination in cases where the margin of dumping is de minimis[11], or the volume of dumped imports[12], actual or potential, or the injury is negligible.

5.9 An anti-dumping proceeding shall not hinder the procedures of customs clearance.

5.10 Investigations shall, except in exceptional circumstances, be concluded within one year after their initiation and shall in any case be concluded within 18 months.

Article 6

Evidence

6.1 All interested parties in an anti-dumping investigation shall be given notice of the information which the authorities require and ample opportunity to present in writing all evidence which they consider relevant in respect of the investigation in question.

> 6.1.1 Exporters, importers or foreign producers receiving questionnaires used in an anti-dumping investigation shall be given at least thirty days

---

[11] For the purpose of this paragraph, a de minimis margin of dumping is considered to be less than 5 per cent, expressed as a percentage of the normal value.

[12] The volume of dumped imports shall be regarded as negligible if the total volume of dumped imports from any one country does not constitute more than 5 per cent of the domestic market for the like product in the importing country, unless countries with less than 5 per cent market share collectively account for more than 20 per cent of the domestic market for the like product in the importing country.

0080

for reply[13]. Due consideration should be given to
any request for an extension of the thirty day
period and, upon cause shown, such an extension
should be granted whenever practicable.

6.1.2 Subject to the requirement to protect
confidential information, evidence presented in
writing by one interested party shall be made
available promptly to other interested parties
participating in the investigation.

6.1.3 As soon as an investigation has been
initiated, the authorities shall provide the full
text of the written application received under
Article 5.1 to the known exporters[14] and to the
authorities of the exporting countries and make it
available, upon request, to other interested parties
involved. Due regard shall be paid to the
requirement for the protection of confidential
information as provided for in paragraph 5.

6.2 Throughout the anti-dumping investigation all
interested parties shall have a full opportunity for the
defence of their interests. To this end, the authorities
shall, on request, provide opportunities for all
interested parties to meet those parties with adverse
interests, so that opposing views may be presented and
rebuttal arguments offered. Provision of such
opportunities must take account of the need to preserve
confidentiality and of the convenience to the parties.
There shall be no obligation on any party to attend a
meeting, and failure to do so shall not be prejudicial to
that party's case. Interested parties shall also have
the right, on justification, to present other information
orally.

6.3 Oral information provided under paragraph 2 shall be
taken into account by the authorities only insofar as it
is subsequently reproduced in writing and made available
to other interested parties, as provided for in
subparagraph 1.2 of this Article.

6.4 The authorities shall whenever practicable provide
timely opportunities for all interested parties to see
all information that is relevant to the presentation of
their cases, that is not confidential as defined in

---

[13] As a general rule, the time limit for exporters shall
be counted from the date of the receipt of the
questionnaire, which for this purpose shall be deemed to
have been received one week from the day on which it was
sent to the respondent or transmitted to the appropriate
diplomatic representative of the exporting country.

[14] It being understood that, where the number of
exporters involved is particularly high, the full text of
the request should instead be provided only to the
authorities of the exporting country or to the relevant
trade association.

0081

paragraph 5 and that is used by the authorities in an anti-dumping investigation, and to prepare presentations on the basis of this information.

6.5 Any information which is by nature confidential, (for example, because its disclosure would be of significant competitive advantage to a competitor or because its disclosure would have a significantly adverse effect upon a person supplying the information or upon a person from whom he acquired the information) or which is provided on a confidential basis by parties to an investigation shall, upon good cause shown, be treated as such by the investigating authorities. Such information shall not be disclosed without specific permission of the party submitting it[15].

6.5.1 The authorities shall require interested parties providing confidential information to furnish non-confidential summaries thereof. These summaries shall be in sufficient detail to permit a reasonable understanding of the substance of the information submitted in confidence. In exceptional circumstances, such parties may indicate that such information is not susceptible of summary. In such exceptional circumstances, a statement of the reasons why summarization is not possible must be provided.

6.5.2 If the authorities find that a request for confidentiality is not warranted and if the supplier is either unwilling to make the information public or to authorize its disclosure in generalized or summary form, the authorities are free to disregard such information unless it can be demonstrated to their satisfaction from appropriate sources that the information is correct[16].

6.6 Except in circumstances provided for in paragraph 8, the authorities shall during the course of an investigation satisfy themselves as to the accuracy of the information supplied by interested parties upon which its findings are based.

6.7 In order to verify information provided or to obtain further details, the authorities may carry out investigations in other countries as required, provided they obtain the agreement of the firms concerned and provided they notify the representatives of the government of the country in question and unless the latter object to the investigation. The procedures described in Annex I shall apply to verifications carried out in exporting countries. The authorities shall,

---

[15] Parties are aware that in the territory of certan Parties disclosure pursuant to a narrowly drawn protective order may be required.

[16] Parties agree that requests for confidentiality should not be arbitrarily rejected.

subject to the requirement to protect confidential information, make the result of any verifications available or provide disclosure thereof pursuant to paragraph 9, to the firms to which they pertain and may make such reports available to the applicants.

6.8 In cases in which any interested party refuses access to, or otherwise does not provide, necessary information within a reasonable period, or significantly impedes the investigation, preliminary and final determinations, affirmative or negative, may be made on the basis of the facts available. The provisions of Annex II shall be observed in the application of this paragraph.

6.9 The authorities shall, before a final determination is made, inform all intested parties of the essential facts under consideration which form the basis for the decision whether to apply definitive measures. Such disclosure should take place in sufficient time for the parties to defend their interests.

6.10 The authorities shall determine an individual margin of dumping for each exporter or producer concerned of the product under investigation. In exceptional cases where the number of exporters or producers involved is so large as to make such a determination impracticable, the authorities may limit the investigation either to a reasonable number of interested parties by using statistically valid samples or to the largest percentage of the volume of the exports from the country in question which can reasonably be investigated provided that this volume is sufficiently large to be representative.

 6.10.1 Any selection of exporters or producers made under this paragraph shall be chosen in consultation with and preferably with the consent of the exporters or producers concerned.

 6.10.2 In cases where the authorities have limited their investigation, as provided for in this paragraph, they shall nevertheless determine an individual margin of dumping for any exporter or producer not initially selected who submits the necessary information in time for that information to be considered during the course of the investigation. The authorities shall not discourage such voluntary responses.

6.11 For the purposes of this Code, "interested parties" shall include :

 i. an exporter or foreign producer or the importer of a product subject to investigation, or a trade or business association a majority of the members of which are producers, exporters or importers of such product;

 ii. the government of the exporting country; and

0083

iii. a producer of the like product in the importing country or a trade and business association a majority of the members of which produce the like product in the importing country.

This list shall not preclude Parties from allowing domestic or foreign parties other than those mentioned above to participate as interested parties in the investigation.

6.12 The authorities shall provide opportunities for industrial users of the product under investigation, and for representative consumer organizations in cases where the product is commonly sold at the retail level, to provide information which is relevant to the investigation.

6.13 The authorities shall take due account of any difficulties experienced by interested parties, in particular small companies, in supplying information requested and provide any assistance practicable.

6.14 The procedures set out above are not intended to prevent the authorities of a Party from proceeding expeditiously with regard to initiating an investigation, reaching preliminary or final determinations, whether affirmative or negative, or from applying provisional or final measures, in accordance with relevant provisions of this Code.

Article 7

Provisional Measures

7.1 Provisional measures may be applied only if:

i. an investigation has been initiated in accordance with the provisions of Article 5, a public notice has been given to that effect and interested parties have been given adequate opportunities to submit information and make comments;

ii. a preliminary affirmative determination has been made of dumping and consequent injury to a domestic industry; and

iii. the authorities concerned judge such measures necessary to prevent injury being caused during the period of investigation.

7.2 Provisional measures may take the form of a provisional duty or, preferably, a security - by cash deposit or bond - equal to the amount of the anti-dumping duty provisionally estimated, being not greater than the provisionally estimated margin of dumping. Withholding of appraisement is an appropriate provisional measure,

0084

provided that the normal duty and the estimated amount of the anti-dumping duty be indicated and as long as the withholding of appraisement is subject to the same conditions as other provisional measures.

7.3 Provisional measures shall not be applied sooner than 60 days from the date of initiation of the investigation.

7.4 The application of provisional measures shall be limited to as short a period as possible, not exceeding four months, or on decision of the authorities concerned, upon request by exporters representing a significant percentage of the trade involved, to a period not exceeding six months. When signatories, in the course of the investigation, examine whether a duty lower than a margin of dumping would be sufficient to remove injury, those periods may be six and nine months respectively.

7.5 The relevant provisions of Article 9 shall be followed in the application of provisional measures.

Article 8

Price Undertakings

8.1 Proceedings may[17] be suspended or terminated without the imposition of provisional measures or anti-dumping duties upon receipt of satisfactory voluntary undertakings from any exporter to revise its prices or to cease dumping so that the authorities are satisfied that the injurious effect of the dumping is eliminated. Price increases under such undertakings shall not be higher than necessary to eliminate the margin of dumping. It is desirable that the price increases be less than the margin of dumping if such increases would be adequate to remove the injury to the domestic industry.

8.2 Price undertakings shall not be sought or accepted from exporters unless the authorities of the importing country have made a preliminary affirmative determination of dumping and injury caused by such dumping.

8.3 Undertakings offered need not be accepted if the authorities consider their acceptance impractical, for example, if the number of actual or potential exporters is too great, or for other reasons including reasons of general policy. Should the case arise and where practicable, the authorities shall provide to the exporter the reasons which led them to consider acceptance of an undertaking as inappropriate, and shall,

---

[17] The word "may" shall not be interpreted to allow the simultaneous continuation of proceedings with the implementation of price undertakings except as provided in paragraph 4.

0085

to the extent possible, give the exporter an opportunity
to make comments thereon.

8.4 If the undertakings are accepted, the investigation
of dumping and injury shall nevertheless be completed if
the exporter so desires or the authorities so decide. In
such a case, if a negative determination of dumping or
injury is made, the undertaking shall automatically lapse
except in cases where such a determination is due in
large part to the existence of a price undertaking. In
such cases the authorities may require that an
undertaking be maintained for a reasonable period
consistent with the provisions of this Code. In the
event that an affirmative determination of dumping and
injury is made, the undertaking shall continue consistent
with its terms and the provisions of this Code.

8.5 Price undertakings may be suggested by the
authorities of the importing country, but no exporter
shall be forced to enter into such an undertaking. The
fact that exporters do not offer such undertakings, or do
not accept an invitation to do so, shall in no way
prejudice the consideration of the case. However, the
authorities are free to determine that a threat of injury
is more likely to be realized if the dumped imports
continue.

8.6 Authorities of an importing country may require any
exporter from whom undertakings have been accepted to
provide periodically information relevant to the
fulfillment of such undertakings, and to permit
verification of pertinent data. In case of violation of
undertakings the authorities of the importing country may
take, under this Code in conformity with its provisions,
expeditious actions which may constitute immediate
application of provisional measures using the best
information available. In such cases definitive duties
may be levied in accordance with this Code on goods
entered for consumption not more than ninety days before
the application of such provisional measures, except that
any such retroactive assessment shall not apply to
imports entered before the violation of the undertaking.

8.7 Undertakings shall not remain in force any longer
than anti-dumping duties could remain in force under this
Code. The authorities of an importing country shall
review the need for the continuation of any price
undertaking, where warranted, on their own initiative or
if interested parties so request and submit positive
information substantiating the need for such a review.

Article 9

Imposition and collection of anti-dumping duties

9.1 The decision whether or not to impose an anti-
dumping duty in cases where all requirements for the
imposition have been fulfilled and the decision whether

0086

the amount of the anti-dumping duty to be imposed shall
be the full margin of dumping or less, are decisions to
be made by the authorities of the importing country or
customs territory. It is desirable that the imposition
be permissive in all countries or customs territories
Parties to this Agreement, and that the duty be less than
the margin, if such lesser duty would be adequate to
remove the injury to the domestic industry.

9.2 When an anti-dumping duty is imposed in respect of
any product, such anti-dumping duty shall be collected in
the appropriate amounts in each case, on a non-
discriminatory basis on imports of such product from all
sources found to be dumped and causing injury, except as
to imports from those sources, from which price
undertakings under the terms of this Code have been
accepted. The authorities shall name the supplier or
suppliers of the product concerned. If, however, several
suppliers from the same country are involved, and it is
impracticable to name all these suppliers, the
authorities may name the supplying country concerned. If
several suppliers from more than one country are
involved, the authorities may name either all the
suppliers involved, or, if this is impracticable, all the
supplying countries involved.

9.3 The amount of the anti-dumping duty shall not exceed
the margin of dumping as established under Article 2.

9.3.1 When the amount of the anti-dumping duty is
assessed on a retrospective basis, the determination
of the final liability for payment of anti-dumping
duties shall take place as soon as possible,
normally within 6 months, and in no case more than
12 months, after the date on which a request for a
final assessment of the amount of anti-dumping duty
has been made except where the party concerned avail
itself of judicial review. Any refund shall be made
promptly and normally within 90 days following the
determination of final liability made pursuant to
this subparagraph. In any case where refund is not
made within 90 days, the authorities shall be
obliged to provide explanation if so requested.

9.3.2 When the amount of the anti-dumping duty is
assessed on a prospective basis, provision shall be
made for a prompt refund, upon request, of any duty
paid in excess of the margin of dumping. A refund
of any such duty paid in excess of the actual margin
of dumping shall normally take place within 6
months, and in no case more than 12 months, after
the date on which a request for a refund, duly
supported by evidence, has been made by an importer
of the product subject to the anti-dumping duty
except where the importer avail himself of judicial
review.

9.3.3 When the export price is constructed in
accordance with Article 2.3, any anti-dumping duties
definitively collected in excess of the margin of

0087

dumping shall be reimbursed upon request. In determining whether a reimbursement should be made, authorities should take account of any decrease in normal value, any reduction of costs incurred between importation and resale, and any movement in the resale price which is appropriately reflected in subsequent selling prices, and should first calculate the export price with no deduction for the amount of anti-dumping duties paid. If the result of this calculation indicates an export price that is equal to or greater than the normal value, and there is verifiable evidence that the amount paid for the goods by the importer is equal to or greater than the normal value, then the anti-dumping duty paid shall be reimbursed. If, however, the export price so calculated is less than the normal value, the export price may be redetermined and the amount of anti-dumping duty paid may be treated as a cost incurred between importation and resale.

9.4 When the authorities have determined margins of dumping in accordance with Article 6.10, any anti-dumping duty applied to imports from exporters or producers not included in the examination shall not exceed

    (a)   the weighted average margin of dumping established with respect to the selected exporters or producers, or

    (b)   where the liability for payment of anti-dumping duties is calculated on the basis of a prospective normal value, the difference between the weighted average normal value of the selected exporters or producers and the export prices of exporters or producers not individually investigated,

provided that the authorities shall disregard for the purpose of this paragraph any margins established under the circumstances referred to in Article 6.8[18]. The authorities shall apply individual duties or normal values to imports from any exporter or producer not included in the examination who has provided the necessary information during the course of the investigation. Where the number of exporters or producers is so large that it is impractical to provide them all with individual margins of dumping within the time frame of the investigation, this shall be done as expeditiously as possible taking into account reasonable administrative limits for the authorities concerned.

9.5 When exporters or producers are able to demonstrate that they are new exporters or producers who have not

---

[18] Parties shall come to a general understanding as to the treatment to be accorded to exporters not included in the sampling exercise where only margins established under the circumstances referred to in Article 6.8 are available.

exported the product during the period of investigation and who are not related (as defined in Article 4.4) to any of the exporters or producers subject to anti-dumping duties, the authorities shall carry out an expedited investigation to determine individual margins of dumping for such exporters or producers. No anti-dumping duties shall be levied while this investigation is being carried out. The authorities, however, may withhold appraisement or request appropriate security (excluding cash deposits) to ensure that, should such an expedited investigation lead to a determination of dumping in respect of such exporters or producers, anti-dumping duties can be collected retroactively from the date of initiation of this investigation.

Article 10

Retroactivity

10.1 Provisional measures and anti-dumping duties shall only be applied to products which enter for consumption after the time when the decision taken under Article 7.1 and Article 9.1, respectively, enters into force, subject to the exceptions set out in this article.

10.2 Where a final determination of injury (but not of a threat thereof or of a material retardation of the establishment of an industry) is made or, in the case of a final determination of a threat of injury, when the effect of the dumped imports would, in the absence of the provisional measures, have led to a determination of injury, anti-dumping duties may be levied retroactively for the period for which provisional measures, if any, have been applied. If the anti-dumping duty fixed in the final decision is higher than the provisional duty paid or payable, the difference shall not be collected. If the duty fixed in the final decision is lower than the provisional duty paid or payable, or the amount estimated for the purpose of the security, the difference shall be reimbursed or the duty recalculated, as the case may be.

10.3 A definitive anti-dumping duty may be levied on products which were entered for consumption not more than 90 days prior to the date of application of provisional measures, provided that no duties shall be levied pursuant to this paragraph on products which were entered for consumption prior to the date of initiation of the investigation, when the authorities determine :

    i.   either that there is a history of dumping which caused injury or that the importer was, or should have been, aware that the exporter practises dumping and that such dumping would cause injury, and

    ii.   that the injury is caused by sporadic dumping (massive dumped imports of a product in a relatively short time period) to such an extent

0089

that, in order to preclude it recurring, it appears necessary to levy an anti-dumping duty retroactively on those imports.

10.4 Except as provided in paragraph 1 above where a determination of threat of injury or material retardation is made (but no injury has yet occurred) a definitive anti-dumping duty may be imposed only from the date of the determination of threat of injury or material retardation and any cash deposit made during the period of the application of provisional measures shall be refunded and any bonds released in an expeditious manner.

10.5 Where a final determination is negative, any cash deposit made during the period of the application of provisional measures shall be refunded and any bonds released in an expeditious manner.

Article 11

Duration and review of anti-dumping duties and price undertakings

11.1 An anti-dumping duty shall remain in force only as long as and to the extent necessary to counteract dumping which is causing injury.

11.2 The authorities shall review the need for the continued imposition of the duty, where warranted, on their own initiative or upon request by any interested party which submits positive information substantiating the need for a review[19]. If, as a result of the review under this paragraph, the authorities determine that the anti-dumping duty is no longer warranted, it shall be terminated immediately.

11.3 Notwithstanding the provisions of paragraphs 1 and 2, any definitive anti-dumping duty shall be terminated not later than five years from the date of its imposition unless the authorities determine, on the basis of a review initiated before that date upon a duly substantiated request made by or on behalf of the domestic industry in accordance with Article 5 within a reasonable period of time prior to that date, that the continued imposition of the duty is necessary to offset injurious dumping and prevent injury from recurring as a direct result of the termination or, if a duty lower than the margin of dumping has been applied, that the injury has not been removed. The duty may remain in force pending the outcome of such a review.

---

[19] The term "review" as used in this Article does not include a determination of final liability for payment of anti-dumping duties as provided for in Article 9.3.

0090

11.4 Any anti-dumping duty extended pursuant to paragraph 3 shall expire after an additional period of 3 years.

11.5 The provisions of Article 6 regarding evidence and procedure shall apply to any review carried out under this Article. Any such review shall be carried out expeditiously and shall be concluded within twelve months of the date of initiation of the review.

11.6 The provisions of this Article shall apply mutatis mutandis to price undertakings.

Article 12

Measures to prevent circumvention of definitive anti-dumping duties

12.1 Without prejudice to the initiation of new investigations under Article 5 and the subsequent imposition of anti-dumping measures in accordance with the provisions of this Code where appropriate, an anti-dumping measure may be imposed on an imported product other than a like product to one which is subject to a definitive anti-dumping duty only in accordance with the provisions of this Article. The authorities may include within the scope of application of a definitive anti-dumping duty on an imported product those parts or components destined for assembly or completion in the importing country, provided that it has been established that:

    i.   the product assembled or completed from such parts or components in the importing country is a like product to a product which is subject to the definitive anti-dumping duty;

    ii.   the assembly or completion of the like product in the importing country is carried out by or on behalf of[20] a party

---

[20] For the purpose of this Article, an assembly or completion operation shall be deemed to have been carried out by or on behalf of a party which is related to an exporter or producer whose exports of the like product are subject to a definitive anti-dumping duty where it is demonstrated that :-

1. the assembly or completion operation has been established specifically to meet the requirement of the exporter or producer ;

2. the product specifications are determined by the exporter or producer and such exporter or producer maintains control of the manufacturing, product design, marketing, distribution, and sourcing of components; and

0091

which is related[21] to an exporter or
producer whose exports of the like product
are subject to a definitive anti-dumping
duty;

    iii. the parts or components have been sourced
in the country to which the original anti-
dumping duties apply and from the exporter
or producer referred to in subparagraph
(ii) above;

    iv. the assembly operations in the importing
country have started or expanded
substantially and the imports of those
parts or components have increased
substantially since the initiation of the
investigation which resulted in the
definitive anti-dumping duty;

    v. the total cost[22] of the parts or
components referred to in subparagraph
(iii) is not less than [G] per cent of the
total cost of all parts or components used
in the assembly or completion of the like
product[23], and include all the principal
components in subassemblies which give the
product its essential characteristics,
provided that in no case shall the parts
and components be included within the
scope of definitive measures if the total
cost of the parts or components referred
to in subparagraph (iii) is less than [H]

---

3. the finished like product is sold under the same
brand name through the same channels of distribution
as the finished like product subject to the
definitive anti-dumping duty.

[21] As defined in Article 4.4.

[22] The cost of a part or component is the arm's length
acquisition price (i.e. price between unrelated parties
and for prices between related parties, they would be
regarded as arm's length if they are comparable with
prices between unrelated parties) of that part or
component excluding all taxes and custom duties, or in
the case of related parties where arm's length
acquisition price cannot be determined and in the case of
parts and components fabricated internally by the party
assembling or completing the product in the importing
country, the total material, labour and factory overhead
costs incurred in such fabrication.

[23] i.e. parts or components purchased in the importing
country, parts or components referred to in subparagraph
(iii), other imported parts or components (including
parts or components imported from a third country) and
parts or components fabricated internally.

0092

per cent of the ex-factory cost[24] of the like product assembled or completed in the territory of the importing country;

vi. there is indication of dumping as determined by a comparison between the price of the product when assembled or completed in the importing country, and the normal value of the original product subject to the definitive anti-dumping order with due allowances and adjustments to ensure a fair comparison in accordance with Article 2 ; and

vii. a determination is made that the inclusion of these parts of components within the scope of application of the definitive anti-dumping duty is necessary to offset the continuation of the injury to the domestic industry producing a product like the product which is subject to the definitive anti-dumping duty.

12.2 The authorities may impose provisional measures in accordance with Article 7.2 when they are satisfied that there is sufficient evidence that the criteria set out in paragraphs 12.1(i)-(vi) are met. Any provisional duty imposed shall not exceed the definitive anti-dumping duty in force. The authorities may levy a definitive anti-dumping duty once all of the criteria in paragraph 12.1 are fully satisfied. The amount of the definitive anti-dumping duty shall not exceed the amount by which the normal value of the original product subject to the definitive anti-dumping order exceeds the price of the like product when assembled or completed in the importing country, with due allowances and adjustments to ensure a fair comparison in accordance with Article 2, as determined in paragraph 12.1(vi).

12.3 An anti-dumping measure may be imposed on a like product to one which is subject to a definitive anti-dumping duty other than when the like product has been imported either directly or indirectly to the importing country from a country in respect of which a final determination of dumping and injury has been made pursuant to the provisions of this Code only in accordance with the provisions of this Article. The authorities may only include within the scope of application of a definitive anti-dumping duty a product exported from a country not included within the scope of a definitive anti-dumping duty and assembled or completed in the

---

[24] i.e. cost of materials, labour, factory overheads and administration costs where appropriate taking into account the company's existing practice of costing inventories.

0093

exporting country, provided that it has been
established that :

    i.   the product imported is a like
              product to a product which is subject
              to the definitive anti-dumping duty ;

    ii.   the assembly or completion of the
              like product in the exporting country
              is carried out by or on behalf[25] of a
              party which is related[26] to an
              exporter or producer whose exports of
              the like product are subject to a
              definitive anti-dumping duty ;

    iii. the parts or components used in
              assembling or completing the product
              have been sourced in the country to
              which the original anti-dumping
              duties apply and from the exporter or
              producer referred to in subparagraph
              (ii) above;

    iv.   the assembly operations in the
              exporting country have started or
              expanded substantially and the
              imports of the like product have
              increased substantially since the
              initiation of the investigation which
              resulted in the definitive anti-
              dumping duty whilst imports of the
              like product from the exporter or
              producer referred to in subparagraph
              (ii) above have correspondingly
              decreased;

    v.   the total cost[27] of the parts or
              components referred to in subparagraph
              (iii) is not less than [J] per cent of the
              total cost of all parts or components used
              in the assembly or completion of the like

---

[25] See footnote 20.

[26] As defined in Article 4.4.

[27] The cost of a part or component is the arm's length
acquisition price (i.e. price between unrelated parties,
and for prices between related parties, they would be
regarded as arm's length if they are comparable with
prices between unrelated parties) of that part or
component excluding all taxes and custom duties, or in
the case of related parties where arm's length
acquisition price cannot be determined and in the case of
parts and components fabricated internally by the party
assembling or completing the product in the exporting
country, the total material, labour and factory overhead
costs incurred in such fabrication.

0094

product[28], and include all the principal
components in subassemblies which give the
product its essential characteristics,
provided that in no case shall the parts
and components be included within the
scope of definitive measures if the total
cost of the parts or components referred
to in sub-paragraph (iii) is less than [K]
per cent of the ex-factory cost[29] of the
like product assembled or completed in the
exporting country;

vi. there is indication of dumping, as
determined by a comparison between
the export price of the assembled or
completed like product, and the
normal value of the original product
subject to a definitive anti-dumping
order, with due allowances and
adjustments including any differences
in assembly costs in the country of
export to ensure a fair comparison in
accordance with Article 2 ; and

vii. a determination is made that the
inclusion of the like product within
the scope of application of the
definitive anti-dumping duty is
necessary to offset the continuation
of the injury to the domestic
industry producing a product like the
product which is subject to the
definitive anti-dumping duty.

12.4 The authorities may impose provisional
measures in accordance with Article 7.2 when they
are satisfied that the criteria set out in
paragraphs 12.3 (i)-(vi) are met. Any provisional
duty imposed shall not exceed the definitive anti-
dumping duty in force. The authorities may levy a
definitive anti-dumping duty once all of the
criteria in paragraph 12.3 are fully satisfied. The
amount of the definitive anti-dumping shall not
exceed the amount by which the normal value
determined under subparagraph 12.3 (vi) exceeds the
export price of the product when assembled or
completed in the exporting country, with due
allowances and adjustments to ensure a fair
comparison.

12.5 The provisions of this Code concerning rights
of interested parties and public notice shall apply

---

[28] i.e. parts or components purchased in the exporting
country, parts or components referred to in subparagraph
(iii), other imported parts or components (including
parts or components imported from a third country) and
parts or components fabricated internally.

[29] See footnote 24.

0095

mutatis mutandis to investigations carried out under this Article. The provisions of Article 9 and 11 regarding review and refund shall apply where appropriate to anti-dumping duties imposed, pursuant to this Article, on parts and components assembled in the importing country and any such review shall examine whether the condition set out in Article 12.1 and 12.3 are still being met.

Article 13

Public notice and explanation of determinations

13.1 When the authorities are satisfied that there is sufficient evidence to justify the initiation of an anti-dumping investigation pursuant to Article 5, the Party the products of which are subject to such investigation and other interested parties known to the investigating authorities to have an interest therein shall be notified and a public notice shall be given.

13.1.1 A public notice of the initiation of an investigation shall contain or otherwise make available adequate information on the following:

i. the name of the exporting country or countries and the product involved;

ii. the date of initiation of the investigation;

iii. the basis on which dumping is alleged in the application;

iv. a summary of the factors which have led to the allegation of injury;

v. the address to which representations by interested parties should be directed;

vi. the time limit allowed to interested parties for making their views known.

13.2 Public notice shall be given of any preliminary or final determination, whether affirmative or negative, of any decisions to accept an undertaking pursuant to Article 8, of the termination of such an undertaking, and of the revocation of a determination. Each such notice shall set forth or otherwise make available in sufficient detail the findings and conclusions reached on all issues of fact and law considered material by the investigating authorities and shall be forwarded to the Party or Parties the products of which are subject to such finding or undertaking and to other interested parties known to have an interest therein.

13.2.1 A public notice of the imposition of provisional measures shall set forth or otherwise

0096

make available sufficiently detailed explanations for the preliminary determinations on dumping and injury (insofar as there is no separate preliminary injury determination and a notice thereof) and shall refer to the matters of fact and law which have led to arguments being accepted or rejected; the notice shall, due regard being paid to the requirement for the protection of confidential information, contain in particular:

i.   the names of the suppliers, or when this is impracticable, the supplying countries involved;

ii.   a description of the product, which is sufficient for customs purposes;

iii.   the margins of dumping established and a full explanation of the reasons for the methodology used in the establishment and comparison of the export price and the normal value under Article 2;

iv.   considerations relevant to the injury determination as set out in Article 3, (insofar as there is no separate notice concerning such injury determination);

v.   the main reasons leading to the determination.

13.2.2 A public notice of suspension or conclusion of an investigation in the case of an affirmative determination providing for the imposition of a definitive duty or a price undertaking shall contain or otherwise make available all relevant information on the matters of fact and law and reasons which have led to the imposition of final measures or the acceptance of a price undertaking, due regard being paid to the requirement for the protection of confidential information; it shall in particular contain the information described in subparagraph 13.2.1 as well as the reasons for the acceptance or rejection of relevant arguments or claims made by the exporters and importers, and the basis for any decision made under Article 6.10.2

13.2.3 A public notice of the termination or suspension of an investigation following the acceptance of an undertaking pursuant to Article 8 shall include or otherwise make available the non-confidential part of the undertaking.

13.3 The provisions of this Article shall apply _mutatis mutandis_ to the initiation and completion of administrative reviews pursuant to Article 11 and to decisions under Article 10 to apply duties retroactively.

0097

Article 14

Judicial Review

Each Party whose national legislation contains provisions on anti-dumping measures shall maintain judicial or administrative tribunals or procedures for the purpose, _inter alia_, of the prompt review of administrative actions relating to initiation, and to preliminary and final determinations and reviews of determinations within the meaning of Article 11 of this Agreement. Such tribunals or procedures shall be independent of the authorities responsible for the determination or review in question.

Article 15

Anti-dumping action on behalf of a third country

15.1 An application for anti-dumping action on behalf of a third country shall be made by the authorities of the third country requesting action.

15.2 Such an application shall be supported by price information to show that the imports are being dumped and by detailed information to show that the alleged dumping is causing injury to the domestic industry concerned in the third country. The government of the third country shall afford all assistance to the authorities of the importing country to obtain any further information which the latter may require.

15.3 The authorities of the importing country in considering such an application shall consider the effects of the alleged dumping on the industry concerned as a whole in the third country; that is to say the injury shall not be assessed in relation only to the effect of the alleged dumping on the industry's exports to the importing country or even on the industry's total exports.

15.4 The decision whether or not to proceed with a case shall rest with the importing country. If the importing country decides that it is prepared to take action, the initiation of the approach to the CONTRACTING PARTIES seeking their appproval for such action shall rest with the importing country.

Article 16

Developing Countries

16.1 It is recognized that special regard must be given by developed countries to the special situation of

0098

developing countries when considering the application of anti-dumping measures under this Code. Possibilities of constructive remedies provided for by this Code shall be explored before applying anti-dumping duties where they would affect the essential interests of developing countries.

16.2 In developing countries, governments play a large role in promoting economic growth and development in accordance with their national priorities, and their economic regimes for the export sector resulting <u>inter alia</u> in different cost structures. This Agreement is not intended to prevent developing countries from adopting measures in this context, including measures in the export sector, as long as they are used in a manner which is consistent with the provisions of the General Agreement, as applicable to these countries.

16.3 In the case of imports from a developing country, the fact that the export price may be lower than the comparable price for the like product when destined for domestic consumption in the exporting country does not <u>per se</u> justify an investigation or the determination of dumping unless the other factors mentioned in Article 5.1 are also present. Due consideration should be given to all cases where, because special economic conditions affect prices in the home market, these prices do not provide a commercially realistic basis for dumping calculations. In such cases the normal value for the purposes of ascertaining whether the goods are being dumped shall be determined by methods such as a comparison of the export price with the comparable price of the like product when exported to any third country or with the cost of production of the exported goods in the country of origin plus a reasonable amount for administrative, selling and any other costs and for profits.

16.4 It is recognized that developing countries may face special problems initially in adapting their legislation to the requirements of the Code, including administrative and infrastructural problems, in carrying out anti-dumping investigations initiated by them. Accordingly, the Committee on Anti-Dumping Practices may grant, upon specific request and on conditions to be negotiated on a case-by-case basis, time-limited exceptions in whole or in part from obligations which relate to investigations undertaken by a developing country under this Agreement.

16.5 Developed countries Parties to this Agreement shall endeavour to furnish, upon request and on terms to be agreed, technical assistance to developing countries Parties to this Agreement, with regard to the implementation of this Agreement including training of personnel, and the supplying of information on methods, techniques and other aspects of conducting investigations on dumping practices.

0099

PART II

Article 17

Committee on Anti-dumping Practices

17.1   There shall be established under this Agreement a Committee on Anti-Dumping Practices (hereinafter referred to as the "Committee") composed of representatives from each of the Parties. The Committee shall elect its own Chairman and shall meet not less than twice a year and otherwise as envisaged by relevant provisions of this Agreement at the request of any Party. The Committee shall carry out responsibilities as assigned to it under this Agreement or by the Parties and it shall afford Parties the opportunity of consulting on any matters relating to the operation of the Agreement or the furtherance of its objectives. The GATT secretariat shall act as the secretariat to the Committee.

17.2   The Committee may set up subsidiary bodies as appropriate.

17.3   In carrying out their functions, the Committee and any subsidiary bodies may consult with and seek information from any source they deem appropriate. However, before the Committee or a subsidiary body seeks such information from a source within the jurisdication of a Party, it shall inform the Party involved. It shall obtain the consent of the Party and any firm to be consulted.

17.4   Parties shall report without delay to the Committee all preliminary or final anti-dumping actions taken. Such reports will be available in the GATT secretariat for inspection by government representatives. The Parties shall also submit, on a semi-annual basis, reports of any anti-dumping actions taken within the preceding six months.

Article 18

Consultation, Conciliation and Dispute Settlement

[to be added]

PART III

Final Provisions

[to be added, including transitional provisions]

0100

ANNEX I

Procedures for on-the-spot investigation pursuant to Article 6.7

1. Upon initiation of an investigation, the authorities of the exporting country and the firms known to be concerned should be informed of the intention to carry out on-the-spot investigations.

2. If in exceptional circumstances it is intended to include non-governmental experts in the investigating team, the firms and the authorities of the exporting country should be so informed. Such non-governmental experts should be subject to effective sanctions for breach of confidentiality requirements.

3. It should be standard practice to obtain explicit agreement of the firms concerned in the exporting country before the visit is finally scheduled.

4. As soon as the agreement of the firms concerned has been obtained the investigating authorities should notify the authorities of the exporting country of the names and addresses of the firms to be visited and the dates agreed.

5. Sufficient advance notice should be given to the firms in question before the visit is made.

6. Visits to explain the questionnaire should only be made at the request of an exporting firm. Such a visit may only be made if the authorities of the importing country notify the representatives of the government of the country in question and unless the latter do not object to the visit.

7. As the main purpose of the on-the-spot investigation is to verify information provided or to obtain further details, it should be carried out after the response to the questionnaire has been received unless the firm agrees to the contrary and the government of the exporting country is informed by the investigating authorities of the anticipated visit and does not object to it; further, it should be standard practice prior to the visit to advise the firms concerned of the general nature of the information to be verified and of any further information which needs to be provided, though this should not preclude requests to be made on the spot for further details to be provided in the light of information obtained.

8. Enquiries or questions put by the authorities or firms of the exporting countries and essential to a successful on-the-spot investigation should, whenever possible, be answered before the visit is made.

0101

<u>ANNEX II</u>

<u>Best information available in terms of Article 6.8</u>

1.   As soon as possible after the initiation of the investigation, the investigating authorities should specify in detail the information required from any interested party to calculate the dumping margin and/or to assess the injury suffered by the domestic industry in the importing country, and the way in which that information should be structured by the interested party in its response. The authorities should also ensure that the party is aware that if information is not supplied within a reasonable time, the authorities will be free to make determinations on the basis of the facts available, which may include as a last resort those contained in the request for the initiation of the investigation by the domestic industry.

2.   The authorities may also request that an interested party provide its response in a particular medium (e.g. computer tape) or computer language. Where such a request is made, the authorities should consider the reasonable ability of the interested party to respond in the preferred medium or computer language, and should not request the company to use for its response a computer system other than that used by the firm. The authority should not maintain a request for response in a particular medium or computer language, and the response need not be given in that particular medium or computer language, if the interested party does not maintain computerized accounts or if presenting the response in a particular medium or computer language would result in an unreasonable extra burden on the interested party, e.g. it would entail unreasonable additional cost and trouble.

3.   All information which is verifiable, which is appropriately submitted so that it can be used in the investigation without undue difficulties and which is supplied in a medium or computer language requested by the authorities, should be taken into account when determinations are made. If a party does not respond in the preferred medium or computer language because of the circumstances set out in paragraph 2, this should not be considered to significantly impede the investigation.

4.   Where the authorities do not have the ability to process information if provided in a particular medium (e.g. computer tape) the information should be supplied in the form of written material or any other form acceptable to the authorities.

5.   Even though the information provided may not be ideal in all respects this should not justify the authorities from disregarding it provided that the interested party has acted to the best of its ability.

6.   If evidence or information is not accepted, the supplying party should be informed forthwith of the

0102

reasons thereof and have an opportunity to provide further explanations within a reasonable period, due account being taken of the time-limits of the investigation. If the explanations are considered by the authorities as not being satisfactory, the reasons for rejection of such evidence or information should be given in any published findings.

7.   If the authorities have to base their determinations, including those with respect to normal value, on information from a secondary source, which may include as a last resort the information supplied in the request for the initiation of the investigation, they should do so with special circumspection. In such cases, the authorities should check the information from other independent sources at their disposal, such as published price lists, official import statistics and customs returns, and from the information obtained from other interested parties during the investigation. It is clear, however, that if an interested party does not co-operate and thus relevant information is being withheld from the authorities, this situation could lead to a result which is less favourable to the party than if the party did co-operate.

0103

외 무 부

종 별 :

번 호 : GVW-2567   일 시 : 91 1206 1200

수 신 : 장관(통기, 경기원, 상공부)

발 신 : 주 제네바 대사

제 목 : UR/반덤핑 관련 수출국 회의

표제 회의가 12.5 아국등 7개 수출국이 참여 홍콩대표부에서 개최된바 요지 하기임.

1. 반덤핑 협상 관련 개별 쟁점에 대한 수출국의 공동기술문안 작성 관련 홍콩이제시한 문제 (91.11.8 GVW-2289 참조)를 기초로 그간 수출국회의에서 논의된 결과를토대로 수정안을 마련함.(파편송부 예정) 동 수정안은 개개 쟁점에 대한 기술적 용어 및 문장의 개선,명료화를 위한 것이며, 수출국 공동입장으로 UR협상에 공식으로 제시기 위한 것은 아니라는 전제하에 작성된 것임.

2. COUNTRY HOPPING 관련 구체적 요건으로 제 3국에 기존 생산 시설의 존재, 원수출국 수출 감소와 조사 개시가 원덤핑 관세 부과후 6개월내에 이루어져야 한다는 3가지 요건을 제시하여야 한다는데 의견을 같이 하고 기술적 문안 작업을 하기로함.

3. RULES OF ORIGIN 에 의한 덤핑 관세 부과

0 아국은 RULES OF ORIGIN 에 의한 덤핑 관세부과는 EC 의 자의적인 동제도 운영, UR 이후 조화된 국제 원산지 기준의 채택 여부 불투명및 채택시에도 어느정도 명료하고 객관적인 국제기준이 설정될수 있을지 등이 의문시되므로 RULES OF ORIGIN 에의한 덤핑 관세 부과제도보다는 제 3국 우회 덤핑이 적절한 요건과 기준이 설정될시 덜 위험할 것이라는 의견을 밝힘.

0 제 3국 우회 덤핑에 관한 MCPHAIL III 초안에 의할시 RULES OF ORIGIN 에 의한 덤핑관세부과가 금지될수 있는지에 대해 각국은 MCPHAILIII (12.3 서문)가 이를 염두에 둔것이라는 점에 대체적으로 같은 의견을 보였으나 이는 추후 더 검토키로 함.

4. 12.8 일 주 반덤핑 비공식 회의 일정

RAMSAUER 규범제정 의장 보좌관 주재로 반덤핑 비공식 회의가 12월 10,- 13일개최 될 예정임.끝

통상국   2차보   경기원   상공부

PAGE 1   91.12.07   08:56 DQ

외신 1과 통제관

0104

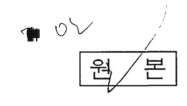

외 무 부

종 별 :

번 호 : GVW-2289 　　　　　　　일 시 : 91 1108 1900

수 신 : 장관(봉기,상공부)

발 신 : 주제네바대사

제 목 : UR/반덤핑 협상 관련

　　　0 반덤핑 협상 관련 홍콩이 작성한 DRAFT 를 송부함.(11.8 파편송부)

　　　0 본 DRAFT 는 브랏셀회의시 작성된 문안(TRANCHE 1 및 TRANCHE 2중 일부)과 주요미결 쟁점에 대한 수출개도국 입장을 토대로 구체적 문장 또는 용어의 기술적 개선및 명료화에 중점을 둔것임

　　　0 주요미결 쟁점사항에 대해서는 MCPHAIL III중 개도국이 선호하는 OPTION 에 기초를 두고 있으며 수출개도국이 주장하는 입장중 MCPHAIL 3 에 반영되어 있지 않은사항이 일부 반영되어있음.

　　　- 구성가격(이윤) 계산시 우선 순위설정(2.2.3CARLISLE 2 에 근거)

　　　- RESIDUAL DUTY 계산시 BIA 불포함 및 영 또는 최소 마진율 포함(9.4)

　　　- SUNSET 의 최대기능 기간을 8년으로 함.(11.3)

　　　- 우회덤핑에 있어 'ON BEHALF OF ' 및 COST개념의 정립(12조)

　　　0 본 DRAFT 는 UR 마지막 단계에서 미국,EC가 공동입장을 제시할 가능성에 대비수출국의 공동입장과 구체적 LANGUAGE 를 제시할 필요성에 대비하기 위한 것으로내주에 본 DRAFT를 기초로 구체적 검토를 하기로 함.끝

　　　(대사 박수길-국장)

통상국　　　2차보　　　상공부

PAGE 1 　　　　　　　　　　　　　　　　　　91.11.09　　09:10 DQ

　　　　　　　　　　　　　　　　　　　　　　외신 1과　통제관

　　　　　　　　　　　　　　　　　　　　　　　　　0105

외 무 부

종 별 :

번 호 : GVW-2372

일 시 : 91 1120 1030

수 신 : 장관(봉이,경기원,재무부,상공부)

발 신 : 주 제네바 대사

제 목 : UR/반덤핑 협상관련

9.19 표제협상과 관련 규범 제정 그룹의장보좌관(RAMSAUER 스위스 공사)과 가진협의 결과하기 보고함.(추준석 상공부 국제 협력관,강상무관 참석)

0 RAMSAUER 보좌관은 반덤핑 분야에 관한 각국입장을 명확히 알기 위해 19, 20 양일간 주요국(16개국정도)과 집중적인 개별 협의를 할예정이라고 하고, 이협의 결과를 토대로 추후 협상전략 및 일정등을 결정할 것이라고 함.

0 동인은 덤핑 협상에 있어서는 목표수준에 대한 공통된 견해가 없다(NO COMMONVIEW ABOUT FRAMEWORKOF SIZE)고 하고 각국이 어느정도의 수준을 요구하고있는지를파악하기를 원한다고 한후 구체적 이슈로는 AVERAGING, 원가이하 판매, 구성가격,피해결정, 제소자 자격, 최소 덤핑 마진 및 시장점유율, SAMPLING (RESIDUEAL DUTY),신규 수출자취급, SUNSET, 우회덤핑 및 소급적용(COUNTRYHOPPING 관련), 분쟁해결이주요미결과제라고 한후 아국의 의견 개진을 요구함.

0 이에 대해 아국은 덤핑협상의 중요성,전통이슈에서 현저한 개선이 있는 경우우회덤핑을 협상할 용의가 있단 점, MINIMUMPACKAGE 는 의미가 없다는 점을 강조하였음.

0 구체적 이슈로는 구성가격(ACTUAL DATA 사용),AVERAGING, 원가이하 판매, 피해누적, DE MINIMUS,SUNSET 가 중요함을 강조하고 기타 제소자 자격,RESIDUAL DUTY, 신규 수출자 취급 문제가 해결되어야 함을 주장하고 개개 이슈에 대해 아국입장을 소상히 개진함.

0 이에 대해 RAMSAUER 보좌관은 우회덤핑,덤핑결정, THE MINIMIS 가 협상의 중요3대요소라고 생각한다고 하고 원가 이하 판매 및 DEMINIMUS 는 미국.EC(특히 미국)가의회문제등으로 받아들이기 굉장히 어려운 문제로 생각한다고 함.

0 이에 대해 아국은 DE MINIMIS 의 경우 기준의 계량화가 중요하므로 미국.EC 가

통상국   2차보   청와대   안기부   경기원   재무부   상공부

91.11.21   08:39 ED

외신 1과 통제관

0106

계량화의 원칙에 찬성하면 구체적 숫자는 협상할 용의가 있음을 밝히고 덤핑 마진의 경우 5 퍼센트, 시장PTWM유율의 경우 3 퍼센트(개별국가 경우) 20퍼센트(전체수출국 경우)를 협상의 기초로제시함.

0 원가이하 판매의 경우는 START UP COST 및CYCLYCAL INDUSTRY(불경기의 경우)의비용조정이 중요함을 강조함.

0 제 3국 우회 수출 및 COUNTRY HOPPING 의 경우 이중 어느것이 받아들이기 용이한지를 RAMSOUER공사가 질의한바, 이에 대해 아국은 기준 및조건의 객관성, 엄격성과 구체수단의 2가지차원에서 이를 검토하여야 한다는 점과 COUNTRYHOPPING 의 경우구제수단은 관세의 소급적용에 한하나 구체저 LPA건과 기준에 대해서는 아직 충분한논의가 이루어지지 못했다는 점이 문제라고 지적함.

0 기타 구체적 이슈에 대해 아국이 밝힌 중요입장은 다음과 같음.

- 구성가격 산정에 있어서 ACTUAL DATA 의 사용이가장 중요하며, 이운 사정시 사용가능한 여러가지방법의 우선 순위 설정도 중요함.

- AVERAGING 의 경우 선진국이 주장하는 3가지유형의 TARGETTING 을 논의할 용의가 있음.

- DE MINIMUS 의 경우 시장점유율은 낮으나 덤핑마진이 큰 경우는 조사 개시 종료 대상에서 제외하는 문제를 검토 용의

- SUNSET 의 경우 원칙적으로 5년으로 하되 어떤 경우에도 최장 8년을 초과하지않는다는 새로운조항 설정 필요

- 우회 덤핑의 경우 원 수출국으로 수입된 부품의총 부품에 대한 비율은 75 퍼센트, 수입국내부가가치의 최종 제품 비용에 대한 비율 20퍼센트를 제시함.

(대사 박수길-국장)

외 무 부

종 별 :

번 호 : GVW-2445   일   시 : 91 1126 1500

수 신 : 장 관(통기, 경기원, 상공부)

발 신 : 주 제네바대사

제 목 : 갓트 규범강화에 대한 공동입장

　　아국을 포함한 30 개국이 UR 협상중 규범강화(세이 프가드, 보조금, 상계관세, 반덤핑, BOP 및 TRIMS 분야등)의 중요성을 강조한 공동입장 을 별첨과 같이 마련하여 11.25(월)던켈 총장에게 전달하였는 바, 동 자료를 국내홍보등에 적의 활용바람.

　　첨부: 공동입장 1부. 끝

　　(GVW(F)-537) 대면정

　　(대사 박수길-국장)

통상국   2차보   경기원   상공부

PAGE 1   91.11.27   15:01 WH

외신 1과 통제관

0108

Gw(21)-537 1126 1500

COMMUNICATION

Gw-2445 청부

ON GATT RULES AND DISCIPLINES

The following countries/participants in the Uruguay Round
negotiations:

Argentina,   Austria,   Brazil,   Chile,   Colombia,
Czechoslovakia, Egypt, El Salvador, Finland, Hong Kong,
Iceland, India, Indonesia, (Korea,) Malaysia, Mexico,
Morocco, Nicaragua, Nigeria, Norway, Pakistan, Peru,
Philippines, Poland, Singapore, Sweden, Switzerland,
Thailand, Uruguay and Venezuela

express their deep preoccupation about the state of the Uruguay
Round negotiation on rules and underline herewith the overall
interests of the trading community for strengthened GATT rules
and disciplines.

The participants to the present statement welcome the political
commitment expressed by the United States and the European
Community at the recent Summit in the Hague to intensify the
negotiation process in order to achieve progress mainly in the
difficult fields of market access, agriculture and services as
well as to strengthen GATT rules and disciplines. In this context participants to the present Declaration support the statement made by the Chairman of the Trade Negotiations Committee at
its last meeting on November 7th, that the strengthening of rules
and multilateral disciplines play an ever more important role in
world trade.

The multilateral trading system based on the principles of
MFN and non-discrimination is confronted today with major
challenges which demand an additional future-oriented negotiating
effort on rules:

- the globalisation of markets requires a predictable and
  stable multilateral trading system, taking account of the
  interests of both importing and exporting countries;

- the most impressive efforts made by many developing
  countries and economies in transition in Central and
  Eastern Europe to reform their economies require a sound
  legal basis in the multilateral trading system, as a
  recognition of their effort and as a guarantee against
  setbacks;

- trade is one of the most powerful engines of growth and
  development. In this context, unambiguous and strengthened
  GATT rules and disciplines are the basis for increased
  market access opportunities, which are so decisive for the
  economic well-being of all contracting parties in GATT;

537-2-1

OAR FGH   UOI   '91-11-27 01:55

2

- and indeed, strengthened GATT rules and disciplines are the
   key to a revitalized multilateral trading system. They
   should bring an end to unilateralism, thereby significantly
   contributing to make the multilateral trading system more
   reliable.

The participants of the present communication, which have
made major contributions in the various areas of the Round, are
of the view that, in the given time frame, an additional
negotiating effort should be directed towards clearer and more
precise rules, with a view to allow a major step forward in the
process of progressive liberalization.

The following elements are particularly important for
success in the negotiations on rules:

First, an unambiguous non-discriminatory safeguard
mechanism and a clear, staged and binding program for
dismantling grey areas measures.

Second, clear, strengthened and balanced disciplines in the
area of subsidies and countervailing measures, with a view
to providing for fair and open competition on the basis of
concepts, elements and the structure contained in the
existing framework proposal.

Third, a revision of the anti-dumping code which ensures
that anti-dumping procedures are not abused either for
harassment or as disguised instruments for protectionism
while at the same time providing that clear and genuine
circumvention of anti-dumping measures would be prevented
and subject to similar disciplines.

Fourth, a strengthened mechanism for the application of
trade measures taken for balance-of-payments purposes.

Fifth, balanced results in the area of TRIMs, which would
effectively address trade distorting investments measures.

A substantial package on rules remains the cornerstone of
the multilateral trading system. Such a package is essential so
as to ensure the efficient functioning of the GATT dispute-
settlement mechanism and to preserve the rights of smaller and
medium sized contracting parties. It is therefore the overall
interest of the trading community that GATT rules emerging from
the Uruguay Round should strengthen the multilateral trading
system.

0110

537-2-2

082 P05   HOI

외 무 부

종 별 :

번 호 : GVW-2477

수 신 : 장 관(통기,경기원,상공부)

발 신 : 주 제네바대사

제 목 : 반덤핑에 관한 WORKING PAPER

일 시 : 91 1127 1900

연: GVW-2464(11.27)

표제건 FAX 송부함.

첨부:반덤핑 WORKING PAPER 1부

(GVW(F)-0549).끝

(대사 박수길-국장)

통상국	2차보	경기원	상공부				

PAGE 1

91.11.28   08:11 WH

외신 1과 통제관

0111

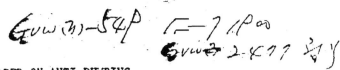

DRAFT WORKING PAPER ON ANTI-DUMPING

The attached paper reflects the present state of the negotiations on anti-dumping. It is an updated version of the draft text on anti-dumping dated 23 November 1990 ("McPhail III") which has been the primary basis for the drafting work done at the Brussels Ministerial Meeting as well as for the informal consultations on anti-dumping that started in September 1991.

The paper includes the results of the drafting process which took place at the Brussels Ministerial Conference as well as further changes resulting from the drafting process of late October this year. The respective paragraphs are marked by a vertical line at the left-hand margin of the pages. Changes made with respect to the original draft text of 23 November 1990 are marked by an asterisk (*).

On a significant number of substantive points discussed in the recent consultations divergent views have been expressed. The relevant parts of the paper are marked by double asterisks (**), or appear in square brackets as in the original draft text.

The major open issues which have emerged from the recent consultations are:

- Averaging;
- Sales below cost of production;
- Constructed value;
- Factors to be considered in the injury analysis;
- Criteria for determining whether a petition is filed "on behalf of" a domestic industry;
- De minimis margins of dumping, quantification of negligible import volumes and cumulative assessment of injury;

- Sampling and residual duties, treatment of new exporters;
- Sunset clause;
- Anti-circumvention measures in case of assembly operations in importing countries;
- Anti-circumvention measures in case of assembly operations in third countries;
- Retroactivity in case of "country hopping";
- Dispute settlement.

Negotiations will have to concentrate on these issues for which urgent political decisions are required.

PART I

ANTI-DUMPING CODE

Article 1

Principles

The imposition of an anti-dumping duty is a measure to be taken only under the circumstances provided for in Article VI of the General Agreement and pursuant to investigations initiated[1] and conducted in accordance with the provisions of this Code. The following provisions govern the application of Article VI of the General Agreement in so far as action is taken under anti-dumping legislation or regulations.

---

[1] The term "initiated" as used hereinafter means the procedural action by which a Party formally commences an investigation as provided in Article 5.

ADC2/NZ.III-2

0113

Article 2

Determination of Dumping

2.1 For the purpose of this Code a product is to be considered as being dumped, i.e. introduced into the commerce of another country at less than its normal value, if the export price of the product exported from one country to another is less than the comparable price, in the ordinary course of trade, for the like product when destined for consumption in the exporting country.

2.2 When there are no sales of the like product in the ordinary course of trade in the domestic market of the exporting country or when, because of the particular market situation or the low volume of the sales in the domestic market of the exporting country, such sales do not permit a proper comparison, the margin of dumping shall be determined by comparison with (a) a comparable price of the like product when exported to an appropriate third country, provided that this price is representative, or (b) the cost of production in the country of origin plus a reasonable amount for administrative, selling and any other costs and for profits.

**2.2.1 Sales of the like product destined for consumption in the domestic market of the exporting country shall be considered a sufficient quantity for the determination of normal value if they constitute five per cent or more the sales of the like product to the importing country.

**2.2.2 Sales of the like product in the domestic market of the exporting country or sales to a third country at prices below per unit (fixed and variable) cost of production plus selling, general and administrative costs may be treated as not being in the ordinary course of trade by reason of price and may be disregarded in determining normal value only if the authorities[2] determine that (a) such sales are made within an extended period of time in substantial quantities and (b) such sales are at prices which do not provide for the recovery of all costs within a reasonable period of time.

Sales below cost

**2.2.2.1 The extended period of time should be long enough to enable the authorities to discern whether there is a consistent pattern, in terms of quantities, of sales below per unit costs. This period should normally be one year but shall in no case be less than six months.

---

[2]When in this Code the term "authorities" is used, it shall be interpreted as meaning authorities at an appropriate, senior level.

**2.2.2.2 Sales below per unit cost are made in substantial quantities when the authorities establish that within the extended period of time the weighted average selling price of all arm's length transactions is below the weighted average unit cost, or the volume of those sales represents a substantial proportion[3] of all sales.

2.2.2.3 Costs shall normally be calculated on the basis of records kept by the exporter or producer provided that such records are in accordance with the generally accepted accounting principles of the exporting country, and such records reasonably reflect the costs associated with the production and sale of that product. Authorities shall consider all available evidence on the proper allocation of costs, including that which is made available by the exporter or producer in the course of the investigation provided that such allocations have been historically utilized by the exporter or producer, in particular in relation to establishing appropriate amortization and depreciation periods and allowances for capital expenditures and other development costs.

[2.2.2.4 In determining whether the prices provide for recovery of costs within a reasonable period of time, taking account of whether prices prevailing at the time of sale are below weighted average costs, the authorities shall be guided by the pattern of prices and costs pertaining to the product and industry in question. In addition, unless already reflected in the cost allocations, the following practices should be observed:

(i)   Producers shall be given an opportunity to identify those non-recurring items of cost which benefit current and future production and authorities shall adjust costs for the period of investigation appropriately.

(ii)   For products in the start-up phase of production the authorities shall determine if prices of the product provide for the recovery of all costs within a reasonable period of time based on actual and verified data of the exporter or producer concerning, inter alia, cost curve, sales volumes and cost recovery period for a prior generation or model of the product subject to the investigation. When this is not possible the per unit costs shall reflect the cost at the end of the start-up phase, or the lowest cost during the period of investigation, if that is earlier.

---

[3]For the purpose of this paragraph, a substantial proportion is not less than [A] per cent.

(iii) In the case of cyclical industries[4], where sales would otherwise be found to be made at prices below per unit cost of production pursuant to paragraph 2.2.2, the following provisions shall apply:

    (a) when capacity utilization and per unit costs of production vary significantly over the business cycle and sales prices vary only moderately the calculation of the per unit cost shall be adjusted to reflect average per unit costs for the exporter's or producer's most recent five-year period for the facilities involved;

    (b) when the sales price varies significantly over the business cycle and the capacity utilization and the per unit costs of production vary only moderately the calculation of the export price shall be adjusted to reflect the average sales price for the exporter's or producer's most recent five-year period for the facilities involved.]

[2.2.2.4 The authorities shall determine that prices below cost provide for recovery of costs within a reasonable period of time if prices below cost at the time of sale are above weighted average costs for the period of investigation. In addition, unless already reflected in cost allocations, the following practices shall be observed:

(i) Authorities may adjust costs appropriately for those non-recurring costs which benefit future or current production;

(ii) For products in the start-up phase of production, costs shall be adjusted to reflect the cost at the end of the start-up period, or the lowest cost during the period of investigation, if that is earlier;

(iii) Costs for cyclical industries[4], for the purpose of this Article, shall reflect fixed unit factory costs adjusted by the ratio of capacity utilization over the period of investigation to capacity utilization over the most recent five-year period for the same facilities.]

2.2.2.5 Nothing in this paragraph shall compel investigating authorities to determine sales in the domestic market of the exporting country, by reason of price, not to be in the ordinary course of trade for the purposes of establishing normal value.

---

[4] Cyclical industries are those characterized by [high sunk costs and] a pattern of recurring periods of sectoral contraction and expansion of demand, sales, and production not associated with seasonal variations or other short-term factors.

**2.2.3 For the purpose of paragraph 2.2, the amounts for administrative, selling and any other costs and for profits shall be based on actual data pertaining to the production and sale in the ordinary course of trade of the like product by the exporter or producer under investigation. When such amounts cannot be determined, the authorities may designate such other method as may be reasonable, provided that the amounts do not exceed the amount for administrative, selling and other costs and for profit normally incurred and realized on production and sales in the ordinary course of trade of other producers and exporters of like products or products of the same general category in the domestic market of the country of export. The provisions of sub-paragraph 2.2.2 shall apply under this paragraph in establishing whether sales are in the ordinary course of trade.

2.3 In cases where there is no export price or where it appears to the authorities concerned that the export price is unreliable because of association or a compensatory arrangement between the exporter and the importer or a third party, the export price may be constructed on the basis of the price at which the imported products are first resold to an independent buyer, or if the products are not resold to an independent buyer, or not resold in the condition as imported, on such reasonable basis as the authorities may determine.

*2.4 A fair comparison shall be made between the export price and the normal value. The two prices shall be compared at the same level of trade, normally at the ex-factory level, and in respect of sales made at as nearly as possible the same time. Due allowance shall be made in each case, on its merits, for demonstrated differences which affect price comparability, including differences in conditions and terms of sale, taxation, levels of trade, quantities, physical characteristics, and any other differences which are also demonstrated to affect price comparability.[5] In cases referred to in paragraph 3 of Article 2 allowance for costs, including duties and taxes, incurred between importation and resale, and for profits accruing, should also be made. If, in these cases, price comparability has been affected, the authorities shall establish the normal value at a level of trade equivalent to the level of trade of the constructed export price, or make due allowance as warranted under this paragraph. The authorities shall indicate to the parties in question what information is necessary to ensure a fair comparison and shall not impose an unreasonable burden of proof on those parties.

---

[5] It is understood that some of the above factors may overlap, and authorities shall ensure that they do not duplicate adjustments that have been already made under this provision.

*2.4.1 When the price comparison under this paragraph requires a conversion of currencies, such conversion should be made using the rate of exchange on the date of sale[6], provided that when a sale of foreign currency on forward markets is directly linked to the export sale involved, the rate of exchange in the forward sale shall be used. Temporary fluctuations in exchange rates shall be ignored and, during the investigation, exporters shall be given at least 60 days to adjust export prices to reflect sustained movements during the period of investigation.

**2.4.2 Subject to the provisions governing fair comparison in paragraph 2.4, in cases where prices vary in both the exporting and importing country, the normal value and the export price shall normally be compared on a weighted average to weighted average or transaction to transaction basis when establishing the existence of dumping margins during the investigation phase. A weighted average normal value may be compared to individual export transactions when the pattern of export transactions to particular customers reveals a distinct pattern of targeted dumping during the period of investigation, provided that the authorities ensure that no margins of dumping are found when there are similar movements in levels of prices at the same time in the two markets, and provided that the authorities give an explanation of the reasons for using such a comparison.

2.5 In the case where products are not imported directly from the country of origin but are exported to the country of importation from an intermediate country, the price at which the products are sold from the intermediate country to the country of importation shall normally be compared with the comparable price in such an intermediate country. However, comparison may be made with the price of the product in the country of origin, if, for example, the products are merely trans-shipped through the intermediate country, or such products are not produced in the intermediate country, or there is no comparable price for them in the intermediate country.

2.6 Throughout this Code the term "like product" ("produit similaire") shall be interpreted to mean a product which is identical, i.e. alike in all respects to the product under consideration, or in the absence of such a product, another product which although not alike in all respects, has characteristics closely resembling those of the product under consideration.

2.7 This Article is without prejudice to the second Supplementary Provision to paragraph 1 of Article VI in Annex I to the General Agreement.

---

[6]Normally, the date of sale would be the date of contract, purchase order, order confirmation, or invoice, whichever establishes the material terms of sale. (Text to be added.)

Article 3

Determination of Injury[7]

3.1 A determination of injury for purposes of Article VI of the General Agreement shall be based on positive evidence and involve an objective examination of (a) the volume of the dumped imports and the effect of the dumped imports on prices in the domestic market for like products and (b) the consequent impact of these imports on domestic producers of such products.

**3.2 With regard to the volume of the dumped imports, the authorities shall consider whether there has been a significant increase in dumped imports, either in absolute terms or relative to production or consumption in the importing country. With regard to the effect of the dumped imports on prices, the authorities shall consider whether there has been a significant price undercutting by the dumped imports as compared with the price of a like product of the importing country, or whether the effect of such imports is otherwise to depress prices to a significant degree or prevent price increases, which otherwise would have occurred to a significant degree. No one or several of these factors can necessarily give decisive guidance.

**3.3 The examination of the impact of the dumped imports on the industry concerned shall include an evaluation of all relevant economic factors and indices having a bearing on the state of the injury, including actual and potential decline in sales, profits, output, market share, productivity, return on investments, utilization of capacity; factors affecting domestic prices; the magnitude of the margin of dumping; actual and potential negative effects on cash flow, inventories, employment, wages, growth, ability to fund research and development or to raise capital or investments. This list is not exhaustive, nor can one or several of these factors necessarily give decisive guidance.

**3.4 It must be demonstrated that the dumped imports are, through the effects of dumping, as set out in paragraphs 2 and 3 of this Article, causing injury within the meaning of this Code. The demonstration of a causal relationship between the dumped imports and the injury to the domestic industry shall be based on the examination of all relevant evidence before the authorities. The authorities shall also examine any known factors other than the dumped imports which at the same time are injuring the industry, and the injuries caused by these other factors must not be attributed to the dumped imports. Factors which may be relevant in

---

[7]Under this Code, the term "injury" shall, unless otherwise specified, be taken to mean material injury to a domestic industry, threat of material injury to a domestic industry or material retardation of the establishment of such an industry and shall be interpreted in accordance with the provisions of this Article.

ADC2/N2-III-2

0119

- 8 -

this respect include, _inter alia_, the volume and prices of imports not sold at dumped prices, contraction in demand or changes in the patterns of consumption, trade restrictive practices of and competition between the foreign and domestic producers, changes or developments in technology and the export performance and productivity of the domestic industry.

3.5 The effect of the dumped imports shall be assessed in relation to the domestic production of the like product when available data permit the separate identification of that production on the basis of such criteria as production processes, producers' sales and profits. If such a separate identification of that production is not possible, the effects of the dumped imports shall be assessed by the examination of the production of the narrowest group or range of products, which includes the like product, for which the necessary information can be provided.

[3.6 Where imports from more than one country are subject to an investigation, the effects of such imports may be cumulatively assessed only under the following circumstances:

(a) such imports will compete with each other and with the like domestic product; and

(b) imports from a particular country represent more than [B] per cent of the total imports of the like product under investigation, provided that such imports may be cumulated if imports from countries whose individual shares of total imports of the like product under investigation is less than [B] per cent but collectively account for more than [C] per cent.]

[3.6 As a general rule, injury caused by dumped imports from different countries shall be assessed separately. However, in exceptional circumstances, the authorities may cumulatively assess the effects of such imports for the purposes of injury determination if the following conditions are met:

(i) the margin of dumping established in relation to imports from each exporter or producer is more than _de minimis_;

(ii) there is evidence that the imported products compete with each other and with the like domestic product: and

(iii) the volume of dumped imports and the injury attributable to the dumped imports from each country is not negligible.

In any case even when the above-mentioned conditions are met, the authorities shall consider the relative magnitudes of the volumes of imports from each country, and in particular whether there are significant disproportions of the volumes and the trends of volumes of imports from each such country in assessing whether imports from each country make a distinguishable contribution to injury or pose a threat of injury.]

ADC2/NZ-III-2

0120

- 9 -

3.7 A determination of a threat of material injury shall be based on facts and not merely on allegation, conjecture or remote possibility.   The change in circumstances which would create a situation in which the dumping would cause injury must be clearly foreseen and imminent.

   **3.7.1 In making a determination regarding a threat of material injury, the authorities should consider inter alia such factors as:

      (i)   a significant rate of increase of dumped imports into the domestic market indicating the likelihood of substantially increased importations;

      (ii)   sufficient freely disposable or an imminent, substantial increase in capacity of the exporter indicating the likelihood of substantially increased dumped exports to the importing country's market taking into account the availability of other export markets to absorb any additional exports;

      (iii) whether imports are entering at prices that will have a significant depressing or suppressing effect on domestic prices, and would likely increase demand for further imports;   and

      (iv)   inventories of the product being investigated.

No one of these factors by itself can necessarily give decisive guidance but the totality of the factors considered must lead to the conclusion that further dumped exports are imminent and that unless protective action is taken, material injury would occur.

3.8 With respect to cases where injury is threatened by dumped imports, the application of anti-dumping measures shall be considered and decided with special care.

- 10 -

Article 4

Definition of Industry

4.1 In determining injury the term 'domestic industry' shall be interpreted as referring to the domestic producers as a whole of the like product or to those of them whose collective output of the products constitutes a major proportion of the total domestic production of those products, except that

(i) when producers are related to the exporters or importers or are themselves importers of the allegedly dumped product, the industry may be interpreted as referring to the rest of the producers;

(ii) in exceptional circumstances the territory of a Party may, for the production in question, be divided into two or more competitive markets and the producers within each market may be regarded as a separate industry if (a) the producers within such market sell all or almost all their production of the product in question in that market, and (b) the demand in that market is not to a substantial degree supplied by producers of the product in question located elsewhere in the territory. In such circumstances, injury may be determined to exist even where a major portion of the total domestic industry is not injured provided there is a concentration of dumped imports into such an isolated market and provided further that the dumped imports are causing injury to the producers of all or almost all of the production within such market.

4.2 When the industry has been interpreted as referring to the producers in a certain area, i.e. a market as defined in sub-paragraph 1(ii),[8] anti-dumping duties shall be levied only on the products in question consigned for final consumption to that area. When the constitutional law of the importing country does not permit the levying of anti-dumping duties on such a basis, the importing Party may levy the anti-dumping duties without limitation only if (1) the exporters have been given an opportunity to cease dumping in the area concerned or otherwise give assurances pursuant to Article 8 of this Code, and adequate assurances in this regard have not been promptly given, and (2) such duties cannot be levied on specific producers which supply the area in question.

---

[8]As used in this Code "levy" shall mean the definitive or final legal assessment or collection of a duty or tax.

0122

ADC2/N2-III-2

/ı͵ —ᴄı

- 11 -

4.3 Where two or more countries have reached under the provisions of Article XXIV:8(a) of the General Agreement such a level of integration that they have the characteristics of a single, unified market, the industry in the entire area of integration shall be taken to be the industry referred to in paragraph 1 above.

4.4 The provisions of paragraph 2 of Article 3 shall be applicable to this Article.

0123

ADC2/NZ-III-2

- 12 -

Article 5

Initiation and Subsequent Investigation

5.1 An investigation to determine the existence, degree and effect of any alleged dumping shall normally be initiated upon a written application by or on behalf of the domestic industry, as defined in Article 4:1.

*5.2 An application under paragraph 1 shall include evidence of (a) dumping, (b) injury within the meaning of Article VI of the General Agreement as interpreted by this Code and (c) a causal link between the dumped imports and the alleged injury. Simple assertion, unsubstantiated by relevant evidence, cannot be considered sufficient to meet the requirements of this paragraph. The application shall contain such information as is reasonably available to the applicant on the following:

[9 For purposes of this Article the term "a major proportion" in Article 4 shall normally mean 50 per cent of the value of total domestic production of the like product. The percentage may be less than 50 per cent, but not less than 25 per cent, provided there is more expressed support than expressed opposition. In the case of fragmented industries involving an exceptionally large number of producers, authorities may determine support and opposition by using statistically valid samples.]

[9 For purposes of this Article the term "a major proportion" in Article 4 shall normally mean 50 per cent of the value of total domestic production of the like product. In exceptional circumstances the percentage may be less than 50 per cent, but not less than 25 per cent, provided there is more expressed support than expressed opposition.]

[9 For purposes of this Article, the authorities shall find that the application has been filed by or on behalf of the domestic industry as defined in Article 4 only if domestic producers expressly supporting the initiation of an investigation account for at least 50 per cent of the domestic production of those producers expressing support for or opposition to initiation, provided that an investigation shall not be initiated if domestic producers expressly supporting the initiation of an investigation account for less than 25 per cent of such domestic production. In exceptional circumstances, including those where the industry is fragmented into a large number of producers that do not have a representative association, authorities may determine level of support among the domestic industry by employing sampling techniques. For purposes of this Article, a recognized representative of the employees of a producer may indicate express support or express opposition to a request for initiation on behalf of that producer.]

0124

ADC2/NZ-III-2

- 13 -

(i)   identity of the applicant and a description of the volume and
        value of the domestic production of the like product by the
        applicant. Where a written application is made on behalf of
        the domestic industry, the application shall identify the
        industry on behalf of which the application is made by a list
        of all known domestic producers of the like product (or
        associations of domestic producers of the like product) and, to
        the extent possible, a description of the volume and value of
        domestic production of the like product accounted for by such
        producers;

(ii)   a complete description of the allegedly dumped product, the
        names of the country or countries of export or origin in
        question, the identity of each known exporter or foreign
        producer and a list of known persons importing the product in
        question;

*(iii) information on prices at which the product in question is sold
        when destined for consumption in the domestic markets of the
        country or countries of origin or export (or, where appropriate,
        information on the prices at which the product is sold from the
        country or countries of origin or export to a third country or
        countries or on the constructed value of the product) and
        information on export prices or, where appropriate, on the
        prices at which the product is first resold to an independent
        buyer in the importing country;

*(iv)   information on the evolution of the volume of the allegedly
        dumped imports, the effect of these imports on prices of the
        like product in the domestic market and the consequent impact of
        the imports on the domestic industry concerned, as demonstrated
        by relevant factors and indices having a bearing on the state of
        the domestic industry, such as those listed in Article 3.2 and
        3.3.

5.3 The authorities shall examine the accuracy and adequacy of the
evidence provided in the application to determine whether there is
sufficient evidence to justify the initiation of an investigation,
provided that the authorities shall not initiate an investigation unless
they are satisfied that the application for the initiation of an
investigation has been made by or on behalf of the domestic industry, as
provided in Article 5:1.

5.4 The authorities shall avoid, unless a decision has been made to
initiate an investigation, any publicizing of the application for the
initiation of an investigation. However, after receipt of a properly
documented application and before proceeding to initiate an investigation,
the authorities shall notify the government of the exporting country
concerned.

0125

ADC2/N2-III-2

5.5 Notwithstanding paragraph 1, if in special circumstances, the authorities concerned decide to initiate an investigation without having received a written application by or on behalf of a domestic industry for the initiation of such investigation, they shall proceed only if they have sufficient evidence of dumping, injury and a causal link, as described in paragraph 2, to justify the initiation of an investigation.

5.6 The evidence of both dumping and injury shall be considered simultaneously (a) in the decision whether or not to initiate an investigation, and (b) thereafter, during the course of the investigation, starting on a date not later than the earliest date on which in accordance with the provisions of this Code provisional measures may be applied.

5.7 A written application under paragraph 1 shall be rejected and an investigation shall be terminated promptly as soon as the authorities concerned are satisfied that there is not sufficient evidence of either dumping or injury to justify proceeding with the case. There [should] [shall] be immediate termination in cases where the margin of dumping is de minimis[10] or the volume of dumped imports[11], actual or potential, or the injury therefrom is negligible.[11]

5.8 An anti-dumping proceeding shall not hinder the procedures of customs clearance.

*5.9 Investigations shall, except in special circumstances, be concluded within twelve months after their initiation, and in no case more than 18 months.

---

[10]For the purpose of this paragraph, a de minimis margin of dumping is considered to be less than [E] per cent, expressed as a percentage of the normal value.

[11The volume of dumped imports shall be regarded as negligible if the total volume of dumped imports from any one country does not constitute more than [X] per cent of the domestic market for the like product in the importing country, unless countries with less than [X] per cent market share collectively account for more than [Y] per cent of the domestic market for the like product in the importing country.]

[11This shall be deemed to occur when the volume of dumped imports account for less than [F] per cent of the total market in the importing country for the like product under investigation.]

ADC2/NZ-III-2

0126.

Article 6

Evidence

6.1 All interested parties in an anti-dumping investigation shall be given notice of the information which the authorities require and ample opportunity to present in writing all evidence which they consider relevant in respect of the investigation in question.

*6.1.1 Exporters, importers or foreign producers receiving questionnaires used in an anti-dumping investigation shall be given at least thirty days for reply.[12] Due consideration should be given to any request for an extension of the thirty-day period and, upon cause shown, such an extension should be granted whenever practicable.

6.1.2 Subject to the requirement to protect confidential information, evidence presented in writing by one interested party shall be made available promptly to other interested parties participating in the investigation.

*6.1.3 As soon as an investigation has been initiated, the authorities shall provide the full text of the written application received under Article 5:1 to the known exporters[13] and to the authorities of the exporting country and make it available, upon request, to other interested parties involved. Due regard shall be paid to the requirement for the protection of confidential information as provided for in paragraph 5.

6.2 Throughout the anti-dumping investigation all interested parties shall have a full opportunity for the defence of their interests. To this end, the authorities shall, on request, provide opportunities for all interested parties to meet those parties with adverse interests, so that opposing views may be presented and rebuttal arguments offered. Provision of such opportunities must take account of the need to preserve

---

[12]As a general rule, the time limit for exporters shall be counted from the date of the receipt of the questionnaire, which for this purpose shall be deemed to have been received one week from the day on which it was sent to the respondent or transmitted to the appropriate diplomatic representative of the exporting country.

[13]It being understood that, where the number of exporters involved is particularly high, the full text of the request should instead be provided only to the authorities of the exporting country or to the relevant trade association.

ADC2/NZ-III-2

42—16

0127

confidentiality and of the convenience to the parties. There shall be no obligation on any party to attend a meeting, and failure to do so shall not be prejudicial to that party's case. Interested parties shall also have the right, on justification, to present other information orally.

6.3 Oral information provided under paragraph 2 shall be taken into account by the authorities only insofar as it is subsequently reproduced in writing and made available to other interested parties, as provided for in sub-paragraph 1.2 of this Article.

6.4 The authorities shall whenever practicable provide timely opportunities for all interested parties to see all information that is relevant to the presentation of their cases, that is not confidential as defined in paragraph 5 and that is used by the authorities in an anti-dumping investigation, and to prepare presentations on the basis of this information.

6.5 Any information which is by nature confidential, (for example, because its disclosure would be of significant competitive advantage to a competitor or because its disclosure would have a significantly adverse effect upon a person supplying the information or upon a person from whom he acquired the information) or which is provided on a confidential basis by parties to an investigation shall, upon good cause shown, be treated as such by the investigating authorities. Such information shall not be disclosed without specific permission of the party submitting it.[14]

    6.5.1 The authorities shall require interested parties providing confidential information to furnish non-confidential summaries thereof. These summaries shall be in sufficient detail to permit a reasonable understanding of the substance of the information submitted in confidence. In exceptional circumstances, such parties may indicate that such information is not susceptible of summary. In such exceptional circumstances, a statement of the reasons why summarization is not possible must be provided.

    6.5.2 If the authorities find that a request for confidentiality is not warranted and if the supplier is either unwilling to make the information public or to authorize its disclosure in generalized or summary form, the authorities are free to disregard such information unless it can be demonstrated to their satisfaction from appropriate sources that the information is correct.[15]

---

[14]Parties are aware that in the territory of certain Parties disclosure pursuant to a narrowly drawn protective order may be required.

[15]Parties agree that requests for confidentiality should not be arbitrarily rejected.

ADC2/NZ-III-2

0128

*6.6 Except in circumstances provided for in paragraph 8, the authorities shall during the course of an investigation satisfy themselves as to the accuracy of the information supplied by interested parties upon which its findings are based.

*6.7 In order to verify information provided or to obtain further details, the authorities may carry out investigations in other countries as required, provided they obtain the agreement of the firms concerned and provided they notify the representatives of the government of the country in question and unless the latter object to the investigation. The procedures described in Annex I shall apply to verifications carried out in exporting countries. The authorities shall, subject to the requirement to protect confidential information, make the reports of any verifications available, or provide disclosure thereof pursuant to paragraph 9; to the firms to which they pertain and may make such reports available to the applicants.

6.8 In cases in which any interested party refuses access to, or otherwise does not provide, necessary information within a reasonable period or significantly impedes the investigation, preliminary and final determinations, affirmative or negative, may be made on the basis of the facts available. The provisions of Annex II shall be observed in the application of this paragraph.

*6.9 The authorities shall, before a final determination is made, inform all interested parties of the essential facts under consideration which form the basis for the decision whether to apply definitive measures. Such disclosure should take place in sufficient time for the parties to defend their interests.

*6.10 The authorities shall, as a rule, determine an individual margin of dumping for each known exporter or producer concerned of the product under investigation.   In cases where the number of exporters, producers, importers or types of products involved is so large as to make such a determination impracticable, the authorities may limit their examination either to a reasonable number of interested parties or products by using samples which are statistically valid on the basis of information available to the authorities at the time of the selection, or to the largest percentage of the volume of the exports from the country in question which can reasonably be investigated.

   *6.10.1 Any selection of exporters, producers, importers or types of products made under this paragraph shall preferably be chosen in consultation with, and with the consent of the exporters, producers or importers concerned.

   *6.10.2 In cases where the authorities have limited their examination, as provided for in this paragraph, they shall nevertheless determine an individual margin of dumping for any exporter or producer not initially selected who submits the necessary information in time for that information to be considered during the course of the investigation, except where the number of exporters or producers is so large that individual examinations would be unduly burdensome to the authorities and prevent the timely completion of the investigation. Voluntary responses shall not be discouraged.

ADC2/NZ-III-2

0129

44-18

6.11 For the purposes of this Code, "interested parties" shall include:

(i)   an exporter or foreign producer or the importer of a product
       subject to investigation, or a trade or business association a
       majority of the members of which are producers, exporters or
       importers of such product;

(ii)   the government of the exporting country; and

(iii) a producer of the like product in the importing country or a
       trade and business association a majority of the members of
       which produce the like product in the importing country.

*This list shall not preclude Parties from allowing domestic or foreign
parties other than those mentioned above to be included as interested
parties in the investigation.

6.12 The authorities shall provide opportunities for industrial users of
the product under investigation, and for representative consumer
organizations in cases where the product is commonly sold at the retail
level, to provide information which is relevant to the investigation
regarding dumping, injury and causality.

6.13 The authorities shall take due account of any difficulties
experienced by interested parties, in particular small companies, in
supplying information requested and provide any assistance practicable.

6.14 The procedures set out above are not intended to prevent the
authorities of a Party from proceeding expeditiously with regard to
initiating an investigation, reaching preliminary or final determinations,
whether affirmative or negative, or from applying provisional or final
measures, in accordance with relevant provisions of this Code.

- 19 -

Article 7

Provisional Measures

7.1 Provisional measures may be applied only if:

(i)   an investigation has been initiated in accordance with the provisions of Article 5, a public notice has been given to that effect and interested parties have been given adequate opportunities to submit information and make comments;

(ii)   a preliminary affirmative determination has been made of dumping and consequent injury to a domestic industry;   and

*(iii)the authorities concerned judge such measures necessary to prevent injury being caused during the investigation.

7.2 Provisional measures may take the form of a provisional duty or, preferably, a security - by cash deposit or bond - equal to the amount of the anti-dumping duty provisionally estimated, being not greater than the provisionally estimated margin of dumping.   Withholding of appraisement is an appropriate provisional measure, provided that the normal duty and the estimated amount of the anti-dumping duty be indicated and as long as the withholding of appraisement is subject to the same conditions as other provisional measures.

7.3 Provisional measures shall not be applied sooner than 60 days from the date of initiation of the investigation.

*7.4 The application of provisional measures shall be limited to as short a period as possible, not exceeding four months or, on decision of the authorities concerned, upon request by exporters representing a significant percentage of the trade involved, to a period not exceeding six months.   When authorities, in the course of an investigation, examine whether a duty lower than the margin of dumping would be sufficient to remove injury, these periods may be six and nine months, respectively.

7.5 The relevant provisions of Article 9 shall be followed in the application of provisional measures.

0131

ADCI.NZ-III-2

- 20 -

Article 8

Price Undertakings

8.1 Proceedings may[16] be suspended or terminated without the imposition of provisional measures or anti-dumping duties upon receipt of satisfactory voluntary undertakings from any exporter to revise its prices or to cease dumping so that the authorities are satisfied that the injurious effect of the dumping is eliminated.   Price increases under such undertakings shall not be higher than necessary to eliminate the margin of dumping.   It is desirable that the price increases be less than the margin of dumping if such increases would be adequate to remove the injury to the domestic industry.

8.2 Price undertakings shall not be sought or accepted from exporters unless the authorities of the importing country have made a preliminary affirmative determination of dumping and injury caused by such dumping.

*8.3 Undertakings offered need not be accepted if the authorities consider their acceptance impractical, for example, if the number of actual or potential exporters is too great, or for other reasons, including reasons of general policy.   Should the case arise and where practicable, the authorities shall provide to the exporter the reasons which have led them to consider acceptance of an undertaking as inappropriate, and shall, to the extent possible, give the exporter an opportunity to make comments thereon.

8.4 If the undertakings are accepted, the investigation of dumping and injury shall nevertheless be completed if the exporter so desires or the authorities so decide.   In such a case, if a negative determination of dumping or injury is made, the undertaking shall automatically lapse except in cases where such a determination is due in large part to the existence of a price undertaking.   In such cases the authorities may require that an undertaking be maintained for a reasonable period consistent with the provisions of this Code.   In the event that an affirmative determination of dumping and injury is made, the undertaking shall continue consistent with its terms and the provisions of this Code.

---

[16]The word "may" shall not be interpreted to allow the simultaneous continuation of proceedings with the implementation of price undertakings except as provided in paragraph 4.

0132

ADC2:NZ-III-2

- 21 -

8.5 Price undertakings may be suggested by the authorities of the importing country, but no exporter shall be forced to enter into such an undertaking. The fact that exporters do not offer such undertakings, or do not accept an invitation to do so, shall in no way prejudice the consideration of the case. However, the authorities are free to determine that a threat of injury is more likely to be realized if the dumped imports continue.

8.6 Authorities of an importing country may require any exporter from whom undertakings have been accepted to provide periodically information relevant to the fulfilment of such undertakings, and to permit verification of pertinent data. In case of violation of undertakings the authorities of the importing country may take, under this Code in conformity with its provisions, expeditious actions which may constitute immediate application of provisional measures using the best information available. In such cases definitive duties may be levied in accordance with this Code on goods entered for consumption not more than ninety days before the application of such provisional measures, except that any such retroactive assessment shall not apply to imports entered before the violation of the undertaking.

*8.7 Undertakings shall not remain in force any longer than anti-dumping duties could remain in force under this Code. The authorities of an importing country shall review the need for the continuation of any price undertaking, where warranted, on their own initiative or if interested exporters or importers so request and submit positive information substantiating the need for such a review.

0133

ADC2/NZ-III-2

- 22 -

Article 9

Imposition and Collection of Anti-Dumping Duties

9.1 The decision whether or not to impose an anti-dumping duty in cases where all requirements for the imposition have been fulfilled and the decision whether the amount of the anti-dumping duty to be imposed shall be the full margin of dumping or less, are decisions to be made by the authorities of the importing country or customs territory. It is desirable that the imposition be permissive in all countries or customs territories Parties to this Agreement, and that the duty be less than the margin, if such lesser duty would be adequate to remove the injury to the domestic industry.

9.2 When an anti-dumping duty is imposed in respect of any product, such anti-dumping duty shall be collected in the appropriate amounts in each case, on a non-discriminatory basis on imports of such product from all sources found to be dumped and causing injury, except as to imports from those sources, from which price undertakings under the terms of this Code have been accepted. The authorities shall name the supplier or suppliers of the product concerned. If, however, several suppliers from the same country are involved, and it is impracticable to name all these suppliers, the authorities may name the supplying country concerned. If several suppliers from more than one country are involved, the authorities may name either all the suppliers involved, or, if this is impracticable, all the supplying countries involved.

9.3 The amount of the anti-dumping duty shall not exceed the margin of dumping as established under Article 2.

*9.3.1 When the amount of the anti-dumping duty is assessed on a retrospective basis, the determination of the final liability for payment of anti-dumping duties shall take place as soon as possible, normally within 12 months, and in no case more than 18 months, after the date on which a request for a final assessment of the amount of anti-dumping duty has been made, except where one or more of the parties have availed themselves of judicial review. Any refund shall be made promptly and in no case more than 90 days following the determination of final liability made pursuant to this sub-paragraph. In any case, where a refund is not made within 90 days, the authorities shall be obliged to provide an explanation, if so requested.

*9.3.2 When the amount of the anti-dumping duty is assessed on a prospective basis, provision shall be made for a prompt refund, upon request, of any duty paid in excess of the margin of dumping. A refund of any such duty paid in excess of the actual margin of dumping shall normally take place within 12 months, and in no case more than 18 months, after the date on which a request for a refund, duly supported by evidence, has been made by an importer of the product subject to the anti-dumping duty. The refund authorized should normally be made within 90 days of the above-noted decision except where one or more of the parties have availed themselves of judicial review.

ADC2/NZ-III-2

0134

- 23 -

**9.3.3 When the export price is constructed, in accordance with Article 2:3, any anti-dumping duties definitively collected in excess of the margin of dumping shall be reimbursed upon request. In determining whether a reimbursement should be made, authorities should take account of any decrease in normal value, any reduction of costs incurred between importation and resale, and any movement in the resale price which is appropriately reflected in subsequent selling prices, and should first calculate the export price with no deduction for the amount of anti-dumping duties paid. If the result of this calculation indicates an export price that is equal to or greater than the normal value, and there is verifiable evidence that the amount paid for the goods by the importer is equal to or greater than the normal value, then the anti-dumping duty paid should be reimbursed. If, however, the export price so calculated is less than the normal value, the export price may be redetermined and the amount of anti-dumping duty paid may be treated as a cost incurred between importation and resale.

**9.4 When the authorities have determined margins of dumping in accordance with Article 6:10, any anti-dumping duty applied to imports from exporters or producers not included in the examination shall not exceed

(a) the weighted average of margin of dumping[17] established with respect to the selected exporters or producers, or

(b) where the liability for payment of anti-dumping duties is calculated on the basis of a prospective normal value, the difference between the weighted average normal value of the selected exporters or producers and the export prices of exporters or producers not individually investigated,

provided that the authorities shall disregard for the purpose of this paragraph any zero or de minimis margins and margins established under the circumstances referred to in Article 6:8. The authorities shall apply individual duties or normal values to imports from any exporter or producer not included in the examination who has provided the necessary information during the course of the investigation. Where the number of exporters or producers is so large that it is impractical to provide them all with individual margins of dumping within the time frame of the investigation, this shall be done as expeditiously as possible taking into account reasonable administrative limits for the authorities concerned.

**[17] The weighted average margin of dumping under this sub-paragraph for a producer or exporter is its total amount of anti-dumping duty liability for the like product, divided by the total value of exports to the importing country subject to such duty. When averaging margins of dumping for a number of producers or exporters, the individual rates of dumping shall be weighted by the volumes of exports to the importing country by each producer or exporter.

0135

ADC2/NZ-III-2

- 24 -

**9.5 Anti-dumping duties shall not be levied on products of exporters or
producers who have not exported the product during the period of
investigation and who are not related to any of the exporters or producers
subject to anti-dumping duties shall not be subject to any anti-dumping
duty until the authorities have carried out an expedited investigation to
determine individual margins of dumping for such exporters or producers.
The authorities, however, may withhold appraisement and/or request
guarantees to ensure that, should such an expedited investigation lead to a
determination of dumping in respect of such exporters or producers,
anti-dumping duties can be collected retroactively to the date on which the
product exported by such exporters or producers was first entered for
consumption in the importing country.

0136

ADC2/NZ-III-2

- 25 -

Article 10

Retroactivity

10.1 Provisional measures and anti-dumping duties shall only be applied to products which enter for consumption after the time when the decision taken under Article 7:1 and Article 9:1, respectively, enters into force, subject to the exceptions set out in this article.

10.2 Where a final determination of injury (but not of a threat thereof or of a material retardation of the establishment of an industry) is made or, in the case of a final determination of a threat of injury, when the effect of the dumped imports would, in the absence of the provisional measures, have led to a determination of injury, anti-dumping duties may be levied retroactively for the period for which provisional measures, if any, have been applied. If the anti-dumping duty fixed in the final decision is higher than the provisional duty paid or payable, the difference shall not be collected. If the duty fixed in the final decision is lower than the provisional duty paid or payable, or the amount estimated for the purpose of the security, the difference shall be reimbursed or the duty recalculated, as the case may be.

10.3 A definitive anti-dumping duty may be levied on products which were entered for consumption not more than [90] days prior to the date of application of provisional measures, provided that no duties shall be levied pursuant to this paragraph on products which were entered for consumption prior to the date of initiation of the investigation, when the authorities determine for the dumped product in question that:

(i)   there is a history of dumping which caused injury or that the importer was, or should have been, aware that the exporter practices dumping and that such dumping would cause injury, and

(ii) the injury is caused by massive dumped imports of a product in a relatively short time which in light of the timing and the volume of the dumped imports and other circumstances (such as a rapid build-up of inventories of the imported product) is likely to seriously undermine the remedial effect of the definitive anti-dumping duty to be applied, provided that the importers concerned have been given an opportunity to comment.

10.4 Except as provided in paragraph 1 above where a determination of threat of injury or material retardation is made (but no injury has yet occurred) a definitive anti-dumping duty may be imposed only from the date of the determination of threat of injury or material retardation and any case deposit made during the period of the application of provisional measures shall be refunded and any bonds released in an expeditious manner.

0137

ADC2/NZ-III-2

- 26 -

10.5 Where a final determination is negative, any cash deposit made during the period of the application of provisional measures shall be refunded and any bonds released in an expeditious manner.

0138

ADC2/NZ-III-2

- 27 -

Article 11

Duration and Review of Anti-Dumping Duties and Price Undertakings

11.1 An anti-dumping duty shall remain in force only as long as and to the extent necessary to counteract dumping which is causing injury.

11.2 The authorities shall review the need for the continued imposition of the duty, where warranted, on their own initiative or, provided that a reasonable period of time has elapsed since the imposition of the definitive anti-dumping duty, upon request by any interested party which submits positive information substantiating the need for a review.[18] Interested parties shall have the right to request the authorities to examine whether the continued imposition of the duty is necessary to offset dumping, whether recurrence of the injury would occur if the duty were removed or varied, or both.   If, as a result of the review under this paragraph, the authorities determine that the anti-dumping duty is no longer warranted, it shall be terminated immediately.

**11.3 Notwithstanding the provisions of paragraphs 1 and 2, any definitive anti-dumping duty shall be terminated not later than five years from the date of its imposition (or from the date of its most recent review under paragraph 2 if that review has covered both dumping and injury, or under this paragraph), unless the authorities determine, on the basis of a review initiated before that date on their own initiative or upon a duly substantiated request made by or on behalf of the domestic industry within a reasonable period of time prior to that date, that the continued imposition of the duty is necessary to offset dumping and prevent the continuation or recurrence of the injury.   The duty may remain in force pending the outcome of such a review.

11.4 The provisions of Article 6 regarding evidence and procedure shall apply to any review carried out under this Article.   Any such review shall be carried out expeditiously and shall normally be concluded within twelve months of the date of initiation of the review.

11.5 The provisions of this Article shall apply _mutatis mutandis_ to price undertakings.

---

[18] A determination of final liability for payment of anti-dumping duties as provided for in Article 9.3 does not, by itself, constitute a review in terms of this Article.

0139

ADC2/N2-III-2   42-28

- 28 -

Article 12

Measures to Prevent Circumvention of
Definitive Anti-Dumping Duties

**12.1 An anti-dumping measure may be imposed on an imported product other than a like product to one which is subject to a definitive anti-dumping duty only in accordance with the provisions of this Article. The authorities may include within the scope of application of a definitive anti-dumping duty on an imported product those parts or components destined for assembly or completion in the importing country, provided that it has been established that:

    (i)   the product assembled or completed from such parts or components in the importing country is a like product to a product which is subject to the definitive anti-dumping duty;

    (ii)   the assembly or completion of the like product in the importing country is carried out by or on behalf of a party which is related[19] to an exporter or producer whose exports of the like product are subject to a definitive anti-dumping duty;

    (iii)   the parts or components have been sourced from the exporter or producer subject to the definitive anti-dumping duty, from suppliers in that country that have historically supplied the parts or components of the like product to that exporter or producer, or a party in the exporting country supplying parts or components of the like product on behalf of such an exporter or producer;

    (iv)   the assembly operations in the importing country have started or expanded substantially and the imports of those parts or components have increased substantially since the initiation of the investigation which resulted in the definitive anti-dumping duty;

    (v)   the parts or components imported constitute a predominant proportion (i.e. not less than [G] per cent of the total value of the parts or components) of the assembled or completed like product, provided that in no case shall the parts and components be included within the scope of definitive measures if the value added in the assembly or completion operation is greater than [H] per cent of the ex-factory cost of the like product assembled or completed in the territory of the importing country;

---

[19] An understanding among Parties should be developed defining the word "related" and the expression "by or on behalf of" as used in this Code.

0140

(vi) there is evidence of dumping, as determined by a comparison between the price of the product when assembled or completed in the importing country, and the normal value of the like product when subject to the original definitive anti-dumping duty, with due allowances and adjustments to ensure a fair comparison in accordance with Article 2; and,

(vii) a determination is made that the inclusion of these parts or components within the scope of application of the definitive anti-dumping duty is necessary to prevent or offset the continuation or recurrence of the injury to the domestic industry producing a product like the product which is subject to the definitive anti-dumping duty.

**12.2 The authorities may impose provisional measures in accordance with Article 7:2 when they are satisfied that there is sufficient evidence that the criteria set out in paragraphs 12.1 (i)-(vi) are met. Any provisional duty imposed shall not exceed the definitive anti-dumping duty in force. The authorities may levy a definitive anti-dumping duty once all of the criteria in paragraph 12.1 are fully satisfied. The amount of the definitive anti-dumping duty shall not exceed the amount which which the normal value of the like product when subject to the original definitive anti-dumping duty exceeds the price of the product when assembled or completed in the importing country, with due allowances and adjustments to ensure a fair comparison in accordance with Article 2, as determined in paragraph 12.1 (vi).

**12.3 An anti-dumping measure may be imposed on a like product to one which is subject to a definitive anti-dumping duty other than when the like product has been imported either directly or indirectly to the importing country from a country in respect of which a final determination of dumping and injury has been made pursuant to the provisions of this Code only in accordance with the provisions of this Article. The authorities may only include within the scope of application of a definitive anti-dumping duty a product exported from a country not included within the scope of a definitive anti-dumping duty and assembled or completed in the exporting country, provided that it has been established that:

(i) the product imported is a like product to a product which is subject to the definitive anti-dumping duty;

(ii) the assembly or completion of the like product in the exporting country is carried out by or on behalf of a party which is related to an exporter or producer whose exports of the like product are subject to a definitive anti-dumping duty;

(iii) the parts or components used in assembling or completing the product have been sourced from the exporter or producer subject to the definitive anti-dumping duty, from suppliers that have historically supplied the parts or components of the like product to that exporter or producer, or a party in the exporting country supplying parts or components of the like product on behalf of such an exporter or producer;

0141

ADC2/NZ-III-

(iv) the assembly operations in the exporting country have started or expanded substantially and the imports of the like product have increased substantially since the initiation of the investigation which resulted in the definitive anti-dumping duty;

(v) the parts or components referred to in sub-paragraph (iii) above constitute a predominant proportion (i.e. not less than [I] per cent of the total value of the parts or components) of the assembled or completed like product, and include all the principal components or sub-assemblies which give the product is essential character, provided that in no case shall the parts and components be included within the scope of definitive measures if the value added in the assembly or completion operation is greater than [J] per cent of the ex-factory cost of the like product assembled or completed in the territory of the exporting country;

(vi) there is evidence of dumping, as determined by a comparison between the export price of the assembled or completed like product, and the normal value of the like product when subject to the original definitive anti-dumping order, with due allowances and adjustments including any differences in assembly costs in the country of export to ensure a fair comparison in accordance with Article 2; and,

(vii) a determination is made that the inclusion of the like product within the scope of application of the definitive anti-dumping duty is necessary to prevent or offset the continuation or recurrence of the injury to the domestic industry producing a product like the product which is subject to the definitive anti-dumping duty.

**12.4 The authorities may impose provisional measures in accordance with Article 7:2 when they are satisfied that the criteria set out in paragraphs 12.3 (i)-(vi) are met. Any provisional duty imposed shall not exceed the definitive anti-dumping duty in force. The authorities may levy a definitive anti-dumping duty once all of the criteria in paragraph 12.3 are fully satisfied. The amount of the definitive anti-dumping duty shall not exceed the amount by which the normal value determined under sub-paragraph 12.4 (vi) above exceeds the export price of the product when assembled or completed in the exporting country, with due allowances and adjustments to ensure a fair comparison.

**12.5 The provisions of this Code concerning rights of interested parties and public notice shall apply mutatis mutandis to investigations carried out under this Article. The provisions of Articles 9 and 11 regarding review and refund shall apply to anti-dumping duties imposed, pursuant to this Article, on parts and components assembled in the importing country.

0142

ADC2/NZ-III-2

(12-7/

- 31 -

Article 13

Public Notice and Explanation of Determinations

13.1 When the authorities are satisfied that there is sufficient evidence to justify the initiation of an anti-dumping investigation pursuant to Article 5, the Party or Parties the products of which are subject to such investigation and other interested parties known to the investigating authorities to have an interest therein shall be notified and a public notice shall be given.

    13.1.1 A public notice of the initiation of an investigation shall contain or otherwise make available adequate information on the following:

        (i)   the name of the exporting country or countries and the product involved;

        (ii) the date of initiation of the investigation;

        (iii) the basis on which dumping is alleged in the application;

        (iv) a summary of the factors which have led to the allegation of injury;

        (v)   the address to which representations by interested parties should be directed;

        (vi) the time-limits allowed to interested parties for making their views known.

13.2 Public notice shall be given of any preliminary or final determination, whether affirmative or negative, of any decision to accept an undertaking pursuant to Article 8, of the termination of such an undertaking, and of the revocation of a determination.   Each such notice shall set forth or otherwise make available in sufficient detail the findings and conclusions reached on all issues of fact and law considered material by the investigating authorities and shall be forwarded to the Party or Parties the products of which are subject to such finding or undertaking and to other interested parties known to have an interest therein.

    13.2.1 A public notice of the imposition of provisional measures shall set forth or otherwise make available sufficiently detailed explanations for the preliminary determinations on dumping and injury (insofar as there is no separate preliminary injury determination and a notice thereof) and shall refer to the matters of fact and law which have led to arguments being accepted or rejected; the notice shall, due regard being paid to the requirement for the protection of confidential information, contain in particular:

0143

- 32 -

(i)   the names of the suppliers, or when this is impracticable, the supplying countries involved;

(ii)   a description of the product, which is sufficient for customs purposes;

(iii) the margins of dumping established and a full explanation of the reasons for the methodology used in the establishment and comparison of the export price and the normal value under Article 2.

(iv)   considerations relevant to the injury determination as set out in Article 3, (insofar as there is no separate notice concerning such injury determination);

(v)   the main reasons leading to the determination.

13.2.2 A public notice of suspension or conclusion of an investigation in the case of an affirmative determination providing for the imposition of a definitive duty or a price undertaking shall contain or otherwise make available all relevant information on the matters of fact and law and reasons which have led to the imposition of final measures or the acceptance of a price undertaking, due regard being paid to the requirement for the protection of confidential information; it shall in particular contain the information described in sub-paragraph 13.2.1 as well as the reasons for the acceptance or rejection of relevant arguments or claims made by the exporters and importers, and the basis for any decision made under Article 6.10.2.

*13.2.3 A public notice of the termination or suspension of an investigation following the acceptance of an undertaking pursuant to Article 8 shall include or otherwise make available the non-confidential part of this undertaking.

13.3 The provisions of this Article shall apply mutatis mutandis to the initiation and completion of administrative reviews pursuant to Article 11 and to decisions under Article 10 to apply duties retroactively.

0144

MTN.GNZ-III-2

- 33 -

Article 14

Judicial Review

*Each Party whose national legislation contains provisions on anti-dumping measures shall maintain judicial, arbitral or administrative tribunals or procedures for the purpose, _inter alia_, of the prompt review of administrative actions relating to final determinations and reviews of determinations within the meaning of Article 11 of this Agreement. Such tribunals or procedures shall be independent of the authorities responsible for the determination or review in question.

0145

ANGR/NZ-III-2

- 34 -

Article 15

Anti-Dumping Action on behalf of a Third Country

[To be added]

0146

- 35 -

Article 16

Developing Countries

[To be added]

0147

- 36 -

PART II

Article 17

Committee on Anti-Dumping Practices

[To be added]

0148

- 37 -

Article 18

Consultation, Conciliation and Dispute Settlement

**18.1 Consultations and the settlement of disputes with respect to any matter affecting the operation of this Agreement shall be subject to the provisions of Articles XXII and XXIII of the GATT, including the Dispute Settlement Procedures as adopted by the CONTRACTING PARTIES, and shall take place under the auspices of the Committee on Anti-Dumping Measures.

[18.2 etc. - to be added]

0149

ADC2/NZ-III-2

42-78

- 38 -

PART III

Final Provisions

[To be added, including transitional provisions]

- 39 -

ANNEX I

Procedures for On-The-Spot Investigations Pursuant to Article 6:6

1. Upon initiation of an investigation, the authorities of the exporting country and the firms known to be concerned should be informed of the intention to carry out on-the-spot investigations.

2. If in exceptional circumstances it is intended to include non-governmental experts in the investigating team, the firms and the authorities of the exporting country should be so informed. Such non-governmental experts should be subject to effective sanctions for breach of confidentiality requirements.

3. It should be standard practice to obtain explicit agreement of the firms concerned in the exporting country before the visit is finally scheduled.

4. As soon as the agreement of the firms concerned has been obtained the investigating authorities should notify the authorities of the exporting country of the names and addresses of the firms to be visited and the dates agreed.

5. Sufficient advance notice should be given to the firms in question before the visit is made.

6. Visits to explain the questionnaire should only be made at the request of an exporting firm. Such a visit may only be made if the authorities of the importing country notify the representatives of the government of the country in question and unless the latter do not object to the visit.

7. As the main purpose of the on-the-spot investigation is to verify information provided or to obtain further details, it should be carried out after the response to the questionnaire has been received unless the firm agrees to the contrary and the government of the exporting country is informed by the investigating authorities of the anticipated visit and does not object to it; further, it should be standard practice prior to the visit to advise the firms concerned f the general nature of the information to be verified and of any further information which needs to be provided, though this should not preclude requests to be made on the spot for further details to be provided in the light of information obtained.

8. Enquiries or questions put by the authorities or firms of the exporting countries and essential to a successful on-the-spot investigation should, whenever possible, be answered before the visit is made.

0151

- 40 -

ANNEX II

Best Information Available in Terms of Article 6:8

1. As soon as possible after the initiation of the investigation, the investigating authorities should specify in detail the information required from any interested party, and the way in which that information should be structured by the interested party in its response.   The authorities should also ensure that the party is aware that if information is not supplied within a reasonable time, the authorities will be free to make determinations on the basis of the facts available, including those contained in the request for the initiation of the investigation by the domestic industry.

2. The authorities may also request that an interested party provide its response in a particular medium (e.g. computer tape) or computer language.   Where such a request is made, the authorities should consider the reasonable ability of the interested party to respond in the preferred medium or computer language, and should not request the company to use for its response a computer system other than that used by the firm.   The authority should not maintain a request for a computerized response, if the interested party does not maintain computerized accounts and if presenting the response as requested would result in an unreasonable extra burden on the interested party, e.g. it would entail unreasonable additional cost and trouble.   The authorities should not maintain a request for a response in a particular medium or computer language if the interested party does not maintain its computerized accounts in such medium or computer language and if presenting the response as requested would result in an unreasonable extra burden on the interested party, e.g. it would entail unreasonable additional cost and trouble.

*3. All information which is verifiable, which is appropriately submitted so that it can be used in the investigation without undue difficulties and which is supplied in a timely fashion, and, where applicable, supplied in a medium or computer language requested by the authorities, should be taken into account when determinations are made.   If a party does not respond in the preferred medium or computer language but the authorities find that the circumstances set out in paragraph 2 have been satisfied, this should not be considered to significantly impede the investigation.

4. Where the authorities do not have the ability to process information if provided in a particular medium (e.g. computer tape) the information should be supplied in the form of written material or any other form acceptable to the authorities.

*5. Even though the information provided may not be ideal in all respects, this should not justify the authorities from disregarding it provided the interested party has acted to the best of its ability.

0152

ADC2/NZ-III-2

- 41 -

6. If evidence or information is not accepted, the supplying party should be informed forthwith of the reasons thereof and have an opportunity to provide further explanations within a reasonable period, due account being taken of the time-limits of the investigation. If the explanations are considered by the authorities as not being satisfactory, the reasons for rejection of such evidence or information should be given in any published findings.

7. If the authorities have to base their determinations, including those with respect to normal value, on information from a secondary source, including the information supplied in the request for the initiation of the investigation, they should do so with special circumspection. In such cases, the authorities should, where practicable, check the information from other independent sources at their disposal, such as published price lists, official import statistics and customs returns, and from the information obtained from other interested parties during the investigation. It is clear, however, that if an interested party does not co-operate and thus relevant information is being withheld from the authorities, this situation could lead to a result which is less favourable to the party than if the party did co-operate.

0153

ADC2/NZ-III-2

외 무 부

종 별 :

번 호 : GVW-2501   일 시 : 91 1129 1530

수 신 : 장 관(봉기,경기원,재무부,상공부)

발 신 : 주 제네바대사

제 목 : UR/규범제정 및 TRIMS(공식)

11.28(목) 표제회의가 MACIEL 의장 주재로 개최되어 동 그룹의 협상 진전상황등에 대해 논의하였는 바, 요지 하기 보고함.(본직, 강상무관등 참석)

0 의장은 오늘 회의 목적은 규범제정 그룹의 협상 진전상황을 참가국에게 알리는 것이라하면서 그동안의 협상결과 반덤핑, 세이프가드, TRIMS 및 BOP 분야에서 WORKING PAPER 혹은 FRAFT TEXT 가 마련되었으나, 동 문서에 대해 여전히 참가국간 의견의 차이가 있으며, 모든것이 합의될때까지 어떤것도 합의된 것은 아니라는 점을 강조함.

0 보조금.상계관세 분야에서는 개도국 특별 취급관련 사항에 대해 다소의 진전이있었으나 합의수준에 이른 정도의 충분한 것은 아니며 동사항에 대해 보다 구체적인DRAFTING 이 필요하며, 세이프가드 조치 관련 몇가지 기술적 사항 및 용어에 대한 수정이 있었으나, 어떤 조항도 합의된것은 아니라고 함.

0 한편 KDUEK은 규범제정 분야중 수입허가 절차, 선적전 검사, 원산지 규정등에대해 기술적인 수정이 일부 있었으며, 기술장벽 협정중 미결사항인 동 협정의 비정부 기관 및 지방정부에의 적용문제는 다음주에 협상을 재개할 예정임을 밝힘.

0 의장은 상기 쟁점 사항(특히, 보조금. 상계관세, 반덤핑, 세이프가드, TRIMS 및 BOP)에 대해 다음주 갓트 총회가 끝난 직후부터 집중적이며 심도있는 협상을 재개하여 12월 20일까지 UR협상의 성공적인 타결을 마무리 지을수 있도록 각국의 협조를 당부함.

0 이에 대해 스위스는 규범제정 분야의 중요성을 강조하면서 아국을 포함한 30 개 국이 규범강화의 중요성에 대한 공동입장을 밝힌점을 상기시켰고 홍콩은 몬트리올선언에 따라 세이프가드 제 22항의 회색조치 철폐가 본 협상의 가장 중요한 요소인바 현 의장안은 수락할수 없으며, 22조 B 항이 개선되어야 한다고 주장하였고, 인도, 알젠틴, 브라질, 우루과이등이 이에 찬성함.

통상국   2차보   경기원   재무부   상공부

PAGE 1   91.11.30   08:11 WH

O EC 는 회색조치 철폐에 대한 상기 국가의 주장에 대해 현재는 어떤것도 합의된바 없으며, 협상의 최종결과를 기다려야 할 것이라고 말함.

O 본직은 상기 WORKING PAPER 마련을 위해 의장 및 RAMSAUER 보좌관이 보인 노력에 사의를 표하고, 규범강화에 대한 30개국 공동 성명서(GVW-2445로 기송부)의 기본정신이 향후 동 그룹 협상에 반영되어야 한다는 점과, UR 협상의 성공적타결을 위해특히 반덤핑 및 세이프가드 제 22항 협상에 적극 참여할 것임을 언급하였음.

O 이에 MACIEL 의장은 30 개국 공동 성명은 규범제정 협상에 긍정적으로 기여할것이라고 언급함. 끝

(대사 박수길-국장)

외 무 부

종 별 :

번 호 : GVW-2615　　　　　　　　　　일 시 : 91 1212 1900

수 신 : 장관(봉기,경기원,재무부,상공부)

발 신 : 주 제네바 대사

제 목 : UR/반덤핑 협상 주요국 비공식 회의

　　12.10 및 11 간 RAMSAUER 규범제정 협상 그룹 의장보좌관 주재로 개최된 표제회의 결과 하기임.(강상무관, 상공부 박과장등 참석)

　　1. RAMSAUER 의장은 향후 협상 일정과 관련,반덤핑 협상에서 관계국간 합의에 의한 TEXT가 내주 월요일(12.16) 까지 마련되기를 촉구하고 이것이 실현되지 않을시 12.18 까지 의장이 TEXT를 준비할수 밖에 없다고 함.

　　2. 의장은 그간의 각종 회의 결과를 반영하여 사무국이 작성한 토론문서를 작성, 배포하고 이를토대로 회의를 진행함.(별첨 참조)

　　가. AVERAGING (2.4.2 조)

　　0 노딕은 사무국안에 자국이 제안한 표준편차의 개념이 충분히 반영되지 않았다고 함.

　　0 아국, 홍콩등은 2.4.2 의 9째줄 'DIFFERSIGNIFICANTLY'의 개념이 불명확한 점을 지적함.

　　0 일본은 10째줄의 ( )된 문장의 삭제를 주장함.

　　0 EC 는 사무국안 11번째 줄의 'IF IT CAN HE,.,.)이하 문장이 적절치 못하다고함.

　　0 호주는 둘째줄 문장중 ' BOTH EXPORTING COUNTRYAND' 의 삭제를 주장함.

　　나. STANDING (5.1 조)

　　0 아국, 일본, 홍콩, 싱가폴등은 침묵을 지키는 회사는 중립적인 것으로 간주해야 한다는 것이 본이슈의 기본 자세임을 강조하고 예외적인 경우의 지지비율은 33 퍼센트로 해야 한다고 주장함.(일본은25 퍼센트 주장) 또한 수출국들은 노조포함을 반대함.

　　0 일본은 예외적인 경우 SAMPLING 사용을 고려하겠다고 함.

통상국	2차보	외정실	분석관	청와대	안기부	경기원	재무부	상공부

PAGE 1　　　　　　　　　　　　　　　　　　　　91.12.13　　08:02 BX

외신 1과 통제관

0156

0 미국은 SAMPLING 의 필요성과 노조 포함을주장함.

0 의장은 각국간 의견의 차이가 심하므로 기준의 계량화가 어려울 경우 일반적 지침을 제시하는 질적 기준을 제시할수 밖에 없다함.

다. NEW COMERS (9.5 조)

0 사무국은 NEW COMERS 인지의 여부를 <u>수출업자가 증거를</u> 제시토록한 점이 MACPHAIL III 와 다른점이라고 함.

0 이에 대해 아국등 모든 수출국은 수출자에게 증거제시 의무를 부과하는 것은 인정하나 NEWCOMERS 로 판명된 수출자에 대해서 담보 제공 및 소급적용에 있어 일반원칙과 다른 특별규정을 적용하는 것은 부당하다고 지적함.

라. 피해 판정(3.6 조)

0 수출국 및 멕시코는 경쟁관계의 고려요소에 품질이 포함되어야 함을 주장하고피해 누적은 동일한 조사를 받고 있는 수출에 한정해야함을 주장함.

0 아국은 사무국안중 둘째줄에 포함되어 있는<u>시간, 지역의 동일성</u>에 관한 요건은FOOT NOTE의 경쟁관계 고려 요소에 포함시키는 것이 기술적으로 더 적합함을 지적함.

0 미국, EC 는 저가상품이 고가상품에 영향을줄수 있으므로 가격을 경쟁관계 고려요소에 포함시키는 것을 반대함.

0 미국, EC 는 최소 덤핑 마진 및 시장점유율에 해당하는 수출도 피해 누적시 포함시켜야 함을주장하고 수출국들은 이에 반대함.

마. 구성가격(2.2.3 조)

0 수출국들은 사무국안중 (III) 의 방법은 (I)및 (II) 의 방법을 사용할수 없을시 최종방법이어야 한다는 점에서 우선 순위 설정을주장함.

0 미국, EC 는 BENCH MARK 사용이 합리적이고 명료한 방법임을 주장함.

0 일본은 (III) 의 방법을 사용시 상한선을 설정하여야 한다고 하고, 이에 미국,EC 는 상한선이 있으면 하한선도 있어야 한다고 주장함.

바. COUNTRY HOPPING (10.4 조)

0 아국, 일본등 수출국은 기존 규범의 강화 및 개선이 있을시에만 COUNTRY HOPPING 을 논의할것임을 강조하고 엄격한 기준의 설정을 요구함.

0 사무국은 COUNTRY HOPPING 의 경우 별도의 덤핑마진 조사 및 피해 조사가 있어야 하며 이에 추가하여 새로운 요건이 필요하다는 점을 분명히함.

PAGE 2

0 아국, 일본, 홍콩, 싱가폴등은 (II) 관련원수출국으로 부터의 수출 감소와 제3국 수출증가사이에는 PROPOTIONAL 한 관계가 추가되어야 한다고 주장하고, 또한 (IV) 관련 'BEFORE ANTI DUMPINGORDER' 라는 문장을 'FACILITIES' 되에 삽입할것을 주장함.

0 미국은 COUNTRY HOPPING 이 반덤핑 협정의 균형을 위해 필수적 요소라고 강조하면서 (II) 의 삭제를 주장하고 (III) 중 '기존 설비 존재' 의 삭제를 주장함.

0 기타 ' CONTROLLING INTEREST' 'FINANCIAL COMMITTMENT'의 개념을 명확히 할 필요가 있음이 지적됨.끝

첨부: GVW(F)-602)

(대사 박수길-국장)

PAGE 3

0158

주 제 네 바 대 표 부

번 호 : GVW(F) - *602*   년월일 : *11212*   시간 : *1P00*

수 신 : 장   관 *(동기. 경기원. 재무부. 상공부)*

발 신 : 주 제네바대사

제 목 : *GVW - 제15 전망*

총 12 매(표지포함)

보 안 봉 제	*(서명)*
외신과 봉 제	

10.12.1991   *(Secretary)*

CONSTRUCTED VALUE: ALTERNATIVE METHODS FOR CALCULATING AMOUNTS FOR PROFITS AND FOR SELLING, GENERAL AND ADMINISTRATIVE EXPENSES

1.   The various drafts on constructed value in the draft papers which have been under consideration in the negotiations contain two different approaches to the question of the definition of alternative methods for calculating profits and selling, general and administrative expenses: one approach, reflected in the drafts submitted in July and August 1990, attempts to describe each alternative method in some detail;   another approach, reflected in the drafts submitted in November 1990, provides for the use of any reasonable method, subject to a ceiling.

2.   The secretariat text in the non-paper dated 26 November 1991 was intended to take into account concerns expressed by some participants regarding the phrase "such other method as may be reasonable" in the draft text dated 23 November 1990.   Thus, the text in the non-paper relied on some of the concepts appearing in the draft papers submitted in July and August 1990 but differed from these draft papers in that it attempted to define the possible alternatives <u>in an exhaustive manner</u>.   As made clear in the discussions on 29 November, an important problem that arises with this approach is the precise definition of what method to use if data pertaining to other producers of the like product or of products of the same general category of products cannot be used.[1]   Reservations were expressed regarding the suggestions in Article 2.2.3.1(iii) of the secretariat draft, in particular with respect to the concept of "cost of capital", while it was noted that there were also problems of definition regarding the test suggested in the first part of that sub-paragraph (publicly available data on the profit realized in the business sector).

---

[1] At the meeting on 29 November use of a company's overall profit was also suggested as a possible alternative.

0160

ADC/CV2

- 2 -

3.   The attached revised version of the secretariat draft provides
alternative language for Article 2.2.3.1(iii), which might perhaps raise
less problems than the language originally suggested.   It should be noted
that this type of formulation could of course also be used in a 'ceiling'
approach of the type reflected in Article 2.2.3 of the draft working
paper.[2]

---

[2] For example: When such amounts cannot be determined, the authorities
may designate such other method as may be reasonable, in light of
historical performance in the industry under consideration, provided that
... etc.

0161

ADC/CV2

CONSTRUCTED VALUE

<u>Note</u>:   This redraft attempts to define, with a greater degree of
specificity than in Article 2.2.3 of the draft text dated
23 November 1990, alternative methods for calculating the amounts
for profit and selling, general and administrative expenses in a
constructed value calculation.   It does not attempt to deal with
the unresolved questions of the inclusion of the terms "in the
ordinary course of trade" and "country of export" and the issue of a
possible order of preference among the alternatives.   The text in
sub-paragraph 2.2.3.1 (iii) is suggested as a possible alternative
for the expression "any other reasonable method" used in Carlisle 2.

2.2.3 For the purpose of paragraph 2 of this Article, the amounts for
administrative, selling and any other costs and for profits shall be the
actual amounts, as verified from the records of the exporter or producer
under investigation, pertaining to production and sales [ ] of the like
product* by the exporter or producer under investigation.

2.2.3.1 When such amount for profit cannot be determined on this basis,
this amount may be determined on the basis of <u>any one</u> of the following
methods, based on actual data:

(i)   the profit realized by the exporter or producer under
investigation in respect of production and sales [ ] of products
of the <u>same general category</u> of products [ ];

(ii)   profit normally realized by other exporters or producers in
respect of production and sales [ ] of the like product* or of
products of the same general category of products** [ ];

---

*It is important that in a final version of a text on constructed
value there should be consistency between the part of the text dealing with
the methodology for determining profits and selling general and
administrative expenses and the first part of article 2:4 of the existing
Code (when there are no sales of the like product in the ordinary course of
trade in the domestic market of the exporting country ...).

**Sub-paragraph (ii) could be made more specific by a reference to the
use of weighted averages.   In addition, a reference to exporters or
producers subject to investigation might be necessary.

0162

ADC:??

- 2 -

(iii) [publicly available data on the profit realized in the business
sector concerned in the country [ ] or, where such data is not
available, a reasonable measure of the cost of capital in that
country.]

or [any other method which reasonably reflects the historical
performance in the industry under consideration.]

2.2.3.2 If the exporter or producer under consideration does not sell the
like product* in the country subject to investigation, the amounts for
administrative, selling and any other costs may be determined in accordance
with the methods described in sub-paragraphs 2.2.3.1(i) and (ii) for the
calculation of profits.

2.2.3.3 The provisions in paragraph .. regarding allocation of costs and
adjustments for start-up operations and cyclical fluctuations shall apply
to cost calculations under this paragraph.

0163

ADC/CW

9.12.1991

CUMULATIVE INJURY ASSESSMENT

1. The attached text is a slightly redrafted version of the text in the secretariat non-paper dated 26 November 1991. The main purpose of this redraft is to clarify how a provision on cumulation could relate to a provision quantifying negligible import volumes.

2. It should be noted that at the meeting held on 29 November several participants pointed to the need for a further consideration of the factors listed in the footnote to Article 3:6 regarding the existence of "competition" between imported products and between the domestic and imported products.

0164

ADC:CIA2

9.12.1991

3.6   When imports from more than one country are subject to [the same] investigation and such imports are reasonably coincident in time and geographic location and compete[1] with each other and the domestic like product, the authorities may, for the purpose of determining whether injury exists, cumulatively assess the effects of such imports (other than imports which have been exempted from the investigation pursuant to Article 3:7) only if they determine in a particular case that circumstances exist warranting such a cumulative analysis.   In making this determination they shall consider, *inter alia*, the relative magnitude of the volume of imports from each country.

---

[1] In determining whether imported products compete with each other and with the domestic like product the authorities shall consider such factors as the existence of common or similar channels of distribution, the existence of sales or offers to sell to the same customers or group of customers and the prices of the products in question ...

3.7   (...)   There shall be immediate termination in cases where (...) the volume of dumped imports (..) is negligible.   The volume of dumped imports shall be regarded as negligible if the volume of dumped imports from any one country does not constitute more than [X] per cent of the domestic market for the like product in the importing country, unless countries with less than [X] per cent market share collectively account for more than [X] per cent of the domestic market for the like product in the importing country.

0165

ADCI:ARTS

Article 10

Retroactivity

10.1 Provisional measures and anti-dumping duties shall only be applied to products which enter for consumption after the time when the decision taken under Article 7:1 and Article 9:1, respectively, enters into force, subject to the exceptions set out in this article.

10.2 Where a final determination of injury (but not of a threat thereof or of a material retardation of the establishment of an industry) is made or, in the case of a final determination of a threat of injury, when the effect of the dumped imports would, in the absence of the provisional measures, have led to a determination of injury, anti-dumping duties may be levied retroactively for the period for which provisional measures, if any, have been applied.   If the anti-dumping duty fixed in the final decision is higher than the provisional duty paid or payable, the difference shall not be collected.   If the duty fixed in the final decision is lower than the provisional duty paid or payable, or the amount estimated for the purpose of the security, the difference shall be reimbursed or the duty recalculated, as the case may be.

10.3 A definitive anti-dumping duty may be levied on products which were entered for consumption not more than [90] days prior to the date of application of provisional measures when the authorities determine for the dumped product in question that:

    (i) there is a history of dumping which caused injury or that the importer was, or should have been, aware that the exporter practices dumping and that such dumping would cause injury, and

    (ii) the injury is caused by massive dumped imports of a product in a relatively short time which in light of the timing and the volume of the dumped imports and other circumstances (such as a rapid build-up of inventories of the imported product) is likely to seriously undermine the remedial effect of the definitive anti-dumping duty to be applied, provided that the importers concerned have been given an opportunity to comment.

10.4 A definitive anti-dumping duty may be levied on products which entered for consumption not more than [X] days prior to date of the application of provisional measures, if:

    (i) the product subject to the investigation is a like product to that in respect of which a definitive anti-dumping duty is in force in the importing country and is produced in and exported from a country not subject to that definitive anti-dumping duty;

0166

ADC2:ART10

- 2 -

   (ii)   imports of the product subject to investigation from the third
        country have increased significantly over a period of not more
        than [X] months since the imposition of the duty referred to in
        sub-paragraph (i), and there is a corresponding decline of
        imports of the product from the country to which that duty
        applies;

   (iii) the party in the country subject to the original anti-dumping
        duty has a controlling interest[1] in the party exporting the
        product subject to investigation from the third country;

   (iv)   production in the third country of the product subject to
        investigation takes place in pre-existing facilities used to
        produce that product; and

   (v)   the authorities determine that the injury caused by the imports
        of the product subject to investigation is such as to seriously
        undermine the effectiveness of the original anti-dumping duty.

10.5 The authorities may, after initiating an investigation, take such
measures (not involving a financial commitment) as may be necessary to
collect anti-dumping duties retroactively as provided for in paragraphs 3
and 4, once they have preliminary evidence that the conditions set forth in
those paragraphs are satisfied.

10.6 No duties shall be levied pursuant to paragraphs 3 and 4 on products
entered for consumption prior to the date of initiation of the
investigation.

10.7 Except as provided in paragraph 1 above where a determination of
threat of injury or material retardation is made (but no injury has yet
occurred) a definitive anti-dumping duty may be imposed only from the date
of the determination of threat of injury or material retardation and any
case deposit made during the period of the application of provisional
measures shall be refunded and any bonds released in an expeditious manner.

10.8 Where a final determination is negative, any cash deposit made during
the period of the application of provisional measures shall be refunded and
any bonds released in an expeditious manner.

---

[1]To be defined.

0167

ADC: ART:?

10.12.1991

AVERAGING

1. Reproduced below is a revised version of Article 2.4.2 of the draft working paper on anti-dumping. This redraft deals only with the problem of the definition of situations in which a comparison of a weighted average normal value with individual export transactions would be permissible and does not address other questions raised in recent discussions.

2. In this revised version an attempt is made to reflect a suggestion (made at the meeting held on 29 November) that the situation in which a comparison between a weighted average normal value with individual export prices would be permissible should be defined by reference to differences between price variations among export transactions and price variations among transactions in the domestic market, rather than, as reflected in the secretariat non-paper dated 25 November, by reference only to differences among export prices.

3. It should be noted that at the meeting held on 29 November it was also suggested to limit Article 2.4.2 to the text of the first sentence.

2.4.2 Subject to the provisions governing fair comparison in paragraph 2.4, in cases where prices vary in both the exporting and importing country, the existence of margins of dumping during the investigation phase shall normally be established on the basis of a comparison of a weighted average normal value with a weighted average of prices of all export transactions or by a comparison of normal value and export prices on a transaction to transaction basis. A weighted average normal value may be compared to prices of individual export transactions if the authorities find a pattern of export prices which differ significantly among different purchasers, regions or time periods (having regard to the

0168

25.11.1991

NEW EXPORTERS

9.5 When exporters or producers in a country exports from which are
subject to anti-dumping duties in an importing country provide evidence
showing that they have not exported the product in question during the
period of investigation and are not related to any of the exporters or
producers in the exporting country subject to anti-dumping duties, the
authorities shall promptly carry out a review for the purpose of
determining individual margins of dumping for such exporters or producers.
Such a review shall be initiated and carried out on an accelerated basis,
compared to normal duty assessment and review proceedings in the importing
country.   No anti-dumping duties shall be levied on imports from such
exporters or producers while the review is being carried out.   The
authorities may, however, withhold appraisement and/or request guarantees
to ensure that, should such a review result in a determination of dumping
in respect of such producers or exporters, anti-dumping duties can be
levied retroactively to the date of the initiation of the review.   If the
authorities find that there is no dumping, the exporters or producers
concerned shall be exempted from the application of the anti-dumping
duties.

0169

- 2 -

relative weight of the transactions in question) and if it can be
demonstrated that, because of the absence of a similar pattern of price
differences among transactions used to establish the normal value, the use
of a weighted average-to-weighted average or transaction-to-transaction
comparison would not be representative of the patterns of export and
domestic prices under consideration.

0170

외 무 부

관리
번호 *91-939*

종   별 :

번   호 : GVW-2655

일   시 : 91 1215 1830

수   신 : 장관(통기,경기원,재무부,상공부)

발   신 : 주 제네바 대사

제   목 : UR/반덤핑(주요국 비공식)

일반문서로 재분류(19*91* . *12.31(.)*)

12.15(일) RAMSAUER 규범제정그룹 의장보좌관 주재로 표제회의가 개최 되었는바, 요지아래 보고함.

1. 의장은 지난 금요일(12.13) 회의 이후, 참가국간 주요 쟁점사항에 대한 논의를 거쳐, 의견을 좁히거나 합의된 사항이 있었는지에 대해 문의하고, 각쟁점사항에 대한 각국입장을 다시한번 확인함

2. 참가국들은 각쟁점 사항에 대해 기존입장을 반복함에 따라 오늘회의에서도 별다른 합의점을 도출하지 못하고 회의가 종료됨.

3. 이에따라 아국, 노르딕, 싱가폴, 홍콩등 수출국들은 12.20 TNC 회의에 제출될 반덤핑 TEXT 마련을 위한 공식.비공식 회의가 사실상 오늘 회의로써 끝난것으로 판단됨에 따라 주요 쟁점사항에 대한 공동입장을 별첨과 같이 마련, 동 문서를 RAMSAUER 규범제정그룹 보좌관에게 제출함으로써 동 그룹의장 책임하에 반덤핑 TEXT 작성시 수출국 입장을 최대한 반영시킬 예정임.

4. 관찰 및 평가

O 미국, EC 등 수입국이 주요쟁점 사항에 대해 계속 강경한 입장을 고수하고 있어 아국이 기대하는 현 CODE 의 상당한 개선은 불투명한 상태이며, 동 코드의 개선정도는 UR 전체 PACKAGE 와도 연계될 것으로 판단됨.

O 현재로서는 관계국간 합의에 의한 TEXT 마련은 실패하였고, 의장 책임하에 TEXT 가 마련될 것으로 보이며 RAMSAUER 가 비공식적으로 제시한 토론문서가 그 기초가 될것으로 보임.

- 동 TEXT 에는 NEW ISSUE 중 COUNTRY HOPPING 과 수입국조립우회덤핑은 포함될 것으로 보이며, 제3국 조립우회덤핑이 포함될지는 미지수임.

- 전통이슈에 대한 수출국 기대 수준의 반영정도는 뉴이슈인 3 가지 유형의

통상국	장관	차관	2차보	경제국	분석관	정와대	안기부	경기원
재무부	상공부							

91.12.16   05:33
외신 2과 통제관 FM
0171

우회덤핑이 모두 포함되는지 여부 및 그 구체적 요건에 좌우될 것으로 판단됨.

  - 또한 쟁점이슈(AVERAGING, 원가이하판매, 구성가격, 피해누적, 제소자가격, 최소덤핑 마진 및 시장점유, 신규수출자처리문제, SUNSET 등)가 동 TEXT 에 모두 포함된다 하더라도 수출국이 기대하는 수준의 질적 정도는 구체적 표현문제에 좌우되므로 현재로선 예측하기 곤란함.

  첨부:[84f첨부:수출공동입장 1 부

  (GVW(F)-0624). 끝

  (대사 박수길-국장)

  예고:91.12.31. 까지

주 제 네 바 대 표 부

번 호 : GVW(F) - *0624*   년월일 : *11/15*   시간 : *1830*

수 신 : 장   관(통기, 경기원, 재무부, 상공부)

발 신 : 주 제네바대사

제 목 : 첨부

총 *10* 매(표지포함)

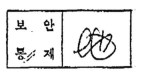

보 안 봉 재	
외신과 봉 재	

C24-1--1

Draft 14.12.1991

COORDINATED POSITION OF A NUMBER OF COUNTRIES
IN THE ANTI-DUMPING NEGOTIATIONS

Note: The following paper represents the coordinated position of Brazil, Finland, Hong Kong, Hungary, India, Korea, Malaysia, Norway, Singapore and Sweden on the issues set out below. It should be seen as part of a general package of overall balance in the Uruguay Round.

1.   Anti-dumping discipline issues

1.1.   Sales below cost

1.1.1.   Ramsauer's text of 26.11.1991 on paragraph 2.2.2, with the end of the text amended as follows:
" --- prices which do not provide for the recovery of all costs within a period of time, which is reasonable for the product and industry under consideration." and including subparagraphs 2.2.2.1 - 2.2.2.3

1.1.1.1   In subparagraph 2.2.2.2 exhange or for and if the value for A in footnote 3 is less than 50 %. If the value is 50 % or more or is acceptable.

1.1.2.   For para 2.2.2.4, take the first text in [   ]. Make the technical correction that in subparagraph (iii)(b) "export price" shall be "normal value".

0174

2.

1.2. Constructed value

1.2.1. Paragraph 2.2.3 of the secretariat's text of 9.12.1991, supplemented with the order of preference provisions in paragraphs 2.2.4.1 - 2.2.4.2 from Carlisle 2, specified as follows:

1.2.1.1. "any other reasonable method" in paragraph 2.2.4.2(ii) of Carlisle 2 shall be replaced by a properly defined method, e.g. as set out in paragraph 2.2.3.1.(iii) of the secretariat's paper of 9.12.1991 and a maximum level shall be indicated for such calculations.

1.2.1.2. The profits shall be specified to refer to weighted average profits.

1.2.1.3. Any reference to "ordinary course of trade" in paragraph 2.2.3. would be unacceptable. Those words should be replaced by a specification that the production and sale are in the country subject to the investigation.

1.2.1.4. In paragraph 2.2.3.2. of the secretariat's text of 9.12.1991 the three last lines should read as follows: "----administrative, selling and other costs may be determined <u>taking into account S, G & A for exports of the product or exporter concerned, where appropriate and in the absence of such data the costs may be determined</u> in accordance with the methods described in sub-paragraphs 2.2.3.1(i) and (ii) for the calculation of profits. (Amendment underlined.)

1.3. Currency fluctuations
Ramsauer's text of 26.11.1991.

0175

624-10-3

1.4.   Averaging

The following text, based on the secretariat's
text of 10.12.1991: "Subject to the provisions
governing fair comparison in paragraph 2.4, in
cases where prices vary in both the exporting and
importing country, the existence of margins of
dumping during the investigation phase shall be
established on the basis of a comparison of a
weighted average normal value with a weighted
average of prices of all export transactions or by
a comparison of normal value and export prices on
a transaction to transaction basis, except as set
out below. When anti-dumping duties are calculated
on a transaction to transaction basis negative
margins of dumping shall be taken into account. A
weighted average normal value my be compared to
prices of individual export transactions if the
authorities find a pattern of export prices which
differs significantly among different purchasers,
regions or time periods (having regard to the
relative weight in terms of volume and price level
of the transactions in question) and if it can be
demonstrated that, because of the absence of a
similar pattern of price differences among
transactions used to establish the normal value,
the use of a weighted average-to-weighted average
or transaction-to-transaction comparison would not
be representative of the patterns of export and
domestic prices under consideration. A constructed
normal value shall be compared to a weighted
average of the prices of all export transactions.

624-10-4

0176

4.

1.5.   Injury, pecially cumulation

1.5.1.   For paragraph 3.6. the following text:

"When imports from more than one country are
subject to the same investigation or to
simultaneous anti-dumping investigations and when
such imports are reasonably coincident in time and
geographic location and compete (1) with each
other and the domestic like product, the
authorities may, for the purpose of determining
whether injury exists cumulatively assess the
effects of such imports (other than imports which
have been exempted from the investigation pursuant
to Article 5:7) only if they determine that the
circumstances in the particular case warrant such
a cumulative analysis (2).

---

(1)   Secretariat text of 9.12.1991, with addition of
           a quality criterion.

(2)   In making a determination regarding a cumulative
           analysis, inter alia the following factors shall be
           taken into account; the trend and the relative
           magnitude of the volume of imports from each
           country and the extent to which imports from each
           country have contributed to the injury.

0177

6>4-10-5

1.6   Standing of petitioners

1.6.1.   Footnote 9 to Article 5.1 should read as follows:
          "For purposes of this article the term "a major
          proportion" in Article 4 shall normally mean
          expressed support by producers representing 50 per
          cent of the value of total domestic production of
          the like product. In exceptional circumstances the
          percentage may be less than 50 per cent, but not
          less than expressed support by 33 per cent, provided
          there is more expressed support than expressed
          opposition."

1.6.2.   In Article 5.3. the words "are satisfied" should be
          replaced by the words "have satisfied themselves".

1.7.   De minimis market share and dumping margin.

1.7.1   Ramsauer's text of 26 Nov. 1991 paragraph 5.7. with
          the following values:

1.7.1.1. In footnote 10, E - 4

1.7.1.2. In footnote 11, X - 3
                         Y - 12

1.8.   Newcomers

          Accept the secretariat's text of 25.11.1991, Article
          9.5, with the proviso that the word "related" on the
          fourth line needs to be defined. Article 4.4. of
          Carlisle 2 contains an adequate definition.

0178

6-4-10-6

1.9.   Termination of investigation and sunset

1.9.1.   Paragraph 11.3 of Ramsauer's text of 26.11.1991, revised to read as follows: "Notwithstanding the provisions of paragraphs 1 and 2, any definitive anti-dumping duty shall be terminated not later than five years from the date of its imposition, unless the the authorities determine, on the basis of a review of both dumping and injury initiated before that date on their own initiative or upon a duly substantiated request made by or on behalf of the domestic industry within a reasonable period of time prior to that date, that the continued imposition of the duty is necessary to offset dumping and prevent the continuation or recurrence of the injury. The duty may remain in force pending the outcome of such a review."

1.9.2.   Add a new subpara 11.4 from Carlisle 2 as follows: "Any anti-dumping duty extended pursuant to paragraph 3 shall expire after an additional period of 3 years".

1.9.3.   Amend paragraph 11.4. of Ramsauer's text of 26.11.1991 to read: "The provisions of Articles 5 and 6 regarding evidence and procedures...."

1.9.4.   Paragraphs 11.4-11.5 in Ramsauer's text become 11.5-11.6

1.10   Adjustments for inflation

1.10.1. Add to paragraph 2.2.2.3. of Ramsauer's text of 26.11.1991 the words "---appropirate const indexation to compensate for distortions caused by inflation ----"

0179

6ฺ-/0-7

1.10.2.   Add to paragraph 2.4 of the same text the words
"---nominal price adjustments to compensate for
disortions caused by inflation ---"

1.10.3. " Temporaty fluctuations in exchange rates, whether
free or induced, shall not themselves lead to ---"

*P Amend the beginning
paragraph
2.1.1 is read as
fellows*

2.   Issues requested by the anti-dumping users.

General comments:
The countries indicated at the outset of the present
document could accept provisions on
anti-circumvention; assembly in the importing
country and one of the two other issues; either
anti-circumvention; assembly in a third country or
retroactivity in connection with country hopping.
However, they have a preference for provisions on
retroactivity in connection with country hopping.
Their acceptance of anti-circumvention; assembly in
a third country is conditional upon having a clear
provision that the relevant code article constitutes
an exclusive remedy to address such circumvention/
Those countries accept the application of general
dispute settlement provisions and procedures to
anti-dumping matters, but they cannot accept any
porposals to qualify or to restrict those provisions
and procedures or to restrict the competence of
panels.

2.1.   Anti-circumvention; assembly in the importing country.

Accept the secretariat's text of 11.12.1991, specified as follows:

2.1.1.   The following figures should apply under article 12.1. (v):

G = 80 %
H = 20 %

2.1.2.   Footnote 18 should be restricted to cover a contractual arrangement only with the exporter or producer in question and only for the purpose of carrying out the assembly or completion.

2.1.3.   In subparagraph (iii) the word "historically" should be qualified so that occasional deliveries a long time ago cannot be included.

2.1.4.   Define "arm's length price" e.g. "Price between unrelated parties, and prices between related parties which are comparable with prices between unrelated parties."

2.2.   One of the following

2.2.1   Anti-circumvention; assembly in third countries

Ramsauer's text 26.11.1991 with values for I and J which are stricter than the values for G and H under article 12.1 to take account of the increased risks of distortions of trade and investments and a clear

0181

624-10-P

9.

provision that measures according to Article 12.3.
constitute an exclusive remedy for such
circumvention measures, which are addressed in that
Article.

2.2.2. Retroactivity in connection with countryhopping

Secretariat paper of 9.12.1991,

0182

외 무 부

종 별 :

번 호 : GVW-2665   일 시 : 91 1216 1200

수 신 : 장 관(통기,경기원 재무부,상공부)

발 신 : 주 제네바 대사

제 목 : UR/TRIM 비공식 협의

12.14(토) MACIEL 의장 주재로 개최된 표제협의 내용 아래 보고함.

1. 의장은 마지막 협의임을 강조하면서 자신의 새로운 안(별첨 1 참조)을 배포하고 타협을 촉구함.

- 10.30 자 의장 제안과의 주요 차이점

0 제 3조의 2(B) 의 추가(수입국내에서의 생산시장에 대한 영향)

0 제3조 2(C) 중 POSITIVELY 를 SIGNIFICANTLY 로개정

0 잠정 조정기간의 연장

당초의 선진국 1년, 개도국 2년 LLDC 3년을 각각 2년, 5년, 7년 으로 개정

2. 토의 내용

- 미국, 일본은 의장의 새로운 안에 실망을 표시하고 수출 이행 의무는 금지되어야 함을 재차 강조하면서 미국은 이에 대한 자국의 안을 서면으로 배포함.

(별첨 2 참조)

- EC 는 의장안 EFFECT TEXT 가 WORKABLE 하지않고 수출 이행의 의무의 전면 금지는 많은 개도국이 반대하고 있음을 감안하여 두안을 조정한 중재안을 배포하고 이를설명함.(별처 3참조)

0 EC 안의 주요 내용

1) TRADE EFFECT 뿐만 아니라 이의 THREAT 까지포함.

2) EFFECT TEXT 의 기준이 되는 제반 규정을 삭제하고 이를 PANEL 의 판단에 맡김.

3) 향후 매 3년 마다 동 협정의 운용 상황점검시 수출 이행의무의 사용 제한 강화 방안 논의

- 이에 인도, 말레이지아등 대부분의 개도국은 EC안에 THREAT 의 포함등을 이유로 강력히 반대함.

통상국	2차보	구주국	청와대	안기부	경기원	재무부	상공부

91.12.17   01:02 FN

외신 1과 통제관

0183

- 의장은 가능하다면 월요일 한번더 협의를 계속할것이나 참가국간 합의가 있던없던 화요일 저녁까지 의장 TEXT 를 제시할 것임을 언급하고협의 종료함.

첨부: 1. 의 장안(12.14 일자)

2. 미국제안

3. EC 중재안. 끝

(GVW(F)-627)

(대사 박수길-국장)

쭈 제 네 바 대 표 부

번 호 : GVW(F) - *0627*   년월일 : *11 2 16*   시간 : *1200.*

수 신 : 장   관 (통기, 경기원, 재무부, 상임부)

발 신 : 주 제네바대사

재 목 : UR/TRIMS 비공식협의

총 *12* 매(표지포함)

보 안 통 제	김 우정
외신과 통 제	

첨부1.

DRAFT

14 December 1991

14.00

TRADE-RELATED INVESTMENT MEASURES

Preamble

The CONTRACTING PARTIES;

Considering that Ministers agreed in the Punta del Este Declaration that following an examination of the operation of GATT Articles related to the trade restrictive and distorting effects of investment measures, negotiations should elaborate, as appropriate, further provisions that may be necessary to avoid such adverse effects on trade;

Desiring to promote the expansion and progressive liberalisation of world trade and to facilitate the movement of investment across international frontiers so as to increase the economic growth of all trading partners, and particularly developing countries, while ensuring free competition;

Taking into account the particular trade, development and financial needs of developing countries, particularly those of the least-developed countries;

Recognising that certain investment measures can cause trade restrictive and distorting effects;

decide as follows:

ARTICLE 1: Coverage

1.   This Decision applies to investment measures related to trade in goods only (hereafter referred to as "TRIMs").

TRIMS23

0186

627-12-2

- 2 -

ARTICLE 2: National Treatment And Quantitative Restrictions

1.   Without prejudice to other obligations under the General Agreement, no contracting party shall apply any TRIM that is inconsistent with the provisions of Article III or Article XI of the General Agreement.

2.   An illustrative list of TRIMs that are inconsistent with the obligation of national treatment provided for in Article III:4 of the General Agreement and the obligation of the general elimination of quantitative restriction provided for in Article XI:1 of the General Agreement is contained in the Annex to this Decision.

ARTICLE 3: Adverse Trade Effects

1.   In the application of any TRIM, which is enforceable or mandatory under domestic law or under administrative rulings and which requires an enterprise to export a specific product or a specified minimum volume, value or proportion of volume or value of local production, a contracting party shall avoid causing direct and significant trade restrictive and distorting effects adverse to the trade of another contracting party.[1]

2.   Such direct and significant trade restriction and distortion shall, subject to paragraph 5 below, be deemed to arise when a TRIM is demonstrated on the basis of positive evidence by the contracting party which considers its trade is being adversely affected by the TRIM, to have caused one or more of the following effects:

   (a)   exports of like products to those subject to a TRIM, from a contracting party other than the one applying the TRIM, are displaced in third country markets;

---

[1] Measures taken within the framework of an export processing zone or of other equivalent schemes (considered for customs purposes as being outside the customs territory of the contracting party) shall not be regarded as being in conflict with this Article. Subsidies contingent, in law or in fact, upon the export performance of an enterprise are not subject to the provisions of this Decision, but to the disciplines on subsidies as applicable to the contracting party in question.
TRIMS23

0187

- 3 -

(b) local production in the market of the complaining contracting
party is displaced;

(c) exports of the product subject to the TRIM from the contracting
party applying it are significantly affected.

3.   The effects referred to in paragraph 2 above must be demonstrated to
have occurred over an appropriate period of time, in normal circumstances
not less than one year, sufficient to make apparent a clear trend in the
trade flows concerned.

4.   In determining the causal link between a TRIM and any of the effects
referred to in paragraph 2 above, due consideration shall be given to the
existence of other relevant economic, commercial and technological factors
(such as contraction in demand, changes in patterns of consumption,
relative competitiveness and exchange rate fluctuations, and
technologically induced changes in demand) which can affect changes in
trade flows and which were present during the period when the direct and
significant trade restriction and distortion is alleged to have taken
place.

5.   Direct and significant trade restriction and distortion in the sense
of paragraph 1 above will be deemed not to have arisen if any of the
following circumstances is demonstrated on the basis of positive evidence
by the contracting party applying the TRIM to have occurred during the
period when such trade restriction and distortion is alleged to have taken
place and to have caused the effects referred to in paragraph 2 above:

(a) prohibition or quantitative restriction on exports, or existence
of other arrangements limiting exports, of the like product from
the contracting party whose exports have been displaced;

TRIMS23

0188

627-12-4

- 4 -

(b)   natural disasters, strikes, transport disruptions or other _force
majeure_ substantially affecting the availability of the like
product for export from the contracting party whose exports have
been displaced;

(c)   voluntary decrease in the availability for export of the like
product from the contracting party whose exports have been
displaced, including, _inter alia_, a situation where that
contracting party, or the exporting enterprises in such
contracting party, autonomously reallocated exports of the like
product to new markets;

(d)   failure to conform to standards and other regulatory requirements
in the importing country.

6.   Each contracting party in whose market the effects described in
paragraph 2 are alleged to arise shall make available to the complaining
contracting party or parties and to the GATT secretariat all relevant
information that can reasonably be obtained as to the pertinent facts,
including trade data on the products concerned and information on the
matters covered by paragraph 5. Nothing in paragraph 2 shall be construed
to require a contracting party to provide information that is not
reasonably available to it.

ARTICLE 4: Exceptions

All exceptions under the General Agreement shall apply, as
appropriate, to the provisions of this Decision.

ARTICLE 5: Developing Countries

1.   A developing contracting party shall be free to deviate temporarily
from the provisions of paragraphs 1 and 2 of Article 2 above to the extent
and in such a manner as Article XVIII of the General Agreement, as
interpreted by the CONTRACTING PARTIES, permits the contracting party to
deviate from the provisions of Articles III and XI of the
General Agreement.

0189

TRIMS23

627-12-5

- 5 -

2. With reference to Article 3 above, it is understood that in
considering actions that should be taken to remedy any effects adverse to
the trade of another contracting party caused by a measure taken by a
developing contracting party, due attention should be given to whether the
TRIM in question is part of a clearly defined and time-bound programme
designed to promote economic development, and to the special development
needs of least-developed contracting parties.

ARTICLE 6: Notification and Transitional Arrangements

1. Contracting parties shall notify the CONTRACTING PARTIES of all TRIMs
they are applying that are not in conformity with the provisions of
Article 2 above. TRIMs of general or specific application shall be
notified, along with their principal features.[2] Notifications shall be
made within ninety days of the entry into force of this Decision.

2. Each contracting party shall eliminate, subject to Articles 4 and 5
above, all TRIMs which are notified under paragraph 1 above within
two years of the date of entry into force of this Decision in the case of a
developed contracting party, within five years in the case of a developing
contracting party, and within seven years in the case of a least-developed
contracting party.

3. On request, the CONTRACTING PARTIES may extend the transition period
for the elimination of TRIMs notified under paragraph 1 above by up to one
year for a developing contracting party and two years for a least-developed
contracting party which demonstrates particular difficulties in

---

[2]In the case of measures applied under discretionary authority each
specific application shall be notified. Information that would prejudice
the legitimate commercial interests of particular enterprises need not be
disclosed.

TRIMS23

0190

627-12-6

- 6 -

implementing the provisions of this Decision. In considering such a
request the CONTRACTING PARTIES shall take into account the special
development, financial and trade needs of the country in question.

4.   During the transition period, a contracting party shall not modify the
terms of any TRIM which it notifies under paragraph 1 above from those
prevailing at the date of entry into force of this Decision so as to
increase the degree of inconsistency with the provisions of Article 2.
TRIMs introduced less than 180 days before the entry into force of this
Decision shall not benefit from the transitional arrangements provided in
paragraph 2 above.

5.   Notwithstanding the provisions of Article 2 above, and in order not to
disadvantage established enterprises during the transition period, a
contracting party may apply any TRIM to a new investment (i) where the
products of such investment are in direct competition with those of the
established enterprises, and (ii) where necessary to avoid distorting the
conditions of competition between the new investment and the established
enterprises, and provided that the TRIM applying to the established
enterprises has been notified under paragraph 1 above. Any TRIM so applied
to a new investment shall be notified to the CONTRACTING PARTIES. The
terms of such a TRIM shall be equivalent to those applicable to the
established enterprises, and it shall be terminated at the same time.

ARTICLE 7: Transparency

1.   Contracting parties reaffirm, with respect to TRIMs, their commitment
to existing obligations in Article X of the General Agreement and to their
undertaking on "Notification" contained in the 1979 Understanding Regarding
Notification, Consultation, Dispute Settlement, and Surveillance, as
interpreted by the CONTRACTING PARTIES.

2.   Each contracting party shall notify the GATT secretariat of the
publications in which TRIMs may be found, including those applied by
regional and local governments and authorities within their territories.

TRIMS23

0191

627-12-7

- 7 -

3.   Each contracting party shall accord sympathetic consideration to requests for information, and afford adequate opportunity for consultation, on any matter arising from this Decision raised by another contracting party. In conformity with Article X of the General Agreement no contracting party is required to disclose information which would impede law enforcement or otherwise be contrary to the public interest or would prejudice the legitimate commercial interests of particular enterprises, public or private.

ARTICLE 8: Committee on TRIMs

1.   A Committee on Trade-Related Investment Measures shall be established, open to all contracting parties to the General Agreement. The Committee shall elect its own Chairman and Vice-Chairman, and shall meet not less than once a year and otherwise at the request of any contracting party.

2.   The Committee shall carry out responsibilities assigned to it by the CONTRACTING PARTIES and shall afford contracting parties the opportunity to consult on any matters relating to the operation and implementation of this Decision.

3.   The Committee shall monitor the operation and implementation of this Decision and shall report thereon annually to the CONTRACTING PARTIES.

ARTICLE 9: Consultation and Dispute Settlement

The provisions of Articles XXII and XXIII of the General Agreement, and the Understanding on Rules and Procedures Governing the Settlement of Disputes under Articles XXII and XXIII of the General Agreement on Tariffs and Trade as adopted by the CONTRACTING PARTIES shall apply to consultations and the settlement of disputes under this Decision.

TRIMS23

0192

627-12-8

- 8 -

ARTICLE 10:   Review by the CONTRACTING PARTIES

Not later than five years after the date of entry into force of this Decision, the CONTRACTING PARTIES shall review its operation and, if necessary, revise its text. In the course of this review, the CONTRACTING PARTIES shall consider whether it should be complemented with provisions on investment and competition policy.

TRIMS23

627-12-9

0193

첨부2.   14 December 1991

V

UNITED STATES PROPOSAL

PROHIBITION OF EXPORT PERFORMANCE REQUIREMENTS

    A contracting party shall not apply any measure, which is mandatory or
enforceable under domestic law or under administrative rulings, or
compliance with which is necessary to obtain an advantage, which requires
that an enterprise export a specific product, or a specific minimum volume,
value, or proportion of volume or value of local production, generally or
to a specific market or region.

TRIMS30   627-12-1   0194

전3 : EC 대응안

Article III: Export Performance Requirements

1.   In the application of any TRIM, which is enforceable or mandatory or compliance with which is contingent on the grant of an advantage under domestic law or under administrative guidance and which requires directly or indirectly an enterprise to export a specific product or a specified minimum volume, value or proportion of volume or value of local production, a contracting party shall avoid causing direct and significant trade restrictive and distorting effects or a threat of such effects to the trade of another contracting party.(1)

2.   Such direct and significant trade restriction and distorsion shall, be deemed to arise when a TRIM is demonstrated on the basis of positive evidence to have caused one or more of the following effects:

   (a) exports, of like products to those subject to a TRIM, from a contracting party other than the one applying the TRIM are displaced in third country markets;

   (b) sale of like domestic products to those subject to a TRIM are displaced;

   (c) exports of the product subject to the TRIM from the contracting party applying it are positively affected.

---

(1) Measures taken within the framework of an export processing zone or of other equivalent schemes (considered for customs purposes as being outside the customs territory of the contracting party) shall not be regarded as being in conflict with this Article. Subsidies contingent in law or in fact upon the export performance of an enterprise are not subject to the provisions of this agreement, but to the disciplines on subsidies applicable to the CP in question.

0195

627-12-11

첨부3

Article XI: Review

Not later than three years after the date of entry into force of this Decision, and every three years thereafter, the CONTRACTING PARTIES shall review its operation and, if necessary, revise its text. In the course of this review, the CONTRACTING PARTIES shall in particular consider whether it should be complemented with provisions strengthening the discipline on export performance requirements.

0196

627-12-12

외 무 부

종 별 :

번 호 : GVW-2689　　　　　　　　　일 시 : 91 1217 1900

수 신 : 장관(통기,경기원,재무부,상공부)

발 신 : 주제네바대사

제 목 : UR/반덤핑 협상 관련

　　0 아국,싱가폴,홍콩등 11개 수출국들 대사들은 반덤핑 협상에 관한 수출국들의 지대한 관심과 핵심 쟁점사항에 대한 공동입장을 MACIEL 규범제정 그룹의장에게 전달함이 필요하다는데 인식을 같이하고 별첨의 공동입장을 마련, 12.17일 이를 MACIEL의장에게 전달함.

　　0 11개 수출국 대사들은 반덤핑 협상의 UR 의 성공을 위해 가장 중요한 분야의 하나임을 강조하고 의미있고 균형된 TEXT 가 마련되기를 희망하며, 반덤핑 협상 결과가 교역과 부자의 자유로운 흐름을 왜곡하여서는 안된다는 점을전달함.

　　0 이에 대해 MACIEL 의장은 TEXT 도 완전할수는 없으나 균형있는 TEXT 가 될것이라 하고 수출국들이 제시한 공동입장을 고려하겠다고함.

　　0 별첨 공동입장의 구체적 문안 작업은 아국 및 홍콩, 싱가폴, 노딕, 일본의 실무대표가 공동으로 작성한 것이나 노딕, 일본은 상기 대사급회의에는 참석하지 않았음을 첨언함.

　　별첨: 공동입장 1부.(GVW(F)-0637)

　　(대사 박수길-국장)

통상국　2차보　외정실　분석관　청와대　안기부　경기원　재무부　상공부

91.12.18　08:52 BX

외신 1과 통제관

0197

17·12·91

AIDE MEMOIRE

From the following countries:

<u>India, Indonesia, Hong Kong, Hungary, Korea, Malaysia, Philippines, Singapore, Thailand, Yugoslavia</u>, Brazil

1.   We want real and meaningful improvements to the Anti-dumping Code.:

    a. Averaging   –   No zeroing down

                     –   Compare constructed normal value with weighted average export price

                     –   Strict conditions for deviation

    b. Standing   –   50% of total domestic production normally, 33% in exceptional circumstances.

    c. Constructed Value   –   Include all actual data available

                     –   Hierarchy in alternative methods with a ceiling

    d. De minimis   –   Meaningful de minimis dumping margin and import in terms of market share

    e. Cumulation   –   Well defined conditions

    f. Sunset   –   One-off, 5+3

    g. Sales below cost   –   Include period beyond investigation for cost recovery

                     –   Consideration of start-up and cyclical industries in downturn

    h. Newcomers   –   Exonerated if no dumping found

637-3-2 2-#

0198

2

after expedited investigation

1.   **Injury**
     Determination - Strengthen causal link

There should be no deterioration in disciplines in the existing Code as may happen in the case of averaging, if exception is not clearly circumscribed.

2.   We see insufficient grounds at the moment for inclusion of all anti-circumvention measures and country-hopping. Furthermore, there is overwhelming opposition to the new proposal to include third country suppliers of parts and components in the scope of anti-circumvention measures.

3.   Balance in the package is most important. It is not a question of matching the number of issues. We look to the Chairman to be fair in drawing up his text. At the end of the day anti-dumping rules should in no way interfere with legitimate trade and free flow of investments.

· · · · ·

gva3/sp/09/aide

0199

637

외 무 부

종 별 :

번 호 : GVW-2698   일 시 : 91 1218 1000

수 신 : 장관(통기,경기원,상공부,공진청)

발 신 : 주 제네바 대사

제 목 : UR/기술장벽 협정

12.17 MACIEL 규범 제정 그룹 의장 주재로 개최된 표제 회의 결과 하기임.

1. 의장은 동 협정 그룹에서 미결 사항이었던 동협정의 지방정부 및 비정부기관에의 적용 조항인 제 3조 및 제 7조에 관해 별첨 제안을 함.(FAX 송부)

2. 상기 제의에 대해 그동안 동 미결 사항에 대해 대립되는 의견을 제시하여 왔던 미국, EC는 의장 제안이 양쪽 견해를 수용한 타협안으로 수락 가능함을 밝힘.

3. 한편 ANNEX I 의 1 TECHNICAL REGULATION 정의 문구중 첫째줄 '--- CHARACTERISTICS FOR PRODUCTS OFRELATED ...' 로 수정하자는 의견이 있음을 밝힘.

4. 이에 따라 TBT 협정은 12.20 TNC 회의에 상기제안을 수용한 합의문서가 제출될 예정임.끝

첨부: 의장 제안서 1 부. 끝

(GVW(F)-643)

(대사 박수길-국장)

통상국   2차보   정와대   안기부   경기원   상공부   공진청

PAGE 1   91.12.18   21:05 DU

외신 1과 통제관

0200

주 제 네 바 대 표 부

번 호 : GVW(F) - 643　　　년월일 : 11218　　　시간 : 1800˙

수 신 : 장　관 (통기, 경기원, 상공부, 공진청)

발 신 : 주 제네바대사

제 목 : GVW-2608 천부

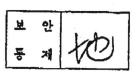

총 4 매(표지포함)

643-4-1

0201

Article 3

Preparation, adoption and application of technical regulations by local government bodies and non-governmental bodies

With respect to their local government and non-governmental bodies within their territories:

3.1 Parties shall take such reasonable measures as may be available to them to ensure their compliance with the provisions of Article 2, with the exception of the obligation to notify as referred to in paragraph 2.9.2 and 2.10.1.

3.2 Parties shall ensure that the technical regulations of local governments on the level directly below that of the central government in Parties are notified in accordance with the provisions of Article 2, paragraphs 9.2 and 10.1, noting that notification shall not be required for technical regulations the technical content of which is substantially the same as that of previously notified technical regulations of central government bodies of the Party concerned.

3.3 Parties may require contact with other Parties, including the notifications, provision of information, comments and discussions referred to in Article 2, paragraphs 9 and 10, to take place through the central government.

3.4 Parties shall not take measures which require or encourage local government bodies or non-governmental bodies within their territories to act in a manner inconsistent with the provisions of Article 2.

3.5 Parties are fully responsible under this Agreement for the observance of all provisions of Article 2. Parties shall formulate and implement positive measures and mechanisms in support of the observance of the provisions of Article 2 by other than central government bodies.

0202

643-4-2

- 2 -

Article 7

Procedures for assessment of conformity by local government bodies

With respect to their local government bodies within their territories:

7.1 Parties shall take such reasonable measures as may be available to them to ensure their compliance with the provisions of Articles 5 and 6, with the exception of the obligation to notify as referred to in paragraph 5.6.2 and 5.7.1.

7.2 Parties shall ensure that the conformity assessment procedures of local governments on the level directly below that of the central government in Parties are notified in accordance with the provisions of Article 5, paragraphs 6.2 and 7.1, noting that notifications shall not be required for conformity assessment procedures the technical content of which is substantially the same as that of previously notified conformity assessment procedures of central government bodies of the Parties concerned.

7.3 Parties may require contact with other Parties, including the notifications, provision of information, comments and discussions referred to in Article 5, paragraphs 6 and 7, to take place through the central government.

7.4 Parties shall not take measures which require or encourage local government bodies within their territories to act in a manner inconsistent with the provisions of Articles 5 and 6.

7.5 Parties are fully responsible under this Agreement for the observance of all provisions of Articles 5 and 6. Parties shall formulate and implement positive measures and mechanisms in support of the observance of the provisions of Articles 5 and 6 by other than central government bodies.

0203

(43 - 4 -3)

Footnote to Article 2.2 TBT:

(1)   This provision is intended to ensure proportionality between
       regulations and the risks non-fulfilment of legitimate objectives
       would create.

0204

643-4-4

외교문서 비밀해제: 우루과이라운드2 8
우루과이라운드 규범 제정 및 투자 협상

초판인쇄 2024년 03월 15일
초판발행 2024년 03월 15일

지은이 한국학술정보(주)
펴낸이 채종준
펴낸곳 한국학술정보(주)
주 소 경기도 파주시 회동길 230(문발동)
전 화 031-908-3181(대표)
팩 스 031-908-3189
홈페이지 http://ebook.kstudy.com
E-mail 출판사업부 publish@kstudy.com
등 록 제일산-115호(2000. 6. 19)

ISBN 979-11-7217-110-0 94340
      979-11-7217-102-5 94340 (set)